The

INDIANS

of

PUGET SOUND

———————————————————

The Notebooks of Myron Eells

Myron Eells, 1880s

The

INDIANS

of

PUGET SOUND

The Notebooks of Myron Eells

Edited with an Introduction by

GEORGE PIERRE CASTILE

Afterword by William W. Elmendorf

UNIVERSITY OF WASHINGTON PRESS *Seattle and London*

WHITMAN COLLEGE *Walla Walla, Washington*

Library of Congress Cataloging in Publication Data
Eells, Myron, 1843–1907.
The Indians of Puget Sound.

Bibliography: p.
Includes index.
 1. Coast Salish Indians—Social life and customs.
2. Indians of North America—Washington (State)—Puget
Sound Region—Social Life and customs.   3. Skokomish
Indians—Social life and customs.   I. Castile, George
Pierre.   II. Title.
E99.S21E35 1985   979.7′700497   85-40355
ISBN 0-295-96262-3

Items illustrated on the following pages are in the Thomas Burke Memorial Washington State Museum, Seattle, and are shown here by courtesy of the Museum: pages 93–96, 99 *left*, 103 *top*, 107 *bottom*, 108, 110 *bottom right*, 123, 133 *center and bottom*, 134 *top*, 136, 139, 142 *top*, 155 *top*, 163 *top*, 164 *bottom*, 167 *top*, 169, 171, 173, 175, 177, 178 *top*, 182, 189 *top and center*, 190 *bottom*, 226 *top*, 229, 236 *bottom*, 238 *bottom*, 297 *bottom*, 379, 384 *top*

Editor's Preface

PUBLICATION OF THIS BOOK is over a hundred years late. Myron Eells began the project in 1875 when Otis T. Mason of the Indian Bureau sent him a questionnaire requesting information on Northwest Coast Indians. Mason was collecting material for the Smithsonian Institution's exhibit at the Philadelphia Centennial Exhibition and his questionnaire went out to Indian agents, missionaries, and others resident on Indian reservations. The response that Eells wrote was published as "The Twana Indians of the Skokomish Reservation in Washington Territory" (1877).

Eells had been living at Skokomish only a year when he prepared the questionnaire, and later, dissatisfied with this premature effort, he began a longer manuscript. In 1879 he sent a copy of the finished work to Major Israel W. Powell, head of the newly founded Bureau of Ethnology. His three-hundred handwritten pages languished at the Bureau for six years and were finally returned to him at his request when Rev. S. D. Peet, editor of *American Antiquarian*, expressed interest in publishing the work.

Eells expanded the manuscript at this point to approximately seven hundred pages and Peet agreed to take it in segments over a period of four years. It was eventually to be bound into a single volume entitled *The Indians of Puget Sound*. Eight articles were published between 1887 and 1890, at which time, according to Eells, Peet "began to make selections here and there as suited him, which was directly contrary to our agreement." Eells asked for the return of the manuscript.

Meanwhile, Otis Mason was seeking more information on Northwest Indians for the Smithsonian Institution, so Eells sent him the 1879 version of the manuscript. Mason extracted portions and, again contrary to the author's wishes, published the result as "The Twana, Chemakum and Klallam Indians of Washington Territory" in the Annual Report of the Smithsonian for 1887. This version, because it is commonly available in libraries, is the most frequently cited of Eells' voluminous writings.

Eells had published in the *Washington Magazine* a number of articles that were versions of one of his earlier papers, "The Worship and Traditions of Aborigines of America" (1885). In 1891 the *Washington Magazine* (now under the name of *Pacific Magazine*) began to publish *The Indians of Puget Sound*, that much-revised large work, but discontinued it after only two articles. The version presented in this volume is dated 1894, although there is reason to believe that Eells added a few notes after that date. After his death in 1907, the handwritten manuscript with drawings, which by then had grown to approximately one thousand pages, came to rest in the Whitman College Library along with his other papers and artifact collections. He had written optimistically of his magnum opus, "It is in such a shape that it can easily be prepared for publication, with hardly any additional writing." Finally, it is here published as he intended.

A selected bibliography at the end of the book lists the articles by Eells that are directly related to this manuscript. Additionally, I have noted many of his other writings on Indians which saw print in journals or were published as books. Myron Eells was a prodigious writer. He left thirty-five bound scrapbooks of his newspaper articles of which six books are primarily concerned with Indians, although non-Indian material is scattered throughout. Some of these articles—spanning 1875 to 1906—are cited in the text or in the Introduction, but no attempt has been made to include them all. At the first of every year, Eells recorded in his journal his previous year's work, and in 1907, the year of his death, he recorded that he had written 1,220 letters in the previous year. Unfortunately, comparatively little of the correspondence was preserved, although journals, manuscripts, and copies of published material are all intact.

The text presented here is as Myron Eells wrote it and as he long tried to have it published. While parts have seen print, they are often difficult to locate and do not convey the whole picture as Eells saw it. I have tried to keep the editing to a minimum. Repetition and interpolations that are not relevant to the text have been eliminated. I have not intruded the attitudes and knowledge of modern historical and anthropological hindsight into the text by correcting Eells' errors of fact or interpretation. Where appropriate, my annotation will be found in the chapter notes. Any substantial change from the original is indicated by a note, but significant departures from the original consist largely in omissions, such as of newspaper clippings by other authors, which Eells included but which did not add to his own observations. A few of these articles have been retained to give the flavor of the intellectual climate in which Eells operated.

Two entire chapters have been dropped, his original chapter 17 ("Languages") and chapter 29 ("The Stone Age of Oregon"). In the opinion of informed readers, the chapter on languages demonstrates only the poor grasp that Eells had of linguistics. The "Stone Age" chapter was made up largely of his naive drawings, which he himself labelled "unnecessary."

Otis Mason eliminated all of the drawings and their references in published form and the other publications of his work have similarly been without illustration. It is in the matter of illustrations that I have taken the greatest liberties with the original, but in a way that I am convinced would have met with Eells' approval. He was not a skilled artist, and the original manuscript is full of his crude sketches in pencil and crayon. In his previously published material a few of these were converted to pen-and-ink drawings and a very few photographs were reproduced. In this edition, the sketches have been replaced by photographs that illustrate his collections.

Not only was Myron Eells a prolific writer, he was also an obsessive collector of Indian material. Virtually every item or type of item he drew or described in the text of his manuscript can be found in his collections, and many of these have been photographed for inclusion here.

Eells had collected for the Philadelphia Centennial and continued to accumulate material when he was made superintendent of the Department of Ethnology for the Washington State Commission, which was preparing for the 1893 Columbian Exposition in Chicago. His personal collections are housed at Whitman College, but most of the Exposition material is now in Chicago's Field Museum of Natural History, while some items came to the Thomas Burke Memorial Washington State Museum. Material at the Burke Museum and Whitman College is included in this volume, along with some photographs taken by Eells that were preserved with the manuscript. In 1983 the Field Museum opened a permanent exhibit on maritime peoples of the Northwest Coast, which includes some of the Eells material on Puget Sound.

I have resurrected this neglected manuscript from the Whitman College archives for a number of reasons. Most obvious is the value of the writer's firsthand observations on the peoples of Puget Sound. His tenure as missionary on the Skokomish Reservation ran from 1874 until 1907 and qualified him to comment on reservation life. He spoke of people he knew and with whom he had worked for most of his adult life.

The Twana and the Klallam, the peoples Myron Eells knew best, are in many ways representative of the numerous small coastal and inland Salish peoples. Few of these groups have received the ethnographic and historical attention that has been paid to the more spectacular Northwest cultures, such as the Kwakiutl. Eells was not always a careful observer and often he did not fully comprehend what he saw, but his detailed notes on a wide variety of topics can be illuminating when compared with other reports and aided by subsequent understanding. He did not, for example, seem to fully understand the nature of the ceremonial life of the people with whom he lived though he recorded a great deal of it. With his data we are free to make our own interpretations.

There is yet another reason to publish the complete work. Robert Ruby and John Brown's *Myron Eells and the Puget Sound Indians*, published in 1976, consists largely of the Eells drawings, with a selection of quotes from his text. The book has flaws and confuses the reader as to which views belong to the nineteenth-century missionary and which to the twentieth-century historians. The authors occasionally elevate Eells to twentieth-century sensitivity when they say, for example, that "Eells did not decry traditional native beliefs" (1976:104). He did, of course, decry them over and over, which was the essence of his missionary work. For a full scholarly review of this work and a discussion of its major deficiencies, see Amoss 1978.

Beyond its ethnographic value, the Eells material has a special significance in that it is a record of American Indian peoples in the midst of change. Although Eells records what he can of the aboriginal nature of the societies, he remarks again and again that some things are gone, changed, or declining. Much of Indian life had already undergone accommodation and adjustment to the Anglo-American society that had engulfed it, and much else was in flux even when he knew it. The Skokomish Reservation was an early center in the rise of the Indian Shaker church (which still flourishes there over a hundred years later), and the events of its formation were observed and recorded by Eells.

In addition to being an observer and recorder of change, Myron Eells was throughout his life an active agent and apostle of change. This manuscript is introduced by an essay that attempts to place him in historical context. The essence of that context is the era in American Indian policy when the reservation system was dominated by the plans and guidance of Christian reformers. Myron Eells is a fine example of these well-meaning missionaries, and his adherence to their themes is reflected everywhere in the text. He and his brother Edwin (who was the Indian agent at Skokomish and later Puyallup) implemented programs of land allotment, education, and Christianization that are faithful mirrors of the sentiments and schemes of the period. Without intending to do so, Myron tells us much about himself and his times in his attempts to describe the Indians.

While the text itself is free of intrusive commentary, I have provided notes to other sources to aid the reader who is not knowledgeable in the details of the history, archeological record, and Indian policy for this time and place. One might come away with the impression, for example, that the potato had been cultivated in the Puget Sound region before the coming of whites. Eells appears prepared to believe that this is the case. The potato is a New World domesticate, but we now know, as Myron did not, that it was a South American plant introduced into the Northwest very early by the whites themselves. The reader who wishes total immersion in the spirit of those past times can save the reading of the notes for later reflection and see the situation as Myron Eells saw it.

Thanks are due to Elaine Downing for a "creative" typing job and to Kathy Connors for her help in sorting out the Eells collections. The photographs were done at Whitman College by Ken Thompson, with additional photography by Larry Paynter. Bill Holm, in addition to allowing us to photograph some of the Eells material in the Burke Museum, gave much helpful advice on the collections and their photographic documentation.

Thanks finally to Whitman College and the Aid to Faculty Scholarship Fund for their support in the research and preparation of this manuscript, and to Will and Sue Thomas, Friends of the College, for a grant in support of publication.

G.P.C.
Walla Walla, Washington
March 1985

Introduction:
Civilization and Salvation
at Skokomish

FRANCIS PAUL PRUCHA, the foremost historical scholar to concern himself with the forces and attitudes governing the development of American Indian policy, called the years from 1865 to 1900 "the most critical period in the whole history of Indian-white relations in the United States" (1976:v). Edwin Eells became the U.S. Indian agent on the Skokomish Reservation in 1871 and was an agent until 1895. His younger brother, Myron, came to Skokomish in 1874 and served as an active missionary on the reservation until his death in 1907. Between them, the two men participated in virtually every aspect of the twists and turns of the dramatic effort to solve the "Indian problem" by the Christian reformers and other "friends of the Indian" (Prucha 1973). Myron Eells attempted to describe in this book the nature and civilization of the Indian peoples whose salvation he sought, and I want in this introductory essay to place him in his historical context.

Cushing Eells, father of Edwin and Myron, came to Washington Territory in 1838 as a Congregational missionary from New England, to aid the work already begun by Marcus Whitman. He set up at Tshimakain among the Spokane Indians in eastern Washington and there remained for nine years until all of the missionaries were driven out of the area by the upheavals surrounding the Whitman massacre in 1847. Edwin was born at Tshimakain on June 27, 1841, and Myron on October 7, 1843.

Both Cushing Eells and his wife, Myra, were devout and dedicated members of their church and this influence on their sons is clear when we observe that Myron followed in his father's footsteps as minister and missionary and that Edwin was involved all his life in temperance activities and church affairs. Neither son left us any evidence of deviation from the stern New England morality they had learned as children. Whether their early experiences at Tshimakain with the Indian peoples who passed in and out of the mission were significant is more to be doubted, not only because of their age but because they were apparently kept apart from the Indian children. Ida Eells, daughter of Edwin, later recorded, "I have heard it said that they did not allow the children to learn the Indian language because their speech was so unclean" (I. Eells 1947:46).

ix

At the time of the massacre Cushing's mission was already in the process of being shut down because of its lack of success. Myra Eells rather despairingly commented, "We have been here almost nine years and have not yet been permitted to hear the cries of one penitent or the songs of one redeemed soul" (I. Eells 1947:46). In their own work the brothers departed considerably from their father's example, since neither at Tsimakain nor elsewhere was he ever to make a significant impact on the Indians. His place in history is in fact a function of his association with Marcus Whitman and his participation in important events in which he did not play the principal part. He was instrumental in the beginnings of much of significance but it was generally others who later brought the ideas to fruition. Whitman College, Pacific University, and Willamette University all owe a debt to Cushing Eells because of his early efforts on their behalf, but at Whitman where he devoted his greatest effort it was in fact A. J. Anderson who put the college on a stable footing. Perhaps some light is shed on Cushing's rather staid approach in a motto attributed to him approvingly in a letter from Edwin to Myron, "When two courses are before you, and one involves an active action, and the other a passive action, and the reasons are about evenly balanced it is safer to take the passive action" (E. Eells 1902).

Myron wrote a book about his father, *Father Eells*, which is revealing in a number of places by its defensiveness about the limited range of his father's deeds. He is reduced to saying, after noting that his father felt his principal efforts to have failed, that "an intimate friend, an associate teacher, said of him that he ought not to feel so, for if he had accomplished nothing more in life than to earn his consistent Christian reputation, his life was a success" (M. Eells 1894a:321). He certainly succeeded in impressing his character upon that of his sons, who respected him and followed his teachings. Myron praised his father's frugality and both he and Edwin sought to emulate it. Myron did so in one form that is frustrating to the student of his papers: he consistently used the backs of letters and other papers he received to write his own notes.

The boys spent most of their childhood in Oregon's Willamette Valley where their father settled after the Whitman massacre. Here Cushing was dismissed by the Missions Board and, while never ceasing to preach, made most of his livelihood as a teacher, first at the Methodist Institute (later Willamette University) and then at the Congregational Tualatin Academy (later Pacific University), while additionally running his own farm.

Edwin Eells, who wrote little for publication other than his agent's reports, has left us a fairly detailed memoir (E. Eells 1916). His literary brother, on the other hand, wrote little about himself except in his rather premature book, "Ten Years of Missionary Work at Skokomish" (M. Eells 1886). We may presume that neither boy could have survived the harsh frontier life without being hardened by it. Some suggestion does emerge, however, that Edwin was the more practical and robust and Myron the more inclined to scholarship. Edwin, when he was twenty-four, for example, rode with the local vigilantes in Walla Walla. His eyesight was bad even as a young man and, prevented from engaging in active gunplay, he was reduced to holding the horses for the other vigilantes. Later, when an Indian agent, he was charged with reckless use of a firearm because he had blazed away with his pistol at an escaping Indian culprit on the reservation. Although Myron was not an active participant in maintaining law and order, he approved of the

justice dealt out in Walla Walla to the "blacklegs" by his brother and other vigilantes (M. Eells 1894a:186).

In his early manhood Edwin also acted as enrolling agent for the draft in the Walla Walla area and encountered and overcame considerable hostility and violence. Perhaps in all of this is some further clue to the unswerving dedication to pursuing the right heedless of opposing voices, which was characteristic of so many of the reformers of this era, and which was implanted in Myron and Edwin by their father. Nowhere in their writings, official and personal, did Myron or Edwin ever express regrets or doubts of other than a momentary kind.

Both Myron and Edwin were launched into the world from Walla Walla, Myron to attend the Hartford Theological Seminary in Connecticut (his father's alma mater) in June of 1868, while Edwin moved to Seattle in August of 1869 to study law. Their respective careers and that of their father, however, came rapidly back together by 1871 when Edwin obtained his appointment as agent for the Skokomish, and first his father and then his brother came as missionaries to that group. It is at this point that they enter into the lives of the Twana and Klallam Indians, the principal groups described in this book.

SKOKOMISH

It is not my intention to describe the Twana and Klallam in this essay, but a few words of background are necessary to allow further discussion of the role that Edwin and Myron played in Indian policy and administration at this time. The standard ethnographies that ought to be consulted are *The Structure of Twana Culture* by W. W. Elmendorf (1960) and *Klallam Ethnography* by Erna Gunther (1927). Although it is not exclusively concerned with the Twana and Klallam, *Indian Shakers* by Homer Barnett (1957) explores the messianic cult that began early on the Skokomish Reservation during the contact period of the nineteenth century. A variety of other sources can be found cited throughout this text.

The Twana and Klallam were both placed on the Skokomish Reservation according to the terms of the treaty of Point No Point in 1855, one of a flurry of nearly identically worded treaties made by the territorial governor, Isaac I. Stevens. The treaty originally envisioned three groups—Twanas, Chemakums, and Klallams—being settled on about four thousand acres of land around the mouth of the Skokomish River, but the largest population actually settled on the reservation lands was Twana, with a very few Klallam. Governor Stevens had apparently thought that all of the Puget Sound peoples could eventually be settled on a single large reserve, and his treaties contained wording that allowed for later removals and the exchange of land. This potential for removal from their lands was a serious threat to the Skokomish peoples in later years. Their attempt to gain assurances that they would not be uprooted from their lands, however, was interpreted by Edwin and Myron as a lust for fee-simple individual ownership—land in severalty—a cause the Eellses promoted along with virtually all reformers of the time.

Figures for the Indian population in these times are probably unreliable, but it appears that in 1871, when Edwin took charge, there were over nine hundred Twana and Klallam who were subject in some sense to the treaty, but only about three hundred, mostly Twana, who were actually settled at Skokomish. A census of the Klallam taken in 1880 by Myron showed only six at Skokomish. The Klallam were scattered in smaller groups and some eventually established their own enclaves; one group at Jamestown purchased their own block of land. These self-established reservations have added still further confusion and legal complexities to those ambiguous land issues built into the original treaty.

The Skokomish Reservation proper eventually comprised 4,987 acres of land around the point where the Skokomish River joins the Hood Canal. The canal (actually a natural inlet despite its name) and the Skokomish River provided the marine food base for the prosperity of the aboriginal peoples. On modern maps the reservation can be found near the town of Union, more ambitiously called Union City in the late 1800s.

THE PUGET SOUND SALISH

The people whom the Eells brothers knew and whom Myron describes in this book had already undergone considerable cultural disruption and change aside from their concentration on "reservations" and placement under Anglo-American administration. White contact was first made along the coast in 1774 with the explorations of the Spaniard Juan Pérez. An active fur trade rapidly developed when the potential of the market for sea otter furs in China was discovered. American ships began to trade along the coast by 1778. Fort Astoria was constructed at the mouth of the Columbia River in 1811, marking a shift to land-based trade and permanent white residence in the area. Although the American fort was taken over by the Northwest Company in 1813, the area only actually began to be seriously exploited under the auspices of the Hudson's Bay Company, which took over Astoria and added other trading sites running up into present British Columbia by around 1825.

There can be no doubt that the Puget Sound Salish people, such as the Twana, who appear to have been limited in range to the general Hood Canal area, and still more the Klallam, who ranged all the way up to the Hoko River, were affected by the early maritime trade through their own trade relations with coastal peoples such as the Makah at the tip of the Olympic Peninsula. There is considerable evidence that trade goods moved inland in advance of actual white settlement, particularly the highly prized steel, which was frequently exchanged in the form of chisels.

The coastal peoples acted to some extent as middlemen diffusing the white trade goods to their inland suppliers. In this area as in others disease, too, seems to have spread in advance of direct white contact, so that the numbers of Salish peoples may have already declined seriously before the time of recording. Still, from the time of first contacts until the middle of the nineteenth century, with the exception of the impact of disease, the native peoples probably did not consciously perceive change as occurring at an unacceptable or disruptive rate.

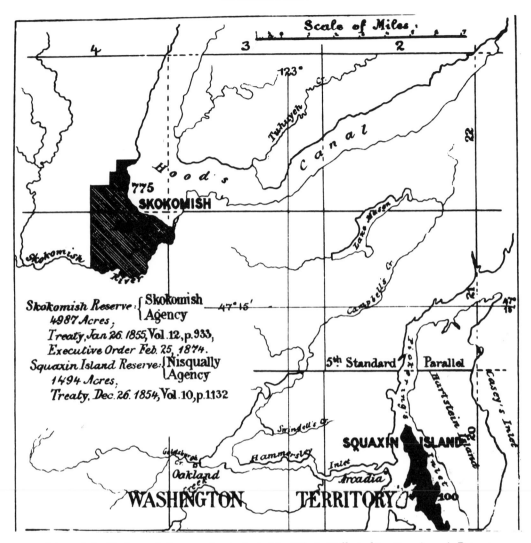

Map of the Skokomish Reservation included by Edwin Eells in his 1879 Agent's Report

In the 1850s the Puget Sound area began to be settled as we have already noted and by 1855 Governor Stevens' treaties were drawn. By 1896, Myron wrote that he already found himself talking of most of the native crafts and customs in the past tense and was hard pressed to reconstruct many of them even from the memories of those still alive. The almost total overturning of the way of life of the Salish peoples was accomplished within a period no greater than a single lifetime. The enormity of this change can be better appreciated if we note that such archaeological sites as Ozette on the Olympic Peninsula show signs of the same basic lifestyle exhibited by peoples known to have been established at least a thousand years before the present. Many of the artifacts recovered from the Ozette site are very nearly identical to those shown in this book but were made many centuries earlier. The inhabitants of the Skokomish Reservation are today still a self-conscious "people" who look upon themselves as distinct from their Anglo-American neighbors though the bulk of their thousand-year pre-Columbian culture was nearly destroyed by 1900. What was it that had vanished? Myron tells us much, but a brief sketch of these early peoples may put his detailed observations into better perspective.

Like the Northwest coastal traditions in general none of these peoples were agricultural but they sustained a stable village existence, relatively dense populations, a rich material culture, and elaborate social arrangements. The Twana were less spectacular in some aspects of this pattern than the better-known Kwakiutl of Vancouver Island, but much of what can be said about a dramatic culture need only be said in a lower key and on a smaller scale to capture the essence of Twana life.

The theme of these cultures is their marine orientation. Subsistence is based primarily on ocean and river resources, especially the variety of salmon running in late summer and early fall. Salmon provided a stable food resource when smoked or dried and stored for the winter months. This reliable food base made possible a complex social organization that is usually associated with agricultural societies. Important supplements to fishing, which was done by the men, were the gathering of shellfish by the women and the collection of plants such as camas, fern, and other roots. Also important was the hunting of sea mammals and water fowl, and, on land, the beaver, bear, deer, and elk.

The technology of the Twana is shown in this volume through photographs and descriptions of the artifacts collected by Eells. Aboriginally, it was indeed a Stone Age culture with no metals apparently known or used. A variety of ground-stone implements such as mortars and pestles were made, along with ground and chipped stone blades and points. As with most others in the Northwest, the Twanas' true skill was in woodworking, making watertight boxes, elaborate canoes, and a wide range of steamed and bent implements, such as fishhooks. Elaborate baskets, including watertight ones, and stone and wood bowls served as containers. The photographs include such items as fish weirs and nets, cords and mats, and woven cloth to illustrate the range of technological skills.

With their secure subsistence base, the Twana and others like them lived in permanent winter villages in one or more large plank houses (see, for example, p. 65). During the warmer months, however, these larger units broke up into smaller groups for fishing and collecting. Smaller mat-covered houses were constructed for these shifting settlements. It was primarily during the winter residence that important social and religious activities took place and the complexities of Twana life were manifest.

Myron Eells never spoke any of the Indian languages except the trade Chinook Jargon of only a few hundred words, which was inadequate for the description of the intricacies of belief and custom. He was able to obtain information from English-speaking Indians, sometimes relayed through bilingual schoolboys, but obviously much was lost in translation coming and going. For this and perhaps other reasons he does not seem to do justice to religion and social life. The reader is again referred to the ethnographies of Elmendorf and Gunther for a more detailed picture than Eells provides.

Most religious and ceremonial activity Eells lumped under the general Chinook Jargon label "tamahnous," though he did make some attempt at sorting out its components. Elmendorf described the importance of a "Guardian Spirit" complex, which is associated with shamanistic power, vision quests, and "spirit" dancing (1960:485). Pamela Amoss has more recently examined similar beliefs of the Nooksack under the title of *Coast Salish Spirit Dancing* (1978). Elmendorf breaks the ceremonial complex down into fifteen types (1960:541). Prominent among these were the potlatch and the secret society initiation, which is apparently what Eells refers to as "black tamahnous." Description of this rich tradition is inappropriate here and I only note that aboriginal religious life was far more complex than Eells gave it credit for being.

Ceremonialism is intimately linked to social organization, an area that appears to have confused Eells. It is only fair to point out that even Franz Boas (with whom Eells corresponded), who is often referred to as the "father of American anthropology," never fully grasped the nature of Kwakiutl kinship relations after years of far more systematic study than Eells was able to conduct on the Salish (White 1963:52). Some of Boas' students discovered that the inheritance of "rank" is a keystone to Northwest social relationships (see Codere 1950). Twana and Klallam, too, shared this fascination with rank and their reckoning of kinship, formation of marriage alliances, and "give aways," all reflect the interests of class or rank. Eells was only vaguely aware of these factors.

By the time Eells began to make his observations, many traditions had already passed away. It would have been very hard for him to have understood the web of reciprocal debts, kin links, and relative rank since these were already in disarray. What he saw was a society already largely under the command of outsiders (such as his own brother), who appointed "chiefs" without knowledge of or regard to the aboriginal system of ranking. Aboriginal patterns of warfare and political alliance had been outlawed by whites.

THE REFORMERS

When Territorial Governor Isaac Stevens hastily concluded treaties and gathered the Indian peoples onto reservations his motives were obvious and simple. It is evident here as elsewhere in the expanding American West that reservations were primarily devices to clear useful land for settlement and isolate the remaining Indians where they could be militarily supervised and kept peaceful. Stevens wanted to settle the Indian "problem" in his capacity of territorial governor and also to promote the feasibility of a northern route for the transcontinental railroad. His role as *ex-officio* superintendent of Indian affairs would seem to have been decidedly influenced by his other capacity as trailbreaker for both settlers and railroad. One biographer titled his work, *Isaac I. Stevens: Young Man in a Hurry,* and it does seem that Stevens had been in too much of a hurry, for a series of wars with the Indians broke out directly on the heels of the treaty making (Richards 1979). These wars started in eastern Washington with the Yakimas and Walla Wallas, but quickly spread to the Puget Sound area. Eells reports on some of this conflict in this volume.

Edwin Eells was appointed Indian agent at Skokomish at the time of the so-called "peace policy" in Indian affairs promoted by President Grant, which contrasted greatly with the policies of Governor Stevens. Northwest Indians were virtually all finally confined to reservations and, with some few exceptions, were in a state of peace. After a flurry of treaty writing by the Peace Commission in 1867, the treaty system ended in 1871 when Congress declared that no more treaties would be made. The key to the new era, however, was the pressures brought on the government by reform-minded religious groups concerned with Indian affairs, particularly Quaker organizations at first. Out of this pressure came a system whereby the Indian agents were nominated by religious organizations, and a board of Indian commissioners also made up of religious leaders was appointed as a kind of watchdog agency over administration and expenditure. The system was established by 1869 and Edwin was nominated by the Congregational Church through the American Missionary Association. Myron received a commission from the same American Missionary Association.

President Grant's policy was aimed at getting reliable employees for the agencies and curtailing the prevalent corruption and mismanagement. The Skokomish Reservation came under Congregational jurisdiction, although the government technically approved all nominees.

The goal of curtailing corruption was at least in this one instance achieved, since Edwin notes that at the end of his career when his books went through their final audit, "I was not short an article of property or a dollar in money" (E. Eells 1916:70). The challenge he faced is illustrated by the statement he says the territorial superintendent made when he was commissioned: "Young man, it makes no difference what your character and reputation has been or how you conducted yourself hereafter—you will be called dishonest and believed to be a thief, and you can just as well make up your mind to it" (E. Eells 1916:70).

Political influence rapidly reasserted itself as a factor in the Indian service and Edwin Eells' survival as an agent for twenty-four years is unique in a period when employees were regularly turned out with each shift in party administration. I have written elsewhere of the trials and tribulations of Edwin Eells' political struggle, which included repeated accusations of dishonesty, all of which he managed to refute (Castile 1981). On one occasion he had to travel to Washington, D.C., to face accusations before the Senate Indian Affairs Committee, and in the end his position on the Puyallup lands was completely eliminated. The American Missionary Association editor said at the time, "His removal is said to be due solely to politics. We are sorry for the Indians, and we are ashamed of a government that will deprive them for partisan purposes of a good agent" (1895:38).

What were the goals of the reformers which Myron and Edwin Eells represent? Above all, they were committed to the assimilation of the Indian peoples into the mainstream of American life. They had no ambitions toward preserving the traditional ways of the Indian peoples whom they, as much as anyone else, saw as barbaric. The founder of the Carlyle Indian School reflects this attitude in his announced determination toward his students: "to kill the Indian in him and save the man" (Prucha 1973:261). The reformers differed from others in their belief that the Indians were in fact capable of civilization and in their determination to bring it about.

The approach was distinctly paternalistic, with goals and procedures set by the agent and coercion used where cooperation could not be obtained. The agent appointed "chiefs" and enforced his policies with Indian police and judges. Law formally establishing an Indian police force was not enacted until 1879, but Edwin was already holding trials for drunkenness and had authorized a police force by 1874. A system for identifying "Indian offenses" and courts to try them, directed primarily at the prohibition of traditional religion and curing, was established by 1883, but again Edwin, like many other agents, had long since been striving to suppress these practices on his own authority. Myron recounts the struggle against the Shaker Church in his *Ten Years of Missionary Work among the Indians at Skokomish*, and describes its suppression by his brother under the heading, "The Victory" (1886:180–237). Edwin deposed the appointed "chiefs" who were supporting the religion, forbad its further practice, and banished Billy Clams, its apparent leader, from the reservation. All of this Myron obviously approved, and deplored later limitations imposed on the power of the agents (Castile 1982).

The centerpiece of the efforts to suppress uncivilized behavior as a step toward civilization and assimilation was the campaign against drinking. Myron organized temperance societies while Edwin arrested and jailed offenders for drunkenness. Edwin made many attempts to have whites convicted for selling liquor to the Indians but with little success. With the Dawes Act of 1887, any Indian who possessed allotted land also became a citizen of the United States. This did not apparently affect Eells' control so long as Washington remained a territory but in 1891, a year after statehood, a court case was brought and Edwin's authority to arrest and try Indians for drunkenness or any other offense was ended. He commented in his memoirs, "Our labor of twenty years, based on force and law, more than moral principle, was swept away" (1916:237). In 1903 in a pessimistic article, "The Decrease of the Indians," Myron attributed that decrease in large part to the "vices of civilization," in particular drunkenness. He agreed with Edwin that "contact between Indians and worthless whites" made inevitable the failure of the efforts of both agent and missionary (1903:149).

In the area of education for Indian children there was a similar concern for isolating the pupils from contamination; however, it was the contaminating influence of their parents and kinsmen that the reformers sought to regulate. Education policy was described in 1875 by the Board of Indian Commissioners, which stated that "the true policy in dealing with the Indian race, as with every other, for the purpose of elevating them to the social and moral conditions of Christian civilization, consists not so much in feeding or governing the adults as in educating the children" (Prucha 1976:269). In general, there was a feeling that the adults might well be beyond salvation and that only the children could hope to become truly assimilated.

Myron echoes prevailing opinion in his support of boarding schools and his comments regarding the influence of the home on the student. "Neatness" of the household seems to have concerned him particularly and he bewails the influence of the elders in dragging down the young. He claims that the young try to restrain the uncivilized behavior of the parents, but "the old folks say: 'your education and civilization are a splendid thing for you, when they make you so above your parents and relatives that you cannot treat them politely. Religion is a pretty thing, isn't it, when it leads you to treat us so.' So with all their honest efforts they are between two fires, and it is a hard place for them. Some get discouraged and fall back into the old ways" (M. Eells 1903:147).

Above all else the reformers saw the distribution of land in severalty and the breaking up of communal ownership as the cornerstone of their civilizing and assimilative crusade. This was embodied in the passage of the Dawes or General Allotment Act, which was praised by Theodore Roosevelt in 1901 as "a mighty pulverizing engine to break up the tribal mass" (Taylor 1971:16). Dawes himself took a more positive attitude, similar to that expressed by Edwin Eells on communal ownership, "there is no enterprise to make your home any better than that of your neighbors. There is no selfishness, which is at the bottom of civilization" (Washburn 1975:17). I have written elsewhere of Edwin's efforts and views noting that by his second annual report he had already begun to ask for land patents and continued to do so every year until 1887 (Castile 1981). In 1887 he rejoiced that "the reservation Indians belonging to this agency are no longer wards of the government, but free-born sovereigns of their native land. With them the Indian problem has been solved" (1887:215).

Myron was in essential agreement but was more cautious. His caution was not over the land itself, for he said in 1893, "From 1874, for many years, we—our agent, other agents in this state and myself—worked earnestly to induce government to give them patents to their land in severalty" (1893:558). But the problem of control over behavior was linked to the granting of citizenship with the land. "This came several years earlier than the Christian workers among the Indians thought wise . . . they need a parent's restraining power yet" (1893:559).

Edwin had the more practical problem of protecting the Indian land. In his 1888 report he noted that "The great and increasing value of the land belonging to the Indians of the Puyallup Reservation makes it an object of desire to the covetous and avaricious" (1888:22). The pressures of the expanding city of Tacoma were irresistible and where there were once 18,000 acres of Puyallup Reservation land only 33 acres remain today in trust status. Being relatively isolated, Skokomish fared better, losing only about half of its original 4,987 acres to non-Indian owners. The impact of this well-meant program was everywhere much the same: it succeeded in separating Indians from their "surplus" lands while having only dubious impact on their civilization.

Myron Eells saw fairly clearly that land, education, or other remedies would have little impact if promises were not kept and "justice" done. In a talk, "Justice to the Indian," he cites the words of an anonymous Portland dentist, "I have no great hankering after the Indians, but if I had made a promise to a dog I would keep it" (1883:1). He says himself, "other plans are good, of treating them as individuals, or giving them land and the like are good if kept in their place, but we must remember that they are not the root but the branches of the tree. Justice is the root. . . . If we make a promise to a dog let us keep it" (1883:8–9). Perhaps more than anything else the quest for just treatment for the Indians, whatever the program, separated the reformers from others.

Myron's specific purpose at Skokomish was, of course, the religious salvation of the Indian not their civilization, although he saw little difference in these purposes. It is curious that, like his father before him, Myron Eells appears not to have had much direct success in the religious conversion of the peoples of Skokomish. Writing in 1894 of services commemorating twenty years of missionary work, he says of his congregation, "During this time one hundred and fifteen have been received into the church on profession of faith, and thirty-one by letter. Of these seventeen have died, forty-five have been dismissed by letter, thirteen have been dropped and six are suspended" (1894b:333). It would appear then that he had only sixty-five members after twenty years and not all of these were Indians. Writing in 1898 he estimated that the Shaker religion had six hundred to eight hundred members, a startling contrast to his own limited success (1898). In fact, in 1894 he wrote in another article that there had been a revival of the Shaker religion, and "they have taken the larger share of the uneducated Indians in the Church with them" (1894c:167).

Since Eells himself is in fact the major firsthand source on the rise of the Shaker Church cited by subsequent students, his own account in this volume will serve to describe that movement and I will not do so here (Barnett 1957; Castile 1982). Myron in some ways seems to have approved of the Church and, writing in 1899, even took credit for its good points, saying, "I assert that nearly all that is good in the Shaker religion is there because of the Christian teaching these Indians have had" (1899:8–9). The claim is probably true and his part in the creation of the fusional faith of the Shakers may well have been his greatest contribution to the well being of the Puget Sound peoples. He himself credits it repeatedly with achieving the aims of promoting and sustaining temperance as well as discouraging gambling, the resort to traditional curers, and other forms of debauchery. Some of his goals were achieved even if not in the way he had intended.

Perhaps this is the point at which to end this introduction with the words of his brother in his memoirs on the occasion of Myron's death: "Although occupying a humble position, he had exerted a wide influence for good, and left that highest of all records—'a good name'" (1916:370).

The

INDIANS

of

PUGET SOUND

The Notebooks of Myron Eells

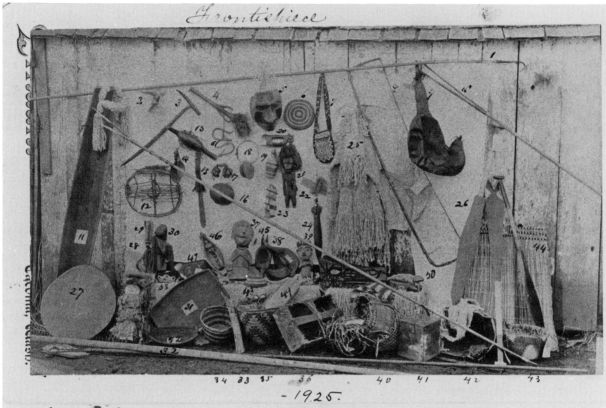

Frontispiece

- 1925 -

Photograph of a number of articles in my cabinet, together with some which I obtained for the Worlds Columbian Exposition at Chicago. Taken 1892.

1. Fish hook with handle
2. Hand adze
3. Camas digger
4. Tamahnous rattle, Quinaielt
5. Mask
6. Table mats
7. Beaded shot pouch
8. Quinaielt fish net
9. Paunch, oil bottle
10. Fish spear
11. Plate
12. Snow shoes
13. Black tamahnous rattle
14. Ladles
15. Copper war club
16. Duck spear
17. Deer hoof rattles
18. Shell rattles
19. Bottle covered with grass work
20. Clallam hand adze
21. Quinaielt doctor
22. Combs
23. Head band of shells
24. Stone war club
25. Wool dress
26. Paddles
27. Clallam drum
28. Baby in cradle
29. Strap for carrying basket
30. Head of Haida canoe
31. Plate
32. Herring rake
33. Canoe
34. Basket, fancy
35. Basket, watertight
36. Twana drum
37. Twana carving
38. Duck floats
39. Haida doctor
40. Basket, flexible
41. Water box
42. Basket, Makah
43. Basket
44. Mat coat
45. Duck float
46. Canoe
47. Box
48. Basket
49. Basket
50. Duck or puffin dish
51. Halibut hooks
52. Dish
53. Cap

DEDICATION

To my brother, *Hon. Edwin Eells*,

who for twenty-two years, since 1871, has been United States Indian Agent among the Indians of Puget Sound, and who, during that time has very greatly aided me in my work among them, these pages are affectionately dedicated.

The Indians

of

Puget Sound.

By M. Eells L. D.

36 years

Missionary of the American Missionary
    Association for twenty years at Skokomish
    Washington.
Associate Member of the Victoria Institute
or Philosophical Society of Great Britain.
Corresponding Member of the Anthropo
    logical Society of Washington D. C.
Author of "Indian Missions on the Pacific
    coast," "Ten Years at Skokomish; the
    Twana Indians"; "The Twana, Chem
    akum and Clallam Indians", "Diction
    ary of the Chinook-Jargon Language."
    Hymns in Chinook Jargon.

Vol 1

Original title page

PREFACE[1]

IN THE FOLLOWING PAGES I have tried mainly to describe the Indians as they formerly were, with frequent allusions, however, to their present condition. They are now in a state of transition, but some are more advanced in civilization than others. In a general way, I should say of the greater part of those under forty-five years of age at the present time, that if they had white skins, talked the English language, if all of them had abandoned their belief in their medicine men, if they travelled in boats instead of canoes, if the women wore hats or bonnets on their heads, and if they were neater, they would be called civilized, at least as much so as the lower class of whites. Consequently in these articles I have often been obliged to use the word "were" instead of "are," and yet, in order to describe the Indians correctly, it has seemed that I ought to make a distinction.

My residence since June 1874 has been in the Skokomish reservation among the Twana Indians. My missionary work has also been among the Squakson and Clallam Indians, and with the few Chemakums who are left. Consequently, my observation has been mainly among them. Indians from nearly all the other tribes on the main part of Puget Sound have either intermarried with those of the Skokomish reservation, lived here from time to time, or made visits here; and I have visited some of these other Indians at their homes, so that I have had an opportunity to see considerable of other tribes, and I have here recorded what I have thus learned. Hence I have entitled the work, *The Indians of Puget Sound*, although the greater part of the work refers to the four tribes first mentioned, for the habits and customs of all the tribes on Puget Sound, although speaking different languages, are much the same.

I have also visited the Indians on the coast at the Quinaielt and Neah Bay agencies, and while not professing to describe them, yet refer to them at times by way of contrast or agreement, thus preserving what I have learned about them.

I have been surprised to see how little has been written about these Indians.[2] As far as I can learn, Vancouver, in 1792, was the first writer who speaks of them, but his notices of them, as a discoverer, are necessarily very meager.[3] Commodore Wilkes in 1841 is the next.[4] Gathering his information largely from the officers of the Hudson's Bay Company, he was more full, yet his statements refer more to the number and situation of the tribes than to their manners and customs.

Dr. George Gibbs made a report in 1854 to Captain George B. McClellan, of the same character, but a year or two later he wrote out by far the fullest account extant of their habits and customs, which, however, was not published until 1877, when it was printed by the Ethnological Bureau at Washington in volume 1 of *Contributions to North American Ethnology*. In it is also given a vocabulary of the Nisqually language. He also prepared a small dictionary of the Clallam and Lummi languages, which was published in Shea's *Library of American Linguistics*, very few copies of which are extant.[5]

In Tolmie and Dawson's *Comparative Vocabularies of the Tribes of British Columbia* (Montreal, 1884) are given short vocabularies of about two hundred words in the Snohomish and Chehalis languages.[6] Early residents among the tribes on the Columbia river, as Ross Cox, G. Franchere, and Alexander Ross, have written fully in regard to those tribes, and Hon. J. G. Swan has described the Indians on the Pacific coast of Washington territory, but no resident among the tribes on Puget Sound has described them, with perhaps the exception of Dr. Gibbs, and his residence was, I believe, more properly among the whites of the Sound than with the Indians, though his eyes and ears were open and he gathered information largely from other whites who had lived among them.[7]

CONTENTS

Volume 1

Volume 2

Volume 3

Volume 4

CONTENTS

Volume 5

Volume 6

VOL. 1

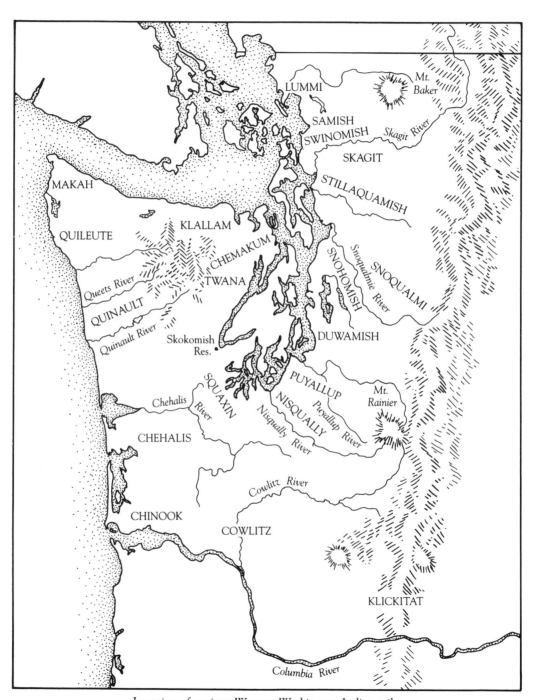

Location of various Western Washington Indian tribes

I

NAMES AND SITUATIONS OF THE TRIBES

THE TWANAS

Their name is spelled Too-an-hooch in the treaty which was made in 1855; the Clallams [Klallams], Squaksons, and other Indians pronounce it Tu-an-hu, and the Twanas call it Tu-ad-hu.[1] These various pronunciations have been shortened to Twana, which is now used in all government reports.*

They originally lived on both sides of Hood's Canal for its whole length and were divided into three bands, the Du-hle-lips [Duhlelap], Skokomish, and the Kol-sids, or Quil-ceeds [Quilcenes].

The Du-hle-lips originally lived at the head of the Canal, where a small stream empties into it, which they called Du-hle-lip but which the whites now call Union creek, and for about ten miles below the head.

Fifteen miles below the head were the Skokomish band, who lived near the mouth of the Skokomish river, where is the present reservation for the whole tribe. Dr. Gibbs, in volume 1 of *Contributions to North American Ethnology*, gives this as the name of the whole tribe, but it was originally only the name of one band. Now, however, as it is the name of the reservation, the whole tribe is better known to the whites by the name Skokomish than by their original one of Twana.

Thirty or forty miles below the Skokomish river lived the Quilceeds, or Kol-ceedobish as they called themselves, but Kol-sin-o-bish as the Clallams pronounced it. Their home was around the Quilceed Bay, the northernmost arm of Hood's Canal, and the mouth of the Duk-a-boos and Dos-wail-opsh rivers.

These three bands were not always at peace but waged petty wars with each other. For more than thirty years, however, most of them have been gathered on the same reservation, have been on good terms with each other, and have intermarried, so that these band distinctions are now practically obsolete. When, however, the older Du-hle-lips

---

*J. K. Townshend in 1835 spelled the word Too-wanne-nos. [The Townshend referred to in this and subsequent footnotes is John Kirk Townshend, *Narrative of a Journey across the Rocky Mountains to the Columbian River . . .* , 1839—Ed.]

leave the reservation for fishing, they are apt to go to their old waters, and the same is true of the Quilceeds.

The dialects of these three bands formerly varied a little: thus, the word for "go" in Du-hle-lip was *bi-se-dab*, while in Skokomish it was *bi-he-dab*. But at the present time I have not found it practicable, in collecting a vocabulary, to separate the dialects. I have gathered most of the words from the older school boys, who have been brought up on the reservation and who have heard all of the dialects, which are rapidly merging into one. Generally I have found it necessary to use English-speaking Indians for the purpose, and the older school boys are the best there are.

At present most of these Indians live on the Skokomish reservation. About a dozen live around Seabeck and Quilceed.

Although the Squakson tribe, by treaty and language, belong to the Nisqually Indians, yet about thirty of that tribe, since the selection of the Skokomish reservation, have moved to it, and have become incorporated with the Twanas. They did so because their own people for a time were scattered, because of the nearness of the reservation to their old haunts and its advantages, and because of numerous intermarriages between them and the Twanas. For the most part they use their own language, but they understand the Twanas and the Twanas understand them. Twenty-five others for a time became connected with the Twanas, but because they did not obtain titles to the land on the reservation as soon as they expected, and as soon as they had a right to expect from government promises, they became discouraged and left.

THE CHEMAKUMS

North of the Twanas were this tribe. In the treaty their name is written Chemakum. Dr. George Gibbs writes it Tsem-a-kum. Hon. J. G. Swan follows the orthography of the treaty, which represents most correctly the way in which both the Indians and the whites of the region pronounce it. The whites call a prairie by the same name. These people call themselves A-hwa-ki-lu, as well as Chemakum.

They formerly occupied the land from the mouth of Hood's Canal to the mouth of Port Discovery Bay. According to their tradition and that of Kwilleutes [Quileutes], they originally came from the latter tribe (who live on the Pacific coast about 30 miles south of Cape Flattery, and 125 miles distant, and from whom they are now separated by the Makahs and Clallams). Hon. J. G. Swan says in regard to this in his work on the Makahs (p. 57) that the Kwilleutes have a tradition that a long time ago, there was a very high and sudden tide which took four days to ebb, after which a portion of the tribe made their way to the vicinity of Port Townsend and are known as Chemakums. The latter have a similar tradition and the numerals of the two tribes corroborate the same.

They are said originally to have been a very warlike tribe, not very numerous, but strong and brave. They had a village near where Irondale or Port Hadlock is now, called Tsets-i-bus, which is said to have been a kind of capital for nearly all of the tribes on the Sound, and where they occasionally collected for various purposes. Dr. Gibbs, in 1852, stated their number to have been ninety, but they are now virtually extinct, there being none left who are not married to white men or into other tribes. The last complete families connected themselves with the Clallam Indiams, but death has destroyed them as families, leaving only scattered individuals, and they use the Clallam language. They say that their diminution was caused by the smallpox, but probably war had much to do with it, as Dr. Gibbs says that they were engaged in wars with the Makah, Clallam, Twana, Snohomish, and Duwamish Indians, by whom their power was broken.

THE CLALLAMS

In the treaty, the name is spelled S'Klallam, but the "s" has been dropped and the "k" changed to a "c," wherever the name is except in government reports. Their own name for themselves is Nu-sklaim. Their territory formerly extended from Port Discovery Bay west to the Hoko river near the mouth of the Straits of Fuca. Many other bands of the same tribe lived on the northern side of the Straits in British Columbia. The treaty with them, made at the same time as with the Twanas, expected them to go to the Skokomish reservation, and the government was to furnish the means to move them there. This has never been done; they have never been moved and probably never will be. At present many of them have moved further up the Sound to obtain work. The following is a description of their villages.

1. Across the bay, opposite Port Gamble, is quite a village of them, named Boston, who earn their money largely at the saw-mills there. Until within a few years, Port Ludlow has had a few, but they are now gone.

2. Near Port Townsend are a few who make their living by fishing.

3. Opposite Port Discovery is a small village of those who live mainly by working in the saw-mill there. They have bought the land on which their houses stand.

4. At Sequim are the last remnants of a band which formerly was of considerable importance.

5. At Jamestown, five miles from Dungeness, is a flourishing village of those who formerly lived at Dungeness and Sequim. It is the most influential village in the whole tribe. They bought land, laid it off into a town and have a school, church, and jail. The home of the head chief is here. They gain their living by farming on their land, canoeing, fishing, and working for the neighboring whites. Twenty years ago, they were a drunken, worthless set, so that the neighboring whites petitioned the Indian agent to remove them to the Skokomish reservation. Hearing of this, the leading ones, as they did not wish to be removed from the land of their fathers, determined to reform. Gathering together $500, they bought 210 acres of land, divided it among themselves, according to the amount contributed by each one, and have since that time been slowly improving. They have also improved in morals, until now they are the most civilized and prosperous band in the tribe.

6. At Port Angeles has been another village of considerable importance. Many years

ago, when the U.S. Custom House was here, work was abundant and the Indian village lively, but as the custom house was washed away, and the business removed to Port Townsend, most of the whites moved away, employment became scarce and nearly all the Indians went away, not to return again, a good share having crossed the Straits to the British side. About a dozen are all that are now left.

7. At Elwha was formerly the largest band of the tribe, but they have now diminished in numbers and strength. Five or six of them have homesteaded land a mile or two back from the beach, the only ones of the whole tribe who live so far from salt water. These Indians live by canoeing, fishing, and what they raise on their places, and, in the later part of winter and spring, go to the Makah waters for seals.

8. About Pysht are a few families who live mainly by fishing and sealing.

9. At Clallam Bay, about 1880, a number bought about a hundred and fifty acres of land in imitation of their Jamestown neighbors. They did not, however, progress as rapidly, as for many years there were very few whites near by to encourage and teach them. There were not enough children among them to warrant the establishment of a school and a greater proportion of them were old and non-progressive. They raised a little on their land, fished, and hunted seals. About 1891 a boom took place in Clallam Bay, two towns sprang up, the lands of these Indians became very valuable, and they sold out, to dwindle away.

According to the census of these Indians, which I took for the United States in 1880, they were then distributed as follows:

Six were on or near the Skokomish reservation, 10 at Seabeck, 96 at Port Gamble, 6 at Port Ludlow, 12 at Port Townsend, 22 at Port Discovery, 18 at Sequim, 122 at or near Jamestown, 57 at Port Angeles or across the Straits from that place, 67 at Elwha, 24 at Pysht, 46 at Clallam Bay, and 3 at Hoko. Since that time, those at Skokomish, Seabeck, Port Ludlow, and Hoko have left those places and nearly all have left Sequim and Port Angeles. I can learn of only two dialects which were spoken by this tribe: those at Elwha, Pysht, and Clallam Bay speaking, it is said, as if with thicker tongues than the others, and so pronouncing some words differently.

THE LUMMIS

These Indians were situated on the east side of the Sound to the extreme northern part of Washington. They speak another dialect of the Clallam language and, for some reasons, ought to be included in the treaty made with the Snohomish Indians and others in that locality, and, hence, have become virtually more distinctly separated from the Clallams than they were before the treaty was made. There were three bands of these: the Lummi proper, who lived about the mouth of the Nooksack river; the Swallah, who lived on Orcas and San Juan islands; and the Buk-sak, who lived up the Nooksack river. According to Dr. Gibbs, this latter band spoke a dialect so different from that of the Lummis as to be almost unintelligible to them.

THE SAMISH

These Indians lived about the Samish river, south of the Lummis. They speak the same language, but are said to be a distinct tribe. There were but two bands of them: the Samish, who lived at the mouth of the river, and the Bis-tla-tlous, who lived up the river.

THE SKAGITS

This tribe lived south of the Samish Indians, and by language are more nearly related to the Snohomish and Nisqually tribes on the south than to their northern neighbors. They lived mainly near the Skagit river. As near as I can learn from the Indians, there were five bands: the Swinomish, who lived on the salt water not far from the mouth of the river, and on Fidalgo Island and on Whidby's Island, opposite; the Do-kwa-tcabsh, who lived on the river at the mouth; the Sba-li-hu, who resided farther up, on what might be called the middle of the river; the Sba-le-hu, whose country was on the northern branch which flows from Mt. Baker; and the Sak-wi-be-hu, who lived on the southern branch of the river. Dr. Gibbs also mentions the Kiliallu, Nukwatsamish, Towahha, Sakumehu, Miskaiwhu, Miseekwigweelis, and Skwonamish, but does not state whether they are villages or bands, or where they lived.

THE SNOHOMISH

These lived south of the last-named tribe, south of the Stillagwamish river to the Snohomish river and on both sides of it and its branches. The Indians speak of four bands: the Du-gwads-habsh, who lived on the southern part of Whidbey's Island; the Snohomish proper, whose home was near the mouth of the river of that name; the Ske-haw-mish, on the north fork of the Snohomish river, which on some maps is marked the Skywhamish, and on others the Skykomish; and the Snoqualmie, who lived on the southern branch of the Snohomish river, called the Snoqualmie river. Dr. Gibbs also mentions the Sk-tah-le-jun, Kwehtl-mamish, and Stolutswhamish bands. While he confirms the statements of the Indians that the Snoqualmie, or Snokwalmu, band was very intimate with and properly belonged to this tribe, he also says that their dialect of the language agrees more nearly with the Indians on their south, that is, with the Nisqually language proper.

THE DUWAMISH*

These lived on the Duwamish river and its tributaries, and on the islands and peninsulas across the Sound, west of the same region. Some of them are on the Port Madison and some on the Muckleshoot reservation. They were divided into several bands, as the Sawamish, Sukwamish, Samamish, Skopahmis, Sk'telmist, and St'kahmish.

THE PUYALLUPS**

These were formerly called Puyallupahmish and lived on the Puyallup river and Vashon island opposite its mouth. The Puyallups proper lived about the mouth of the river; the T'kaw-kwa-mis, on its upper branches; and S'ho-ma-mish on Vashon island. They were formerly not very important, but have of late years become so, because their reservation is the most valuable on the Sound.

THE NISQUALLY, OR SQUALLIAMISH

These lived mainly about the Nisqually river, south of the Puyallups and about Olympia and some of the bays west of it. The bands were the Stulakumamish, who lived near where Steilacoom now is; the Segwallitsu, the S'hotlemamish, of Case Inlet, or North Bay; the Sahehwamish of Hammersly Inlet, or Skookum Bay; the Sawamish of Totten Inlet, or Oyster Bay; the Skwaiaitl of Eld Inlet, or Mud Bay; the Stehtsasamish of Budd Inlet, where Olympia now stands; and the Nusehtsatl of Henderson's Inlet, or South Bay. Dr. Gibbs includes the Puyallups with these as one tribe and probably this was correct formerly, but they have now become separated into two tribes owing to the reservation system.

THE SQUAKSONS

East of the Twanas and west of the Puyallups at and around the base of the great peninsula between Hood's Canal and the main Sound, were the Squaksons [Squaxin], or Skwaksnamish. They speak a dialect of the Nisqually language and were included in the treaty with that tribe at Medicine Creek, but owing to their nearness to the Skokomish reservation (about twenty miles) and their intermarriages with the Twanas, their children have been largely brought to the Skokomish reservation to school.

*J. K. Townshend in 1835 spelled this name Toughnowamish.
**Townshend spelled this name Poo-yal-aw-poo.

THE CHEHALIS

The Upper Chehalis Indians live on the upper branches of the Chehalis river as far down as and including the Satsop. Their proper name is not Chehalis; they have given me Kwai-ailk as their name. Dr. Gibbs says that they are known by the Sound Indians by the name of the Staktamish, by others as the Nuso-lupsh, and by the Willowpah as the Kwu-tch-ni. The Chehalis proper live near the mouth of the Chehalis river, and they thus gave their name to the stream, the whites having first visited it at the coast; after that the Indians on the upper branches became known as the Upper Chehalis Indians. I have not been able to learn that they were divided into bands, but one Indian has given me the names of forty-eight villages which they once occupied between the Satsop branch and the Cascade mountains. Those below the Satsop were called the Lower Chehalis Indians.

All of these three Indians belong to the Salishan family. This family is quite large and includes also the Quinaielts [Quinaults] on the west; the Tilamooks [Tillamooks] and Siletz Indians in Oregon on the south; the Spokanes, Okanogans, Colvilles, and Flatheads of eastern Washington; the Coeur-d'Alênes and Pend d'Oreilles of northern Idaho; and the Thompson River, Nanaimo, Cowichan, and other tribes in British Columbia to the 53rd parallel.

These Puget Sound Indians are bounded on the northwest also by the Makahs and Quillehutes [Quileutes], on the southeast by the Cowlitz Indians, and on the east by the Oakamas [Yakimas] and Klikitats [Klickitats].

II

HISTORY

THEIR OWN ACCOUNT OF THEIR ORIGIN AND HISTORY

They believe that all except the Chemakums were created where they now live, and also that nearly all other tribes and nations were created where they now are. They have hardly any reliable knowledge of their own history earlier than the recollection of the oldest Indians. Even in obtaining their names for various articles, I have often found that persons of twenty or twenty-five years do not know their names for stone arrow-heads, axes, chisels, anchors, rain stones, and the like, which went out of use soon after the coming of the whites. This shows how quickly the past is forgotten by them.[1]

I give the following stories, in which I presume there are more or less grains of truth, most of which were written for me by a Twana school boy, as they were told him by his father, and which are about all I have learned from them about their history.

The Quinaielt and Quilceed Indians. "While the Quilceed Indians were at peace in their habitations, a girl went out and looked into a house and saw (in her mind) many of their enemies getting ready to go into every house of the Quilceeds. She returned and told her master's family, but they would not believe her. The same day a boy went to get some water; when he looked into the water he saw some shadows, which were smiling, and these were the Quinaielt Indians. So he went home in haste to tell his parents, but they would not believe him. The girl took one of her master's sons and hid in the woods. Hence these Indians were not afraid, and so were all killed except the girl, the little boy, and one man, for the Quinaielt Indians went into every house and slew the Quilceeds. One man took his small babe and ran away. His enemies pursued him, and when he saw that they were about to overtake him, he laid down his child and began to swim across the bay. The Quinaielt Indians knew that they could not swim after the man, so they took his child and cut it in pieces. When the girl came back, she found her master dead, because he would not believe her."

The Victoria Indians and two families. "Two families were travelling together and at night they lodged. While they were there some one shot from the woods, and when they looked they saw some Indians. One family went off as fast as it could, but the other had left their child near a log. The Victoria Indians took him, but his father got ready and fired at them, and they restored the child. My father thought that if they should shoot at their enemies, they would think them brave and be afraid. The child that was taken captive is still living, and the daughter of the brave is also alive."

The Quinaielt Indians again. "After the battle the Quilceeds went out to search for their enemies, whom at last they found. Then they made a great shelf over their own beds. Their enemies came and were placed under the shelf, and one of them took a wife of the daughters of the Quilceeds. After a long time they laid themselves down on their beds, and the Quilceeds cut the ropes which held up the shelf. It fell down on the heads of the Quinaielt Indians and none of them escaped.

"Once the Quilceeds bored some holes in the bottom of their canoes, as their enemies came to see them. As they went home the Quilceeds started to take them across the bay. When they were in the middle of the bay, they took out the sticks, and the water came into the canoes and filled them. The Quinaielt Indians were drowned, but the Quilceeds were not drowned because their neighbors went to them and helped them. So the Quilceeds prevailed over their enemies and peace was once more restored."

Story of another family. "There was a man with his wife and children. One woman who was very fair was walking with a babe, and some boys and girls. She was the daughter of a sick man, but when she came home she found some other Indians killing the family, and her father was killed. These took hold of her; one wanted her, another wanted her, and all wanted her; so they killed her and none had her. The man's wife dug deep in the ground, put one of her daughters there, and covered her over; she did also the same for herself, and another person climbed a tree, and none saw her. So three were saved alive. The man was sick, yet they showed him no mercy."

A fight with a grizzly bear. "A long time ago a man came to the Canal to marry a wife. He found one and gave something to her father. The woman loved the man, but the man did not like his son-in-law, but threw the things away, which the man had given him; hence the man went home. After a while the woman went to gather some berries; my mother's mother was among them. The woman had a companion, and the two went away from their comrades, where they saw the bear, but they did not fear it; they simply talked about it and made fun.

"The bear went off, but after a time they saw it again, when they talked just as at first. The bear went around the woman who had wished to marry the man, and suddenly jumped at her. The other woman went to help her, but soon received some wounds, so that she left and went to tell her other comrades, while this woman kept fighting with the bear. Poor woman! She called aloud to her companions to help her, but they ran home to tell the news. She was soon killed; but her friends told her parents, and that night very many people gathered together with spears, arrows, and knives to fight the bear. When they reached the place they told the woman's parents to stand on a fallen tree where they would be safe. Then they surrounded the bear and had a great fight; they shot the bear and wounded her on each side, but after a while she ran away, and they ran after her. After a time they had no more arrows or spears, with the exception of two or three young men who still followed her. When they reached a muddy place, she stood on her hind legs and danced; the young men became frightened and ran back. When they looked at the dead woman they found very many wounds on her."

Thus far I have given the stories as they were written for me by a school boy, A. P. Peterson. The last one is in the main true, as I have heard it from several parties.

23

The Twanas relate that a long time ago they were camped in a scattered condition on Hood's Canal, nearly ten miles south of Seabeck. The Clallams came and killed those farthest north and took four or five girls captive. Those farther south were afraid and some wished to flee, but others said no. The Clallams, however, did not come to them, but returned.

Again I add some war stories as written for me by A. P. Peterson. "For some cause the Quilceeds and Skokomish Indians got mad with each other and got ready for battle. I do not know all about it, but my father tells a part of it. The Quilceeds were in a canoe going home with my mother, whom they took from my father, when my father took his gun and would have killed all of them if some one had not taken the gun away from where it was pointing, and it shot off another way. The Quilceeds then went home, and they became friends again." Thus, what was called war ended without any bloodshed.

The following traditions have also been related to me, which may have a few grains of truth in them for a foundation. A long time ago a large number of Indians came up Hood's Canal and ended near Eneti, on the beach west of the mouth of the Skokomish river, instead of going up the river, as they were not acquainted with the country. The Twanas were camped on the Skokomish river, about four miles above its mouth. Their enemies intended to surprise them, and so conquer them, but owing to their ignorance of the country, they proceeded to march overland to where the Twanas were camped, and consequently fell into a great swamp, which still exists and is considered impassable. Here they stuck and could not get out, until at last they were stung to death by multitudes of mosquitoes. Tradition also says that long afterwards some of the Twanas visited the place and saw the bones, bows, arrows, and spear-heads of their enemies, still there.

The Twanas also say that many years ago, perhaps eighty or a hundred, nearly all the Indians on the Sound leagued together to fight the Indians of British Columbia. This league included the Twanas, Squaksons, Chemakums, Clallams, Snohomish, Puyallup, Nisqually, and Skagit Indians, who went in hundreds of canoes and with thousands of warriors. They intended to surprise their enemies. When near Victoria, however, they met a large number of the Northern Indians in canoes, but they were many fewer in number than the Sound Indians.

The Sound Indians urged the others to fight, but they did not wish to do so, and only consented after a large amount of urging. The battle continued all day, when the Sound Indians were defeated with great slaughter, the British Columbia Indians being by far the best fighters. Only a few of the defeated Indians ever lived to return; in some cases only three or four of a tribe. One or two are reported as having escaped by swimming. Having swum for a long time, they reached a floating tree, upon which they remained for nearly a month, without clothes or food, yet they did not perish. At last they drifted to land on the southern side of the Straits and so returned home.

HISTORY BY THE WHITES

Dr. Gibbs, in volume 1 of *Contributions to North American Ethnology*, has probably given the most correct history extant of the early visits of the whites to this region, of which I make a short synopsis. The first visit of which we have any knowledge was in 1789 by Captain Kendrick of the American vessel *Washington*, or in 1790 by Lieutenant Quimper of the Spanish vessel *Princess Royal*. They came as far as Dungeness. The Indians thought them and their vessel to be Dokibatl, the great deity of the Puget Sound Indians, as they then knew nothing of the white men. Accordingly, when they visited the ship, they painted their faces and prepared themselves for a tamahnous. Captain Kendrick came as far as the entrance to Admiralty Inlet. Two other vessels came a year and a half later, but they did not come further than Port Discovery bay.[2]

In 1792 Lord Vancouver came, who gave the first account extant in regard to the Indians. He visited all of the Indians on the Sound, and gave names to the various places, most of which remain to the present time. The people did not seem surprised at his expedition. With one exception they were all quiet and peaceable. Those who showed signs of hostility were "some distance up the first arm leading to the westward above the Narrows" above Vashon Island, evidently among the Squakson Indians, but owing to precaution, all trouble with them was avoided.

After these explorers in the early part of the present century, the Hudson's Bay Company came, and the great part of the intercourse which these Indians had with the whites was with that company previous to 1850, though a few Americans came to the Sound in the forties. The Methodist missionaries and Catholic priests came in 1839, the latter to stay and have missions among the Indians, more especially among the northern tribes. The Hudson's Bay Company had one trading post on the Sound, Fort Nisqually, established in 1833, while the one at Victoria, B.C., was so near that many of the northern Indians on the Sound traded there.

After 1850 the influence of Americans began to increase, and that of the Hudson's Bay Company to wane with the Indians, and in 1854, the next year after Washington was organized as a territory, the United States sent Governor I. I. Stevens, Col. M. C. Simmons, and a few associates to make treaties with them.

Treaties

December 26, 1854, a treaty was made at Medicine Creek with the Puyallup, Nisqually, and Squakson Indians, together with a few small associate tribes. By the terms of this, three reservations were set apart for the use of these Indians, the Puyallup reservation, at the mouth of the Puyallup river; the Nisqually reservation, about six miles above the mouth of the Nisqually river; and the Squakson reservation, consisting of the Squakson Island.

The Puyallup reservation now consists of 18,062 acres, and is the most valuable reservation on Puget Sound, as it consists mainly of rich bottom land, adjoining Tacoma, the terminus of the North Pacific Railroad. In 1886 these lands were patented to the Indians in severalty. The school for the benefit of the Indians belonging to this treaty is situated here, their physician and other employees reside here, and it is now the headquarters for the agent of all the Upper Sound Indians.

The Nisqually reservation consists of 4,717 acres, which in 1884 were patented to these Indians in severalty.

The Squakson reservation consists of 1,494 acres, all of which is timbered land not far above the level of the sea, and a large share of it may be called second-class land. In 1884 these lands were patented to these Indians in severalty.

January 22, 1855, at Port Elliot, a treaty was made with the Duwamish, Etakmur, Samish, Skagit, Lummi, Snohomish, Sukwamish, Swinomish, and Port Madison Indians. By it, four reservations were set apart for their use. The Tulalip or Snohomish reservation comprises 22,490 acres. Here is the school and the residence of the agent and most of the other employees. In 1885 and 1886 these Indians received patents for their lands—most of which is second quality land.

The Swinomish reservation consists of 7,170 acres. About five hundred acres of this is first quality, tide marsh land. The rest is gravelly and upland and very poor.

The Lummi reservation lies at the mouth of the Nooksack river, not far from the northern boundary of Washington Territory, and comprises 12,312 acres for which the Indians received patents in 1884. More than half of this land is very valuable—first quality.

The Port Madison reservation lies on the opposite side of the bay from the town of Port Madison. There are 7,284 acres in it. It is mostly land of a poor quality.

The treaty of Point No Point was made January 26, 1855, with the three tribes of Chemakums, Clallams, and Twanas. By it, but one reservation was set apart for the Indians—the Skokomish, consisting of 4,987 acres—three-fifths of which is number one bottom land, and the rest is hilly and gravelly. In 1886 these lands were patented to the Indians.

By orders of the President, the Muckleshoot reservation was set apart for the benefit of the Muckleshoot Indians, January 20, 1857, and April 9, 1874. This reservation consists of 3,367 acres on White river, a branch of the Duwamish, and attached to the Tulalip Agency. This is good bottom land.

An attempt was made by Governor Stevens in February, 1855, to negotiate a treaty with several tribes of Indians on and adjoining the Chehalis river, consisting of the Cowlitz, Upper Chehalis, Satsop, Lower Chehalis, Chinook, Quinaielts, and Queets, but it was a failure and consequently no reservation was given them by treaty. By an order from the Secretary of the Interior, dated July 8, 1864, the Chehalis reservation was set apart for the benefit of the Upper Chehalis Indians. This consists of 4,225 acres, is situated on the Chehalis river, at the mouth of Black river, and is attached to the Nisqually Agency. About one-fourth of this reservation is number one bottom land; most of the rest is gravelly upland, and not good for much except pasture. These lands, not being granted by treaty but by an order from the President, could not be patented to the Indians in severalty as the other reservations were, but were thrown open to settlement about 1886. They were immediately entered as homesteads by the Indians, who had the first right to enter them, and very soon they proved up and received their patents.[3]

Hostilities

The first bloodshed on the Sound as far as I can learn was in 1849, at which time an American settler, Leander C. Wallace, was killed at Nisqually by the Snoqualmie and Skehwamish Indians. Six of these were soon afterwards taken and tried, two of whom were found guilty and executed.

In 1855 and 1856, soon after the treaties just mentioned were made but before most of them were ratified, the Yakima war occurred, which was the most widespread Indian war that ever devastated the North Pacific coast. It extended from southern Oregon, about Rogue river to the Yakimas on the north, and from Puget Sound on the west to the Burnt river and the Grand Ronde Valley in eastern Oregon. A part of the Indians on Puget Sound were engaged in it, mainly those living around Steilacoom, Tacoma, and Seattle, namely the Nisquallies, Puyallups, Duwamish, and White River Indians. These were led by Leschi, the greatest war chief Puget Sound has produced, a Nisqually Indian, his brother Quiemuth, Kitsap, Nelson, and Stehi. The Snohomish Indians led by Pat-kanim assisted the whites. The other tribes on the Sound did not engage in the war, and people lived among the Twanas in safety during the whole of the time.

The worst massacre was on White river, though the country around Tacoma and Se-attle was devastated, to what amount I cannot learn; but in 1886, bills for damages by the people of King County alone remained unpaid to the amount of $50,666.81. Vol-unteers were raised, several battles were fought, and the hostiles were driven across the Cascade mountains. There the leaders were taken. Leschi was convicted and hung. Quie-muth was assassinated by the son-in-law of Lieutenant J. McAllister, whom he had mur-dered, and the rest, after trial, were acquitted.

Before the war closed a number of Indians from British Columbia came to engage in it. They committed depredations near Steilacoom, and then started to return, but were overtaken by a United States war vessel under Commander S. Swartout at Port Gamble. The Indians numbered 117 fighting men, and after several offers of peace if they would leave the Sound, which they rejected, they were attacked and completely conquered, with 27 killed. This was the closing act of the drama on the Sound.

The only act of hostility which was ever committed on Hood's Canal, as far as I can learn, was by a Clallam Indian, many, many years ago—how long is not known. I have heard the tradition both among the whites and Indians and know of no reason to doubt its truth. The report is that a person named Captain Hood had excited the enmity of this Indian, who followed him closely, yet secretly, in order to take his life. Hood seems to have been aware of this intent, and one night when he encamped on Hood's spit six miles above Seabeck, he stationed two men to guard him. However, they all fell asleep, whereupon the Indian stole up and killed him, and fled to the other, the western, side of the canal. A bare place, which the Indian is said to have ascended in order to look out for possible pursuers, has been pointed out to me by one of the oldest Indians. The Clallams call the name of the place where he was killed, Hwi-a-ne-ta, a corruption they say of the words "white man." The name of the murderer was Kwainaks.

It is a common belief among the whites that both Hood's Canal and Hood's Spit were named because of this event, but after considerable investigation, and a little newspaper discussion, I think that the spit was named because of this event; but Vancouver in his voyages says that he named Hood's Channel—now changed to canal—in honor of Lord Hood of England, who was never here to be killed.

Agencies

The treaty with the Nisqually and Puyallup Indians was ratified soon after it was made, and proclaimed April 10, 1855, but the other two treaties were not ratified for four years afterwards, that with the Snohomish and confederated bands having been proclaimed April 11, 1859, and that with the Clallam and Skokomish Indians, April 29, 1859. According to these treaties, the Indians connected with the treaty of Medicine Creek were to receive $32,500 as annuities in diminishing installments for twenty years, and $3,250 more to enable them to move to their reservation; the Indians connected with the treaty of Point No Point were to receive $60,000 as annuities in the same manner, and $6,000 to enable them to remove to the reservations; and those connected with the treaty of Point Elliott were to receive $150,000 as annuities, and $15,000 for removal and settlement.

According to these treaties all rights to take fish at their accustomed grounds were secured to the Indians, and also to erect temporary houses for curing fish, also to hunt and gather berries on unclaimed lands; annuities were not to be taken for debts of individuals; the tribes were to preserve friendly relations, not to make war except in self-defense, and not to conceal offenders against the laws of the United States; they were to free all their slaves and not to purchase any more in the future; nor were they to trade outside of the dominion of the United States, nor to allow foreign Indians to reside on their reservations. The President reserved the right to remove the Indians, whenever their own or the interests of the Territory might require it, to other suitable places in the Territory where he might see fit, on remunerating them for all expenses and improvements abandoned, or at his discretion might cause the whole or a portion of their lands to be surveyed and allotted in severalty to them. The United States was, under each treaty, to maintain for twenty years a carpenter, blacksmith and necessary shops, a farmer, a physician with necessary medicines, and to support an agricultural and industrial school with proper instructors.

Soon after the ratification of each treaty the United States began to fulfill her part, and, as far as I know, fulfilled it faithfully to the end of the twenty years. Most of the time, until 1882, there were three agents, each one of whom had charge of the Indians represented by one treaty. In 1882 they were all consolidated under one agent, whose headquarters were on the Snohomish reservation, while the Indians were allowed to reside on their several reservations. The next year the agency was divided in two, one agent to have charge of the Snohomish, Swinomish, Lummi, Port Madison, and Muckleshoot reservations, with headquarters at the first named one; and the other to have charge of the Puyallup, Nisqually, Chehalis, Squakson, and Skokomish reservations, with headquarters on the Puyallup reservation.

The principal boarding and industrial schools have been at the Snohomish, Puyallup, Skokomish, and Chehalis reservations, with day schools, more or less, at Port Madison, Port Gamble, Jamestown (near Dungeness), and Lummi. After the expiration of the twenty years most of the employees were discharged, except the school employees and the physicians. By special appropriations these have been continued to the present time.

By the terms of the Dawes bill, passed by Congress and approved February 8, 1887, all Indians who acquire land in any way or have severed their tribal relations become citizens, hence nearly all of the Indians on Puget Sound became citizens at that time, the large share of those living off the reservations having obtained land in some way.

RELIGIOUS HISTORY

Religiously, the Indians belonging to the Snohomish, Port Madison, Muckleshoot, Lummi, and Swinomish reservations have been under the teachings of the Catholics for about forty years; the Puyallup, Nisqually, and Upper Chehalis Indians have been chiefly under the Presbyterians for twenty or twenty-five years, though the Catholics have given some instructions to the Puyallup and Nisqually Indians, and the Twanas, Clallams, and Squaksons have been chiefly under the Congregationalists for twenty years.[4]

III

MAN

POPULATION

These Indians have greatly decreased since the coming of the whites, though reliable data are difficult to obtain.[1] The earliest census of which I can learn was taken by Commodore Wilkes in 1841, but it comprises only a part of the tribes on the Sound. His estimate was 2,920 persons. The next was a census by Dr. W. F. Tolmie of the Hudson's Bay Company, for many years in charge of their fort at Nisqually. It was taken in 1844, but comprised the tribes on the east side of the Sound, and he numbered 4,389 persons. Dr. G. Gibbs, in 1855, gives a complete census by tribes and bands, taken when the treaties were made. His number is 6,374. The first census, published in the report of the Commissioner of Indian Affairs, to which I have had access, is that of 1862. I append also those for 1871, 1878, 1881, 1885, and 1892 from the same authority.

In preparing Table 1, I have found some difficulty, because some of the names used forty or fifty years ago are so different from those now used, but I have done the best I could. It is, however, quite unsatisfactory. The earlier censuses of 1841 and 1844 are partial and incomplete. It is probable also that those of 1862, 1878, and 1881 are too high in some of their estimates, while those of 1885 and of 1892 are too low, as in some cases the latter only report the Indians on the reservations and actually under their control. It is likewise unsatisfactory to trace any one tribe, as, owing to the reservation system, some have been removed, become divided and mixed up, parts of the tribes of forty years ago going to one reservation, a part to another, and a part to not any. Most old settlers among the Twanas and Clallams, with whom I have conversed, estimate that thirty-five years ago there were from 2½ to 5 times as many of those Indians as there are now. Though this may be an exaggeration, yet they have greatly decreased. Some of the tribes, too, which seem to hold their own quite well, have not actually done so. The Puyallups are an instance of this. The mortality among them during the past twenty years has been great, but immigration has kept up their numbers, owing to the value of their land on the reservation, some of which can be obtained by outsiders as the owners die, these outsiders being the heirs of the deceased.

Causes affecting population. Intemperance has been one of the greatest foes to the lives of these Indians. The Clallam head chief, Lord Jim Balch, said at one time that the saloons of Dungeness had killed five hundred Clallams in twenty years. This is probably an exaggeration, yet the mortality has been great. Consumption and the diseases consequent upon consumption have caused the death of a large number, consumption carrying off probably far more adults than any other disease. At an early day, 1852 or 1853, small pox killed many, while the measles and whooping cough have swept many of the children away. All of these except consumption, which is caused largely by the dampness of the climate, have been introduced by the whites.

Many have died from diseases caused by the transition from a savage to a civilized life. Especially has this been the case among the children. A permanent house with a floor is built for them. The old-fashioned house with the ground for a floor drank up the grease as it was spilled, and if it became too filthy, it was easily removed a short distance. But the new house is too costly to be removed, while its floor, which receives plenty of dirt, grease, and saliva, cannot absorb it. Poisonous air is the result, which often causes the little ones, weak by nature, who have to lie in it and breathe it, to waste away. The parents, fearful that the little sick ones will be cold, keep up a large fire, making it often too warm, and this increases the poison in the air. Thus, many have died when it has been difficult to tell what disease had hold of them—literally poisoned to death.

TABLE 1

	1841	1844	1855	1862	1871	1878	1881	1885	1892
Treaty of Medicine Creek									
Puyallups	500	325				606	547	560	609
Squaksons		135	893	1150		100	91	120	119
Nisqually	200	563				278	158	180	90
Upper Chehalis	200	207	216	300		205	165	190	157
Total	900	1230	1109	1450	1650	1189	961	1050	975
Treaty of Point Elliott									
Snohomish		695	997	3400				467	460
Swinomish	650	195	1475	700				222	257
Lummi	300	244	680	1300				248	401
Port Madison	150	525	807	1000				142	161
Muckleshoot									161
Total	1100	1659	3959	6400	3383	2900	2817	1164	1440
Treaty of Point No Point									
Twana	500		290	450		250	243	201	227
Clallam	420*	1760†	926	1300		550	481	380	331
Chemakum			90	100					
Total	920	1500	1306	1850	825	800	724	581	558
Grand Total	2920	4389	6374	9700	5985	4889	4502	2795	2973

*A census of about half the tribes
†A census by Mr. Finlayson of the Hudson's Bay Company taken in 1845

They also naturally love to be in the water or to go somewhere, especially when it rains heavily, as they cannot read at home, so they get wet. When they went barefoot, wet feet were felt but little, but when they put on socks and shoes and wet them, they have not always been careful to dry them, and so colds and rheumatism are far more common and fatal than when they were uncivilized.

As the subject of the increase and decrease of the Indians has been quite widely discussed I submit the following ideas. On first contact with the whites they decrease. If the tribe is large and kept together somewhat compactly, and there is comparatively little intercourse with the whites except on the outer edge, and wholesome efforts are made to civilize them, they do not rapidly diminish; and when somewhat civilized, they begin to increase, as Doctors Riggs and Williamson testify has been the case among the Dakotas, and as has been the case also among the large tribes in the Indian Territory. But where the tribes are small and the intercourse with worthless whites is considerable, their decrease is rapid, and sometimes a tribe will become extinct before it has time to rally. This has been the case with the Chemakums, many tribes in the Willamette valley of Oregon, and in the states east of the Mississippi. In this respect each tribe is somewhat like an army fighting for its own existence. If it can hold its own a certain length of time, it may conquer, but if it is small and the attack severe, it is cut to pieces.[2]

PHYSICAL NATURE

In 1875 with the assistance of R. H. Lansdale, M.D., and Hon. E. Eells, Indian Agent, eleven Twanas were measured and weighed, and Table 2 shows the average, both before and after deducting what we thought to be right on account of clothes, and also the extremes under each head.

The color of the eyes and hair is black. As to blushing, they are similar to white people, but not so sensitive; as to muscular strength and speed, they are inferior to white people, but in regard to climbing, they are superior; their growth is attained early in life, and their decay also begins early. Their child bearing is generally very easy, although there are occasional exceptions, which have increased as they become civilized, and some deaths in childbirth have occurred; their reproductive power is less than with whites; sterility prevails considerably, caused in early life by various kinds of abuse; the age of puberty in males is about fourteen, and with females not far from thirteen; they cross with all races, there being some children who are half-Indian and half-Negro, and a few who are half-Indian and half-Chinese. Their teeth come about the same as with white children, but wear down early in life, and the more they become civilized, owing probably to the sugar and syrup which they eat, the more they decay. Their length of life is probably ten years less than with whites, at least that was Dr. Lansdale's opinion, and I agree with him.

In 1880 I was employed to take the United States census among the Clallams, and was surprised to find how much younger most of them were than they looked to be. Although very few of the older ones knew their ages, yet all could tell how large they were when the treaty was made, twenty-five years previous, from which I could make a fair estimate. In only one or two cases did I guess them to be younger than they were. One man, whom intimate acquaintances had guessed to be sixty, was found to be forty-five. There are a few gray people and a few partially bald among them, but only a few of either.

DISEASES

The principal diseases are scrofula, scrofulous swellings, and abscesses, all of which are grafted on a scrofulous diathesis, consumption and bleeding of the lungs. They are also largely troubled with acute and chronic bronchitis, catarrh, diarrhea, dyspepsia, conjunctivitis, skin disease, syphilis, gonorrhea, tooth ache, and chronic rheumatism. Their diet habits and the climate have produced a scrofulous diathesis from generation to generation, thus shortening their lives. The dampness of the climate also produced rheumatism and consumption. The above facts were given me by R. H. Lansdale, government physician at the Skokomish reservation from 1874–76.

An examination of the reports of the Commissioner of Indian Affairs for 1883–85, gives the following figures in regard to the diseases treated by the three physicians on the Sound, namely at the Tulalip, Skokomish, and Puyallup agencies. Total numbers of cases treated, 4,599: of these 18 percent were mismatic diseases, including fevers, diarrhea, and tonsillitis; 1¼ percent were enthetic diseases, as syphilis and gonorrhea; 9 percent were diathetic, of which rheumatism was by far the most common; 4 percent were tuber-

TABLE 2

	Before deducting		After deducting	
	Average	Extremes	Average	Extremes
Weight	151⁷/₁₁lbs	124½–174½ lbs.	142 lbs.	114¹⁹/₂₂–164¹⁹/₂₂ lbs.
Height	5 ft. 6 in.	5 ft. 3¾ in.– 5 ft. 9 in.	5ft. 5 in.	5 ft. 2¾ in.–5 ft. 8 in.
Circumference of head	21⁸/₁₁ in.	21–23 in.	21 in.	20³/₁₁–22³/₁₁ in.
Circumference of chest	35 ³¹/₂/₁₁ in.	32–38 in.	34½ in.	31²/₁₁–37²/₁₁ in.
Circumference of pelvis	35²¹/₂/₁₁ in.	33½–37 in.	34 in	32³/₁₁–35⁸¹/₂/₁₁ in.
Circumference of arm	10²/₁₁ in.	9–11 in	10 in.	8⁹/₁₁–10⁹/₁₁ in.
Circumference of fore-arm	9⁵/₁₁ in.	8½–11 in.	9³/₁₁ in.	8²¹/₂/₁₁–10⁹/₁₁ in.
Circumference of thigh	18¾ in.	17–20 in.	17 in.	15¼–18¼ in.
Circumference of leg	13½ in	12–14½ in.	13 in.	11½–14 in.
Length of upper extremities			27⁸/₁₁ in.	26–30 in.
Length of lower extremities			31³/₁₁ in.	29–34 in.
Length of trunk			23⁷/₁₁ in.	22–25 in.

cular, as consumption and scrofula; 1 percent were parasitic, as worms; 8 percent were nervous diseases, of which head ache was the most common; 13 percent were diseases of the eye; 1¾, of the ear; one quarter of 1 percent, of the circulation; 19 percent, of the respiratory organs, of which bronchitis was the most common; 8 percent, of the digestive organs, diarrhea being the most general; 1¼ percent were of the urinary and genital organs; 1¼ percent were diseases of the bones, nearly all being of the teeth; 7 percent were skin diseases; and 7 percent were wounds, injuries, and accidents. Of the whole number sick, 134 died—nearly 3 percent.

Cuts and wounds heal easily. Scrofulous diseases are very difficult to cure. [These Indians] are not nearly as sensitive to pain as the whites; they will cut themselves in their religious ceremonies, with apparently little suffering, while the same wounds would throw a white person into a fever; and they can easily endure a number of fleas, which would torment a white person beyond endurance. Very few are deformed. Three Clallams have been hump-backed, two of whom died while children.

INSANITY

Two cases of insanity have I known in twenty years, the one a Clallam, the other a Twana. It is said that the Clallam in early life was chopping, when a tree fell on his head and split it open so that some of his brains ran out, but he recovered. In after years he was badly addicted to drinking, and on account of this was removed from Port Discovery to the Skokomish reservation in the winter of 1880. Some months previous to this removal he is said to have shown some signs of insanity for a few weeks. For some months after the removal, whiskey was kept from him. Having secretly obtained it, however, in July 1881 he became insane. He was doctored both by the Agency physician and Indian medicine men, but was not cured. He was then allowed to return to his old home, but died soon afterwards. Probably the early injury, the liquor, and the removal from his old home were the causes of his insanity.

The Twana case was caused by none of these reasons. The only reason I could ever give was a long series of troubles of twelve or fifteen years with different wives. Toward the last he cut his foot so that it never healed thoroughly so that he could work much or earn money for his support. Then his wife left him, but relatives cared for him and a mild, harmless kind of insanity attacked him, from which he suffered for about a year. In March 1892 he wandered away into the mountains. His relatives heard of him a few times from white men who saw him, but although they tried to find him, they could not do so. Evidently he lived on roots, bark, or berries for two or three months, and then in trying to cross a river on two logs, he fell between them and was drowned. In August he was found there by his nephew, who was fishing, and he had apparently been there six to eight weeks.

SUICIDE

I have known of only two cases of suicide, both of whom were women. One was an aged Clallam of Dungeness, who had some unhappy troubles with her husband, which caused her to hang herself; the other was a young woman of Port Madison who was compelled by her relatives to marry a man whom she did not wish, and she likewise hung herself. Gibbs says that instances are not rare of young women destroying themselves on the death of a lover.*

FLATHEADS

The custom of flattening the heads by pressure was almost universal among these Indians. It was done in infancy with a pad made of cedar bark, beaten and pressed steadily on the forehead for months. It has been described so often by numerous writers that no

*Contributions to North American Ethnology, vol. 2, p. 198.

Puyallup Indian boys at the Forest Grove Training School

further description is necessary. School teachers here have been unable to see any difference between the intellect of those whose heads have been thus flattened and those which are natural, which could be attributed to this cause. Some of the Indians, however, believe that it has caused numerous headaches among them in later life. Very few infants are thus treated now.

MENTAL PHENOMENA

In school, the children acquire in primary lessons, on an average, as rapidly as white children in the same school who have had the same advantages, but do not progress as well in the more advanced lessons, as a general thing. A few of them have done well in advanced studies, but the proportion is much less than with white children. Heredity seems to have its influence.

Their memories are generally better than those of white people, but their reasoning powers are usually much poorer, though occasionally they reason very sharply. The strength of will among a few is quite great, and these become leaders, but the common people have not much.

In tracking game and obtaining fish, they have a large amount of patience and good habits of observation. Generally they are quite industrious, and a trip over most reservations on pleasant days shows that most of the men are at work; on rainy days it is different, as they have but little indoor work to perform. The women, however, are generally busy, rain or shine, as they can make mats and baskets when not otherwise busy.

MORALITY

Their moral ideas were formerly quite low, especially in regard to theft, lying, murder, intemperance, and chastity, but of late years they have greatly improved. Formerly they would say it was wrong to steal, but if not found out it was apparently all right. Now there are very few who are ever accused of stealing, and murders have of late been almost unknown. Lying is much more common. In regard to chastity they have improved much, but still there is room for improvement. Intemperance greatly decreased after good Indian Agents were appointed under President Grant's policy, especially among the southern Indians of the Sound, the Twanas, Puyallups, Chehalis, Nisqually, and Clallam Indians. But since the Indians have become citizens there has been a reaction, liberty has become with many license, and intemperance has increased. In different localities these vices of unchastity and intemperance abound more than in others, owing to different causes but chiefly to their proximity to our towns and cities.

Their emotions and passions are often very strong, though generally not as lasting as with whites.

PROGRESS

While this subject shows the character of the Indian mind, it is so large that it cannot well be described here in detail. Very frequent remarks will be made about it in the following pages, in connection with the various subjects treated. Still, to a missionary like the writer, whose time is devoted to it, it has seemed so large that he has described it among the Twanas and Clallams in a separate volume entitled "Ten Years at Skokomish," published by the Congregational Sabbath School and Publishing Society at Boston, Massachusetts, to which the reader is referred for much that is of value in regard to this class of ethnological facts.

Joseph Spar

Martha Spar

Mary Adams

Milton Fisher

Mrs. Joseph Campbell, noted by
Myron Eells to be "one half white"

William Miller, brother of Mrs. Campbell

Mrs. Campbell's two children, "three fourths white"

Frank H. Peterson

Miss Emily Atkins, "one half white"

John Williams and his wife, Nellie. He is an Olympia; she a Twana

David Charley and his wife, Susie Charley

Charlie Jackson and his wife, Lucy Jackson

George G. Bridges,
"half white; age 26, height 5 ft. 9 in."

Louis Amor, *"half Clallam-half Italian"*

44

David Hunter and Mary Hunter, his wife; and Henry and Emma Johnson and their two children

Tillie Atkins

"Steilacoom Indians," from a stereoptican photograph

Skokomish Indian School, 1892

Skokomish boys, 1888

Frank H. Peterson, a Twana, and Mrs. Mary Adams at her father's grave

"Pow Wow" of Puyallup Indians

IV

SURROUNDINGS

NEARLY THE WHOLE OF PUGET SOUND is surrounded by mountains; the Cascade range on the east, the Black hills on the south, and the Olympic range on the west.[1] From these mountains numerous streams flow into the Sound. Among these the larger ones are the Nooksack river in the land of the Lummi Indians; the Skagit in the land of the Skagits; the Snohomish and Stillaquamish in the Snohomish land; the Duwamish, Puyallup, and Nisqually in the lands occupied by those several tribes. All of these come from the Cascade mountains. The Chehalis river also comes from the Cascade mountains, flows through the land of the Chehalis Indians, south of the Black hills and empties into Gray's Harbor. From the Olympic mountains flow the Skokomish, Dosewailopsh, and Dukaboos into Hood's Canal in the land of the Twanas, and the Dungeness, Elwha, Pysht, and Clallam rivers into the straits of Fuca in the land of the Clallams.

Nearly all of the land occupied by these tribes is heavily timbered, the prairies being small and so gravelly as to be of but little value for cultivation. Hence, these Indians have always lived mainly on the salt water and streams, using the forests and mountains only as hunting grounds.

MINERALS

The mineral substances which have been of practical value to the Indians, besides the soil for cultivation, as far as I know, are as follows: agate, basalt, chalcedony, and jasper for arrow-heads, though very seldom, however; volcanic rock and beach stones for anchors, hammers, sinkers in fishing, and tanning stones; black mud of the salt marshes for dyeing; clay stones for pipes and rain stones; clay of a red and clay color for paints; metamorphic rock for axes and adzes; quartzite and sedimentary rock for hammers and whetstones; and slate for knives.

Copper was also obtained from British Columbia or Alaska, and copper ornaments and a few such implements found their way to Puget Sound. Vancouver, in 1792, speaks of seeing a number of copper ornaments at Port Discovery. I have a copper war club, which came from the tribes of British Columbia.

Bancroft[2] says that the Nootka Indians have a tradition of a supernatural teacher, an old man, who came from the Sound long ago with a canoe of copper and paddles of copper, and everything else he had was of the same. He told them that he came from above, that they should all die, but after death rise and live again above. On account of this, they became angry at him and killed him, and because of this crime their descendants obtained great benefits, for they have had copper ever since.*

PLANTS

The following fifty native plants are of practical use, besides cultivated plants and grass for stock.[3]

Alder. The wood is used for firewood, for making dishes, plates, paddles, bailers, and masks; and for building fish traps and rough houses; and the bark is used for medicine and dyeing.

Barberry. The bark is used for medicine, and the wood for firewood.

Blackberry. The berry is used for food, the juice for paint and medicine and the young leaves for tea.

Cat-tail rush. The blades are used for making strings, ropes, mats, and one kind of basket; the mats which are made from them being one of their most useful articles. The head of this rush was formerly used in making blankets.

Red cedar. This is the most useful vegetable production of their country. Its wood is used for planks for houses and burial enclosures, for rails, shingles, shakes, posts, and the like; also for canoes, oars, baby boards, buoys, spinning wheels, boxes, torches, arrow shafts, fish traps, tamahnous stocks, and firewood; the limbs for baskets and ropes; the bark for baskets, mats, sails, infant head protectors, strings, and bailers, and when beaten, for women's skirts, beds for infants, wadding for guns, napkins, head bands, blankets, and for gambling purposes; the gum and leaves for medicine, and the roots for making baskets.

Cherry. The bark is used for strings and medicine.

Cottonwood. The wood is used for firewood, the bark for medicine and strings, and the buds for medicine.

Cranberry. The berry is used for food, the juice for paint, and the young leaves for tea.

Crab-apple. The wood is used for wedges, hoes, mauls, mallets, and firewood; the fruit for food; and the bark for medicine.

Currant. The berry is occasionally used for food.

Dogwood. The wood is manufactured into gambling disks and hollow rattles, and is used for fuel.

Elder. The wood is made into arrow-heads, which are used as playthings; the bark is used for medicine, and the berry for food.

Fir, red. The wood is valued for firewood, lumber, masts, spear handles, spits, and oars; the bark is preferred to everything else for fuel, as it is often three inches, and sometimes six inches, thick and pitchy; the pitch wood is good for fire pots, torches, and kindling, and for the latter purpose is sometimes sold to the whites; the pitch is used for fastening on arrow- and spear-heads, and for cement.

*Bancroft's *Native Races of America*, vol 3. p. 151.

Gooseberry. There are two varieties, both of which are used for food.

Grass. (specific name unknown). It is used extensively in making and ornamenting baskets, and is found in swamps.

Hazel. The nuts are used as food; the wood is used for rims to snow shoes, nets, and the like; and the bark for strings.

Hemlock. The wood serves for firewood and halibut hooks, the leaves for tea, and the branches for covers in steaming food.

Huckleberry, black, blue, and red. The berries of all varieties are used for food, and the juice occasionally for paint.

Ironwood. The wood is used for arrow-shafts, arrow and spearheads, and mat needles, and the bark for medicine.

Indian onion. The bulb is eaten.

Kelp. Strings and ropes, especially fish-lines, are made from the root.

Kamass. The root is edible.

Laurel. The wood is used for making spoons, vessels, and fancy articles; the leaves are used for medicine.

Liquorice. The root is medicinal.

Maple. The wood is useful for hacklers, mat blocks, paddles, oars, bobbins, seine blocks, combs, fish and duck spear-heads, fish clubs, rails, and firewood. The leaves are used in steaming. A smaller variety of maple is also used for firewood.

Moss. This is used to wrap around wood while steaming it to make bows and the like, the whole being buried in the ground.

Nettle. The fiber is used in making strings, a twine, the strongest they had.

Oregon grape. The root and bark are valuable as a medicine, and the root for dyeing yellow.

Peuce-da-num. The stem is used for food, and the seeds, when ripe, as a medicine, being peppery.

Raspberry. The berry is used for food, and the juice as a paint.

Rose. The roots and leaves are a medicine.

Rush. A round kind of rush is used in making mats.

Sallal berry. The berry is used for food.

Salmon berry. The berry and young shoots are eaten.

Skunk cabbage. The leaves are used for medicine, and the roots occasionally for food.

Strawberry. The berry serves as food.

Thimble cap. The berry and young shoots are eaten.

Spruce. The wood is burned, and is also carved; the roots are used in making halibut hooks; and the leaves serve as medicine.

Vine maple. The wood is burned for fuel.

Willow. The bark is used for strings, and the wood occasionally for fuel.

Yew. Paddles, bows, arrows, and fish clubs of the best kind are made of the wood.

Fern. The roots, beaten, were formerly used as food.

Kinnikinnik (Arctostaphylos). The berry is used for food, and the leaves, dried, are occasionally mixed with tobacco for smoking when the latter article is scarce.

Fireweed (Epilobium). The cotton-like down from the seed was formerly used in making blankets.

Plants not identified. The roots of two varieties, the top of one of them, and the root of another variety are eaten. One of them is a rush (*Equisetum*).

BEASTS

The following seventeen kinds of beasts are useful to them.

Bear, black. The flesh is eaten, the skin is used for robes and arrow quivers, and is sold to the whites.

Bear, grizzly. Though scarce, its skin was used for robes, and the Indians believed it to be a very strong tamahnous animal, which was supposed to be used by the medicine men in making people sick.

Beaver. The meat is good for food, the skin for furs, and the teeth are used in the women's game of gambling.

Cat, wild. The flesh was occasionally eaten, and the skins were used for robes. It was also a tamahnous animal.

Dog. The common dog is of use for hunting, domestic purposes, and the like. The hair of the wool dog was used for making blankets; this breed is now extinct.

Deer. This is probably the most useful wild animal known to them. The flesh is used for food, the skins for robes, strings, fringes, moccasins, clothes, shot-pouches, and the like. The fawn skins are sometimes made into buoys for whaling; formerly they made shirts, which answered the purposes, or shields or suits of armor from the skins; the sinews they use for thread, the hoofs for rattles in religious dances, and the brains in tanning.

Elk. The flesh serves for food; the skins for robes and shield-shirts, and, when dressed, for strings and clothes; and of the horns they made wedges, chisels, and paint. The animal is in most respects used much as the deer, but is not so common by far.

Mink. The skins are useful as furs.

Muskrats. The skins are useful as furs, and the teeth in gambling, occasionally.

Otter. The flesh is eaten. The skins of the sea otter are among the most valuable furs.

Panther. The skins are made into robes and clothes. It is also a tamahnous animal.

Raccoon. The skin is used for furs, and the flesh for food.

Sheep, mountain. The flesh is used for food, and the horns for dishes and ladles.

Wolf. The skin is used for robes, quivers, and caps. It is likewise a tamahnous animal.

The intestines of several of these animals are used for holding oil, and the bones for various articles, such as awls, arrow- and spear-heads, combs, fasteners, and the like.

BIRDS

There are seventeen kinds of birds, which they utilize as follows: The crane, seven varieties of ducks (i.e., the mallard, pin-tail, wood-duck, scoter, teal, diver, and canvasback), the grouse, goose, two varieties of loons, and the pheasant are used as food, while the feathers serve as beds, pillows, and ornaments for the hair at festivals. The gull also occasionally serves as food for old people, and the feathers are used for beds, though they are rather coarse.

The feathers of the eagle, hawk, and red-headed woodpecker are useful for feathering arrows, and in tamahnous head-bands.

A piece of the kingfisher skin where the tail or wing feathers enter it was formerly used in fishing, attached to the line near the hook, as it was superstitiously supposed that it would attract the fish.

FISH AND OTHER MARINE ANIMALS

Thirty-six kinds of marine animals are used by them. The following are eaten: three varieties of clams, two of crabs, two of codfish, and their eggs; the dogfish when food is very scarce; two kinds of flounders, the halibut, herring, mussels, and oysters; porpoise; five varieties of salmon with their eggs, namely, silver, red, dog, black, and hump-backed; the hair seal occasionally; smelt, sea eggs, scallops, sturgeon, trout, whale, cuttlefish, and one called *tse-kwiets* by the Twanas.

The shells of the abalone, dentalia, and occasionally the olivella were useful as money and ornaments.

Large clam shells were of use as drinking dishes.

The skin of the dogfish is used as sandpaper.

The dogfish, porpoise, hair seal, shark, and whale furnish valuable oil, some of which is eaten, some used in painting, and some sold to the whites.

From the skin of the hair seal are made buoys used in sealing and hunting, small sacks, hunting pouches, and the like.

Scallop shells are used as rattles in tamahnous.

From the bones of the whale, war clubs and a part of codfish hooks are made, and its sinew is used as thread.[4]

Boarding house and shops at Skokomish Agency, 1892

Flats at the mouth of the Skokomish River, with the Indian Agency showing in the distance

Skokomish River and part of the Agency

House of J. M. Spar, a Skokomish Indian, on the Skokomish River

Two views of The Dalles of the Skokomish, a "great fishing resort of these Indians"

The upper falls

The lower falls

Betsy Boston, a Puyallup Indian

V

SUBSISTENCE

FOOD

Food formerly consisted of the spontaneous products of the land and water, such as roots, berries, game, fish, and other marine animals.[1]

Fish

The fish eaten are of at least twenty-one different varieties, namely two varieties of codfish; two of salmon, smelt, skate, hair seal, trout; whale, sturgeon, halibut, herring, porpoise, cuttlefish; two varieties of flounders, one called by the Twanas *tse-kwiets*; and the dogfish, the latter, however, only when food is very scarce.

The fish called *twe-kwiets* is peculiar looking, seeming to be covered with soft horns. I believe it does not swim, but crawls on the bottom in salt water, and is speared where the water is shallow. What I have seen were taken where the bottom is quite muddy. The Twanas do not clean them in their canoes where they catch them, but wait until they go to land, for they believe if they were to throw the entrails into the water, no more such fish would go to that place.

Of these, the salmon, smelt, herring, and halibut are dried, as well as eaten fresh. The herring and smelt are dried whole, the salmon after being cut open and the head and back bone removed, and the halibut after being cut into strips.

The whale and cuttlefish seldom visit the waters of the upper Sound, and the halibut do not usually go very far up, and so are not used much by the Indians of that region.

Besides the flesh of the dogfish, porpoise, seal, and whale, their oil was formerly eaten, and still is to some extent.

The eggs of the salmon and codfish are considered a luxury. Salmon were formerly the staff of life, and a large business of the summer was to dry them for the winter. They are now often salted.

Shellfish

Ten kinds at least of shellfish are used for food: four varieties of clams, two of crabs, one each of mussels, oysters, sea eggs, and scallops, the two latter not being usually found much above Port Townsend.

Of these clams alone are dried. In doing this, the Indians first build a large fire, in which they heat a large number of stones, and when the fire has burned down they remove the brands and large coals, pour on the clams, perhaps several bushels of them, and cover the whole with several thicknesses of mats. They are then steamed until they are cooked, the shell is then opened thus, and they are taken from the shell, spitted on slender sticks two or three feet long and put above their fires in their houses to dry. When dried they are stored away in baskets. Fish eggs are dried by being placed on small frames made of split sticks or bark and placed over their fires. A frame of cedar sticks is made by tying small sticks at each end to a cross piece. Often, too, the eggs are hung up without any frame, in bunches. The eggs are spread over the frame, and the whole is hung over the fire.

There are some kinds of fish in their waters all the year long, though some varieties they do not eat unless food is very scarce, but as long as there is any kind of fish with the clams and mussels, which always abound, there is never any need of real suffering for want of food. The only suffering to which they almost voluntarily subject themselves is from improvidence. Sometimes they live from hand to mouth, not having much food beforehand, and so when severely inclement weather in the winter came, the old ones were obliged to go for clams in the cold storms, and this caused some suffering.

Vegetables

Vegetables are the kamass, formerly highly prized, but as it grows only in certain localities, which are not numerous, they seldom use much of it now; the root of the skunk-cabbage, steamed; the Indian onion, the peucedanum stem, a kind of rush root, the root of an unknown plant and of the fern were also eaten. The fern roots were dried, laid on a rock, and beaten with a club into a kind of flour, which was mixed with fish eggs and made into a cake, called by the Clallams, *skeve u*. The young shoots of the thimble cap, salmon berry, and a plant of which I do not know the name, were and still are eaten. Of all these the kamass, Indian onion, and fern cakes, as far as I know, were alone put up for future use.

The blackberry, three varieties of huckleberry—black, red, and blue—salal berry, cranberry, gooseberry, hazel-nut, salmon berry, strawberry, raspberry, crabapple, currant, elderberry, and blueberry, and berry of the kinnikinnik, or *Arctostaphylos*, are all used as food. The blackberry, two varieties of huckleberry, raspberry, and sallal berries are dried for winter use, the first being made into a kind of cake. Beginning with the young shoots early in the spring, and following on with the berries, the huckleberry hanging on the bushes until they freeze solid in December, together with the roots, they had a vegetable diet more or less abundant from early spring to early winter with a little laid up for the rest of winter as a luxury.

Beasts

The black bear, deer, elk, otter, wild-cat, raccoon, and occasionally the mountain sheep were used for food; all except the mountain sheep and wild-cat being still used. When a bear is killed, it is very common to invite friends and have a feast in honor of the event. The flesh of the deer, elk, and bear are dried. They were formerly not so much accustomed to this kind of food as they were to fish, as before the introduction of fire arms it was much more difficult to obtain it.

Birds

The cranes, grouse, gull, light and dark loon, pheasant, and seven varieties of ducks are eaten. It is said that the grouse and mallard were not eaten until the whites came, the former because they fed on snails. None of these were put up for future use, but now ducks are sometimes salted down by the barrel. I am not aware that they ever used any flowers, seeds, insects, or worms for food. Large animals were too abundant.

Salt

Salt was never used until the whites came, and even now they do not use it on much food which whites think they cannot eat without it. There is no place in this region where salt could be obtained, except from the salt water of Puget Sound. It seems singular that they did not use it in some way, since there is so much in the water, but they did not even have a word in their language for salt, though they had terms for salty and salt water. Since its introduction by the whites, they have preferred to adopt the English word salt into several of their languages as its name, rather than to give a name derived from any of their words. I have occasionally seen some of them drink salt water with a relish, and it is possible that thus they satisfied the demands of nature. No other spices were used.

At present they use every kind of food possessed by whites; flour and sugar being very largely used, and without which a large share of them think they cannot live. In 1889 the agents reported that the Squaksons obtained 75 percent of their living by labor in civilized pursuits; the Clallams 85 percent; the Tulalip, Port Madison, Swinomish, and Lummi Indians 90 percent; and the Muckleshoot, Puyallup, Nisqually, Upper Chehalis, and Twana or Skokomish Indians their entire living in the same way.

Cooking

The food which they do not eat raw is cooked in much the same manner as the whites cook it, roasted in the ashes and on spits, boiled, stewed, and baked. They formerly steamed large quantities, especially meat at their feasts, and it was done in much the same manner as that described in steaming clams, but green branches of trees were used in connection with the mats. In boiling, too, they heated stones, and put them with the food to be cooked in their water-tight baskets.

Storing

Cultivated roots when stored are commonly cached on or in the ground, covering them with boards and earth, regular cellars being uncommon among the Twanas, Clallams, or Squaksons. Formerly they had no food which they needed to keep from freezing, hence they stored what they kept for the winter use in baskets in their houses.

DRINKS

I cannot learn that formerly they had any drink except water, unless occasionally they made a tea of the leaves of the blackberry, cranberry, or hemlock. At present they are greatly addicted to the use of tea and coffee. The large share of them as yet use but little milk or butter, for while many of them have cows, they think dairying too much trouble.

Ardent Spirits

Drunkenness is and always has been a besetting sin among Indians, although they boast that they do not make and never have made intoxicating drinks. Those are the effect of civilization. (!) The law and the gospel have both been used to prevent drunkenness, and in some places with good effect. This has been more especially noticeable on some of the reservations, before the Indians became citizens, where drunkenness was considered a crime and punished as such, than among those Indians who have lived around our towns where there is more temptation and less fear of punishment, and those on the reservations who have become citizens; though some of the latter have stood up well against temptation.

MEDICINES

I have obtained the following information in regard to their remedies, though it is by no means complete.

Alder buds. They eat them, and afterwards drink salt water as an emetic in cases of colds and biliousness.

Alder bark. This they grind in water, and drink the infusion as a tonic.

Barberry bark is prepared in the same way as the last, and used to purify the blood.

Blackberry root is used for colds.

Cedar gum is chewed for toothache.

Cedar leaves are chewed and bound on cuts.

Cherry bark is prepared as alder bark for a physic and tonic.

Cottonwood bark, thick from the body of the large trees, after having been soaked in salt water, is ground and used as a medicine.

Cottonwood buds are also used as a medicine.

Crabapple bark. A cold tea is made from this as a wash for the eyes.

Elder bark. An infusion taken internally and in a vapor bath is used for diarrhea.

Licorice is used for colds, and as a tea for gonorrhea.

Oregon grape. The root and bark are used in the same way as alder bark for skin diseases, as a tonic, and for venereal disease.

Rose bark and roots are used as medicine.

Potatoes, scraped, are used for burns and scalds.

Skunk cabbage leaves. They heat rocks, throw water over them, place leaves on them, and get over the steam for strengthening general debility.

Earth is sometimes bound on bruises.

Cautery. Rheumatism is sometimes treated by taking a red-hot iron, or a stick, or small bunch of cedar bark or rag, twisted into the shape of a stick, setting fire thereto and burning a hole in the flesh to the bone. I have seen one Clallam, who had dozens of scars on him from this mode of treatment.

Blood-letting is done by scarifying the body in various places.

Soap and sugar are applied as a salve for boils.

The following is from Dr. Gibbs in *Contributions to North American Ethnology*, pages 207, 208:

A decoction of the white flowering or poisonous kamass furnishes an emetic.

Cucumber vine (white) (Sieyos Oregonus). A decoction is used as an emetic and cathartic.

Skunk wood. The inside bark, chewed up, serves as a poultice.

Colt's foot. The juice is used as a fomentation for bruises and sprains.

Hemlock-spruce. Women during their periods of menstruation bind the twigs around their bodies, perhaps as a species of charm. They are also used as a bed for the sick.

For gonorrhea, the females smoke themselves over a fire made of certain plants or wood.

Swellings produced by injuries they sometimes scarify.

Sores that are slow in healing they sometimes cauterize. They employ moxia by the application of coals of fire, and the powder left by worms under the bark of trees, is also strewn over them to dry them up. This and potter's clay, dried and powdered, is used for chancres. Suction by the mouth is a remedy to alleviate pain.

NARCOTICS

I cannot learn that they ever used tobacco or anything else in this line, until the whites came, though since their advent, the Indians have made some pipes, different from those of the Americans. Native pipes have been found on the Columbia river, near the mouth of the Umatilla, and some of the Puget Sound Indians had considerable intercourse with the Yakima and Klikitat Indians, and it is a little strange if they did not learn to smoke; still I cannot learn that this is so.

Nearly all the Indians now use tobacco more or less, except a few who have broken off from principle. The Twanas, however, I believe use it much less than the other tribes, it being uncommon to see one with a pipe or cigar in his mouth, while it is common among the other tribes. Some of the pipes will hereafter be figured. When tobacco is scarce, they sometimes mix with it the leaves of the kinnikinnik (*Arctostaphylos*). I have never known of their smoking the pipe of peace.

VI

BUILDINGS

HOUSES

Their houses for human occupancy, either permanent or temporary, are as follows:

The potlatch houses. These are the only public buildings among the Indians. They are not always built on a uniform plan. One was built on the Skokomish reservation in 1875–76, which was about 40 by 200 feet. The figures, opposite, are the exterior view of this building and the inside view of the four sections at one end, there being nine in all. Large tamahnous posts (a a a), about 9 feet long, from 1½ to 2¼ feet wide and 5 or 6 inches thick, support the sides of the building. Smaller posts (b b b) support the cone of the roof. A platform for beds (c c c), about 3½ feet wide and 2 feet above the ground, runs entirely around the inside of the building. A kind of shelf (d d) is overhead for storing various articles.[1]

Small walls are made, one on each side of the doors (e), to keep the wind and cold from making the bed platforms too uncomfortable, and they often serve to divide the people who come from different localities from each other. Low seats (g g), about 6 inches high, are made in front of the bed-platform, on which also their beds are sometimes spread. Fires (f f f) are made in front of these seats. Occasionally a post (h) extends from the ground to the ridge pole to support the latter. Large round cross beams (i i i), considerably larger in the middle than at each end, extend from one side of the house to the other, resting on the top of the large posts (a a a), and on these are placed most of the posts (b b b) which support the ridge pole. There are three doors on the front side facing the water, one at each end, and none at the back, which is against a hill.

Another potlatch house, at Dungeness, will be described in Chapter XXI in the description of potlatches. One built by the Twana Indians about 1868 was similar to the one just described, but larger, having been about 50 by 300 feet. One at Squakson and one at Port Angeles were also similar, and none of these was used much for dwellings after the potlatches. The one just described so fully was used for potlatches in 1876, and again in 1878, but was afterwards crushed by the snow and destroyed.

One at Sequim and one at Port Gamble were more nearly like the one at Dungeness and afterwards were used as dwellings.

Sweat houses. These are very uncommon. The only ones I have seen were used by the medicine man, but have long since gone out of use. They were 3 or 4 feet in height, a little more in diameter, and conoidal. Sticks were driven into the ground in a circle, bent over and fastened together at the upper end, or if long enough, the other end was put

A potlatch house, from a stereoptican photograph

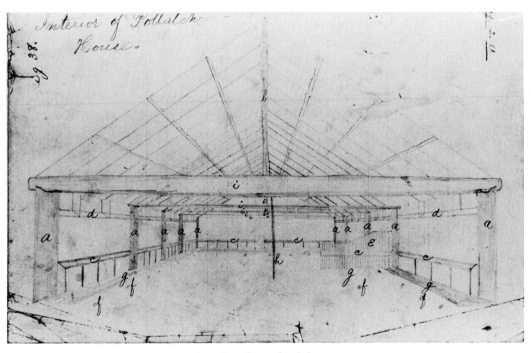

Interior of a potlatch house

Potlatch house at Port Hadlock, "raised by 'Old Patsy' in 1891"

into the ground. These were covered with large leaves of maple or evergreen and the whole was then covered with earth. They were intended for only one person at a time.

Large dwelling houses. These are usually 25 or 30 feet wide by 30, 40, or 50 feet long, though occasionally they are nearly twice as long. Each house is owned by one man, but intended for several families, usually his friends and relations, who pay no rent. There is no floor but the ground. The doors are either at each end, as in the figure, or in the middle of one side. There are small walls on each side of the entrance, inside, similar to (e) in the potlatch house.

Each corner is intended for one family, though sometimes it is occupied by more. On the inside, all around the building, is the bed-platform, similar to the one in the potlatch house. A part of this, however, is used for storing their effects. Underneath it, many things are also kept, especially their bark and firewood, if they have any in advance.

Below and in front of the platform is a low seat, 6 inches high and 3 feet wide, which is also similar to the one in the potlatch house. The fire is in front of this, and the smoke escapes by holes in the roof. Immediately over the fire and about 7 feet from the ground, sticks are placed in various positions, where food, especially fish and clams, is hung to dry. This class of houses has now gone largely out of use, except by a few of the least civilized old ones.

The flat-roof dwelling house. The sides are made of both upright and horizontal boards, and the roof is composed of two parts: first, a section made of cedar shakes or clap-boards, and which generally has quite a steep pitch; and, second, another part made of long boards with barely enough pitch to carry off the rain. Such houses are not large, usually not far from 20 by 25 feet, and are intended for only one or two families. The inside arrangement is very similar to those of the large dwelling houses. Twenty years ago there were several of these among the Twanas; ten years ago they had all disappeared.

A dwelling house of this type, which I had made in 1892 as a sample of the old dwelling houses, was sent to the World's Columbian Exposition [see page 68, bottom]. It was only 7 feet square, and about the same in height. The long roof boards extend completely from one side to the other. This is said to have been the most common mode of building houses previous to the coming of the whites. Only a single one now remains on the Skokomish reservation.

Civilized houses. The first on the Skokomish reservation were built about 1874 by the government carpenter, with lumber bought by annuity money. They had floors and two or three rooms similar to small cottages for whites. Hence no further description is needed. They were generally about 16 by 22 feet. Since then the greater part of the Indians on the Sound have built for themselves civilized houses of some kind, often very much better than those first built by government. Very few people now live on the ground and in the smoke.

The summer house or mat house. These are made of mats, with occasionally a few boards. Generally they are built at fishing places during the summer. Inside, the beds are laid around the side on boards a few inches from the ground. The fire is in the middle; most of the space overhead is occupied with fish which are being dried. People and things are stowed where any room can be found, and the whole atmosphere is filled with smoke. In 1892 I had one made for the Columbian Exposition, about 7 feet square, but wholly of mats, only four mats being used in the construction.

The half-circle camp. When travelling in stormy weather, they often place poles in the ground in the form of a semicircle to the windward and fasten mats to them, the whole standing so as to answer both as wall and roof. Under this shelter they sleep. The fire is to the leeward, which is open.

Tents of cotton cloth. Tents are now often used in travelling, and sails are also spread over poles so as to form a kind of low tent.

Of these houses, numbers 3, 4, and 5 may properly be called permanent, but are occasionally torn down and moved, perhaps only a short distance, because of vermin and dirt.

The size as given in the figures is that of representative houses, but it varies.

The residence of Chief Sitwell on the Puyallup Reservation

A flat roof dwelling house, which Eells had made for the Columbian Exposition

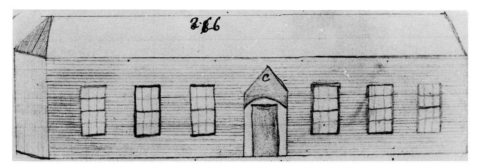

The house of Head Chief Balch, "well above average"

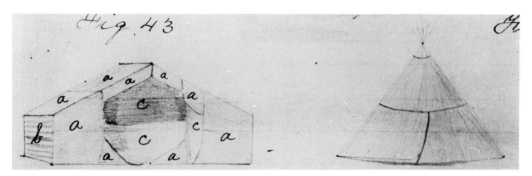

Summer house and mat house

Puyallup smoke house

OUTBUILDINGS

These consist of barns, stables for horses, stables for oxen when they are logging, cellars and caches for roots (chiefly potatoes), woodsheds, and hen houses, the last two of which are rather scarce. They often take their canoes into their large houses. These outhouses are all built after the style of those of the whites, though not usually as substantial. None of them was in use, as far as I know, before the coming of the whites.

VILLAGES

Their houses were originally near the beach in small villages, but arranged with no order. Those at Jamestown are now on one straight street and those on the reservations are scattered on their farms.

APPURTENANCES TO DWELLINGS

Doors. An ancient form of door was a circular aperture cut through the building. The only one I have seen, in their houses, was in a Clallam house at Sequim. It was 3¼ by 3¾ feet. It was closed by sliding other boards over the aperture. In the house sent to the Exposition, the door is of the same style, but is closed by a single board a little larger than the aperture which hangs over it, being held there by a thong. In their summer houses and occasionally in those of style number 4, the doors consisted of mats, hung over the entrance. At present all doors to their permanent houses are made after the style of the whites and are hung with good iron hinges, or, when these cannot be obtained, with some kind of a rough, wooden one.

Fire places. (1) Anciently the Clallams, at least, dug a circular place about a foot deep and five or six feet in diameter in the ground, in some of their houses, heaping up the dirt around the edge, upon which they sat or lay. There are none of these in use now, nor have there been for twenty years. (2) In houses classed 1, 3, 4, and 6, they build their fires on the ground, without any preparation except making the smoke hole in the roof. This often was about three feet square, and generally had a cover, which might be used when a severe storm occurred or when the occupants were absent. In class 4, where long boards extend from one side of the house to the other, this smoke hole is made simply by removing to one side from one to three of these long boards.

Occasionally in the houses, which have floors of lumber, holes are cut in them for fire places, three or four feet square, about the middle of the room, the space from the ground to the floor being filled with earth, and perhaps the edges of the floor around the fire place are lined with tin, while a hole is made in the roof where the smoke may escape. (3) Another form has occasionally been adopted from the white logging camps. The fire place is like that last described, but the place for the escape of the smoke is quite different. A truncated pyramid is made of boards, hollow, so that the base, which is about five feet square, hangs some five feet above the fire, while the smaller end passes through the roof. The draught through this is sufficient to cause the smoke to pass through it, and thus the room is kept tolerably free from it. These have been used but seldom, and I have seen none for several years. They have been a transition affair from smoke to chimneys and stoves, when the Indians were unable to procure the latter. (4) A chimney, wholly of boards at the end of the house, was another transition style. The hearth is of earth, raised to the level of the floor. Its peculiarities are its size and material. It is large, for two reasons: that the boards may not take fire, and, as an additional preventative, sometimes an old piece of iron (as sheet-iron or the side of a broken stove) is placed against the side of the chimney, and so much care is exercised that I have never known a serious fire to result therefrom; second, that the occupants, especially the sick, may lie inside the chimney near the fire. (5) Civilized chimneys, like those used by the whites, of sticks, dirt, and stones, similar to those in use on the frontiers, or of brick, are occasionally made, but not very often, as it is too difficult for the Indians to make them with a good draught. Hence, stoves have of late become very common.

Material for building. This in all permanent buildings is entirely of wood. Of late, sawed boards are usually obtained. Barns and other outhouses are generally made of split cedar boards from 3 to 10 feet long. Formerly planks were made of cedar boards, and as cedar decays very slowly, some of these are still in use among the older and less civilized Indians. The largest which I have seen were among the Clallams at Elwha. One was 2½ feet wide and 40 feet long, and another 3½ feet wide and 20 long. Such boards were split with wedges and trimmed by hewing. Gibbs says he saw a board 4½ feet wide and 24 long.

Ladders were uncommon. I have seen a single native one. It was among the Clallams. It was 8 or 10 feet long, and was made of a split slab in which steps were cut, an inch or two deep.

Totem posts were not known. The nearest approach to them is the tamahnous posts, which will be described in Chapter XXV.

Locks, latches, and hinges. As anciently their doors did not require these, they did not have them. They now commonly use those of American make, or else make rough latches and hinges of wood, and often nail up their doors, when they have no lock.

Structures for burial are common, and will be described in Chapter XXII.

Cupboards. These were probably not in use until the coming of the whites.

Tables. These, like the last, are an innovation from the whites. They are now very common. In fact, it is uncommon not to have them.[2]

VOL. 2

VII
FURNITURE,
VESSELS, AND UTENSILS
OF HOUSEHOLD USE

FURNITURE

Beds. These were made from common mats and blankets. The mat is partly rolled up, which forms the pillow. The rest becomes the bed. When there are several thicknesses of these mats, the bed is quite soft and comfortable. Old-fashioned blankets of dog's hair and other material, and skin, were used for covering. But a bed entirely of these materials is never seen now, although the mats are used to some extent now by the poorer and older Indians as the lower part of the bed. Those of feathers and straw, springs with sheets, quilts, American blankets, and feather pillows are very common. Their bed-steads—the bed-platform—have been described in Chapter VI, in connection with the potlatch and large houses, but as those houses are becoming obsolete, so those bed-platforms are being largely supplanted by bedsteads of American style, both home made and boughten.[1]

Rugs. These are of three kinds, all introduced since the whites came, yet the Indian women are almost the exclusive makers of them in this region. All are made principally of rags.

1. The rags, cut in strips, are braided and then sewed into rugs of a circular or oblong form.

2. They are torn in strips, and these are woven with a warp and woof. They are both rectangular and circular or oblong, and are made with a little taste in the arrangement of colors, more than with the first style, but far less than with the third. They are by far the most serviceable of the three kinds. Both the rectangular and circular are made on the floor. The rectangular ones may also be made while hanging on the wall. I have two or three times also seen them in a kind of loom, similar to the ones anciently used in making blankets.

3. The most ornate kind is made by taking a piece of burlap, as the ground work, stretching it on a frame, and then drawing rags through it by means of an instrument

Rag table mat and miniature rugs, Twana

similar to a large crochet needle of iron. By so doing they can draw rags of any color into any place, and thus they often make rude forms of men, animals, trees, and various figures. I can learn of no different names in the Twana language, by which the three kinds are called. They use these in their own houses and sell them to the whites.

Mats.[2] These are of seven kinds.

1, 2, 3. The first, second, and third kinds are made of the grass of the cat-tail rush. This grass is cut by the women in July and August, dried in the sun, and tied in bunches, as large as can be comfortably carried. When a woman finds time to make mats, she assorts her rushes into three lots according to size. Of the longest rushes she makes the largest mats, which are about 5 feet wide and 12 to 20 feet long. Of rushes of medium length, she makes mats about 3 feet wide, and from 8 to 15 feet long. Of the smaller stalks she makes mats about 2 feet wide and from 2 to 4 long. The largest mats are used chiefly for lining wooden houses and in constructing mat houses. Those of medium size are used at times for the same purpose, for the half-circle camps, for beds, pillows, seats, table covers, and as substitutes for umbrellas and oil-cloth, two layers forming an almost complete protection from the rain. The narrowest mats, usually from 3 to 4 feet long, are used mostly for cushions, as in canoes, and for the paddlers to kneel on. While sorting over the rushes, she splits off a small part from the base of the stalk, of which she makes a string, which she uses in sewing the mat together.

Cattail rush mats, Twana

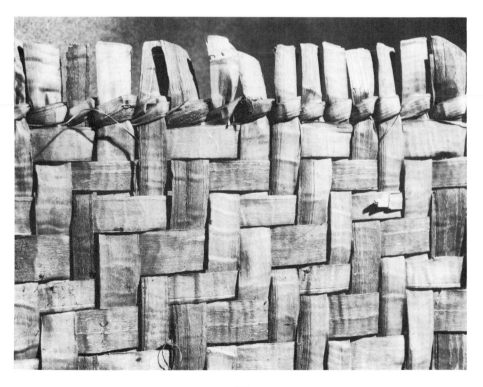

The two wider kinds are also quite an article of commerce with the Makah and some British Columbia Indians, who make none of this kind, but who value them as superior to those of their own manufacture, which are cedar bark. The raw material is also used as an article of trade.

Their manufacture was originally a large part of the indoor work of the women and is as follows. The rushes, having been sorted, are cut so as to be of a uniform length, as long as the mat is to be wide. The ends of the rushes are first temporarily fastened together in the shape of the mat, then strings made of the same material, shredded and twisted, are passed transversely through these rushes, and about 2½ inches apart. This is done with a needle of hard wood, 3 feet long, ½ inch wide, three-cornered, and with an eye in one end, in which the string is placed. After the string is passed through, a small piece of wood with a crease in it is pressed over the mat where the strings are, to render it firm and of good shape. The edges of the mats are fastened by weaving the ends of the transverse threads firmly together.

4. Another mat is made and used in a manner similar to the medium-sized cat-tail mat, but is made from a round rush, which usually grows to a height only sufficient to make mats about 3 feet wide. This rush is about a third of an inch in diameter. It is not very common.

5. A rough mat is made from the inner bark of the cedar, split into strips half an inch wide or thereabouts and woven together at right angles. It is used chiefly to lay fish upon when they are cleaned or to place on a frame over a fire on which food is placed to dry.

6. A good mat is made by the Makah and British Columbia Indians from the inner bark of the cedar. This is split into strips a quarter or a third of an inch wide, and woven in a manner similar to the last, but much larger, more firmly, and with carefully finished edges. Sometimes the strips are colored black, which are woven in at regular distances, or else the border is made of black strips. These mats are rectangular and usually about 4 feet by 7 or 8, though some are larger and some are smaller. They are used for lining houses, and on floors, and are placed on the ground for tables and seats. For bedding they are considerably inferior to the rush mats, as there is far less elasticity to them; neither are they good as a protection against rain, but they are superior for sails, as they are far lighter.

The four kinds first described are made almost exclusively by the Sound Indians and those farther south, and this is not strange, as the Makah Indians have, I believe, none of the material growing in their land. But the same reason does not hold good with the Sound Indians, that they should not make cedar bark mats, as cedar is very abundant with them and cedar bark is used by them for many other purposes. Yet, it seems to be understood that the dividing line between the Makahs and Clallams about the Hoko river, is also the dividing line between the manufacture of these different kinds of mats. When made, however, they do not remain on their respective sides of the line, but are often traded with each other, as their respective merits are fully recognized by the different tribes.

7. A small table mat is also made by the Makahs and Quinaielts, but it finds its way

Grass table mats, Twana

among the Sound Indians, and is also highly prized by the whites. They are both round and oblong in shape, seldom more than 15 inches long or less than 6 inches in diameter. They are made from a very fine grass, woven very firmly, and colored very prettily, at present with aniline dyes. They make a useful ornamental and substantial article for the table. I have seen a few similar to these made by the Puyallup and Twana Indians, but they were far inferior to those made by the two tribes on the coast.

Seats. No chairs, stools, or benches were formerly used, their seats having been the ground, their mats, the bed-platform, and the low seats in front of them, described in connection with their ancient houses in Chapter VI. At present American chairs, stools, benches, and a few sofas are in common use.

Tables. They formerly had none, except a mat spread on the ground. Now good tables are in use.

Cradles. These will be described in Chapter XVIII in connection with the care of infants.

VESSELS AND UTENSILS

Tubs and washing vessels. The only native kind of which I know was the water-tight basket to be described in this chapter. American tubs are now very commonly used. Occasionally they make one by sawing a barrel in two, and sometimes, as in ancient days, go to a spring, river, pond, or the salt water and use nature's tub. I presume, however, that formerly they had but little use for tubs, as they had very little, if any, material which could be washed, except their hands, faces, and bodies.

Brooms and fly brushes. Brooms were formerly not much needed, for the Indians lived in the dirt. If at any time they wanted anything of the kind, they found it in the limbs and leaves of a tree. At present American brooms are common, and might be much more so, with advantage.

Lights. Torches were the only kind used. These were made of pitch fir wood, split somewhat fine; or in the absence of these, they were made of cedar wood, split up in much the same way. They now use candles, coal oil, and lanterns as we do.

Baskets. These were of twelve kinds, some of which were made by these Indians, and some of which, though made by other tribes, were imported and used here.

1. The water-tight basket. I have seen only one which is angular at the rim. It was so old when I saw it that I was unable to make out the figures on it. With this exception, they are oval at the rim. They are made from cedar roots and grass, woven and sewed together, are very stiff, and are the most useful and substantial baskets they have. All the Sound tribes give them the same name, *spa-tco* or *spu-tco*, except the Nisqually-speaking tribes. They are made only by a very few women, and are still valued highly, from three to five dollars apiece for those holding half a bushel or more. They usually hold from two quarts to a bushel, though a few very small ones are made, holding only about a pint. They are very useful for carrying water and juicy berries. Formerly they were used for cooking, stones having been heated and placed in the water in them, with the food. They are also used for carrying and storing dry articles as potatoes, apples, dry fish, and the like. They are usually ornamented with some artistic figures.

2. A stiff basket, but not water-tight, about the same size as the last, is made of grass and cedar bark. This kind is woven, not sewed, and is used for carrying and storing dry articles, and for work less wearing and round than the water-tight basket. They are not much ornamented.

3. The cedar limb basket. Cedar limbs are split and, the bark having been taken off usually, are woven together, and thus a common basket for carrying and storing common dry articles is made. They generally hold from half a bushel to a bushel and a half.

4. The fancy basket. This is made entirely of small grass, woven and tightly pressed together, often with a small bone implement or some similar instrument. A part of the grass is colored, and with this the basket is ornamented. It usually holds from two quarts to a bushel, and is used as a ladies' work basket, or for storing cloth and fancy articles. Very few have handles.

Small "fancy" basket, Twana

Basket, Twana, with "round and round animal design"

Watertight basket, Quinaielt

Basket, Twana, with "round and round design"

Twana woman's work basket

Twana fancy basket

Large watertight basket with leather thongs

Rectangular carrying baskets, Makah and Quinaielt

Head strap for carrying, attached to basket

Medium-size fancy basket (unidentified)

Large basket (unidentified)

Large basket (unidentified)

Large Twana basket with handle

Twana mat grass basket

Basket with "round and round" design

Clockwise from top center: small Clallam basket; Makah fancy basket;
unlabeled; small Makah fancy basket

Clockwise from top: Twana basket; Clallam rush basket; unlabeled; Twana watertight ("old") basket

Large Twana basket

Makah fancy basket

Small Twana bark basket

Fine grass baskets, unidentified in collection (probably Tlingit)

Miniature baskets (unidentified)

Makah fancy table basket

Fine oblong basket with Makah table mat

*Basket with hinged cover, obtained from
a Twana but made by a Snoqualmie*

Fancy wall pocket

Nittinat basket

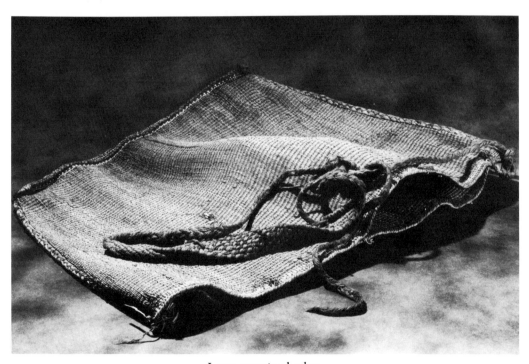

Large carrying basket

Basket made partly of cattail rushes

Basket (unidentified)

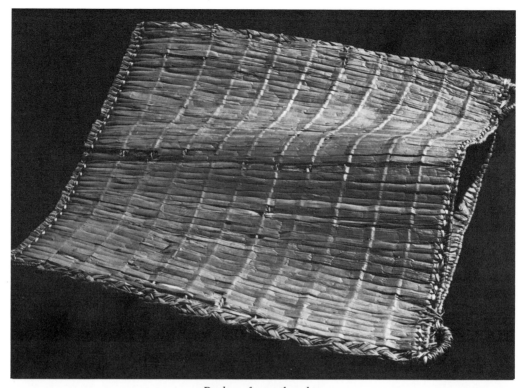

Basket of cattail rushes

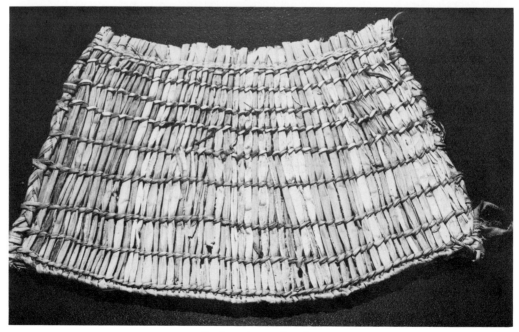

Basket of cattail rushes

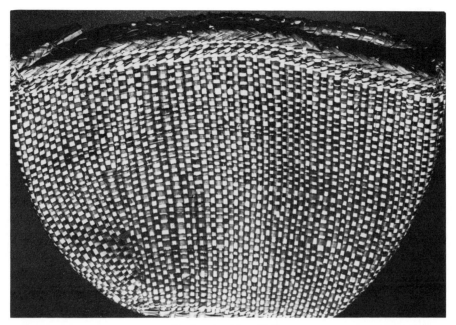

Basket (unidentified)

Small fancy basket

Small fancy basket

5. Another basket is made of a bush, as the hazel, split and shaved on both sides. The pieces are from a third to half an inch wide, and are woven together at right angles. This kind is used rather more by the whites than the Indians as a clothes basket, and was, I think, originally a copy from some American basket.

6. Another kind is made from the grass of the cat-tail rush, woven together. It usually holds about a bushel. It is not durable, as the rush is easily broken. It is not often made or used, except as a temporary affair, and occasionally for storing their effects.

7. A large carrying basket is made by the Makah and Quinaielt Indians, and imported by those on the Sound, those living nearest these two tribes naturally using more than the more distant neighbors. These are made of small round sticks, about an eighth of an inch in diameter, split in two, and placed about a quarter of an inch apart. Others are placed somewhat similarly to these, but at right angles with them, and then they are fastened together with bark. They are thus more open than any other basket made, but are very serviceable. They usually hold near a bushel, and are used for carrying and storing nearly all kinds of dry articles.

8. The Makahs also make a fancy basket, which does not usually hold over two quarts. It also finds its way up the Sound, and is also prized quite highly by the whites for it is the best made fancy basket in use on the Sound. It is, however, made in a variety of shapes and often with covers. It is made of a fine grass, the same that is used in making their table mats. It is highly ornamented, some of the grass being colored with aniline

dyes. Formerly they used their native colors for this purpose, but they have been entirely abandoned as inferior. They are used by the women for holding sewing material and similar articles.

9. A basket is made by the Makah and British Columbia Indians, of cedar bark, split into strips, a third or half an inch wide, and woven together in much the same way as the cedar bark mats. They often hold a bushel or more, though some are much smaller and are used for storing light articles. They are not strong, and will not bear much rough usage. On this account, very few find their way far up the Sound, the Clallams being the principal importers.

10. A basket is made by the Quinaielt Indians of a fine grass, which looks as much like a bag as a basket. It holds from half a bushel to a bushel, and is used for storing cloth and similar articles. Only a few find their way to the Sound, they being more abundant among the Chehalis Indians than those farther north.

11. Another which looks like the last, but which is made of another kind of grass, comes from the Klikitat Indians, east of the Cascade mountains. It seems to be made in a similar manner, and to be used for similar purposes to the last. Both are quite substantial.

12. I have seen one or two baskets made by the Sound Indians, of alder bark. The bark is simply taken from the young growth, 5 or 6 inches wide, and doubled together, the sides being fastened with a string. They are a frail affair, and only made as a temporary basket when in the woods, for want of something better.

Water buckets. These were of two kinds: (1) The water-tight basket, described in the previous section (no. 1) and (2) the water box. The latter is made water-tight, with the exception of the hole in the upper part into which the water is poured, and another one out of which it is poured or drunk. The size of this usually, though not invariably, is about 8 inches square and of the same height. The box has advantage over the basket in that it keeps out the dirt. The manufacture is peculiar. The four sides are made of one board; where the corner is to be, a small miter is cut, both on the inside and outside, partly through. Then the corners are steamed and bent at right angles, and the inside miter is cut so perfectly that it fits water-tight when the corners are bent. The corner where the two ends of the board meet are than fastened with wooden pegs driven in diagonally. The top and bottom of the box are fastened on with pegs similarly inserted. A cement is also used where these pegs are used to help to make it water-tight. They have now gone entirely out of use, having been superseded by pails, buckets, and barrels of American make, though the water-tight baskets are still occasionally used.

Boxes and chests. A box in which to keep shell money and small valuables was made of cedar, as indeed all their boxes were. It consisted of two parts, the box proper, and the cover, which covered the box to the base. The constructive principles of the four sides are the same as the water box just described, and the top and bottom are fastened on in the same manner, except that they are not cemented or water-tight. The one here figured [page 99] is 5 inches high, 5½ wide, and 7 long, and was made especially for me. In 1892 I procured one from Quinaielt, which was 2 or 3 feet long, and of proportionate size, and they were often thus made large enough to contain blankets. Wilkes speaks of seeing

Water pail of wood, Twana

boxes 3 feet square, 1849. When the Hudson's Bay Company came, they brought a trunk, covered with red leather and ornamented abundantly with nails having large brass heads, which the Indians valued highly, and which many of them still prize as superior to American ones, although they now get no new ones of that kind. Except for the native ones just mentioned I have not seen one on the Sound in twenty years.

Dishes. These were of three kinds: wood, horn, and stone. All were used mainly for holding fish and oil. Those of wood—alder being the most common—are the most abundant. I have one made by the Indians of British Columbia, and imported by the Clallams. It is 9½ by 11 inches, and 3½ inches deep, with the upper edges ornamented with shells inlaid. The ends are ornamented with the head of the Thunderbird. I have never seen any made by the Sound Indians, which are thus ornamented. Another which was made by a Clallam, is 6 by 7½ inches, and 3¾ inches deep. The wood was so saturated with oil, that although I have had it about eighteen years, it now shines with oil on the outside about as when I first obtained it. Still another I have is 3½ feet long by 6 inches wide, with about the same depth as above. These two are about the extreme in size. They are both Clallam dishes, either having become extinct farther up the Sound, or never having been made, probably the former.

Others were made of the horn of the mountain sheep. This kind was made by the Indians of British Columbia, the Klikitats, and probably by some of the Sound Indians

Wooden water bucket

Money box, Clallam

on the east side, who hunted high up in the Cascade mountains. One [page 102, top] was found among the Twanas, and I have seen a few others among them, but they were imported. One of mine is circular, about 8 inches in diameter by 3¼ deep. In making them, the horn was first cut open, then steamed and spread open, which accounts for the great size. There is no paint on them, but the figures are carved, the deeper shades being more deeply cut than the others. These dishes were used for holding food as well as grease, and were valued very highly, five dollars being the common price fifteen years ago.

I have seen but one stone dish among these Indians. I obtained it from a Clallam. It is the shape of a quarter of a sphere whose diameter was about 7 inches, and is very regular in shape. It is said to have been used for holding oil. How it was made I do not know, but from what the Indians say, I think it is largely due to the natural formation of stones which they find. I have heard that some others were formerly used by them, also that the Lower Chehalis Indians have some. It seems a little strange that there are not more of them, as mortars were very common about the Columbia river on the south and east of the Cascade mountains.

I also have a natural dish of clay stone, found by a white man at Port Angeles, Clallam County, who gave it to me. It is of much softer stone than the preceding and is of the shape of half a sphere.

99

Grease dish with shell inlay, made by Indians of British Columbia and imported by the Clallams

Ornamental "puffin" dish, Haida

Dish, horn of mountain sheep, Klikitat

Ornamental dish with shell inlay, Quinaielt

Grease dish, Clallam

Grease dish, Clallam (probably an import from the Kwakiutl)

Grease dish, unidentified

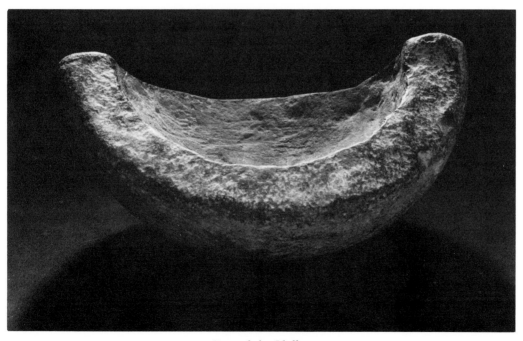

Stone dish, Clallam

Mortars. Mr. P. G. Collins of Whatcom, where the Lummi Indians formerly lived, has found in that region a few stone mortars, which hold from a third of a teacupful to half a pint. One of basalt is in the shape of a bird with a man's face. It is 7½ inches long, 5⅜ high, and 3¼ wide. Another is 2½ inches high, 5½ across the top, 3 inches across the bowl, which is ⅞ deep. Both were found in Whatcom County. The last has carving around the edge which resembles a head. He thinks these must have been used for mixing paints. He has also found a few animal specimens, with the body of an animal, and a mortar in the back. One of these is 5½ inches high, with the body of a bird and a human face, the mortar holding two thirds as much as an egg. One of these is very small, 3 inches long, 1½ at the top, and 1⅞ at base. One has four circles around it at the top.

Cranes. An iron crane is often used, on which to hang kettles when boiling food over a fire. Often sticks of wood are used for the same purpose. Usually they are from 4 to 6 feet long.

Bottles. For holding oil, they use, especially the Clallams, the paunches of seals, porpoises, and some other animals.

Spits. One kind is a single straight stick, nearly round, about half an inch or less in diameter from 1 to 2½ feet long, and sharpened at both ends. By using several of these, some set at right angles to the others, a salmon is stretched out so as to be either dried or roasted. On a single one clams are impaled and dried, and smelt or other small fish are roasted. The other is a stick about ¾ of an inch wide, 1¼ inches thick, and 3 or 3½ feet long, which is split for about 2 feet and then tied with grass to prevent its splitting further. The three ends are sharpened. On the two smaller ones the fish is fastened, and the other is stuck into the ground before the fire.

Plates and troughs. These are made of wood and are quite shallow. Alder wood is preferred. They are generally from 9 to 12 inches wide, and from 16 inches to 6 feet long, the larger ones generally being the deeper. The shorter ones are used for family eating, the larger ones for feasts. I once saw a very rough one, 24 feet long, and about a

Wooden plate, Twana

foot wide, filled with potatoes, crackers, and the like, and set before a number of men at a potlatch at Dungeness. In 1870 and 1878, I saw a number of troughs made of sawed lumber, 6 inches wide, so that the trough, three-sided, was 6 inches wide by 5 deep, and from 8 to 12 feet long. These were filled with dry food at potlatches on the Skokomish reservation. Still, all of these are now almost entirely superseded by American plates, dishes, bowls, and the like, except with a very few very old Indians.

Another kind of plate for the poor or as a temporary affair was made of cedar bark, split into strips a quarter to a half inch wide, and woven together crosswise as a mat. The one I have is 15 or 16 inches square.

Ladles. The common form of ladles or large spoons are made of wood, maple or laurel being preferred, and the horns of cattle. Before the introduction of cattle, a few of horn came with horn dishes, from the north and east. The bowl of these ladles is generally 5 or 6 inches long, 3 or 4 wide, and an inch deep, though those for children are much smaller. These ladles are used for semi-liquid food; but are not always placed in the mouth, but near the mouth, and the food is pushed from them into the mouth with a small stick, or taken from them with a smaller ladle, which is placed in the mouth. They are going out of use but not as rapidly as the plates, as they are occasionally used at their feasts. Our spoons are generally used.

Table cutlery. I am not aware that they ever had table knives or forks, unless at times they used their hunting knives. Fingers were made before forks, and used, too. Now American ones are very common.

Horn spoon, Twana

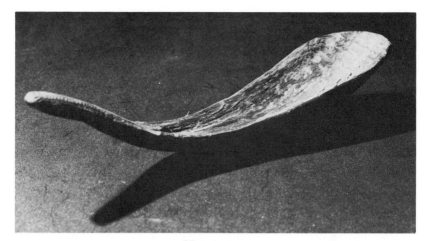

Horn spoon

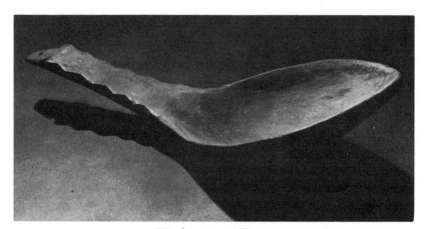

Wooden spoon, Twana

Spoon from horn of mountain sheep

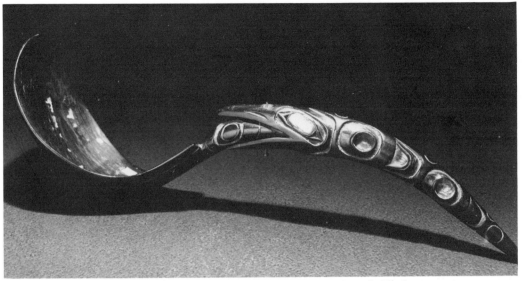

Horn spoon carved and inlaid with mother of pearl, Haida

Wooden spoon

Napkins are seldom used except at feasts. One form and the only native one I have seen is made of cedar bark, slightly beaten, about 2 feet long and tied into bunches an inch in diameter. I have seen also a piece of calico 30 or 40 feet long stretched by two individuals from end to end along a row of feasters, behind their backs. When they had finished their meal, with a sudden jerk it was flopped over their heads in front of them, when all at the same time wiped their hands and mouths, when it was flopped back as suddenly, and the work was done. Their food is often so greasy that with fingers for forks, and mouths for knives, they needed something of this kind, but after an ordinary meal, they often use any rag or towel which is near. Sometimes, too, after a meal, a pail or pan of water is brought in and set down, not far from the eaters, in which they wash their fingers and mouths. Very few, if any, of them as yet have taken kindly to the napkins of their civilized neighbors.

Pottery. No vessels of pottery or of gourds were made or used by them, nor as far as I know any of skin.

Pipes. I have seen a number of stone pipes among them. They are made from a soft clay stone. All are intended to be used with wooden stems. I once saw one with two faces, one on the side of the smoker, and looking toward him, and the other on the opposite side, and looking from him. American pipes are now very common. For remarks about tobacco, see Chapter V, "Narcotics."

Judge J. Wickersham has a pipe of regular pipe stone, which was found at Oyster Bay, Mason County, Wash., among the Squakson Indians. I presume it was brought to the country long ago by some person connected with the Hudson's Bay Company. Parts are lead, which prevent the stone from breaking.

Stone pipe, Twana

Eating and Feasting

Generally, like their white neighbors, they eat three times a day, and most of them use a table, knives, forks, spoons, plates, and dishes in a civilized way. For the last few years, the Twanas and most others have made long tables for their Fourth of July and Christmas feasts. The old style of eating was to take in the hands food which could be held. Semi-liquid food was taken in the ladles, which have just been described, while they sat around the kettle or basket in which it had been cooked, the food and eaters all being on the ground in an informal manner.

At their feasts they spread two long rows of mats, two or three feet apart, on which the feasters sat, while the food, either in kettles, pans, baskets, long wooden plates, troughs on another mat, was set between them. I was present at one feast at Port Gamble in February 1878, with about 75 Twanas, when the Clallams furnished the food. They feasted three times during the evening and night, dozing at two or three o'clock in the morning. The different feasts were given by different persons in the village, and were interspersed with gambling, singing, conversation, and the giving of presents.

Stone pipe, Makah

Stone pipe, Clallam

Stone pipe, unidentified in collection

Straight stone pipe, Clallam

Pipe listed as "pipe of peace"

Stone pipe, Clallam

I was present also at one feast at Sequim in December of the same year, where the Dungeness and Port Discovery Indians were the guests, both guests and hosts being Clallams. The feast lasted two nights. They feasted at one house, then tamahnoused and made presents; after which they went to a second house where they did the same, and then to a third house, where they did likewise, closing about two A.M. On the second night the same acts and ceremonies were repeated. Fourteen large boxes of biscuits, a barrel of sugar, besides a large amount (unmeasured) of clams, fish, and similar food, were consumed or carried away by 125 persons at this time. Quite an amount was carried away, that being the custom, as none must be left. It would be an insult to refuse to eat, even after having partaken once, if a second or third meal is prepared. He must go to all and eat, or offend his host. Very often, however, feasts occur in the day time and consist of only one meal. There is more or less feasting at nearly all their gatherings, including those for religious purposes. Even of late when they meet for Christian services at each others' houses on the Sabbath they feel as if they must have a feast.

VIII
CLOTHING

THE MATERIAL OF WHICH THEIR CLOTHES were formerly made was deer, elk, bear, and wild-cat skins, dog's hair, hawk and eagle feathers, duck and geese down, the down or cotton from the fireweed, cedar bark and roots, wool from the mountain goat, cat-tail rush, and sinew from the whale and deer.[1]

To save repetition, I will here say that nearly all the Indians in Puget Sound now dress in civilized clothing, much as Americans, with the following exceptions. A large share of the older women seldom wear hats or bonnets. They either go bareheaded or put a handkerchief or shawl over their heads. Once in a long while, one is seen with a native hat. The old men and a good share of the women go barefoot, as well as many children, when they are not at school, and once in a long while a person is seen with moccasins. Occasionally a man is seen with a blanket on over his other clothes, but not often. Young children are often more scantily clothed than with the whites. Hence the articles here described nearly all belong to the past.

HEAD CLOTHING

Hats. One kind was made by the Makahs, but many of them found their way up the Sound. It was water-tight, very serviceable, and seems to be made in a manner similar to the water-tight baskets, described in the last chapter [VII]. Other hats, somewhat similar, were made by the British Columbia Indians, especially the Nittinats and Nanaimos, which were likewise imported. They were much flatter at the top. These were worn as much by the women as the men, but commonly the Puget Sound Indians went bareheaded, as they made nothing of the kind.

Infants' head dresses. One kind, and the only native kind I have seen, was made of cedar bark, split into strips about half an inch wide and woven at right angles, nearly into the shape of a bonnet. These were placed over the head and face of the infant, when fastened on to its board, to keep out the smoke and dust. Gibbs (1885) speaks of some fur caps.

Head dress of ceremony. One kind was made of beaten cedar bark. A band of this, a half an inch to an inch in diameter, was made long enough to go around the head. Two bunches of the same material hung down behind, and two long feathers of eagles or hawks stood erect on each side of the head. Still another style I have seen was made of

Painted basketry hat, Makah

Painted basketry hat (probably imported from Kwakiutl or farther north)

cloth, a cloth band being placed around the head, with strips of red cloth, a foot or more long, hanging down all around so thickly that the face and neck were entirely concealed.

Wilkes adds, "Although the dress of these natives would seem to offer some conceal-ment to the body, few are seen that wear it with any kind of decency. Their persons are usually very filthy and they may be said at all times to be covered with dirt.[*]

Gibbs (1855) adds, "They also wore on occasions, robes made of small animals, such as the rabbit, sewelell (*Aplodentia leporina*), muskrat, or of larger ones, as the cougar and beaver. The women universally wore a breech clout of strands gathered round the waist, and falling usually to the knees, which served the purpose of concealment. With the men no idea of immodesty prevailed. Decency had not even its fig leaf. The clout was some-times made of twisted grass, at others of cedar bark, hackled, and split into a fringe. The ordinary dress however of the men, when they saw fit to use any was a deer skin shirt, leggings and moccasins."[†]

[*]*U.S. Exploring Expedition* (condensed), p. 286.
[†]*Contributions to North American Ethnology*, vol. 1, p. 219.

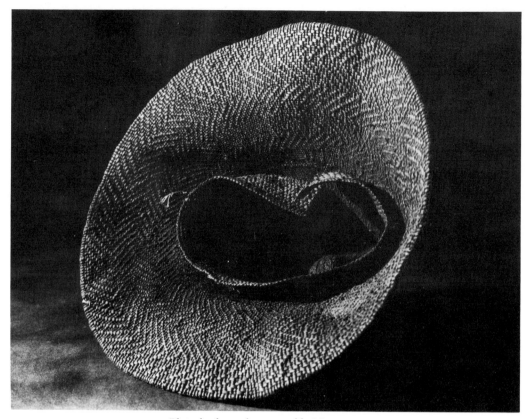

Plain basketry hat, possibly Nanaimo

BODY CLOTHING

When Vancouver first visited the Clallams in 1792, he reported those Indians as clothed in skins of deer, bear, and other animals, but principally in a woolen garment of their own maufacture, well made. Probably this was the woman's woolen skirt, which will soon be described. Wilkes, in 1841, says that the leathern hunting shirts were fringed with beads or shells, and a very few had leggings. Coats and pants were made of deer and elk skin, but whether such were made before the coming of the whites has been a question with me, or, whether they followed the fashion they obtained at an early day from the whites, using their own material. These, however, are now entirely out of date.

A coat was made of the cat-tail rush. It extended down before and behind from the shoulders half-way from the hips to the knees, and was fastened together at the sides. There was a hole for the neck, and one for each arm, and it was put on over the head. It shed rain well. I never saw any until 1892, when I had two made for the World's Columbian Exposition.

Same hat as shown on facing page

Cattail rush coat

*John Haiten, a Nisqually, with "ceremonial shirt of deer skin
and tamahnous articles in hands"*

Annie Williams, "in woman's ancient dress and bonnet of wool of mountain goat, with silver bracelets made by Makah Indians on her wrists." In foreground, blanket of same kind of wool; Makah basket; Waterbox

Annie Williams, "in woman's ancient dress and head band of wool of mountain
goat. Doctor's rattle and tamahnous shell in the hands." (1) Mat coat; (2)
Blanket of same wool; (3) Gorgets of dentalia shell

Annie Williams, "in woman's ancient dress and mantle of mountain goat. Deer rattles in her hands. Head bands and gorgets of dentalia shell." (1) Mat coat; (2) Blanket of mountain goat wool

The dresses for the women were of at least two kinds of cedar bark and the wool of the mountain goat. The latter was the dress of the wives and daughters of the chiefs, the former of the common people. It consisted of a skirt fastened in front around the waist. This was made by fastening to a band, which went around the waist, twisted strings of the same material, which hung down for a foot and a half to two and a half feet. A cape was made of the same material. The one represented in the figure [page 119] was made for the Columbian Exposition in 1892, by a Twana woman from a blanket of the wool of the mountain goat, which had recently been brought to the reservation by some Sno-homish Indians. I afterwards obtained one at the Quinaielt reservation which was much shorter, about a foot and a half long, but very much heavier, the strands being much thicker. It was very old, and was evidently the old fashion.

The one of cedar bark was of the same pattern, but of beaten cedar bark. Another kind was of cedar bark, but only a foot or so wide, and hung down in front like an apron. It was worn by the very poorest and the slaves.

Blankets. There were at least three kinds. One was made of dog's hair, geese or duck down, and the cotton from the fire-weed. These were twisted into strings and woven together. This special breed of dog was kept for its hair, but is now extinct. It was not large, but the hair was long, and a woman's wealth was often estimated by the number of such dogs she owned. I have never seen any of these blankets. Vancouver speaks of two as resembling those of Pomerania, but larger. They were white.

Another kind of blanket was imported from the Makahs who made it. It was made from the inner bark of the cedar, slightly beaten, so as not to be too stiff, and woven with strings of goose down, twisted. The only one I have seen was at Dungeness in 1878, and had a border or fringe of black hair. The third kind was of the wool of the mountain goat, twisted into coarse strings and woven together.

All of these blankets were woven on a loom.

A kind of bonnet was made of the wool of the mountain goat, woven. It was for the wives and daughters of chiefs.

A woman's head dress was made from the wool of the mountain goat. Another kind was made of the dentalia shell, strung together from eight to a dozen wide, with beads or leather between the different rows.

Robes. These were made of the skins of the deer, elk, bear, whistling marmot, and wild-cat, the latter being sewed together. Occasionally a buffalo robe was obtained from the Klikitat Indians.

Hand and arm clothing. I cannot learn of any special covering for the arms and hands. Some parts of the blankets and body clothing already described would naturally protect these parts.

Leg and foot clothing. Moccasins were occasionally used, but the climate is too wet to admit of their being worn with much comfort, nor is the cold in the winter so great that they need them long. They generally went barefooted. At present, the Twana women spend much time in knitting woolen socks, which they sell to the whites. Wilkes and Gibbs speak of leggings occasionally.

Indian towel of cedar bark

Woman's ancient apron or slave's dress, Twana

Woman's skirt of mountain goat wool

Parts of Dress

Fastenings for blankets and shawls are and were made of wood, bone, iron, and brass, sometimes very plain and common, and sometimes with ornamental heads, as dogs, birds, and the like. They were five or six inches long.

Fringes were appended to the buckskin coats, pants, and shirts. They were about an inch long, and made likewise of buckskin.

Receptacles for dress. Some of the baskets described in the previous chapter, and the boxes mentioned in the previous chapter, were used for storing clothing.

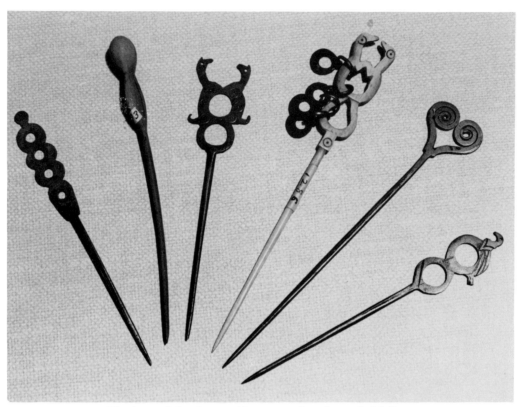

Blanket and shawl pins of bone, wood, and metal, Clallam

IX
PERSONAL ADORNMENTS

SKIN ORNAMENTATION

Painting. During their religious ceremonies, and often at their feasts, potlatches, and at their gambling performances, they painted their faces.[1] Red was the universal color, except at their black tamahnous ceremonies, when black was used. The women sometimes paint to prevent their being tanned, and if they have done something which will make them blush in company, they sometimes paint to prevent these blushes being seen. They generally use their fingers for brushes, and have no especial pattern. Commonly, they paint their cheeks and foreheads smoothly, but sometimes in streaks, these running both ways of the face, also in spots in a very irregular manner. Formerly in time of war, they also painted profusely.

Tattooing. This was common, but the younger ones do but little of it, as the whites, whose example they follow, do not tattoo. I doubt whether anciently they did this work, but probably began it when the whites first came, sailors and some of the employees of the Hudson's Bay Company having been accustomed to do so. I have copied one from the hand of a Twana man, the others from the hands and wrists of women [overleaf].

It is much more common on hands and wrists than on other parts of the body. I cannot learn that there is any special meaning to the figures than mere ornament. In doing the work, they use a needle and thread, blackening the thread, and drawing it under the skin as deeply as they can bear it.

BODY DECORATION

Ear pendants. Native ones are of three kinds, two of them being made from their money, the same as whites. One is of the dentalia shells, a number of which are fastened together. Small pieces of black or red cloth are often fastened in the lower part for greater ornament. The other is of abalone shell. I have seen only one of stone. It was found in a grave at Hoodsport, in the land of the Twanas. Both the men and the women used them. With the exception of a very few old Indians, they have been supplanted by American ones. One Clallam has become quite expert in making them of silver.

Head bands. I have a head band of dentalia shell, formerly used. Threads are run through the shells, and then through the leathers which keep the shells in their place. These are very scarce now, but the very few there are, are valued highly.

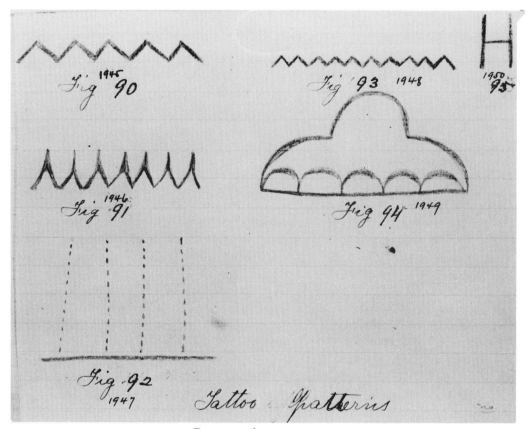

Drawings of tattoo patterns

I have a cap band once worn by a Twana Indian. For other descriptions of head bands, see "Head dress of ceremony" in Chapter VIII. Occasionally at their potlatches they sprinkle their heads with the white down of ducks for ornament.

Neck ornaments. Necklaces were formerly made by stringing the dentalia and olivella shells. Sometimes these strings were five feet long, and were doubled several times. Dogfish bones and bear's claws were also strung for necklaces, the latter being used as charms. Beads of various styles, shapes, colors, and sizes have taken the place of these old ornaments, some being very large. At first blue ones, introduced by the Hudson's Bay Company, were almost exclusively used, but now these are going out of date and are almost as seldom used as the old native ones. Most of the girls now use but few more, or any different ones, from white girls. They now usually keep their long strings of blue beads in their trunks, or hanging in their houses, with their keys fastened to them. The women and girls used these necklaces almost exclusively.

Stone ear pendants

Hudson's Bay Company beads collected from the Twana

Breast ornaments. Gorgets of dentalium shell were formerly used. I have seen a few among the Indians on the Sound, but when in 1892 I wished to procure some for the World's Columbian Exposition, I had to send to Quinaielt for them.

Nose ornaments. Formerly they bored a hole through the septum of the nose, in which they inserted polished bone or wood, quills or the dentalium shell, but they abandoned the practice so long ago that in twenty years I have only seen two or three very old ones with this hole, and none with the ornament.

Ornaments of the limbs. I am not aware that before the whites came they ever had any rings, bracelets, or anklets, but they may have had them of copper, as copper was brought from British Columbia. Certainly as soon as the first whites came, they gladly obtained and used them, and made them from the best material they could procure, valuing them highly and burying both finger rings and bracelets with their dead. They make many from brass and copper and buy silver ones, which are excellently made by the Makah and British Columbia Indians, as well as those of American make.

Dentalia shell gorget with thimbles

Copper bracelets, Clallam (found at Sequim, Washington)

TOILET ARTICLES

Combs. These were made both of wood and bone, the former being the most common. I have seen only one of bone, which was found at Port Angeles. The teeth are usually about 2½ inches long, there being about five to the inch, though they vary. Sixteen teeth are the most I have seen on any single comb. Single ones are more common than double ones. The heads are sometimes carved somewhat artistically. I have one with the representation of a small man on it.

Soaps. I am told that formerly they used a kind of sugar-colored clay, and the leaves of certain trees, as a substitute for soap, but now only American soaps are used.

Tweezers. They have made such of steel and tin for pulling out the beard, and sometimes they pull it out between a knife and finger. They are now abandoning the habit of eradicating the beard, and allow the beard and whiskers to grow, as their white neighbors do. Though their beard is not long, it is jet black and sometimes quite thick on the face.

Perfumes. Formerly they used sweet-scented roots, it is said, though I have never seen them in use, and have never been able to learn the kind, as their use was abandoned long ago for those of civilized manufacture.

Pomades. They have often used bear's oil and other oils for softening the hair, but nothing for coloring it.

Wooden combs, Twana and Clallam

Paints. Before the introduction of American paints, which they now generally use, black paint was made from coal, especially that used in painting their faces. The bottom of their canoes was made black by burning them carefully.

One kind of red paint was made from a red clay obtained on the east side of Hood's Canal, seven miles below the reservation. This was ground and mixed with oil, but is so full of grit that it is far inferior to some obtained by the Clallams.

There is a tradition about this clay as follows. Long ago before Dokibatl, the Great Changer and deity of these Indians first came to the Sound, this bank was Klikitat Indians', and the bank opposite on the other side of the Canal was Twanas'. There was a great contest of gambling between the two tribes, and the Klikitats won the game. When Dokibatl came, he changed them all to land. Because the Klikitats won, the Twanas now use this paint as a kind of charm in their dancing, gambling, and religious ceremonies, that they may be successful. Because the Twanas were then beaten, they are still beaten in their contests with other tribes, i.e., once beaten, always beaten.

Another red paint was obtained from some clay bank farther down the Sound by the

Clallam Indians, which was of a superior quality. I have seen the paint, but not the mine, and do not think it was properly in the Clallam country.

Another red paint was obtained from the gnarl of a certain tree found in the mountains. It is passed through some process underground, but what I cannot learn. Neither can I learn what tree it is taken from, I have simply obtained a few specimens of the paint. The process does not destroy the grain of the original gnarl.

The juice of blackberries, raspberries, and similar ones is often used to paint faces.

A white or yellowish paint was obtained by burning elk horn, grinding it, and mixing it with oil.

A clay-colored paint was obtained from a clay-colored earth found in the Twana land. These latter two were never used in painting the body, but are here mentioned as so many of the paints were used for toilet purposes.

Pin cushions. These are often made, and made very neatly and prettily, but necessarily after patterns furnished by the whites.

COPPER ORNAMENTS

In 1792 Vancouver reported many copper ornaments on the Indians up near the main Sound, but does not state on what part of the body they were worn. At that early day I presume the copper was obtained from British Columbia, or Alaska, where it is said to have been mined.

Commodore Wilkes (1841) says that the hunting shirts of some of the men were fringed with beads or shells, and that the women ornamented themselves with brass bells and other trinkets. They were all fond of wearing brass rings on their wrists and fingers. A few were tattooed and they disfigured their bodies by the manner in which they daubed themselves with red ochre mixed with salmon oil, which besides being disgusting in appearance, was exceedingly so in smell.* Gibbs says that anciently a few porcupine quills were imported from eastern Indians, to adorn their moccasins, but this ceased when beads were brought.

U.S. Exploring Expedition (condensed), p. 286.

X

IMPLEMENTS

IMPLEMENTS OF GENERAL USE

Knives. These were of several different kinds. One now in common use among the older Indians has a bone handle with a curved blade of steel. It is of native make, though it is plain that they never made any such until the introduction of steel by the whites. Old rasps are generally used for this purpose. It is especially convenient in finishing canoes or anything hollow, but is used for all purposes in cutting wood. The person using it generally whittles towards himself, and not away from himself. The handle is about 5½ inches, and the blade about 4½ inches long.[1]

A hunting knife of native make is likewise made from an old rasp, with a bone handle. It is double-edged. The handle is of two pieces of bone, which is riveted around the iron, the latter generally extending beyond the former. The blade is nearly 6 inches long and 1½ inches wide, and the handle about 4 inches long.

Another kind is made entirely of bone. I have one which was found at Point Wilson, near Port Townsend. It is 7½ inches long, tapering to a point, and was intended mainly for cutting open skins, in dressing slain animals.

Another kind was of slate stone. I have two, one of which was found near the last specimen, and the other at Dungeness. Each weighs about ⅝ of an ounce, is flat on both sides, about 2¾ inches long, 1½ wide, and 5/32 of an inch thick. I am not aware that slate is found in this region, and this found its way here possibly through the whites, or distant Indians.

Another stone knife of a different form was owned by a Twana Indian, but after repeated efforts I failed to get it, or even to see it before it was lost. It is said to have been about 6 inches long.

Still another style is a cleaver, the handle being of wood and the blade of sheet iron. Consequently, it was made after the coming of the whites. The blade is about 2 inches wide and 6 long.

Another style was made entirely of bone, and was used for taking cedar bark from the trees. It is about 17 inches long, 1½ inches wide, and ¼ inch thick. It has a hole in the handle for a string. It is double-edged, but dull. I obtained it of a Twana, and have never seen another like it. American knives are now in common use.

Axes, adzes, celts. At present they use those of civilized manufacture, and also make one style of hand adze. The old style was made of stone, of which I have obtained about twenty-five. I believe that these represent about all shapes and sizes which were in general

Twana hunting knife

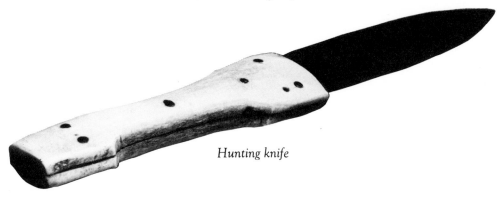

Hunting knife

Hunting knife

Curved knife for making paddles

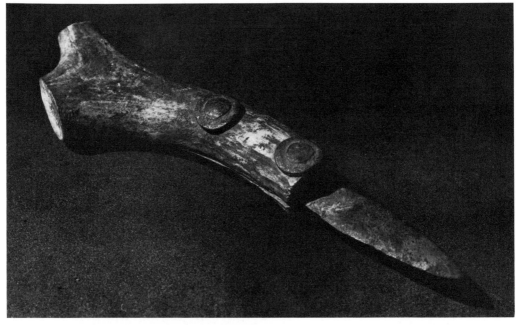

Twana knife

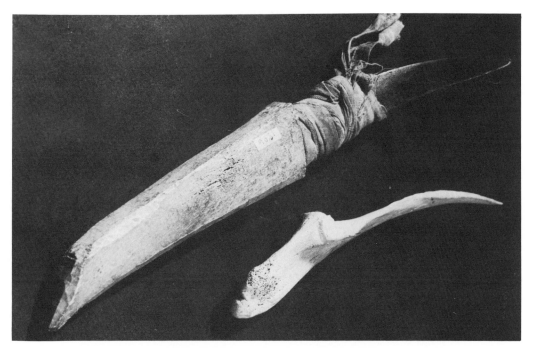

Clallam bone knife and Twana curved knife

Drawing knife

Drawing knife

use. They vary in length from 3 to 7 inches, in width from ¾ to 3¼ inches, in thickness from ⅜ to ¾ of an inch, and in weight from 1½ to 12 ounces. All are polished, with one exception, and that one is unfinished. Most of them are of metamorphic rock, a few of sedimentary, and two of hard sandstone. Generally they are sharpened by being ground more on one side than on the other, but a few are sharpened entirely on one side.

I have obtained them from Clallam, Twana, and Squakson Indians from Clallam Bay to the head of Hood's Canal, and across the Isthmus to Squakson island. Generally they are flat on one side and rounded on the other, but two are rounded on both sides. Mr. J. Y. Collins has found about twenty of these axes about Whatcom, one of which is 1⅝ inches wide, 6½ long, ⅝ thick, and is a double-ender. Some Indians say that these were used as hatchets or axes for ordinary chopping, and there are trees near Dewatto and Doswailopsh which have been partially or wholly cut down by such axes. Others say that they were used as hand adzes, with which to hollow their canoes, after they had been hollowed by burning. Such adzes are now in common use, only they are made of old rasps, and hafted with wooden handles. Both statements are probably true. I had one hafted as an adze for the Columbian Exposition, but have not seen an Indian who professed to know how to haft them as an ax.

Sometimes those of this style of handle are ornamented with carved figures, and I have seen one with a bird's head at one end. I have also seen among the Twanas a solitary instance of one of these hand adzes being hafted by splicing the blade made from an old rasp to a straight stick, for a handle somewhat similar to a chisel.

Twana fishing knife

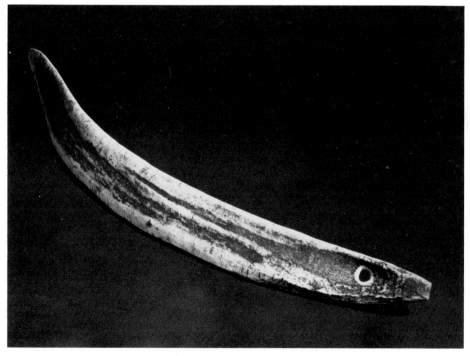

Bone knife for cedar bark removal

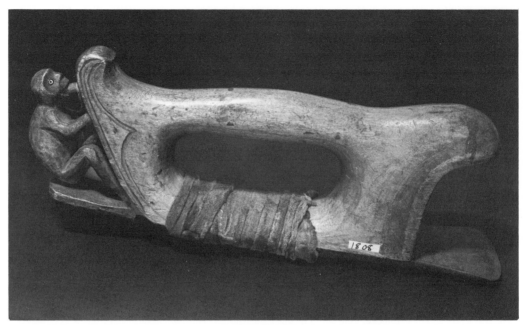

Clallam adze

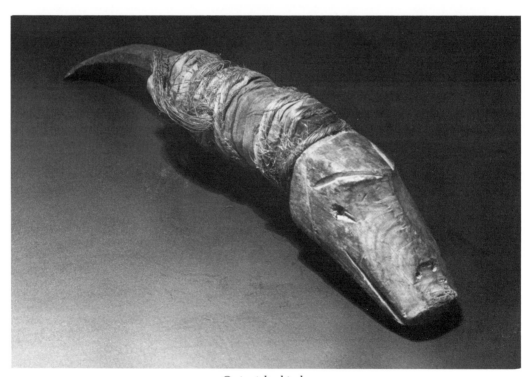

Quinaielt chisel

138

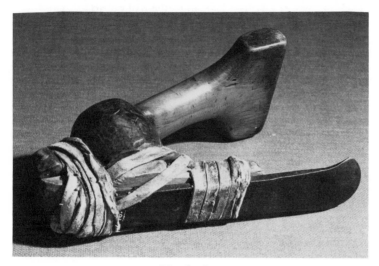

Hand adze

Hand adze with bone handle

Twana adze

Quinaielt adze handle, unfinished

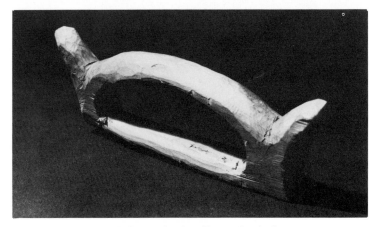

Clallam adze handle, unfinished

Whetstones. I have often seen them use for this purpose a small black rounded, irregular stone, similar to many beach stones in shape though I have not seen such on the beach. It has a very firm smooth grain. Some Indians have told me that they find them on the beach, while others say that they bring them from the northern shores of the Straits of Fuca. It is plain that they had no use for exactly such before the introduction of metallic tools by the whites, though they did probably use something similar to sharpen their stone axes.

An article of stone was found by an old Indian on the beach near the mouth of the Tahooya Creek near the Skokomish reservation. He thought that it was a stone wedge, stating that such were in use long ago, though not in his days or those of his father. This

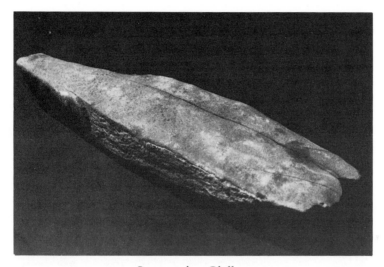

Stone wedge, Clallam

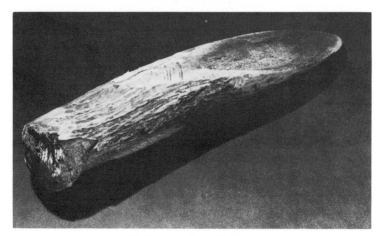

Elk horn wedge, Clallam

Elk horn chisels

Hammer stones

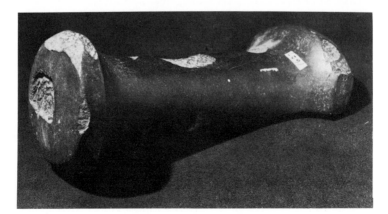

Hammer stone, Twana

may be true, as many such are found south of the Columbia river and east of the Cascade mountains, but I doubt whether this is one as it is of soft material, gray sandstone, and bears no real marks of human workmanship. It is well waterworn.

At present, wooden wedges and iron ones are in common use with old ax heads, which are the most common.

Hammers. Occasionally native ones of stone are used by the old Indians, but it is seldom, as American ones of iron and steel have superseded them. The native ones were commonly in the shape of a pestle. Generally they weigh from 3 to 3½ pounds, and are 6 or 7 inches long. One small one, however, from Dungeness, very regular in shape, is only 3¾ inches long, and weighs ¾ of a pound.

One from Elwha, evidently unfinished and irregular in shape, though but 7 inches long, weighs 7 pounds. They are of sedimentary, trap, quartzite, and basaltic stone. Generally they are smooth and polished, but some are rough. One different from the others was much larger. It was used by pounding on the side, while the previous ones were used by pounding on the end. It was 15 inches long, 5 wide, and 2½ thick. It was of sedimentary rock, was not polished, and was the only one of the kind which I have seen. It has been lost. It was owned by a Twana Indian.

Another kind of hammer or mallet was found on the Skokomish reservation. It was of sedimentary rock not polished, 8 inches long, 3½ wide, 2 thick, and weighs 3½ pounds. It is evidently a water-washed stone, being altered only by having had the groove made around the middle, so that a wooden handle might be fastened to it. The ends have been battered. I have never seen another like it on the Sound. It is now lost.

Another stone tool found on the Skokomish reservation is somewhat similar to the last. It is in much the same state that the water left it, but bears marks of having been worked a little in the middle for a handle. It is 6½ inches long, 2½ wide, and 2 thick, weighing 2 pounds. The Indians believe that it was either used for rubbing deer skins when tanning, or preparing food.

. . . .

Awls. The only ones I have ever seen were of wood or bone. I have one of bone which was found near Port Townsend. It is about 3 inches long, ⅝ inch thick at the larger end, and three-cornered.

WAR AND THE CHASE

War, when possible, was carried out only by treachery and stealth. About twenty-five years ago the Clallams of Dungeness had what they called a great battle with the Tsimpsheans [Tsimshians] of British Columbia. September 21, 1867, eighteen of the latter were camped on Dungeness spit, when a Clallam was sent apparently as a friend to visit them. In reality he was a spy. When he returned, he reported their strength. In the night when the Tsimpsheans were asleep, the Clallams went to their camp and massacred all but one of them who escaped, she having been left for dead, but she recovered. This was a great battle. For full account, see Swan's "Pioneer Address" in Washington Pioneer Association, p. 107.

The whole twenty-six were afterwards taken through the help of Hon. J. G. Swan, and carried to the Skokomish reservation, where they were placed in irons and kept at hard labor by Charles King, the Indian Agent. The Tsimpshean woman was kept by the wife of Benjamin Ranie of Dungeness, who was also a Tsimpshean, until she fully recovered, when she was sent to her home with a large number of presents from the United States Government, which satisfied them so that they never retaliated.

Weapons for Striking

War clubs were used for this purpose, especially when the Indians could creep up in some stealthy way, and surprise their enemies. They were of four kinds: copper, stone, bone, and wood. I have one of copper. It was found on the Skokomish reservation, but its owner was afterwards found, who had lost it. It could be traced back to British Columbia. It is 22 inches long, 2 wide at the widest place, and 7/16 of an inch thick at the handle, but much thinner in most places, tapering to a dull edge at the sides. It weighs three pounds and was formerly worth three slaves, as it could not be broken. The copper probably came from British Columbia or Alaska. I have never seen any other like it.

I have a second of stone. It was also found on the Skokomish reservation. When shown to an old Indian, it made his eyes sparkle, and seemed to fill him with new life, as he went through the warlike motions and showed in how still a manner they formerly crept up to kill a sleeping enemy. It is 16 inches long, 2½ wide, and 2 inches thick, tapering to a blunt edge at the sides. It weighs 3½ pounds, is very regularly made, and smooth. An aperture was made to admit a string, which was to assist in holding it. This hole tapers from both sides of the club to the middle of the handle.

I have obtained two fragments of other stone clubs, one from Doswailopsh, polished, and the other from Dungeness, which is rough; both of these were regularly made, but are not quite as thick as the whole one.

I have also the handle of one of a whale rib, which was found near Dungeness. It evidently extended much longer, similar to the last two, and also in the handle, which is a little broken.

The carvings on all of them are intended to represent the head of the Thunderbird, an emblem of power, and was thus carved to inspire the warrior with courage.[2]

....

Battle axes. I have been told that they did use these. They are at least said to have been made of stone, and when hatchets were introduced by the whites, they were used for a similar purpose—not for throwing, but for cutting and striking.

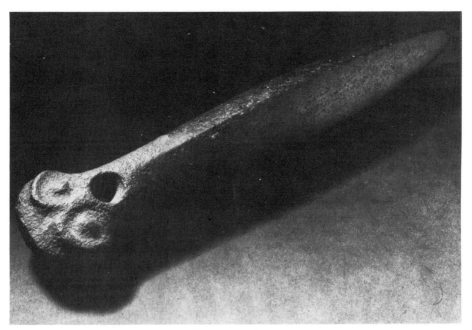

Stone war club

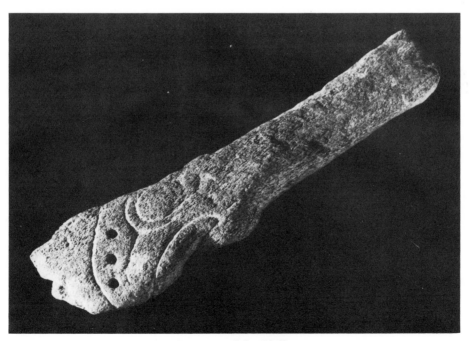

Bone war club, Clallam

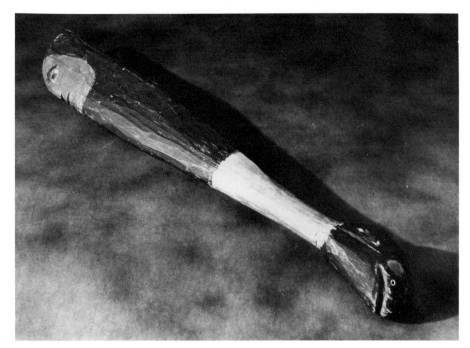

Wooden war club

Weapons for Cutting and Thrusting

Knives. A hunting knife has been described in this chapter. . . .

I lately obtained from a Twana Indian, an English sword bayonet, which originally was held as of great value. I could trace it back to the Chehalis reservation, and I presume it came from the Hudson's Bay Company. It has been excellently kept.

Spears. Two war spears were drawn for me. The head of one is said to have been made of lead, if so it was made since the coming of the whites. The head of the other was of bone. I have also a spear-head or lance-head of stone, which came from the Chehalis. It is very smooth, and is 7½ inches long, 1 inch wide, and ½ inch thick, and weighs 3¼ ounces. A few others like it have been seen in this region.

One of obsidian was found near the head of Hood Canal. This must have been imported, probably from the Umatilla region or southern Oregon, as I know of no obsidian on the Sound. It is very regular and well made, much better than the Sound Indians make. Most of them are very poorly made and of poor stone.

The duck spear. Usually the handle is 15 or 20 feet long, and it has three or four prongs, with notches in them, fastened to the handle at one end. They are notched. They branch so far apart as not to injure the body of the duck, being intended simply to catch in the feathers. Generally the prongs are made of hard wood, but occasionally of

Wooden knife/club, Clallam

Spear head, Chehalis

bone. I obtained one of bone for the Columbian Exposition. One of bone which I have was found near Port Townsend, and one which is owned by J. Y. Collins of Whatcom was found on the Lummi reservation. It is 10½ inches long, and ¾ inch thick. Iron is now often substituted both for bone and wood. However, the use of firearms has so frightened the ducks that they can hardly be caught with these spears and they are seldom seen.

A Twana boy wrote me twelve or fifteen years ago:

> Some people may think that ducks cannot be caught at night with a spear and fire, for they think that if the ducks should see the light they would fly away, but Indians do catch them as follows. When it is a good night then is the time for catching them. Then two men go in a canoe one in front, to use the spear, the other behind to paddle. The fire of pitch wood is also behind. The ducks see the light, but suppose that is afar off. Hence the men come upon them and catch them. Geese are caught in the same way, and fish are also caught at night with a light and fish spears.

Many years ago at times I have seen many lights on the water, of those thus catching ducks and fish when it is very dark, and the scene is quite beautiful. Sometimes, especially in foggy weather, the Indians cover their canoes with green boughs, among which they hide, and then paddle quietly among the ducks, and shoot them. The silly birds imagine that it is a tree which is floating toward them.

Bird Nets

When Vancouver visited the Clallams in 1792, he saw at Port Discovery some very long poles set up in the ground, which he pictured, but the use of which he could not discover. Wilkes saw the same in 1841, and learned that they were for the purpose of suspending nets for taking wild fowl that frequented these shores in great numbers. On these poles the nets were set up at night at which time the geese searched the ground for food. Fires were then built which alarmed the birds and caused them to fly against the nets, by which they were thrown to the ground, where, before they had time to recover themselves, they were caught and killed.

Projective Weapons

Slings. Slings, with stones for shots, are sometimes used by the boys as playthings, and were formerly used occasionally by the young men in killing ducks.

Fire pots. These are said to have been formerly used to set on fire houses into which an enemy had fled. Some vessel, perhaps a basket, was filled with pitch wood. A part of the besieging party would attack one side of the house, in order to draw the attention of the besieged to the opposite side, where the force, which had these fire pots, would approach, set fire to them, and throw them on the roof; and as the besieged attempted to escape, they were killed with clubs, spears, bows, and arrows.

Bows and arrows. These were very common, though they have now gone out of use, except as playthings for children. Yew wood was preferred in their manufacture. These are not wound or bound with anything.

Hon. J. Wickersham obtained nearly a hundred arrows from a Nisqually Indian, which were made for the purpose of killing white persons in the war of 1855–56. These were pointed with iron, but the heads were fastened firmly in the shaft. The shaft was of cedar wood, except about [?] inches at the lower end, which was of bone in order to make that end heavier and so more sure of hitting the mark. The iron arrow point or head was fastened to this piece of bone.

He also has a bow, obtained at the same place and made for the same war, the back of which is covered with sinew cemented on, which renders it very strong and elastic.

Vancouver, in 1792, says that on the back of the bows at Port Discovery, among the Clallams, were strips of hide or serpent skin, exactly the shape and length of the bow, fastened by a cement so adhesive that no change of weather would separate them. I have never seen any such.

The shaft of the common arrow was either of cedar or ironwood. The head was of ironwood or bone, and often 6 or 7 inches long. Lately they have made them of wire, about $\frac{3}{16}$ of an inch in diameter, and 5 or 6 inches long. Sometimes those with a single head had a serrated edge to catch in the feathers of a bird. Others were made for birds,

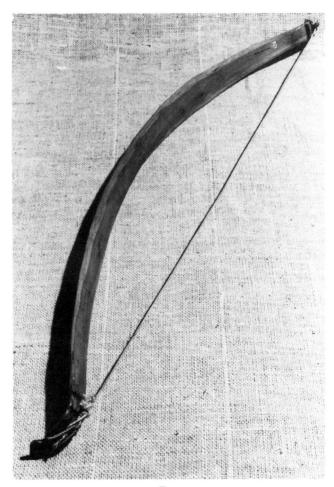

Bows. Left: Quinaielt; center and right:
no tribal identification

Bow

with double or forked-heads, some of whose edges were serrated and some of which were not. One style they used at their shooting games when the contest was to see who could shoot the farthest.

Another style had quite blunt heads, which were made of elder wood and which were used mainly by the boys as playthings, but sometimes to knock over a squirrel.

Another arrow was made of bone (now of iron), and was preferred in war. The head was fastened in so loosely that it would come out of the shaft after it had been shot into a person, remaining in the wound.

Stone arrow-heads are very scarce. This seems very strange, as south of the Columbia river and east of the Cascade mountains they were very abundant. Dr. D. Raffety of East Portland, had a few years ago a hundred and fifty. H. C. Stevens of Oregon City has hundreds, most of which he has found at that place, where there was a manufactory of them. Mr. J. H. Kunzie of Seattle has about four thousand, most of which he collected about the mouth of the Umatilla river. J. J. Durant and D. W. Owen of Pasco have many which they have found near that place. Mrs. Charles Pond of Ellensburg has about five thousand, which she found farther up the Columbia, near White Bluffs or Priests Rapids. Many in all these collections are very delicate and regular and it seems as if they could not be excelled in any possible manner.

But while the region bounding Puget Sound was so rich in stone arrow-heads, the Sound was very poor. Vancouver, in 1792, says of the Clallams of Port Discovery that their spears, arrows, and fish gigs were pointed with flint, agate, and bone, and yet that more of them were pointed with iron and they preferred to exchange those pointed with iron rather than any of the others. This is singular in two respects in regard to the iron and stone points. It would not have been strange, that in advance of the coming of the whites, they should have obtained a few of iron of other Indians. The only way I can account for it is that they must have used all the iron they obtained from the one or two vessels which visited Port Discovery during the three or four years previous to 1792, in making arrow-heads. If stone points were then common, the query arises where they have gone. I have six rough large ones, but they are so large, uneven, and rough that I do not believe they could have been used for arrows, but rather for spears. Otherwise I have obtained only three in twenty years. The first is of agate, and was found near the Chehalis river. It weighs a quarter of an ounce. The two others were found in the Twana land, one of jasper and a good one, the other of chalcedony.

The Twana Indians have a tradition that these of stone were made by the wolf or panther, while those beasts were men before they were metamorphosed by the Great Changer, Dokibatl. They also say that when broken into small pieces and shot into animals, they are sure to cause death. For this reason one old Indian was anxious to give me a high price for one, so that he might break it in pieces, shoot it from his gun, firmly believing the above superstition.

This tradition, in connection with those about Dokibatl, has sometimes raised the query in my mind, whether perhaps a former race of Indians did not live here, who were driven away by the later one, who did make these points. These Indians say they did not make them, plainly they were not made by the wolf, they must have been made by some one, either the ancestors of these Indians, another previous race, or have been imported.[3]

It seems also strange that when they were so abundant to the east and south, that more of them were not imported, and also that some of these Indians did not learn the art of making them.

Dr. J. G. Hoffman, in the *American Anthropologist* for January 1891, says that "the Clallams made arrow points from native copper, or from fragments of this metal, obtained from the sheathing of vessels, which were afterward dipped in sea water, and permitted to corrode" so as to render them poisonous. "The Old chief, the Duke of York, stated, however, that these arrows were never used against human beings. Such a statement may be taken for what it is worth, as I have yet to find an Indian, who will admit the use of alleged poisoned arrows in warfare against man."[4]

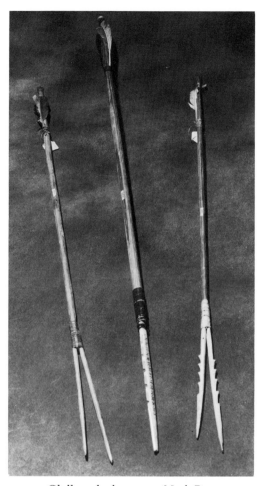

Clallam duck arrows, Neah Bay

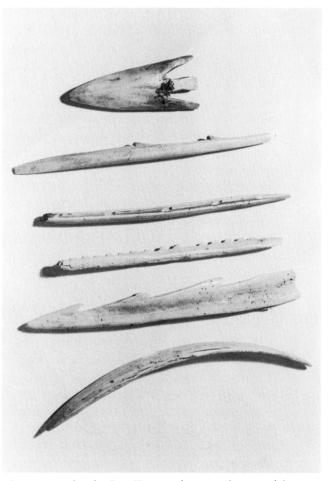

Bone arrow heads, Port Townsend, except for second from bottom, which is identified as a Clallam duck spear

Cases for Projectiles

Arrow quivers. These were made of bear and wolf skins. They are now very scarce. The only one I have seen was among the Clallams, of bear skin, 8 inches wide by 34 long.

Shot pouches. One kind was made of the skin of the hair seal. I obtained one from a Clallam. I have another similar in shape, which came from a Chehalis Indian, but it is of buckskin, fringed. Commonly, however, they are made of strong, plain cloth, without ornaments.

Defensive Weapons

The only armor of this kind of which I have learned was a shirt of dried skin covering the whole body. Ross Cop mentions the same, which he says was remarkably thick, doubled, and thrown over the shoulders, with holes for the arms. It descended to the ankles and from its thickness was arrow-proof. He adds that the head was covered with a species of helmet, made of cedar bark, bear grass, and leather, which was also impenetrable by arrows. The neck, therefore, was the only vital part of the body exposed to arrows. He says that they also had another kind of armor—a kind of corset, formed of thin slips of hard wood, ingeniously laced together by bear grass, and much lighter and more pliable than the former, but not covering as much of the body. * I presume, however, that they depended much more on trees, rocks, and similar natural objects, coupled with a good share of prudence, than upon manufactured articles.

Forts

Wilkes, in 1841, says that the Skagit tribe "are obliged to provide for their defence against the more northern tribes, by whom they are frequently attacked for the purpose of carrying them off as slaves. For protection against these attacks they have large enclosures, 400 feet long and capable of containing many families, which are constructed of pickets, made of thick planks, about 30 feet high. The pickets are firmly fixed into the ground, the spaces between them being only sufficient to point a musket through. The appearance of one of these enclosures is formidable, and they may be termed impregnable to any Indian force: for in the opinion of the officers, it would have required artillery to make a breach in them. The interior of the enclosure is divided into lodges, and has all the aspects of a fortress."†

Gibbs (1856) says that the "Sound Indians, more particularly those on the Straits of De Fuca sometimes fortify their dwellings by stockades, made of heavy puncheons twelve or fifteen feet high, set in the ground and strengthened by large posts, and cross pieces. They were loop holed, and calculated very well to serve even against muskets."**

During the past twenty years I have neither seen nor heard of such forts, but this is not strange as their wars ceased long ago, and the forts consequently have disappeared.

*Contributions to North American Ethnology by G. Gibbs, vol. 1, p. 192.
†Wilkes, U.S. Exploring Expedition, condensed, p. 286.
**Contributions to North American Ethnology, vol. 1, p. 192.

IMPLEMENTS FOR SPECIAL USE

Tools for Working Stone

The number of stone axes, hammers, and the like, which still exist, show that some such tools were used; but the art has been so long buried in the past, that I have seen no such tools, nor have I heard of any, except that the Indians say that one stone was used to break, grind, or polish another. This was undoubtedly true.

Implements for Making Fire

Formerly, a fire was made with two sticks, holding one perpendicular to the other, letting one end of it press on the side of the other, and rubbing it briskly between the hands. Fire was then very valuable, and was often carried very carefully long distances from one camp to another by enclosing it closely between two sticks, so that very little air should strike it. This process was used forty or forty-five years ago. Afterward, when they obtained flint-lock muskets, they struck fire with them. Of late years, they use matches almost entirely. Fir pitch-wood is also very common in helping to start the fire, and also for a light out-doors, especially when fishing in the night. They frequently bring small bundles of it to the whites for sale.

Bow and Arrow Making

Their wedges must have been used in splitting out their arrows, and their bone and stone knives for finishing them. There was but little need of implements for straightening them, as both cedar and arrow wood are so straight that hardly anything was needed for this purpose, except the hands. For fastening the arrows to the shaft, a string of some thin bark as the hazel or cherry was used; and in securing the heads, in addition to these strings, a cement of the pitch of the red fir was used.

The ends of the bows were bent, by being wrapped in seaweed or moss, and buried in the warm ground near the fire, thus steaming them. After which they were easily bent. Strings made of the fiber of the nettle, the entrails of the deer, and the like were used for bow-strings.

Fishing Implements

Spears and hooks. Living as these Indians do on the shores of Puget Sound, a large portion of their food has always been obtained from its waters. The Clallams practice most of the methods used by the Indians who live farther up the Sound, and also have some different devices, as there are some animals, such as the fur seal, halibut, and whale, which live in or near the Straits of Fuca, but which generally do not go much farther up. They have adopted most of the methods used by the whites, as the hook and line and seine, which they purchase and also make from material they buy. In addition, they practice the following native methods.

A very common fish spear is made with a long straight handle, 15 or 20 feet long, and not far from an inch in diameter. It has two or three prongs, which are about 2 feet long. The handle is of fir on account of its strength, as well as being straight, and the prongs are of some hard wood, as maple or ironwood, sometimes hardened in the fire, and lately of iron. They are used in spearing skates, crabs, flounders, salmon, and the like, and for bringing up cod fish eggs, when they are in water that is not too deep. When thus fishing, one person, sitting in the stern of the canoe, will quietly paddle, while another, sitting or kneeling in the bow, uses the spear. Because of long practice they will see a fish partly buried in the mud, where an unpracticed eye will fail to discern it, and having seen it will rarely fail to secure it.

A hook is made of iron, which is fastened into wood by means of bark strings. This has a hole which fits on to the end of a handle, 15 or 20 feet long, similar to the one just described. It is also fastened to the pole by two thongs. The hook is moved around in the water by the pole, and when the fish is caught, the hook slips off of the pole and is held by the thongs. Thus breakage is prevented.

Another form of native spear-head or hook is used in somewhat the same way as the last. The point is of iron. This point is fastened to two side pieces of bone or wood by strings covered with pitch. This, like the last, is fastened to a pole with thongs, the lower end of the pole also fitting into the heads or hooks. This pole is forked at the lower end so as to receive the two hooks. Another part is made of cedar, as it is light, with two wings of white wood, as dogwood. This, like the last, is attached to a pole by thongs, the lower end of the pole also fitting into it. This is first thrust down into the water with the pole, which is then drawn out, leaving it to rise gradually. The shape is such that when rising it whirls around, and the white wood, shining in the water, attracts the fish, on the same principle as the spoon hook of the whites. When the fish comes within reach the Indian spears it with the hook first described.

A spear for taking herring and smelt is made somewhat like a rake, only the teeth are fastened into the lower part of the handle, usually on one edge, but sometimes on both. The handle is made of fir wood, 15 or 20 feet long, flattened about 2½ inches wide. Nails, or strong wire, 1½ or 2 inches long, sharpened, are fastened into the edge at the lower end, for about 3 feet. When fishing, usually two persons go in a canoe to a place where these fish are abundant. One sits in the stern and manages the canoe. The other sits near the bow, takes the rake, and strikes it down among the fish, brings it up behind, and with a peculiar twitch, throws whatever fish he may get on the sharpened points into the hind part of the canoe; it may be one, and it may be a half dozen, or none. Sometimes one person will manage the whole affair alone paddling with the rake.

The following fishing implements are used by the Clallams mainly, but not much by

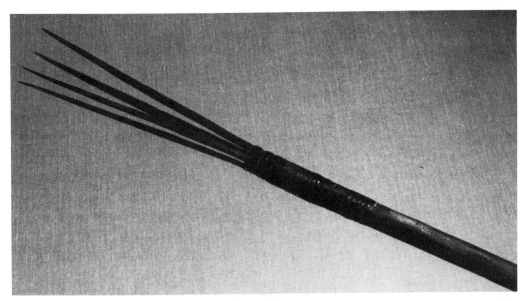

Pronged spear

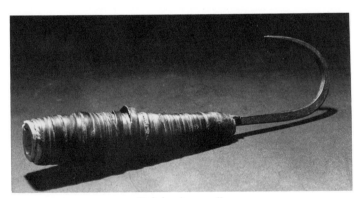

Fish hook or gaff

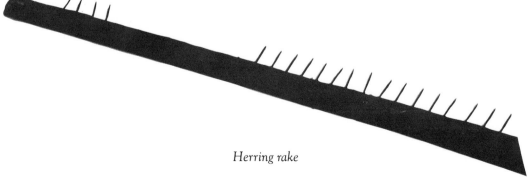

Herring rake

the Indians farther up the Sound, as the whale, halibut, and fur seal are not found much, if any, in those waters.

The halibut hook is made for taking halibut. It is of hemlock roots steamed and bent into the required shape, much like the letter "u". At one end, a piece of bone about 3 inches long is fastened by means of bark, so as to make a hook. Hard wood is also occasionally used. Two of these are then attached, one at each end to a small piece of wood, about 5 feet long, by a string fastened to the side of the "u" opposite the hook. The bait of meat is tied on the hooks, and they are hung horizontally in the water by a line fastened in the middle of the stick, as the halibut will not take a hook when hung perpendicularly. The other end of the "u" prevents the fish from getting away.

The codfish hook is made of a piece of bone 4 or 5 inches long fastened with a string of bark to a piece of whalebone about 2 feet long. The bait, often a small fish, is slipped on the other end, hence the necessity of the loop at that end so that it can easily be fastened to or unfastened from the line.

Sealing spears are made of long wooden handles, similar to those described as belonging to fishing spears, and a head of iron, formerly of bone. I have never seen the process of catching these fur seals, as among the tribes here described it is known only to the lower Clallams, and they go to the ocean off the Makah coast to do so. Generally in this work, they are employed by white men, who own schooners on which they take the Indians, with their canoes, to the seal fields in the ocean. A few Indians of late years have also obtained such schooners, at least among the Makahs.

The Indians with canoes are generally paid a certain share of the skins they catch. Two Indian men go in each canoe, and eight or ten canoes go with each schooner. Other Indians are also taken in the schooners to take care of the pelts. With these schooners they go far out into the ocean, much farther than they did before schooners were used. Generally they live on board the schooners except when at work. On a fine day, when they see the seals, they go to work. One Indian acts as a steersman, and the other as spearsman in each canoe. The heads fit over the ends of the spear handles as with the fish spears, and are also fastened with thongs and lines so that after the head is in the animal, the handle comes out, but the seal is held by a line attached to the head and held by the person. I have seen two iron heads as just finished at a blacksmith shop. The Indian told me that usually he threw two of these spears, one just after the other, but why he did so and why the heads were of a different shape, I could not learn. This business of sealing is generally very profitable. Forty or fifty years ago, the Indians did almost the whole of it without schooners, not going a great distance from land. Then came the schooners, with Indian employees. But of late white people are doing a large share of the work in all departments.

Whaling spears. These are quite similar to the last, but the handles are much larger, being about 2 inches in diameter. The point is of bone. As the handle is so large, it requires great strength to throw it. A buoy is attached to them, made of the skins of fawns or hair seals turned wrong side out and filled with air. With fifteen or twenty of these buoys attached to a whale, he cannot go down and stay very long. Very little, however, is done in this business, as it is too dangerous and whales are too scarce. I have

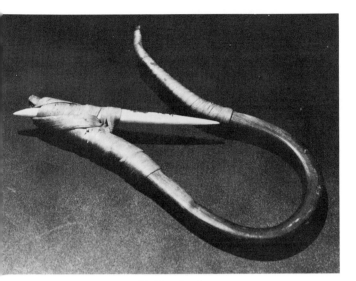

Halibut hook

Fish hook, indicated only as "Alaska"

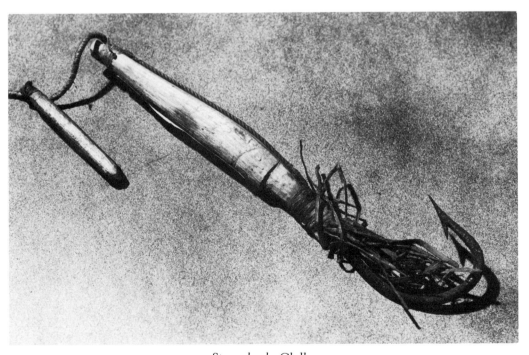

Spoon hook, Clallam

157

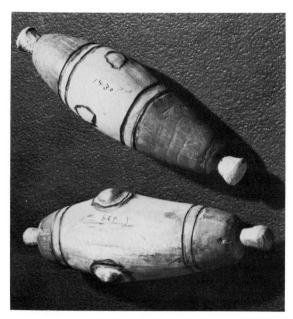

Model of sealskin whaling buoy, Clallam

never seen any of these spears except at Clallam Bay, the settlement of the Clallams farthest west.

Traps and nets. One way of taking salmon in rivers is to build a trap across the stream. I include a drawing of one halfway across the Skokomish river; the other half being similar. A great number of small sticks ¾ inch in diameter and 6½ feet long are fastened together 1 or 2 inches apart as to form a weir. Long sticks are placed across the stream and secured by braces. The small sticks or weir are placed so as to lean against these larger ones, the upper end slanting down-stream and tied to the poles; while for additional security the gravel of the bed of the river is shoveled on around the bottom of them. The weir prevents the fish from ascending the stream.

Nets are then provided, about 6 feet broad and 2 feet deep, made of strings and secured to a rim of wood. Native strings of this sort are made of nettle or alder bark twisted, but American twine is now often used. During the day-time these nets are pulled up, but let down at night when the fish are running, one man watching each net. The fish striving to ascend get into these nets, and their presence is immediately known by the moving of the string. The net is then pulled up, the fish killed with a club and laid on a platform. These clubs are often common sticks, but are sometimes fancifully carved. There are usually four nets let down at once to form the trap.

Another trap is made in a similar way as regards the weir, but otherwise differing across the stream. Up-stream from the weir several pens are built, in which doors are made V-

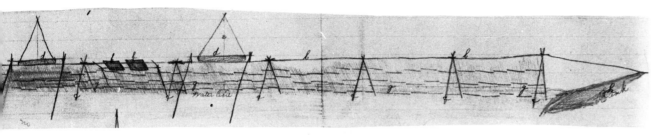

Drawing of fish trap

shaped, opening from below. The fish easily enter this, but, unable to find the way out, are speared. A shovel is used in shoveling the gravel onto the bottom of the trap.

Another style of net is made of twine. It is about a foot broad, 16 inches deep, tapering to a point, fastened at the upper edge to a rim of wood or hoop of iron. It is attached to a handle about 10 feet long, and is used in gathering sea eggs and small fish. I have seen it in use more among the Clallams than the other tribes.

Common large American seines are now commonly used in taking fish in the salt water and in the larger streams.

In making large seines of twine like those used by the Americans, they first wind the twine on a bobbin shaped something like the figure eight, but open at both ends so as to receive the twine, yet almost closed so as to easily run through the loops when tying the knots. These knots are tied over a rectangular block, so as to secure a uniform size of the loop. These blocks may be 3 by 4 inches, or less, according to the size of loop required. I have seen some hardly an inch wide.

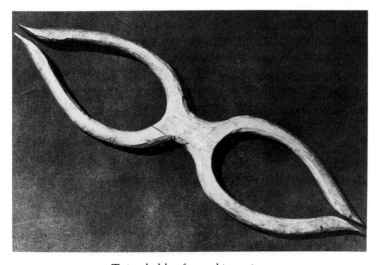

Twine holder for making seines

Line reel

Buoys. These are usually made of cedar, as it is very light. Sometimes a large number of sticks, 10 or 12 inches long, are tied together, so as to make a bundle about 4 inches in diameter.

Another kind is made of a single block 5 inches long and 3 inches in diameter more or less with a hole through it, lengthwise, by means of which it is attached to the seine.

Another style is made of a single cedar block not far from the size of the last, but with a kind of handle at the upper end, through which is a hole across the wood. By means of this the buoy is fastened to the seine.

A fourth kind is made in the shape of a duck. It is used especially as a decoy for porpoises. It is held by a string and floated far behind the canoe. The porpoise seeing it, thinks it may be a duck and comes to the surface in order to be sure, when it is shot. It

Porpoise buoy, Twana

160

Buoy (seine), Twana

may be about 10 inches long, 5½ wide, with a body 1½ inches thick. They are also made much larger than the one described, as I have seen one about 2 feet long or more and correspondingly large other ways. I have two: one a double-headed one with an animal on its back like a bear or coon, 15 inches long, 7 wide, one head 6 and the other 4 inches high, the bear or coon being 3½ inches long, 1½ high, and 1⅛ thick; the other being three-headed, 13½ long, 5 wide, with the heads 2½ and 3 inches high, and the body 2 inches high on each side, but hollow like a bowl between the sides.

A fifth kind, used in catching seals and whales, made of the skins of the hair seal or fawns, has just been referred to while describing the whaling spears. These skins are taken off whole, turned wrong side out, every hole is tied up, except in one or two places into which the air is blown, when air-tight stopples are put in. The one I have of seal skin is 27 inches long and 9 in diameter.

Sinkers. These were of stone, oval, and usually 3 or 3½ inches long by about 2 in diameter. Strings of bark are fastened around this stone both lengthwise and crosswise, to which the line is affixed. These stones are not manufactured for the purpose, but those of about the right size are selected from beach stones.

Another kind, much larger, is used for a sinker to a seine. Like the last it is a natural beach stone, though very regular but the groove around the middle is artificial. It is 9¼ inches long, 6½ wide, 4 thick.

These sinkers are very different from those of the surrounding tribes. I have one from the mouth of the Umatilla river southeast. It is 3½ inches long, 2½ wide, ¾ thick and weighs 7 ounces. It is a natural stone except that it is notched at each end, so that it can be fastened to the line.

Fish clubs. Generally any common stick, 2 or 3 feet long is used for killing salmon, but sometimes they are carved somewhat fancifully.

Porpoise decoy buoys

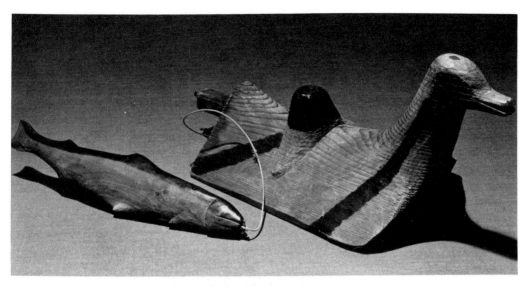

Wooden duck and fish (porpoise buoy?)

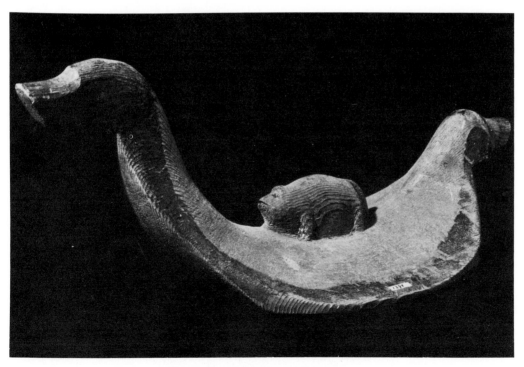

Decoy float for salmon and porpoise

Stone sinker, Twana

Fish club from Skokomish, Twana

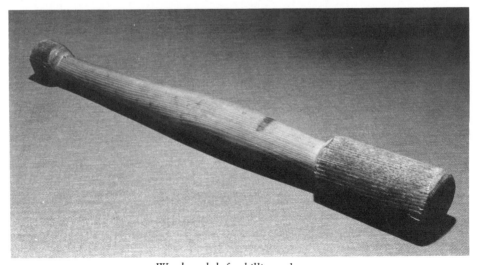

Wooden club for killing salmon

Hunting Implements Other Than Weapons

American steel traps are used in catching mink, beaver, and similar animals. A special bait is sometimes made by cutting off the base of the horn of an ox, filling it with beaver grease, and putting in a stopple of wood. When used, the stopple is taken out, some of the grease is rubbed on the trap, and the bait is hung over it. The scent of the bait attracts the beaver, and in trying to get it, he accidentally puts his foot in the trap. This bait will hold its scent a long time—a year or two.

Leather Working and Tools

Besides the knives already described in this chapter, a stone, sometimes fastened to a handle and sometimes not, and a stick, one end of which is fastened in the ground, are all the tools of which I know. This stone is not made for the purpose, but picked up, and of various shapes—rough, angular, broken, or worn smooth by the water. If there is a handle to it, it is about 3½ feet long and rather rough. It is split at the end, and the stone is fastened to it in an irregular way with thongs. The stick on which the skin is placed so as to remove the hair is about 4 inches in diameter, with about an inch taken off on the under side. It is curved and is 4 or 5 feet long. It is placed in the ground so as to stand in a slanting direction.

Beaver bait, Twana

In tanning it, the deer or elk hide is soaked for two days and the hair removed by scraping it with a rough iron. It is then soaked a half day with the deer brains in hot water over the fire, the brains being rubbed over something like soap. It is then stretched and rubbed with rocks until it becomes soft and pliable, when they dig a hole in the ground, build a fire of rotten wood or cedar bark, stretch the skin over it, and over it with blankets, thus smoking it, after which it is fit for use.

Procuring and Manufacturing Food

Sticks of various kinds of hard wood, about 2 feet long, and a little curved, are used for digging roots, clams, and the like.

An implement for digging kamass was made of a stick about 2½ feet long, an inch or a little more in diameter, a little curved. It was sharpened at one end and at the other a handle of deer horn was fastened at right angles. This handle was about 10 inches long, with a hole in it, which fitted onto the end of the wood. These have entirely gone out of use on the Sound. In fact, I lived here eighteen years before I saw one or even learned of their existence. An old handle was found then and I was told of its use and the stick was fitted to it for me. This stick is of the hardest wood, iron wood, and then hardened in the fire. They are still used on the Yakima reservation, but are made largely of iron. Singularly enough, while the handle is of iron they have it still made in the same shape of the ancient deer horn.

A bone implement, 12 for 14 inches long, the handle of which was from 1 to 1¼ inches wide and ½ to ¾ of an inch thick, the rest probably having been wider and

Clam digger

166

thicker, was used for beating fern roots. I have never seen any such implements, but have the handles of two of them, which were found at Port Wilson, near Port Townsend. Probably such were also made of wood.

The roots, after having been beaten, were made into a kind of meal, and then into a sort of cake.

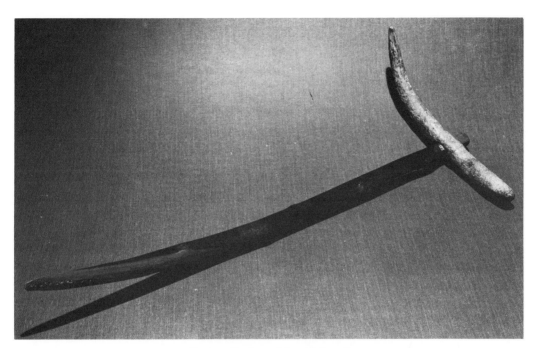

Camas digging stick with handle

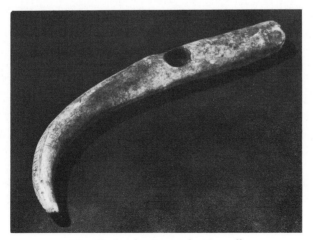

Handle for digging stick, Umatilla

167

Tools for Working Wood

The knives, axes, celts, and the like, already described were used for this purpose.

An article for smoothing wood, after the use of sandpaper, was the skin of the under side of the dogfish. It is quite rough, and answers the purpose well.

Agricultural Implements

The only native farming implement I have ever seen is a hoe, made for me of crabapple wood, by a Clallam. The handle is about 4½ feet long, and not far from 2 inches in diameter with the blade, which is a large limb, at an acute angle, and hardened by fire. It is about 2½ inches wide. Middle-aged Indians say it was used long ago, before the whites came, for cultivating potatoes; but I cannot learn that they ever had potatoes before the advent of Europeans. I think it probable that they had potatoes long before

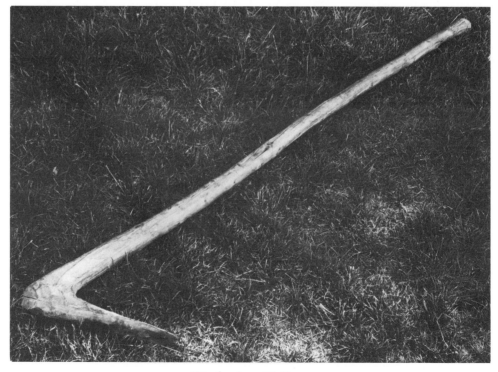

Wooden hoe, Clallam

they had civilized hoes with which to cultivate them. Probably before these Indians can remember such hoes were made to help in the work. It is possible that they had somewhat similar articles in connection with their Indian potato or wapato or onion, and adopted it to American agriculture when the potato was introduced.

Mr. Tudor, formerly engineer of the steamer *Favorite*, once told me that on the Sky-komish river, on the eastern side of the Sound, there are three small prairies of a half an acre or an acre each, which the Indians say they cleared before the whites came, so as to plant potatoes. This is all the evidence I have that agriculture was carried on by these Indians previous to the coming of the whites, and I consider it very slight. A little agriculture may have been carried on after the first advent of whites—the discoverers—who only visited the Sound for a short time, and before the region was settled by the Hudson's Bay Company. There was really not much need of it, as the soil naturally produced so many berries and roots, and the waters abounded in so many fish, that the Indians could easily be supported without the labor of tilling the soil.[5]

Basket Working

The only tools which I have seen in use are the knives for preparing the material, awls for sewing the water-tight baskets, and a bone implement for presssing the woven parts very firmly and closely together. Such were about 6 inches long, about an inch wide at the handle, tapering to a width of about a quarter of an inch at the other end. It was not thick, and the edges were dull. A cloth was wound around the handle to prevent it hurting the hand. Such tools were also made of hard wood.

Making Rugs

The only implement I have seen besides the loom is a sort of rough crochet hook, iron, with a handle of wood, with which to draw the strips of cloth through the burlap in making the fancy rugs.

Crochet hook

Implements for Working Fiber

Hacklers. These were usually made of hard wood, and were about a foot long by 6 inches wide. Some had a single handle, some two handles. They were especially used for beating cedar bark fine, which to them was a very useful article. I have seen one among the Clallams, which was made of the bone of a whale.

Spinning wheels. A small one, at present used for spinning yarn but formerly used for spinning the material which was used in making blankets and woolen clothes, consists of a circular board or whorl, 6 or 7 inches in diameter, through the center of which is a stick about 2 feet long and ½ inch in diameter tapering toward each end. The material to be spun is fastened to one end of the stick, the other end is taken in one hand; the wool, which has first been twisted a little by hand, is taken in the other hand, and the wheel is rolled over and over quite rapidly on the thigh, with the hand which holds it. The yarn is not as even as that spun by machinery or even by American spinning wheels, and yet it is so good that hundreds of pairs of socks made from it are sold to the whites every year from the Skokomish reservation alone.

Occasionally of late tin whorls have been used, made from the covers of tin lard pails. On the Yakima reservation they are sometimes made of leather, but I have never seen any such on the Sound. These have held their own with the women against the inven-tions of the whites as well as most implements. Twenty years ago, the Indian Agent introduced some American spinning wheels among the annuity goods on the Skokomish reservation. But while a few learned to use them to some extent, they did not seem to care much for them, and they have been broken, until hardly one remains; and those who used them have very generally returned to the use of their native ones. Within a few months, an Indian from the Snohomish reservation introduced a new kind, which he saw there and which the Indians can make. It is run with the foot, and seems to be gaining favor.

Wooden hackler for cedar bark, Twana

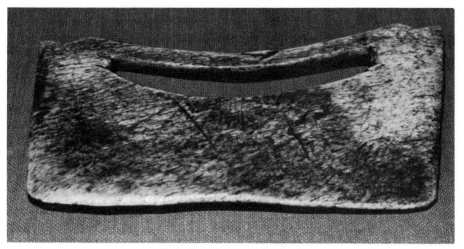

Bone hackler for cedar bark

Hand spinning wheel

American cards are universally used in carding the wool.

Looms. One was formerly made, which was used in the manufacture of their blankets. I have seen one of them in use by a Clallam woman in making a rug. Two posts about 4 feet long, 6 inches wide and half as thick, were sharpened at one end and driven into the ground, as far apart as the length of the article to be woven. Two holes were made in each of these, one towards the upper end and the other towards the lower, in which two bars were inserted, thus joining the posts together. The article to be made was fastened to these bars.

Needles and mat blocks. Wooden ones are used in making blocks. The needles are usually made of iron wood, about 3 feet long, ½ inch through, three-cornered, and considerably curved. They have an eye in one end.

The blocks are of wood, alder or maple being preferred, 5 to 7 inches long, about 3 the other way in the middle, and about ½ inch thick. There is a handle on the upper side. They are curved on the under side so that often they are not more than half an inch wide at the ends, which are sometimes made to resemble a bird's head slightly. Sometimes they are of different shape, with a double handle and painted red. One I obtained on the Skokomish reservation but it came from British Columbia. Judge Wickersham of Tacoma has one similar of stone which he obtained of a Puyallup Indian. It is 2⅛ by 4¼ inches. The use of these articles has been described in Chapter VII in the article on mats. The crease is on the under side.

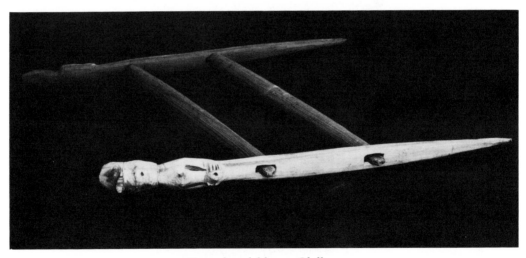

Carved model loom, Clallam

Bone awl or needle

Net needle

"Mat block" (mat creaser) used in dressing rushes

Mat creaser, Twana

Mat creaser, Twana

Twana mat creaser imported from Victoria, B.C.

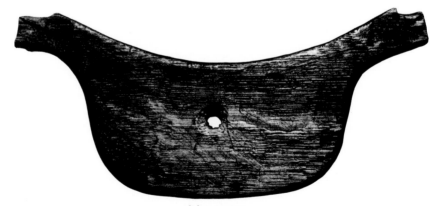

Mat creaser

Mat creaser

Mat creaser

Paints and Dyes

The paints used have been described in Chapter IX. Cedar bark and grass are dyed black for ornamenting baskets by being buried in the black mud of the salt marsh for two or three days. To color the same yellow, they are boiled with the bark of the Oregon grape root. To color them dark red, they are soaked with alder bark. To color them brown, another bark is used, but my informant could not tell me what kind without showing me, and she said it was some distance away.

Baskets are imported from the Makahs and Quinaielts in which the grass is dyed purple, orange, crimson, and different shades of blue, but American dyes are used for these colors. American dyes and paints are often used by the Sound Indians.

Grass trimming tools used for basket making, Clallam

Ropes and Strings and Fishing Lines

Of vegetable material. The largest ropes I have seen made by these Indians are of cedar twigs twisted in much the same style as our own hemp ropes, but they look coarser. These are very strong and lasting. The largest are made on the buoys employed in catching seal, and are ¾ inch in diameter. Some ½ inch in diameter are used for fastening canoes, and those ³⁄₁₆ of an inch are utilized in fastening cross-pieces to canoes.

Of braided cat-tail, they make a flat rope, not very durable, about ⅜ of an inch thick by ¾ of an inch broad, which is used for tying paddles into bundles. The only ones I ever saw used were at a potlatch for this purpose. And of the beaten fiber of the same material twisted, they make strings from ⅛ to ³⁄₁₆ of an inch thick, which are used in sewing mats together. They are not very strong, but for this purpose are good enough.

The ropes at the ends of the head-bands used in carrying baskets are made of tough bark braided. They are about ⅜ of an inch thick and ⅝ broad. Of the inner bark of the alder, split and twisted, a kind of string is made which is manufactured into fishing nets. Another string ¹⁄₁₆ to ⅛ inch in diameter, also used in making nets, is made by hackling and twisting the outer fiber of the nettle. This is strong and looks much like linen twine. The Clallams make, without special preparation, lines out of the smaller part of the kelp root of about ⅛ inch diameter. When dry it is brittle, but when soaked a short time in water it becomes quite tough. It is used for a fishing line.

Cherry, willow, and hazel bark, the inner bark of the cedar, and some kinds of grass are used without preparation as a thin flat strap to wrap around various articles as fastening heads on to arrows, spears, fish hooks, and the like.

Of animal material. Ropes used as hitching ropes, bridles for horses, and the like, are made by braiding the long hair of the manes and tails of horses. They are usually about ½ inch in diameter, and are strong and serviceable.

Elk, deer, and other skins, both tanned and raw, were cut into thongs which were used for various purposes. Sinew from the deer, elk, and whale was used for sewing and bow lines.

Nearly every kind of tool, paint, and rope and string now in use by their white neighbors are also used by the Indians. A large share of their native ones have already gone out of use, and most of the rest will soon belong to the past.

Cord made of cedar bark

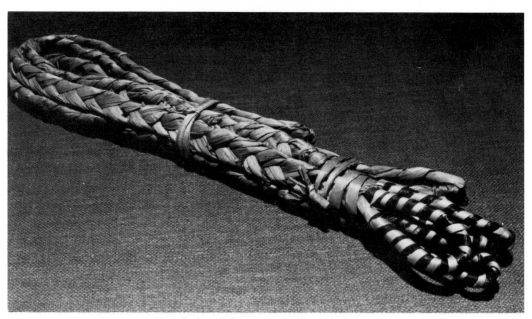

Cord of cattail rush used in mat making

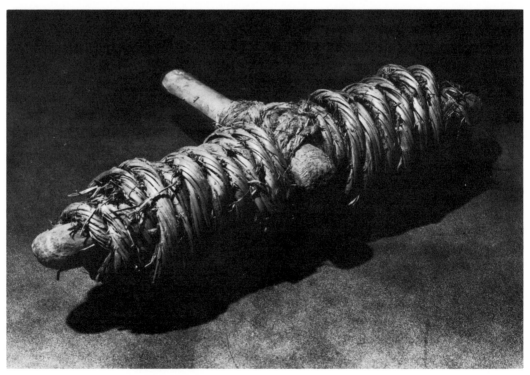

Cedar limb rope binding head of implement used to clean debris from fish weirs

VOL. 3

XI

LOCOMOTION AND TRANSPORTATION

TRAVELLING BY WATER

This is the chief mode of travel, as, with the exception of the Chehalis tribe, their land is all situated on the shores or tributaries of Puget Sound. The Clallams own larger canoes and are better navigators than the Indians farther up the Sound, as they live on the Straits of Fuca, where there is less protection from the ocean winds than in the upper Sound.[1]

Canoes[2]

For this purpose, the canoes are the friends of these Indians as much as the horse is of the Indian of the prairie, or of the Arabian, or the sledge is of the Eskimo. These are dug-outs made from cedar trees. In making them, they formerly burnt them out and finished them with the hand-adzes of stone, but now they universally use American axes and adzes for the first part of the work and the hand-adzes or rasp for the second part, although the finishing touch is put on sometimes with the curved knife. After this they are steamed by filling them with hot water and throwing in heated stones to keep it hot so that they can spread the sides farther apart. They are fastened thus with cross-pieces or thwarts, which are round or flattened, and 1¼–2 inches in diameter, the size varying with the size of the canoe.

Holes bored through the ends of the cross-pieces and the sides of the canoe admit ropes of cedar which keep the cross-pieces in position. A rim or gunwale is often made for the upper edge of the canoe, about an inch in diameter, which can be replaced when worn out. This is of fir, a harder wood than the cedar of the canoe, as the wear on the rim while paddling is considerable.

The canoes in common use are of three kinds. Only once have I seen a fourth kind.

The large or Chinook canoe. These are made chiefly by the Indians of British Columbia and imported; they are used very extensively by all the Indians on Puget Sound for carrying large loads and for dangerous travelling, the square stern being said to be a means of safety in rough seas. One of good size costs one hundred dollars when new. It was 35 feet long, 5 feet wide at the center, with a perpendicular height from the ground of 3 feet at the stern, 22½ inches a quarter of the way from the stern to the bow and also in the middle, 2 feet at a place 6 feet from the bow, 4 feet 6 inches at the top of the head, a foot from the end, and 4 feet 1 inch at the extreme end of the nose. There are two places for masts: near the middle, and near the bow. Near the stern is a seat for the steersman.

The head of this kind of canoe is a separate piece of wood. Such vessels are made both larger and smaller than this one; the largest I have known is the one exhibited at the Centennial Exhibition at Philadelphia in 1876, which is 60 feet long and 8 feet wide. None as large as these, however, is owned by these Indians, but a few of the Clallams have some very large ones for whaling. None as large as this, however, is used on the Sound, the largest I have seen among them being 36 feet long, 6 feet wide, and 3 feet deep. When travelling with it, it was not hauled up on land, when camping, but anchored as a sloop. The smallest I have seen was 8 feet long, but such small ones are not common.

In travelling in these, I have never learned that there was any special place for any person, except in regard to the steersman. Formerly he was a slave. When time with them was worth very little, they preferred to wait for favorable winds. They put a slave to steer, as wind or no wind, he must be at his post.

The shovel canoe, sometimes called the river canoe. These are scarce. They are made in much the same manner and of about the same size as the next kind, and differ from them mainly in that the ends are from a foot to a foot and a half wide, instead of tapering to a point. They are considered safer in swift rivers.

The fishing or small canoe. These are very common and are made all over the Sound. They are entirely of one piece of wood, except that some have the fir rim, mentioned as

Canoe model

being on the Chinook canoes. They are used for fishing, hunting ducks, travelling on rivers, and even on the Sound when it is calm and they wish to take only a small load. I have travelled thirty miles in this kind on Hood Canal, though we preferred to keep near shore if possible. Still I have crossed the Canal in one, when it was quite rough and we were in the trough of the sea, for the larger ones will stand considerable waves. In rough water, however, the Indians are very careful in them.

[A fourth kind] varies in length. It is known that no Puget Sound Indians are in it. Even the Makah and Quinaielt Indians on the ocean shores do not use them, and I do not know that any tribes of the Salish family do.

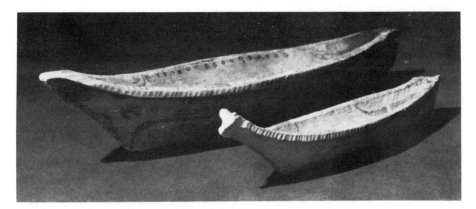

Canoe models; bottom is identified as Chinook

Canoe model

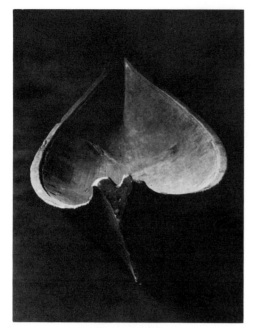

Canoe model

Canoe model

Boat model

Boats

A good many Indians own boats of American make, though boats have not taken the place of canoes as much as most other articles of civilized manufacture have taken the place of their uncivilized relation. The reason probably is that most Indians do not see the superiority of our boats. They are heavier, generally travel slower, and the person propelling one sits looking backward and continually twists his head around to see where he is going. The canoe is light, and one person often travels as fast in one with one paddle, as the white man does with two oars. He looks forward and sees where he is going, and all the snags. True we think the boat is safer, with its keel, but the Indian, accustomed to his canoe from infancy, feels safe in it as we do in our boats. In fact considering the amount the Indians are on the water, they meet with far fewer accidents than the white man does.

I have known but one Indian who could make a good boat. He was brought up by his step-father, a white man, lived mainly with the whites not far from a shipyard, and although he took no regular lessons in the art, picked up so much knowledge by careful observation that he built himself a very good sloop.

A very few Indians have procured sloops, and manage them well, but they are not common as there is not business enough for them. Steamers and cars have in the main rendered them unprofitable both for whites and Indians.

Fishing canoes, Tacoma

Paddles. The common man's paddle, most generally used on the Sound, is about 4½ feet long, with the blade 2½ feet long and 5 inches wide at the broadest place. The woman's paddle is a little shorter and a little broader in the blade, as the stroke of the men is deep and pushing, while that of the women is quicker and more splashing. They are generally made of maple. Yew is preferred on account of its strength, but it is too scarce.

The Makah paddle is imported from that tribe, and is used considerably by the Clallams and some by the Indians farther up the Sound. The larger ones are about 5 feet long, with the blade 3 feet long and 7 inches wide; though many are smaller. They are commonly of yew, and are used by the Sound Indians especially for steering in rough water because of their size and strength.

The Haida paddle. Once in a long while a Haida paddle is seen among the Clallams. The large ones are 5½ feet long, and the blade 3⅓ feet by 6 inches wide. They differ from those already described in having wider handles, and round instead of pointed ends. Some of them are very fancifully painted, with the eye of the Thunderbird and the like,

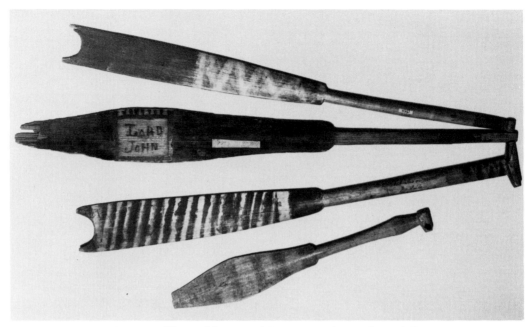

Canoe paddle models; second from top is identified as Clallam

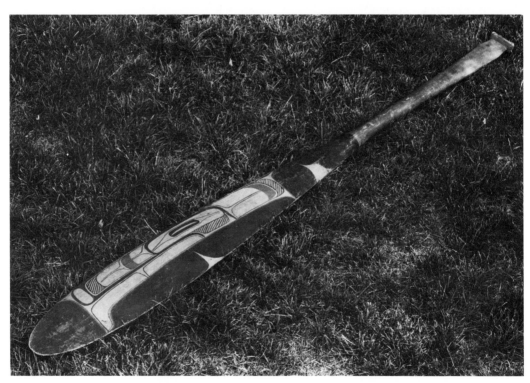

Painted canoe paddle, Haida or Bella Bella

though I do not remember ever having seen one such in use. They evidently are thus painted to sell.

The Chehalis, or river, paddle is about the same size as those first described, fully as long, but it differs in having the end of the blade cut out, leaving it somewhat in the shape of the letter "u". They are used with advantage on rivers where logs are numerous, the end of the paddle fitting on to the log, and so enabling the rower to push the canoe away from it easily. They are not, however, in common use on the Sound. They take their name from the Chehalis Indians, who live on the river of that name. The disadvantage of it is that they do not cut the water as well as the other kinds, on account of their blunt ends.

These four are all the varieties I have seen in use on the Sound.

Oars. They knew nothing of these until the whites came, but now use them considerably with the larger canoes when they have a steersman to look forward. Row locks, either of metal or of two pins of wood fastened into the edge of the boat, are used in connection with them. In dangerous waters, however, they lay aside the oars and use paddles entirely as being safer, for when a wave strikes the side and there is danger of upsetting, they strike the paddles into the water and hold them there, thus holding the canoe from tipping. They both buy oars and make them of fir or cedar. The small canoes are propelled entirely by paddles.

Sails. These are used with the larger canoes of all kinds, and the largest ones often have two sails. The smallest ones have none. Formerly the cedar bark mat was used, but they have now gone entirely out of date, and those of cloth, fashioned and fastened after the style of those in our skiffs, are used. Many a sail has been made entirely of flour sacks, and the flour brands on them, in various shapes, often are very comical.

Poles. In travelling against a strong wind, especially around points of land where the wind is very strong and the water not deep, likewise in ascending swift shallow streams, poles—ten or fifteen feet long—are often used very effectively for pushing. They have no separate poles especially for this purpose, but use those belonging to the sails.

Rudders. A very few have adopted our style of fitting rudders to their large canoes, but only a few. They prefer the old way of steering with the paddle, for they can steer and paddle at the same time, and the shape of the stern, especially of the fishing and shovel canoes, is not adapted for the fitting of rudders to them. Usually the best paddles are used for steering. The steersman is selected according to circumstances. If the water is rough the strongest and most experienced navigator steers, but if the rowing is hard and the steering easy, the strongest person rows, and perhaps a boy or woman steers. I have more than once been in canoes, sailing, when the wind was so strong that it required two persons with oars to steer.

Anchors. These were formerly made of stone, but now some kind of old iron is used, probably some good-sized ring. The only stone anchor I have ever seen (though others similar to it were often used) was found in a shell bed and burying ground at Doswailopsh on Hood Canal. It is evidently a natural stone, except that the groove around the middle, around which the rope was fastened, was hammered out with other stones. This groove is about 2 inches wide, and a little over 2 inches deep. The anchor is about 14 inches long, 7½ wide, and 4½ thick, and weighs 25½ pounds.

Mr. E. P. Brinnan of that place, who found this one and gave it to me, found another near the same place, which has been lost. It was somewhat in the shape of a grindstone, about a foot in diameter, and 4 inches thick, with a hole through it, much nearer one side than the other, for the rope.

Bailing vessels for canoes. These are of three kinds:

1. Of wood, with a handle. Alder or maple or laurel is preferred. It is usually from 5 to 7 inches wide, 9 long, exclusive of the handle, and 1–1½ inches deep. The dipper is diamond-shaped.

A modified form of this has the dipper oval and quite shallow. I have seen but two of this kind and both among the Twanas. The bowl was 8½ by 10 inches, and 1¼ deep. The end of the handle is a head similar to that of a horse.

2. Of wood, without a handle. It is rectangular in shape at the rim, the sides and ends tapering almost to a point inside. It is usually about 10 inches by 6 inches, and 2½ inches deep, but varies some. There is a groove nearly half an inch deep on the bottom on the outside, and the band is clasped to this and the rim. This kind is more commonly used by the Clallams, and the former kind by the Twanas and those up the Sound, but the rule is not invariable.

3. Of cedar bark. This style is not often used. A Clallam made for me the only one I have seen. The handle only is of wood. The bailer is about 6 inches long, 4½ across, with a depth of near an inch. It is in the shape of about an eighth of a cylinder, just as the bark is taken from the tree. The bark, as soon as taken from the tree, is cut into a strip about 4½ inches wide and 14 long, 4 inches of each end are bent at right angles and gathered and fastened to a stick which is parallel to the main part and is the handle. It is not very strong and hence is not much used.

Many times water is also thrown out of the smaller canoes with a paddle or the hand.

TRIPS

The following are accounts of two trips I made with Indians from Skokomish to Dungeness, showing many of the characteristics of their mode of travel.

On Janury 30, 1878, I started with about sixty-five Twana Indians, in seven canoes, to attend a potlatch. We paddled until it began to rain, and also to blow favorably, so that nearly all except those who steered spent the time in trying to keep dry. A few had oil-cloth coats, a few umbrellas, but most of them used their common mats, which are almost water-proof. It was rather comical to see a number of persons, mostly women and children, sitting in a canoe with a mat stretched over them, extending almost from one end of the canoe to the other. From a side view, only their heads were visible. Towards evening, after travelling seven and a half hours and making a distance of thirty miles, we arrived at Seabeck.

The next day it rained heavily until noon, and they decided not to start again on the

Canoe bailer

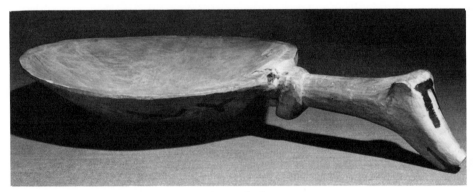

Canoe bailer

Twana bailer

189

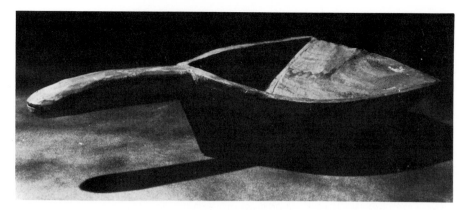

Bella Bella bailer

Canoe bailer

voyage until the following day, as there was a head wind which would prevent their reaching shelter before night, and moreover they did not wish to be the first at the potlatch. Some of them made a fire of pitch wood and cedar on a board, then putting their canoes on blocks about a foot high, they placed the fire underneath, moving it along the whole length of the canoes so as to burn off the moss and other material which might have accumulated on the outside of them, but not leaving the fire long enough in one place to burn the canoe. They do this to make the canoe run more easily.

On Friday morning the messenger came to me at seven o'clock, saying they were about to start. I hurriedly ate a part of my breakfast, and taking the remainder in my hand I started to their canoes. Four of them had gone, but the one in which I was travelling had not even been loaded. This it took them fifteen minutes to do. Then it was said one of the company was sick, so they stopped to tamahnous over him, and it was half past eight before we started. One more canoe with ten persons was here added to our company. The wind blew favorably and strongly, as much as our crafts would bear. There was a fellow-feeling among all, for no single canoe of either set of four was allowed to be far away from the rest, for fear of some accident. If one could not keep up, the rest waited for it.

In eight hours we travelled about thirty-five miles, and arrived at some Indian houses, where all camped within three miles of Port Townsend. It had rained most of the day. We did not stop for dinner, but all ate a little dry lunch at noon. At morning and night they had warm meals. The next morning they had a short tamahnous to obtain fair wind and weather. It consisted of singing and pounding on the drum and on sticks. About eight o'clock we started and reached Port Townsend in about an hour. Here they spent nearly two hours in purchasing things to present to the principal men at the potlatch, and the day being pleasant we went on, having a race in which nearly all the canoes took part. As there was little wind it was a trial of strength and endurance, and was engaged in for mere sport. It was kept up for two or three miles, until one canoe had passed all the rest and the losers were satisfied that it was useless to contest further. At about half past five we reached our destination, having made the entire trip in twenty-two travelling hours.

We set out on our return to Skokomish on the 11th of February at eleven o'clock. They intended to travel only six miles, camp at Sequim and visit these Indians, but the wind and weather proving favorable, they passed Sequim Bay without going into it, and encamped within five miles of Port Townsend. They would have gone farther, but the wind was blowing so strongly they were afraid to round Point Wilson, which is a dangerous place when the sea is rough. Here they camped out, away from the houses, for the first time on the trip. This they often do in summer, but not so in winter if the women and children are along. It was a calm night, and they did not make much preparation for camping. Some slept in their canoes, but most of them lay on the ground, and some fixed up their sails and mats so as to shelter themselves from the wind.

The next morning I was up at six o'clock and called them, but they heard the wind blowing and thought it would not yet be safe to go around Point Wilson, so they did not get up, but in an hour it had calmed down and they concluded to start; fearing though that it would rise again (as it did soon after), they rose and started without any breakfast.

Reaching Port Townsend they remained there until about noon. Then most of them went three miles farther and camped; but the owners of the smaller canoes feared to go across the bay, as it was very rough.

About eight o'clock the following morning we again started and to shorten the distance some of our party took a route where we were obliged to make a short portage. Often in doing this, when there are but few persons along, they unload the canoes and take the articles and canoes separately across, but this time there were so many along that they were able to pull the loaded canoes across, having first laid down sticks over which they were dragged. During the day there was another race.

We reached Port Gamble about two o'clock in the afternoon and some thought it best to proceed, but the Port Gamble Indians invited my companions to spend the night with them and partake of a small feast, which invitation they concluded to accept. The feast consisted chiefly of potatoes and rice, cooked in kettles, around which they sat, taking the food out with their large ladles. After dark the women assembled in one house and sat down in two rows opposite each other, singing for an hour or more, accompanied by the drum and the pounding of sticks. When this was over, two of the Port Gamble women made presents of from 5 to 12 yards of calico to each of the Twana women, and after ten o'clock some of the Twanas and Clallams began to gamble and kept up their game until three o'clock in the morning.

The next morning there was another feast of bread, crackers, and coffee, some of which was carried away. It was half past ten o'clock before we left Port Gamble, hoping to reach Seabeck, twenty miles distant, by night. But soon after starting we met a strong head wind which grew stronger. Sometimes, especially in rounding small points, we used poles to push the canoes. The Indians seldom carry poles for this purpose, but generally use spears. About three o'clock in the afternoon the Indians got tired and encamped, only one canoe reaching Seabeck that night, and that was the one which belonged there. The rest were scattered, singly and in groups of two to four for a distance of about four miles, and were not together again after this; but the Indians were now in familiar waters and no longer felt uneasy concerning the safety of each other.

I was camped with a party having four canoes. The wind blew violently that night, the trees constantly falling near us, and it rained so that it was almost impossible to make a fire. A few had tents, others used their sails as shelter, and the rest arranged their mats on poles placed in a slanting direction so as to keep off most of the rain and wind. About three o'clock the next morning an unusually high tide arose, covering all the beach where we were encamped, compelling us to leave. The water was 6 to 12 inches deep in our camp before we could get our things into the canoes. So we went back to Seabeck for breakfast, reaching the place about seven o'clock. It was a cold ride, as we were wet and the wind was blowing somewhat against us. We had to take turns at paddling to prevent our suffering from cold. Other canoes came in later.

Remaining here until half past ten o'clock we again started, and though there was some head wind, we travelled fifteen miles more before five o'clock, about which time we made camp. Six of our canoes were in company, the other having remained at Seabeck until the next day. That night I witnessed a silent tamahnous over a sick woman.

We encamped on as high ground as we could find along the beach, but next morning about four o'clock the tide was so high as to compel us to run for fear of being again submerged. The water came only to the edge of our beds.

Some of the canoes started about five o'clock and with a fair wind part of the time they reached Skokomish about half past ten o'clock. Others waited until after daylight and did not arrive until two or three hours later. Thirty-three hours were occupied in our return trip.

In July 1876, I made another trip over the same route with these differences in circumstances: The latter trip was with one canoe and in the summer. With one man to steer, one to row, and two women to paddle, we left Skokomish about six o'clock in the morning and at six o'clock we camped on the beach without tents, having travelled thirty-five miles. The next day, the crew wishing to start early, I gave them permission, and we were off about three o'clock in the morning. They took a cold lunch at about seven o'clock, and at 4 P.M. we were at Port Townsend, thirty-five miles from the last camp; but the wind was so strong around Point Wilson that they did not dare to venture there, although they were accustomed to the place, for they were Clallams and were at home in these waters. We were obliged, therefore, to remain at Port Townsend all day.

The following day the wind died down and they wished to go, but as it was Sunday I forbade them; but on Monday, at 2 A.M., we continued our journey and arrived at Dungeness about 8 P.M., having rowed twenty miles that day. We had no favorable wind during the whole trip and made ninety miles in thirty-one travelling hours, though there was little head wind to oppose us.

In returning we started at half past four o'clock, and were at Port Townsend by ten o'clock, where we remained four hours and then set out for Port Gamble, which place we reached by 6:30 P.M. There we remained for the night with the Indians of that place. The next morning, on account of missionary work, we did not leave until nine o'clock, and during the day we were detained about two hours in the same work, so that we travelled only thirty-two miles. The next day by 1 P.M. we reached home, eighteen miles farther. Having had a favorable wind most of the time, we made the whole distance in twenty-three travelling hours.

One of the quickest trips I ever made was with a Clallam man and woman. We went thirty miles in five hours, before a strong wind, and with two sails a part of the time. But at last the wind was so strong we only dared to have one sail. At this time I had a good canoe and experienced navigators, or it would not have been safe. I also once went eight miles in one hour. Few of the Twanas would have dared sail in such winds.

In addition to the tamahnous for wind, mentioned in the account of former trips, they would, especially in a calm, when they wished for a fair wind, pound on the canoe with their paddles or strike the water with them, spattering it forward. They also whistled for wind.

TRAVELLING ON FOOT

They generally travel only short distances on foot, seldom more than ten miles, except in hunting. In coming to the Twana potlatch of 1878, however, the Quinaielt Indians came about a hundred miles, much of it on foot. There was too much land travel to allow them to come entirely by water, and too much water travel to admit of bringing horses. So they brought their canoes as far as they could and walked the rest of the way.

In their short journeys they often, the women especially, carry large loads. The way they usually prefer to do this is to tie the ends of the carrying strap, which are several feet long, around the load, when it is of wood, mats, and such articles; or into the handles of baskets filled with potatoes, fish, apples, and other small objects. They then place the load on the back, and the flat part of the strap around the forehead. Formerly these straps were made of some tough bark, such as that of alder, braided. Now they use straps woven of strings and rags. This strap is from a foot to a foot and a half long, and two to three inches wide, with ropes at each end perhaps five feet long.

Snow-shoes. These are scarce, and not often used, except for hunting in the mountains in the winter, as the snow is not usually deep, nor does it commonly lie long on the ground on the shores of Puget Sound. They are commonly oblong, oval, about 14 by 18 inches with a rim of hazlewood, across which thongs of dried hides are passed. The heel is near the center, the toe extending to the edge. It is fastened to the foot by means of thongs.

Land Conveyances

Horses are used much more by the Twanas and other tribes up the Sound, than by the Clallams. The land of the latter was so mountainous, and disconnected with the land of the other tribes on account of mountains, that until lately they have had comparatively little use for them. In fact prior to the coming of the whites, water travel was so easy and roads so poor, owing to the heavy forests, that all the Sound tribes used horses but very little. Hence, they took very little pride in adorning their saddles and horses with trappings. Since the country has been settled they have adopted the saddles used by the whites, which also have no special trappings.

I think that without doubt horses were introduced to the Sound by Indians from east of the Cascade mountains. The same word, *sti-a-ke-o,* is used for "horse" by all the tribes on the Sound except the almost extinct tribe of Chemakums. The plural is formed differently in the different languages, according to the rules of each, but the singular is the same. It is evidently derived from the Nisqually word, *stick-ai-o,* meaning wolf, probably because it resembled that animal more than any other they knew. For the same reason the Spokanes called it *sintel-ska-ha,* or a great dog, their word for dog being *ska-ha,* as it resembled a dog more than any other animal of which they thought. Plainly, the horse first came to the Indians on the east side of the Sound, who named it; and then when it was seen by those speaking the other languages, the Chehalis, Twana, and Clallam, they adopted the word into their languages.

Sleds. These were almost the only vehicle used by the Twana and Clallam Indians when I came among them in 1874, both for oxen and horses. In fact, the government had no wagon on the Skokomish reservation, their only wheeled vehicles being heavy carts. But the Indian Agent soon after introduced a wagon, and these have become very common now. Buggies are also often seen, the Puyallup Indians having more and better ones than most of the other tribes, because of their proximity to Tacoma and their wealth.

TRAVELS

The limit of their travels was mainly among the tribes among which they intermarried.[3] All of the tribes bordering on the Sound had more or less intercourse with each other, owing to the ease with which they could travel the waters of the Sound, which lay between them. In addition, the Clallams visited the Makahs, Quillehutes, and tribes bordering the Straits of Fuca in British Columbia. The Skokomish Indians went to the Chehalis and Quinaielts. The Chehalis travelled to the Quinaielt, Cowlitz, and Chinook region, and sometimes went to the Columbia river and Williamette valley. The Nisqually and Puyallup Indians went south, likewise to the Columbia, and east across the Cascades to the Klikitat and Yakima country. In fact, after the Indians were conquered in the war of 1855–56, the chiefs fled to that region.

The Duwamish and Snohomish Indians likewise went east, while the Skagits and Lummis travelled north to the tribes of British Columbia. Soon after the coming of the whites, the Duke of York and a few other Clallams went on a ship to San Francisco, and John Palmer went from Port Townsend to San Francisco, and then to the mouth of the Amour river. Of late years a number of the children on the Sound have been taken to Forest Grove and Chemawa, Oregon, to school and a few have been to institutions in the Mississippi valley, while a few Puyallup men have been to Washington on business connected with their reservation.

XII
MEASURING AND VALUING

THE NUMERAL SYSTEM OF THE INDIANS goes by tens. Herewith I give some of their numerals, and add for the sake of comparison those of several neighboring tribes, which I have gathered. Those here given comprise nearly all of those in western Washington north of those bordering on the Columbia River.[1]

NUMERALS

	Twana	*Nisqually*
1	Dá-kûs	Dû-teo
2	Es-sa-lĭ	Tsá-li
3	Téo-ûs	Klé hu
4	Bú-sŭs	Bos
5	Twa-hwĕs	Tsĭl-áts
6	I-a-pá-teĭ	Dyĭl-á-tei
7	Tu-kš	Tsoks
8	Tŭ-ká-teĭ	Tû-ká-teĭ
9	Kwáil-ĭ-a	Hwail
10	O-pa-ditc	Pá-dats
11	Opadite hwĕtl dakus	Padats yâkwi dutco
12	Opadite hwĕtl essali	Padats yákwi dutco
20	Twûb-ᶜcklá ᶜk	Tsá-la-teĭ
30	Tcá-da-ᶜklo ᶜk	Sle-hẃû-tcĭ
40	Sktĭb-bú-sŭs	Tsbos-śû-teĭ
50	Te-tĭts-a-hẃûs	Steĭl-ats-sˆu-teĭ
60	Téit-ti-a-pá-tŭ	Sdzil-a-teĭ-sˆu-teĭ
70	Teĭt-ĭt-tu-ᶜkós	Stsoks-sˆu-teĭ
80	Teĭt-tū-ká-teĭ	Sti-ka-teĭ-sˆu-teĭ
90	Teĭt-tū-hwáil-ĭ-a	S-hwail-sˆu-teĭ
100	Da-kate-tu-pal-áuls	Dûtco-sûb-kẃa-teĭ
200	Essali-teĭt-tu-paláuls	Tsalĭ-sûb-k̓wa-teĭ
300	Tco-us-teĭt-tu-paláuls	Klehu-sub-kwa-teĭ
1000	Opadĭte-teĭt-tu-palauls	

	Snohomish	Skagit	Kwi-nái-ĕlt
1	D-teó	Du-teo	Pau
2	Sá-lĭ	Sá-lĭ	Sá-lĭ
3	Klé-hu	Kle-hu	Kat-la
4	Bos	Bos	Mos
5	Tsi-áts	Sĭ-läts	Tsé-luks
6	I-a-láts	I-läts	Sĭ-tû-teĭ
7	Tsoks	Tsoks	Tsops
8	Tû-ká-tcĭ	Tŭ-ka-teĭ	Tsa-mus
9	Hwûl	Hwûl	Tûǵ-wĭ-hu
10	O-lob	O-lop	Pá-naks

	Upper Chehalis	Lower Chehalis	Chemakum
1	Ot-sus	Pau	Kwetl
2	Sá-lĭ	Sal	Klak-we
3	Teá-tle	Teatl	Kwáil-lĭ
4	Mos	Mos	Me-és
5	Tsi-lutes	Tse-é-lĭtes	Tea-a
6	Tá-hûni	Sé-dĭte-ĭ	Tsĭt-las
7	Tśâ-ops	Tecpo	Tskol-kwûnt
8	Tsa-mos	Tsa-mós	Kwai-kwunt
9	Tó-hu	To-hu	Kwelts-hail
10	Pa-nates	Pa-nĭtes	Tce-ta
11	Tcet-otsus	Tal-pau	Tceta-kûskwa-kwĕtl
12	Tcet-sa-lĭ	Tal-sal	Tceta-kûskwa-klakwe
20	Tsûm-tó-mĭsh	Tsûm-tomĭsh	Hwie-tati-tcĭlo
30	Tcá-nĭs-tó-mĭsh	Tca-nis-tomĭsh	Kwilla-kwûmlo
40	Nós-ûl-tó-mĭsh	Nosĭtl-tomish	Nees-kwûmlo
50	Tsé-lĭts-tómĭsh	Tseelits-tĭtl-tomĭsh	Tcaa-kwûmlo
60	Tahûm̀-ûl-tómĭsh	Seedite-tĭtl-tomĭsh	Tsiltas-kwûmlo
70	Tsaóps-ûl-tómĭsh	Tsops-titl-tomĭsh	Tskol-kwûnt-kwûmlo
80	Tsaḿos-ûl-tómĭsh	Tsamos-tĭtl-tomĭsh	Kwai-kwunt-kwûmlo
90	Ta we-ûl-tomish	To-we-hwi-tĭtl-tomĭsh	Kwelts-hail-kwûmlo
100	Panátes-ûl-tómĭsh	Panites-tĭtl-tomĭsh	Teet-kwûmlo
200	Salĭts-panates-ûl-tomĭsh	Salts-panĭtes-tĭtl-tomish	Kwait-la-teĭ-kwûmlo
300	Tca-tle-panates-ûl-tomĭsh Panates-panates-ul-tomish	Teatl-panĭtes-tĭtl-tomĭsh Panĭts-nauĭts-panĭte-tĭtl-tomish	Kwud-la-teĭ-kwûmlo

Kwil-lĭ-ut		Hoh	Makah
1	Welt	Lĭʼk-i	Tsark wark
2	Klá-we	Klä-u	Attl or ûtl
3	Kwá-lĭ	Kwail	Wi
4	Ma-es	Bái-yas	Boh
5	Stäs	Tá-si	Shút-tce
6	Teĭl-äs	Teĭ-tlas	Tce-patl
7	Kla-ók-us-ĕs	Kla-wak-tsĭs	Atl-po
8	Klau-ŭtl	Kla-wĕ-tûl	A-tlĕs-sûb
9	Wetl-tatl	Wetl-lûtl	Sa-kwas-sûb
10	Kû-shetl	Tcetl-tat	Kluh

Lummi		Cowichan	Chinook Jargon
1	Nût-sâ	Nût-sûs	Ikt
2	Tels-sâ	I-sé-lĭ	Măkst
3	Kle-hu	Kle-hwûs	Klone
4	Ngas	Hûs-si-nûs	Lăk-it
5	Ti-ka-teĕs	Tû-káts-ûs	Kwĭu-nûm
6	T-hŭng	Tû-hûm-mûs	Tá-hûm
7	Tsá-kwŭs	Tsáks-ûs	Sĭn-a-măskt
8	Tats	Táts-ûs	Etokĭu
9	Tŭk-hu	Tó-o-hwûs	Kwist
10	A-pĕn	O-pans	Tăt-lum

Klallam					
1	Nût-sˆa	9	Tŭ-k̓-ho	60	Tlk̓ûngĭl-sha
2	Teĕs-sa	10	O-pen	70	Tsáks-ĭl-sha
3	Klé-hu	11	Open-ĭt-nutsa	80	Táts-il-sha
4	Nos	12	Open-ĭt-tcessa	90	Tûk̓-hûl-sha
5	Ti-ká-tes	20	Nûts-a-kwis	100	Ná-tcu-ĭtc
6	Tû-hûng	30	Tlûl-shá	200	Tsang-ate
7	Tsoks	40	Nĭsl-shá	300	Kle-hwe-ĭte
8	Tats	50	Tlkûfcl-sha	1000	Opĕns-natcuĭte

In the Twana, *schùch-há-chĭ* (and in the Nisqually, *ska sûk-a-chĭ*) means "hand"; hence, we have from the same root, *i-a-pá-chĭ* for "six" in the Twana, and *dzil-á-chĭ* in Nisqually, and a word for "six" of similar derivation may be found in the Snohomish, Skagit, and Quinaielt; *tukachi*, "eight," from the same root, is found in Twana, Nisqually, Snohomish, and Skagit; *ki-tats* is the Clallam word for "hand," and *tats* for "eight," and this is found in the Cowichan of British Columbia and Sûmmĭ; *hul-kwunt* is the Chemakum word for "fingers," and it is seen as the origin of their words for "seven" and "eight." In the Upper and Lower Chehalis, the word for "eight" seems to be derived from those for "four" and "two," that is, twice four.

Sa-lĭ, "two," runs with little variation through the Twana, Nisqually, Snohomish, Chehalis, Quinaielt, Cowichan, and Skagit, and an examination of volume 1 of *Contributions to North American Ethnology*, pages 262 and 280, and Tolmie and Dawson's *Comparative Vocabularies of British Columbia*, shows that a similar word is in the Shooswaap, Okinaken, Shwoyelpi, Skoyelpi, Spokane, Kullispelm, Coeur d'Alene, Flathead, Tait, Kuwaltisk, Snanaimu, Kwantlin, and old, regular Chinook. The Hoh, Kwilleute, and Chemakum would fall into a separate class in regard to this word.

Kle-hu-for, "three," slightly varied, is in the Nisqually, Snohomish, Clallam, Cowichan, Summi, and Skagit, also in the Tait, Kuwalitsk, Snanaimo, Kwantlin, and Songis. In this word, as in the former, the Hoh, Quillehute, and Chemakum languages agree. In this word, the Upper and Lower Chehalis, Quinaielt, Shiwapmukh, Skooswap, Nikutemukh, Okinaken, Wakynakine, Shwoyelpi, Skoyelpi, Spokane, Piskwans, Kalispelin, Kullispelm, Coeur d'Alene, Flathead, Lilowat, and Komookhs are similar.

The word for "four," however, in slightly varied forms, easily traced, combines more of the languages given than any other numeral; *baies, bu-sus-bos, boh, nos-mos-me-es, nos-ngos*, and similar variations, are seen in all the languages of which I have here given the numerals, except the Chinook Jargon. It is the only numeral which connects the Makah with the others, and shows relationship also in the following languages, Coeur d'Alene, Spokane, Skoyelpi, Shwoyelpi, Okinaken, Kullispelm, Piskwans, Regular Chinook, Bella Bella, Ahts, Songis, Tait, Shooswap, Nikutemukh, Lilloet, and Komookh, twenty-nine in all.

The Chinook Jargon is connected with the others, only through the Upper Chehalis, Clallam, Lummi, and Cowichan languages, by the word for "six."

It is singular that in the six languages which I have studied considerably in this region, namely the Twana, Nisqually, Clallam, Chemakum, Upper and Lower Chehalis, none are similar in the number one, while there is a similarity in every other of the first ten numbers. Between the Upper and Lower Chehalis, also between the Nisqually and Skokomish, there is a similarity in eight of the numbers; between the Lower Chehalis and Skokomish, also between the Lower Chehalis and Nisqually, each in six of them; between the Upper Chehalis and Clallam, also the Nisqually and Clallam, also between the Upper Chehalis and Skokomish, also the Upper Chehalis and Nisqually, each in five; and between the Lower Chehalis and Clallam, also the Clallam and Skokomish, in four of them. The Upper and Lower Chehalis, the Skokomish, the Nisqually, and the Clallam are similar in regard to the numbers two, seven, and ten.

There had been considerable discussion as to whether words which sound alike show a similarity of origin in the tribes speaking them; but Professor W. D. Whitney says that numerals and words indicating relationship are of more value as evidence on this point than any others. A further comparison of the four languages which accompany this shows that the Twana and Nisqually agree in many points, and the Clallam is similar to them in some, but the Chemakum, except in a few instances, is different from all the others, and these instances are such that the words may have been adopted from the Clallam, their neighbors. Dr. Gibbs is doubtful whether the Chemakums ought to be included in the Salish family or not. There is no doubt but they are connected with the Hohs and Kwilleutes, judging from the numerals and their traditions. Dr. Gibbs is also of this opinion.

In this connection I would say that a comparison of the manners and customs of all the above-named tribes, as far as I have been able to learn them, show that they are much the same, varying only as their different environments compel them.

Whether or not similarity of customs shows a similarity of origin seems to be an open question. If any customs do, it is to my mind their religious rites, for experience and observation prove that they are less likely to change these than any others. In customs there is little difference among these tribes, the more northern Indians being a little more savage.

The Twana language has another form of numerals for counting money, stones, and small round things, which differs from the form given entirely in the word for "one," *pal-auls*, and in other words by adding to the word given, *s, lis, elis, alis,* or *talis,* as a termination: thus the word for "two," *essali,* becomes *essalis,* and "six," *iapatei, iapatcilis.* Nisqually does the same by adding in the same way, *els,* thus *klehu,* "three," becomes *klehulis,* and *bos,* "four," *bosels.* The Upper Chehalis likewise adds generally *aus, is* or *ts: mos,* "four," becomes *mosis,* and *tahum,* "six," *tahumts.* But for "one" and "two" entirely different words are used, which are *na-tcaus* (one) and *tsamis* (two). The Clallam for the same purpose uses the suffix, *aiuthu,* or *kuthu: nutsa,* "one," becomes *nutsakuthu,* and *tats,* "eight," *tatsaikuthu.* This language also has a third form for counting animals, which consists mainly of using the suffix *eks* or *eiks: nutsa* becoming *nutseks,* and *tats, tatseiks.*

Numeral adverbs. For the numeral adverbs, once, twice, and the like, the Twana adds *olshid* or *tolshid: dakus,* "one," becoming *datcoshid; bos,* "four," *bosolshid;* and *tsahwes,* "five," *tsahwestolshid.* The Nisqually for the same purpose adds *atl,* except with once and twice: *bos,* "four," becoming *bosatl,* and *tukatci,* "eight," *tukatciatl;* but "once" is *ditcahu,* and "twice" *tsubab.* The Upper Chehalis adds generally to the termination *shin, tashin,* or *ushin,* except for "once" which is *natcushin,* and "twice" which is *tsamshin,* the first part of the word being entirely different.

TIME AND SEASONS

Formerly the Twana divided the year into moons, or lunar months, and months into days.

Moon	Slo-khwill'-um	June	Tāk-kā-chid
Star	Kla-kla-chīs'	July	Kwī-o-wăt-id
Sun	Klo-kwāt'	August	Klā-lăcḣ-rid
January	Hā-hāt	September	Kā-ka-bat
February	Stāh-kwâl'-deb	October	Kwā-lā-kwobe
March	Sī-ai-kwúdst	November	Kwā-kwa'-chid
April	Stā-kó-lit	December	Yă-shūtl
May	Stā-klá-chid		

These are the names as well as I can find out. They are nearly out of use and the young men who understand English do not know them. The older ones can only begin at the present month, November, and count backward and forward, and hence they may be a little inaccurate as to the order. The beginning and end do not exactly agree with ours, but are nearly as indicated.

There are no names for the points of the compass; but the following are the names for the winds:

North wind	*Tō-lō‾'tsād*
South wind	*T‾'o-lā-chūl-lā*
East wind	*(no word)*
West wind	*Tōz-b‾'a-dit*

Before the Americans came, they had no weeks, but simply numbered the days in each moon. Since that time they have used the following

Sunday	*Hā-ha-āt'-lis*
Monday	*Tsiā-pāt'-lis*
Tuesday	*Tsib-bĭ-ās'-sab*
Wednesday	*Chā-dā-kwi-sub*
Thursday	*Būs-sā-tli'-sub*
Friday	*Su-kus-tli'-sub*
Saturday	*Sā-chub-its*

The first means, literally, holy day; the second, past (one day past); the third, second day; the fourth, third day; the fifth, fourth day; the sixth, fifth day; and the last, alongside (that is, of Sunday).

The Indians also had names for spring, summer, fall, and winter.

Originally they had no names for the days, and knew nothing about the division of weeks. They say they first obtained the idea of Sunday from the Klikitat Indians. After this they often met on Sunday, talked, prayed, danced, tried to purify themselves, throw away their bad, and make their hearts good. On that day they also married wives. Since they have obtained this knowledge of weeks, they have often given names to the days of the week. . . . The day-time was divided into dawn, sunrise, forenoon, noon, afternoon, sunset, and dusk, and the night had only the division of midnight. Each of these different divisions had its name.

MEASUREMENTS

Length. They had four standards of measurement of length: (1) from end to end of the middle finger outstretched; (2) from the shoulder to the end of the corresponding hand, arm extended; (3) from the shoulder to the end of the opposite hand, arm extended; and (4) the fathom. In travelling, the standard was the distance which a person could travel in one day.

I do not know that land was measured, but in all square measure the above linear measures were used.

Quantity. In measuring articles in bulk their baskets were used, but I know of no basket of standard size being used. A person making a bargain for a certain number of basketsful would have to see the basket.

TRADE

Valuing currency. The dentalia shell and the abalone shell, or parts of it, were the nearest thing to money which they had, the former being the most valuable. A species of olivella shell, found in Clallam waters, was sometimes brought to the Twanas, by whom it was used partly for money. Slaves, skins, and blankets were also used for a similar purpose, or rather for barter, but I have been unable to learn what value they put upon them or on the shells, as their values have changed greatly since the whites came. The value of the dentalia shell depended on the size as well as number, a long one being much more valuable according to size than a short one. It was found in the ocean off British Columbia, and was used as money from Alaska to California, and east to Dakota. Like our money it was also used for ornament. For a myth in regard to it, see Chapter XVIII.

Their modes of trade were both direct and indirect. A direct trade was immediate quid pro quo and plain. An indirect one was peculiar. A person made a present to another, of something the latter did not want but could not refuse lest he should give offense. Still, the giver would soon name the amount he wished in return, and if he did not receive it in the course of time, there was trouble. Often, too, after a direct trade, and the article, as a horse, had been used for six months or longer, if there was trouble about the pay, the animal or article was returned, even if the seller did not wish it, the bargain not being considered binding. This was so, even if a part payment had been made. If a horse, not paid for, should die after having been used a long time, the buyer would claim that the seller must lose part of the price. It was too hard "to pay for a dead horse," or other article destroyed.

Debts. These are the failing of the Indian. When they can get into debt to a white person, they generally seem to be glad to do so; and even when they have the money with which to pay, they keep going into debt often, even though there is no probability of their ever being able to pay if they are allowed to do so. Unless asked to pay, they seldom offer to do so, unless they are obliged to pay in order to get more, as at a store. Still, if pressed a little they generally are willing to make effort to pay. In the financial crash of 1893, the trader J. McReavy, at Union City, failed, and put his property into the hands of a receiver. The Indians of the Skokomish reservation owed Mr. McReavy $5,000 to $7,000; the whites $20,000 to $25,000. Most, both whites and Indians, found it very difficult to pay money and many could not, but the receiver told me that the Indians made less trouble and more honest effort to pay than the whites, as a whole.

I once thought that this disposition of the Indians to get into debt to the whites was evidently a race prejudice, as if all they could get from the whites was clear gain. But the more I have learned of their habits, the more I believe this is not the real cause. That lies in their native training from infancy. They are generally in debt to each other, and these debts are often of very long standing, ten years or more. It is only when there has been trouble among them, that I have been able to learn of some of these debts. One man gets vexed, and so wishes to collect what is due him. The other brings up another debt as an offset. Next the first party brings up another older debt; then one is brought up in which the wife is involved, and so on, they remind the court of unsettled transactions of ten or fifteen years previous. Even a debt of relations and wife's relations is brought up, to be considered as much as if it were a personal one.[2]

At one time an old man at Seabeck was invited to a potlatch at Skokomish nearly thirty miles distant. He accepted the invitation and was away from home for about two weeks. While he was thus absent his house was broken into and robbed of property of considerable value. As he could not find who did it, he claimed that the man who invited him to the potlatch ought to pay him, because if the giver of the potlatch had not induced him to leave home, he would not have lost his articles.

Commerce. They have dishes made from the horn of the mountain sheep, which are said to have come from the Stikine Indians of British Columbia, six or eight hundred miles to the north; the dentalia shell, their ancient money, also came from the same region. They occasionally obtain articles from the Haida Indians of Queen Charlotte's Island. They get pipes, horn dishes, buffalo robes, and baskets from the Klikitats and Yakimas of eastern Washington, one or two hundred miles to the east; baskets from the Cowlitz Indians, a hundred miles to the south, and from the Shoalwater Bay and Quinaielt Indians on the coast, about the same distance to the west and southwest. The distance mentioned is nearly in a direct line, the way in which the articles come is much farther, sometimes twice as far.

The northern commerce is mainly by water, but that with the Klikitat, Yakima, Cowlitz, Shoalwater Bay, and Quinaielt Indians by land, which accounts for the difference in the distance. I have an obsidian spear head, whose travels cannot now be traced, but which I presume came from southern Oregon, if not farther south, while J. Y. Collins of Whatcom has found bird-shaped articles of stone in that region, which seem to be similar to some found at the Dalles and mouth of the Umatilla in Oregon. These were evidently not made there but are believed to have come from Arizona or Mexico. Stone articles could, however, easily thus travel in time, if not lost, as they would never wear out, for the Walla Walla Indians within the memory of the white man, at least no further back than the forties, went to California for trade.

The articles from these distant tribes are, however, limited in number, and many of them are obtained through intermediate tribes who serve as carriers. The great bulk of trade was between the tribes who surrounded Puget Sound, in the United States and British Columbia. These often met at potlatches, and quite an extensive trade was carried on.

For the past twelve or fifteen years, thousands from these tribes—the Yakima region, the Makah reservation, and British Columbia as far north as the Stikine region and sometimes even to the edge of Alaska—meet annually at the hop fields of the White and Puyallup rivers, near Seattle and Tacoma, for picking hops, and at these times they do considerable trading.

As an article of historical interest, A. B. Rabbeson of Olympia has given in the *Tacoma Ledger* the following schedule of prices for Indian labor and other things, which was established by the first Americans in the forties.[3]

One day's work	1 cotton handkerchief
One week's work	1 hickory shirt
One month's work	1 to 3 point blanket
Use of canoe to Nisqually and back	1 cotton handkerchief
Each Indian in canoe	1 cotton handkerchief
1 deer ham	1 load powder and ball
3 ducks	1 load powder and shot
1 barrel cranberries	5 yards white cotton cloth
50 Chinook salmon	1 hickory shirt
1 good horse	1 musket

XIII
GAMES AND PASTIMES

GAMBLING

Gambling has been until within a few years very common, there having been but very few who did not engage in it, and even now they are by no means wholly free from it.[1]

There are also professional gamblers, who, like the whites, generally visit large gatherings, especially potlatches, to ply their trade. Among the women it is not so common as among the men.

There are three native modes:

1. With round disks. This is the men's game generally, though sometimes both sexes engage in it. The disks are about two inches in diameter and a third of an inch thick. They are made of hard wood, quite smooth, and by long continued use become highly polished. One edge of most of them is partly painted, either red or black, while one is left unpainted; or else the edge is entirely painted. There are ten blocks or disks in a set.

Cedar bark is beaten up fine and the disks are divided into handsful of five each, and each handful is then placed under some of this cedar bark on a mat, while the players face each other. But two persons engage at the same time in shuffling the disks, though others are generally around and bet on it, and one of them occasionally changes with one of the players, if his friend should be unlucky. A number of small sticks about four inches long are placed on a board for a tally. At first they are evenly divided, but are changed as one party wins or loses. The object is for one party or person to win them all. Usually from twelve to twenty-four of these sticks are used; the number used depends on the amount of the bet. As one party may win and lose, and continue to do so, it is plain that the game may last a long time, for four days and nights and then be a draw game.

When all is ready for a game, the parties sit down on the ground about twelve feet from each other, and one selects one out of his half a dozen or more sets and shuffles them around considerably; then, under cover, divides them evenly so that five are in each hand, and places each handful under some of this cedar bark. They are then shuffled around on the mats for a time, the opposite player watching all this as closely as possible. His wish is to guess under which hand the disk is which has the painted rim or the unpainted one. With a motion of his hand he indicates under which hand he thinks this one to be, and the player rolls them out. If he guesses aright he wins and plays next; but if he guesses wrong he loses, and the other plays again. They have several sets of these blocks, so that if bad luck attends one set for a time, they may change and use another set.

Gambling disks, men's game

These different sets are marked a little differently on the sides, or else are made slightly different in size to distinguish them, all of each set being alike. They are usually about two inches in diameter and a quarter of an inch thick.

Another form of the game is called the tamahnous game. A large number of people, including women, who have a tamahnous, take part in it, but the men only shuffle the disks. Sometimes it is one tribe against another. The only difference between this form of the game and that just described is in invoking the aid of their tamahnous. While one man plays, another member of his party beats the drum or tomtom, or possibly two of these are used, and the rest of the party clap their hands and sing, each one as I am told singing his or her tamahnous song, to invoke the aid of his or her special guardian spirit. There is certainly no uniformity in their songs, as different persons sing different songs at the same time.

Very seldom do they play for mere fun. There is usually a small stake, and sometimes from one to four hundred or even a thousand dollars are bet, and in former years it is said that sometimes they bet everything they had, even to their clothes on their backs. Outside parties sometimes bet on the game, as white people bet on other person's games.

They have a tradition that a long time ago a great supernatural being called Dokibatl came here and told them to give up all bad habits, these disks being among the things that they were to give up. He took the disks and threw them into the water, but they

Bird bone tally sticks, Clallam

Wooden tally sticks

Pins used to secure gambling mats

came back; he then took them and threw them into the fire, but they came out; he threw them away as far as he could, but again they came back; and so he threw them away five times, and every time they returned; and so, as they conquered him, he told the Indians that they might retain this kind of gambling for fun and sport.

2. Games with bones. A small bone about two inches long and a half inch in diameter is used, or sometimes two of them, one of which is marked. They also at times use two much larger ones, two and a half inches long and an inch or more in diameter, one of which is marked. Occasionally also pieces of wood of the same size are used, but they are considered a poor affair.

Six or eight persons on each side usually play this game, but more may be really engaged in it on the outside, and even the whole tribe, as in the previous game. The drum and the tamahnous are also occasionally used. The players sit in two rows opposite each other, about six feet apart. In front of each set of players is a long stick or rail and all of them except one have small sticks about a foot and a half long, with which, while the one on their side is playing, they pound on the rail, singing at the same time to induce good luck. The one who has no stick in his hands takes the bone or bones in his hands, under cover either of a blanket or some such thing, arranges which shall be in each hand, if both are used (or in which hand, if one is used), and then in sight very rapidly changes them from hand to hand. This is done so quickly, by long practice, that the bones cannot be seen. After a time one of the opposite players by a motion indicates in which hand he thinks the bone is, if one is used, or, if two are used, in which hand the marked one is. If he guesses aright, he wins and plays; if not, he loses and the other one continues to play. When he wins, the other persons stop their noise and singing and his parties take it up. Sometimes it is said that a person will become so expert that if his opponent guesses aright, he will change them without being seen.

Single gambling bone, Clallam

Wood gambling cylinders, Clallam

Bone cylinders for gambling

Metal shells for gambling

Gambling bones, Clallam

The tally is kept with [small sticks] about a foot long, which are stuck into the ground, but on the same principle as in the previous games. I have known a game to be played for four days and nights, and neither party to win, it being a draw game. If one person on a side is peculiarly successful, he will play for a long time, but if he is very unsuccessful, another of his party will take the bones.

Hon. J. Wickersham of Tacoma has a pair made of brass, purposely made for cheating. It is made so that it will look like the one that is not marked, but by a slide can be changed while in the hand so as to look like the one marked. Its mate is a little longer than this one when closed and a little shorter than when open, so that the difference would hardly be noticeable. He also has some similar to mine, only there are two circles on the marked one, one toward each end, instead of only one circle in the middle.

Usually the amounts bet in this game are small, some pins or matches, fifty cents or a dollar and a half, but sometimes the stakes are quite large. For some of the songs sung at these times see Chapter XIV.

3. The women's game. Beavers' teeth are usually used for this, though sometimes those of muskrats. Commonly only one person on each side plays, but sometimes there are two or three. The teeth are marked on one side so as to form two pairs of two each, one of them having a string tied around it. They are all taken in one hand and thrown up, and the manner in which they fall shows how the game goes; it being somewhat on the principle of throwing dice. If the marked side of the one which has the string on it is down and all the rest up, or up while the rest are down, it counts four; if that side of all is up or down, it counts two. If the marked side of one pair is up, and that of the other pair down, it counts one; and if the pair, one of which has the string on it, is up or down and the other pair is divided, it counts nothing. To get thirty is a game, but generally they play three games and bet money, dresses, cloth, and the like. The women sometimes learn to throw them very expertly, although quickly, by holding the one with the string on it a trifle longer than the others, and then give it a peculiar turn so as to make it fall differently from them.

They usually keep tally with small sticks about four inches long, but, if they can, they use the bones of birds of about the same length. But the women play this game very little, as compared with the time devoted by the men to the other games.

4. Cards. In addition to these [games mentioned], a considerable number of men, at least the younger ones, have learned to play cards, on which they bet considerable amounts at times. It is about the only kind of civilized (!) gambling which they have learned, with a few exceptions.

For ten years most of the Twanas, Squaksons, Puyallups, and Chehalis Indians gave up almost entirely their gambling, though many of the other tribes clung to it. Within a year, however, some of them have revived it.

Beaver teeth for women's gambling, Twana

Bear's teeth for gambling, Twana

Incised bear tooth for women's gambling

DANCING

Another amusement which the Indians occasionally follow is dancing. No partners are chosen, but both men and women dance; the men holding on to each other's hands by themselves and the women doing the same; though all in the same room. White people would hardly call it dancing, for it is simply a jumping up and down, sometimes in the same place and sometimes all move along together, in the house and out of it, while they keep time to the drum and sing. Generally this dancing is a religious perform-ance, a part of their tamahnous, but occasionally it is practiced for mere sport. I have seen them do so until they were entirely exhausted by their laughing and sports.

HORSE RACING

As far as I know, the Clallams have very little if any of this, as their horses are few. At least they have no race track. The other tribes mentioned have practiced it largely for many, many years, as their outdoor summer sport, the gambling having been their indoor winter sport. They do not do as much of it now by any means as they did twenty years ago, still at times, especially at their Fourth of July celebrations and at hop-picking, they have large races, sometimes one tribe being against another. As far as they can, they usually practice it, as the whites do, without a book of rules.

SHOOTING

A field sport which is now entirely out of date was the shooting of arrows, the object being to see who could shoot the farthest, and large bets were made. The winning arrow would sell for a large price. One arrow of this kind was made for me. Both head and shaft were made of wood. The head was split and the shaft inserted into it. I have never learned that this was common with arrows for other purposes, as usually the shaft was split, and the head inserted. It is fletched with two feathers, as ordinary arrows.

BASEBALL AND DANCING

As their ancient sports have been abandoned, these as practiced by the whites have in a measure taken their places, though by no means is as much time spent with them as was spent with their ancient games. There is too much work to be done.

CHILDREN'S GAMES

Indian children, like white children, have their own special plays, and also imitate the ways of their superiors. Among the former are ball, shuttle cock, shinny, and a native game in which there are two parties. One side holds some article, while a person from the other side advances to get it. The members of the first side say all the funny things they can, and the opposite side cannot have the article unless their representative can get it without laughing.

In games of imitation they go through all the motions of gambling and tamahnous, and these seem to be the principal ways in which they mock the older Indians.

In imitating whites they sometimes have several post offices a short distance from each other, with as many postmasters, and a mail carrier who carries bits of paper from one to the other; or they will hold a council in remembrance of the time when some distinguished person from Washington has been here, when they will make speeches, have an interpreter, and all things in regular order. Again, it will occasionally be a church, while they go through with the services, or a court with judge, jury, lawyers, witnesses, and a criminal. An odd occurrence took place at one of these mock courts some time ago, which happened to be overheard by their teacher. A boy was on trial for drunkenness. When the proper time came the criminal arose and said substantially as follows:

213

Gentlemen, I am a poor man and not able to employ a lawyer, so I must plead my own case. The court has been slightly mistaken about the case. I am a white man; my name is Captain Chase (a white man living near the reservation). I came to church on Sunday. The minister did not know me; as I was well dressed, he thought I was a good man and might have something to say, hence he asked me to speak. I knew I was not a suitable man to address the congregation, but I could not well refuse. So I rose and went to the platform, but I had some tobacco in my mouth. I tried quietly to take it out and throw it down without being seen, but the Indians noticed it, and thought a minister should not chew tobacco, and beside I did stagger a little. These are the reasons I am on trial here.

XIV

MUSIC

Music among these Indians consists more of noise than melody.[1] As a rule the Clallams are far more musical than the Twanas. The women sometimes sing alone when at work, at funerals, and when tending the children; but in nearly all their gambling, war, boat, and religious songs, the men take the lead, the women, however, joining. Usually all persons sing the same melody, though sometimes the pitch varies considerably. At some of their tamahnous ceremonies, I have heard nearly all singing a different song; each one, as I have been told, sings his or her tamahnous song. At a distance of a few hundred yards, however, all of these seemed to blend into one harmony.

INSTRUMENTS

Instruments are intended more for noise than anything else. Indeed, no single one can vary the tone, the only modifications being loud and soft. They are used chiefly in their religious performances, hence a description of them will be given in Chapter XXV.

They consist of the drum, deer-hoof rattles, scallop shell rattles, and hollow rattles made from wood. Those who have no instruments pound with small sticks on larger ones, and clap their hands.

SONGS

Songs consist of work, patriotic, and boat songs, and songs for gambling and the nursery, for love and war, for funeral and religious ceremonies. I have known of instruments being used only with those for war and gambling, the boat songs, and religious songs, and in all of these the aid of their spirits or tamahnous was invoked, which made them really religious songs. In their singing, the songs are continually repeated.

Boat songs. When travelling in a common way they are not accustomed to sing much, but sometimes when on a parade before friends, generally on the arrival of several canoes at a council or great festival, there is considerable singing, accompanied by drumming, clapping of hands, pounding with sticks and paddles on boards and canoes, and sometimes by rattling with the hollow wooden rattles. This occurs just before the landing, beginning sometimes when the canoes are two or three miles away, as far as they can easily be heard. Song number 1 is a song of this kind, which I heard in 1875, when the

Clallams of Elwha arrived at a council at Dungeness, and number 2 is another sung by the same Indians when they arrived at the same place at a potlatch in 1878 (Chapter XXI, "Potlatch no. 2").

Patriotic songs. At one time in travelling with a large number of Twana Indians, one of whom was a Chemakum woman whose husband was a Twana, we passed through the Chemakum country. When we reached it, she began singing something, but at first I did not understand what she was doing. I asked the other Indians about it, and they said, "Hush." I did so, as they all kept still. They afterwards told me that she was singing an ode in the Chemakum language to her native land. None of them understood her, but out of respect to her they kept silent. This has been the only song of the kind I have ever heard.

Gambling songs. When gambling according to the second method described in Chapter XIII, singing is universal, accompanied by the pounding of small sticks on the larger ones. Numbers 3 and 4 are songs of the kind which I have heard among the Twanas; number 3 having been sung by one party in the game, and number 4 by the opposite one. The words have no meaning. Numbers 5, 6, and 7, I have heard sung by the Clallams in the same kind of game, and as sung by both Twanas and Clallams in the same game.

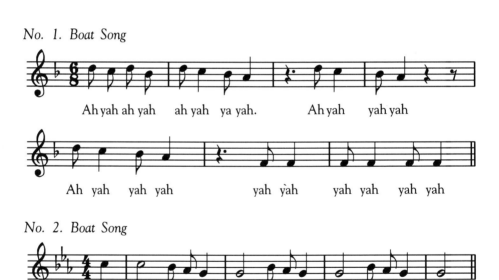

No. 1. Boat Song

Ah yah ah yah   ah yah ya yah.   Ah yah   yah yah

Ah yah   yah yah   yah yah   yah yah   yah yah

No. 2. Boat Song

No. 3. Gambling Song

Hĭ - nĭ hai nĭ   ha   hai nĭ

No. 4. Gambling Song

Hi - ha - hi

No. 5. Gambling Song

Havi - a - ho

No. 6. Gambling Song

Ha   ha   ha   ha   ve.

No. 7. Gambling Song

Hi - ye - ha - la - la.

No. 8. Gambling Song

No. 9. Tamahnous Gambling Song

No. 10. Baby Song

Ta - ka - tas skûl - le - e

No. 11. Mourning Song

No. 12. Mourning Song

Oh - d - da - d - da d - da

No. 13. War Song

Ho ya chi chis ho ya chi chis ho ya chi chis

No. 14. Tamahnous Song for Wind

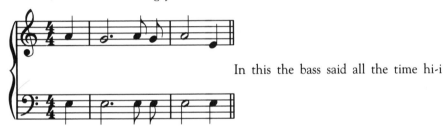

In this the bass said all the time hi-i

No. 15. Tamahnous Song for Sick

No. 16. Tamahnous Song for Sick

Hi - i - e - hi - i - a - hi - e

No. 17. Tamahnous Song for Sick.

He - he - e - a he - e - a he - e - a he - e - a

No. 18. Dance Song

Hni - ni - a - wa - hi - hit

No. 19. Dance Song

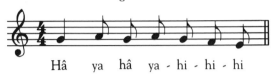

Hâ ya hâ ya - hi - hi - hi

No. 20. Dance Song

No. 21. Black Tamahnous Song

Ho-ho - hoi - ho - hoi

No. 22. Black Tamahnous Song

Hâ hâ hoi Hui hi - hi

No. 23. Black Tamahnous Song

No. 24. Black Tamahnous Song

Ha hoi hie hi ni

In gambling, the singing is unversal in the first method described, and is accompanied by the pounding on large sticks with smaller ones, different songs being sung by opposing parties. The words have no meaning. When gambling in the second method, there is usually no singing unless it becomes a tamahnous game, when a drum, one for each party, is brought in, and there is pounding on sticks and clapping of hands and singing. In this singing each person sings his or her tamahnous song, thus invoking the aid of his or her tamahnous, so as to win the game. I was once present at such a game, and from inside the house the singing was a confused medley on different keys and I could catch nothing of it, but when I was a few hundred yards away the sounds had blended into number 9, though different keys mainly in chord were distinguishable.

Nursery songs. The common ones, to soothe a crying child, or hush one to sleep, I have never been able to obtain, but I have been told of one special one, number 10, by a Clallam.

Funeral songs. At all funerals, and often for several days afterwards, there is a crying kind of singing, with no accompaniment. Generally, however, all do not sing the same melody at the same time in unison. One may sing alone, or several may sing at the same time, and perhaps the same melody, but perhaps each will begin and finish as he or she may wish, paying no attention to any of the rest. Often for weeks or even months after an especially dear friend has died, someone, almost universally a woman, will sit near her house and cry or sing by the hour. At the funerals, usually both men and women sing. Number 11, I have heard frequently sung by the Twanas, some time after the funeral, and number 12 at the time of the funeral. Often these notes are sung in the order I have written them, and sometimes in a different order, but in some order the notes, *do*, *la*, and *mi*, in the minor strain are sung, and sometimes other words, such as "my child, why did you die," or the word father, mother, or friend, are substituted for child, as the case may be.

War songs. As wars have ceased—long ago—I have heard these songs only very rarely and then at some great festival, as a potlatch in memory of former days. Number 13 I heard sung at a potlatch (see Chapter XXI, "Potlatch no. 2"). It was sung by the Clallams, and frequently repeated, closing each time with the word *ho-ya* in very loud tones, when all squatted nearly to the ground. This was done with blackened faces, accompanied with the drums and hollow wooden rattles.

Religious songs. At their religious ceremonies, whatever be the occasion, singing is almost universal. Number 14 I heard when a party of Twanas were camped and were tamahnousing for a fair wind for the day's journey (see Chapter XI, "Trips"). It was accompanied by the beating of the drum and pounding on sticks.

Numbers 15, 16, and 17 are Twana songs used when a medicine man is attempting to cure a sick patient. Number 17 had a kind of bass on the letter "c" in the same time. They are sung by all present, and with the same accompaniments as number 14. Number 18 was sung by the Twanas, and 19 and 20 by the Clallams at a religious dance, accompanied by the drum, number 20 being a solo to 19, the chorus. Number 21 is the chorus only of a Clallam song, sung at a black tamahnous performance. The solo varied so that I could not get it.

Numbers 22, 23, and 24 are black tamahnous songs of the Twanas. Generally, each of these three was begun by a leader, then another person took it up, the first one stopping, then all from twenty to forty persons joined in it, with a small drum and hollow wooden rattles, and lastly the large drum was used. The song was repeated several times, and it ended with a great *hi* or *ho* meaning "done." When 24 was sung, an extra voice sang a solo, higher and quite varied at times. Of the songs for dancing and tamahnous, I give the simpler ones, which I have heard. I have been unable to note the more varied ones before they would cease.

Work and love songs I have been unable to obtain.

Church songs. It has been found impracticable to translate our hymns into the Chinook Jargon languages, or to compose any that will rhyme. Hence, all that has been done has been to teach some truth that can be sung to one of our tunes.

In 1871 I prepared a small hymnbook in the Chinook Jargon language, which was copyrighted by G. H. Himes of Portland, Oregon, and published by him. A second edition, enlarged, he published in 1889. From its introduction I take the following:

> These hymns have grown out of Christian work among the Indians. They repeat often, because they are intended chiefly for Indians who cannot read, and hence must memorize them; but as soon as they learn to read, they sing in English. It will be noticed that often two syllables must be sung to one note. The chief peculiarity which I have noticed in making hymns in this language is, that a large proportion of the words are two syllables, and a large majority of these have the accent on the second syllable, which renders it almost impossible to compose any hymns in long, common or short metres.

With the assistance of some of the Indians I have also prepared a few in the Twana, Clallam, and Nisqually languages. Herewith I give one—not in the Chinook Jargon hymnbook—and one in each of the other languages, also one in the Snohomish dialect of the Nisqually language taken from a prayer book and catechism in that language by Rev. J. B. Boulet, Catholic priest on that reservation.

Chinook Jargon

Tune: "Saviour, breathe an evening blessing"

1. Saghalie Tyee, yaka mamook
   Konoway illahee, konoway kah. (Repeat both lines)

   Chorus: Yaka mamook, yaka mamook
              Konoway illahee, konoway kah.

2. Saghalie Tyee, yaka mamook
   Konoway tillikums, konoway kah. (Repeat both lines)

   Chorus: Yaka mamook, yaka mamook
              Konoway tillikums, konoway kah.

Translation

1. God made
   All the earth, everywhere.
   He made, he made
   All the earth everywhere.

2. God made
   All the people, everywhere.
   He made, he made
   All the people everywhere.

Other verses are made by changing the second word in the second and fourth lines to *iktas*, "things"; *muckamuck*, "food"; *moosmoos*, "cattle"; *kuitan*, "horses"; *tupso*, "grass"; and the like.

Twana

Tune: "The Hebrew children"
Dĭ-tcád, dĭ-tcád ká-owe klits Noah. (Repeat twice)
Ko-wá ate klits ái-ĭ tûb-bé hu.

Chorus: At-só-ĭ, at-só-ĭ hoi klĭs-hé-dab sûb-la-bad (Repeat twice)
         Ko-wá ate klits ái-ĭ-tûb-bé-hu

Translation
Where, where is Noah.
Far away in the good land.
Soon, soon we will go and see him,
Far away in the good land.

Other verses are made by substituting Moses, Daniel, Jesus, and similar names for Noah in the first line. Four hymns have been made in Twana.

Clallam

Tune: "John Brown"
1. Jesus tá-tcĭ tci-á-tci Teicl. (Repeat twice)
   Jesus tsi tu hatl.
2. Jesus kwâ-kwĭ á-tcu hêín-me. (Repeat twice)
   Jesus tsi tu hatl.
3. Jesus kẃâ-kwĭs aú-ĭts ká-kûng. (Repeat twice)
   Jesus tsi tu hatl.
4. Jesus kwâ kwĭs aú-ĭts ka-yatst. (Repeat twice)
   Jesus tsi tu hatl.

Translation

1. Jesus came from Heaven.
   Jesus is good.
2. Jesus taught the people.
   Jesus is good.
3. Jesus said, do not lie.
   Jesus is good.
4. Jesus said, do not steal.
   Jesus is good.

Six hymns have been made in this language.

Nisqually

O hatl sta-hél lt sahkweb etiêb
Tu-hwál te tsa hu le i-á kt-hwál kwe-shiêk
To-lal i hu as ga-kél djó-a hûte
s-ás i-áts ûds bûk hu aas kweb a hu tcatl.

Chorus: Hatl sla-hél, hatl, sla hél
         Al-kwe klos tsa-givûds ku-bûk tzû-ûś dzûk hu
         Tu-o-gosts hwal tzas hó-ĭ a hu klob.
         Tu-hwal hwe kl tz-as djo-el bûk sla-hél
         Hatl sla-hel hatl sla-hel
         Al-kwe klos tsa-kwûds ku-bûk tzû-ûs dzûk hu.

Translation

O happy day that fixed my choice
On thee my Saviour and my God.
From a shining heart
Tell its raptures all abroad.

Chorus: Happy day, happy day
         When he will wash my sins away.
         He taught me how to watch and pray
         And live rejoicing every day.
         Happy day, happy day,
         When he will wash my sins away.

Two have been made in this language by the Indians on the Snohomish reservation, and a number of others by the Squakson, Mud Bay, Puyallup, and other Indians, who speak Nisqually. Many of these are used quite extensively, some being sung to tunes, and some being chanted.

Snohomish

Hymn for the funeral of adults. "O Sherk Siam! O Sherk Siam!"

1. O dgwe hath Shehu! Tlabotebitobolh,
   Hob chahu o trod ku astilhtalbihu,
   Tolal di hud hoyud helle,
   Hoyud helle ku seles halgwa

   Chorus: Ashabit te v ate-ed
           At silhtalbihu ate stsilhdalbs

2. O dgwe hath Shehu! Rara Shesu Kri,
   Tlabotebitobolh vc.

Chorus: Ashabit te v ate-ed
        At silhtalbihu ate stsilhdalbs

XV
ART

<hr/>

THERE IS NO SPECIAL CLASS OF ARTISTS among them as there is among the tribes to the north in British Columbia; still, they make considerable work that is quite artistic on baskets, cloth, leather, wood, etc.[1]

Their work as a general thing does not equal that of more northern tribes, but is fully equal to that of the tribes east and south. Little, however, is wasted on the desert air or made merely for ornament, but it is generally put upon some useful article.

On Baskets

All of the figures on these are woven in with colored grass. . . .

The Clallams and tribes farther up the Sound import bottles made by the Makahs and Quinaielts, bottles of various sizes, from vials to quart junk bottles, covered with fine grasswork, which are beautifully figured. These are covered simply for the beauty of it or for sale.

On Cloth

The straps, with which they carry their baskets and other loads are ornamented by weaving different colored cloth strings into the strap as it is made. These are common to all the tribes on the Sound, and might be largely multiplied.

Their fancy rugs are also covered with figures, woven in. In the one drawn two dogs are seen; on others I have seen a dog, a tree, chicken, deer, and some soldiers. Many more illustrations might be given. In some of them the figures mean something and are quite distinct; in others, they mean nothing and are often blended together.

Their shot pouches of cloth are sometimes covered with bead work, though not often. It is said that formerly, after the whites first came, they ornamented with beads to a great extent, but of late the art is almost entirely neglected.

Pin cushions of patch work and patch work quilts, some of which are very artistic, are becoming common. I have seen a pin cushion made by an Indian girl, between the sides of a clam shell, which was well done. In mittens they often knit figures, though they are rarely of any significance.

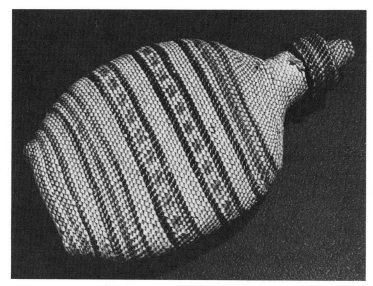

Grass woven-work covered bottle

Walking stick covered with grass woven work, Quinaielt

Carrying strap, Twana

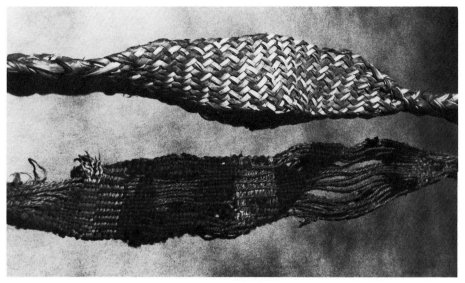

Carrying strap, Twana

Bead work on shot pouch

Drawing of rug design

228

Quiver front of beaded work (collected from Quinaielt but originally from eastern Plateau)

On Skin

On a very few Clallam drums, I have seen some painting. One seemed to represent nothing, being simply for ornament. Another had a deer. But paintings on leather are not common.

Taxidermy. A squirrel skin and a young bear skin, each stuffed quite neatly, the former with paper, the latter with straw, are the only specimens of taxidermy which I have seen among them.

Tattooing has been described in Chapter IX.

On Wood

Carvings. These are quite common. Sometimes it is done for mere amusement. Occasionally the handle of a fish spear is ornamented. On a long board, formerly on a house at Dungeness, were carvings which were supposed to represent moons and cats. No one now knows when they were made. An Indian, who had a grandson, married, said that they were there when he was a boy. They are flat, intaglio, half an inch deep. The house was destroyed a few years ago, and I secured a part of the board.

Occasionally they carve a person in wood for mere ornament. One woman at Skokomish has owned the wooden figure of a man thus carved, about 12 inches long and of proportionate size, dressed in white man's clothes. Her sister had its companion, a woman dressed like a white woman. These were carved by their father, a Port Madison Indian. A Clallam carved for me a man, about 9 inches long and dressed as they sometimes do when performing at their potlatches. He has on very little clothing. The face below the nose, the upper part of the chest, and the hair are painted red. The latter is done up in a knot which projects in front. He holds in his hands across his stomach a carved face.

A Twana man carved for me a small man, 6 inches long and dressed as Americans do. The same person also prepared for me the face and chest of a man. The face is about 8 inches long by 7 wide, and is a natural growth on a maple tree. It looked very much like an old Indian, so much so that he said he would fix it up for me if I wished. So he smoothed the face, a very little, put some brass headed nails in the eyes and nose, earrings in the ears, and put on a small body.

One canoe, formerly owned by a Twana, had on its head a carved figure, supposed to be a monkey in bas-relief, the joint of the foreleg being raised 1¼ inches, and that of the hind leg 2 inches, but the middle of the body is in very low relief. The figure appears the same on both sides of the prow. The canoe was obtained from the Haida Indians. It has been broken, but I obtained the head.

A Clallam chief at Elwha, Cultus John, had a few years ago two large side posts in his house, 2 to 2½ feet wide and 6 or 8 inches thick, each carved so as to represent a large man, one of whom held a frog in his hands. The work was excellently done by a regular carver of the Nittinat tribe of British Columbia. On account of the death of his son, the chief destroyed his house, but moved the posts to the grave, where they remained a few years. The last time I visited the place the chief had died, and the posts were gone. When he set them in the ground at the grave, he put them in nearly to the elbows. Above that, I made the following measurements. From the elbow to the top of the head was about 5 feet. The face was 32 inches long from the top of the forehead to the top of the chest, there being hardly any neck. It was 26 inches wide. The eyes were 3½ inches in diameter. The mouth was 9½ inches long. The lower part of the nose projected 5½ inches from the face.

The post was about 10 inches thick. One of the carvings represented a man, who held in his hands clasped on his stomach, a frog, 18 inches long by 11 wide. The other represented a woman, who was a trifle larger than the man. A mask was nailed on the side of the forehead of each, projecting in front, one representing the face and head of a pig, the other of a bird. Another opening and shutting mask was divided, one half being nailed on the other side of each forehead. . . .

Their wooden dishes are sometimes ornamented with carved figures. One which I have was imported by the Clallams from British Columbia. A part of the carving is intended to represent the head of the Thunderbird.

But the Haidas excelled all other tribes in carving. Their totem posts in wood and imitations of them in stone are renowned all over the United States and Canada.

Paintings. Both the Twanas and Clallams ornament the blade of their paddles sometimes, with paintings, most of which are meaningless, but sometimes they represent the owner's tamahnous.

One Clallam at Port Gamble had formerly a large canoe, which had painted on it something which seemed to be a double-headed alligator; but where the idea of such an animal was obtained, I cannot learn, unless it may have been from some picture. The figure was as long as the canoe, but only 8 or 10 inches wide. In the middle was the rough representation of a man's face, or possibly that of the Thunderbird—it was difficult to tell which.

A Twana man with paint drew three very good representations of ships on a post at a potlatch house about twenty-five years ago, which I have obtained. . . .

On Horn and Bone

A number of horn dishes, which the Twanas have imported from British Columbia and the Klikitat Indians, have carvings and carved lines traced on them, some of which represent faces, and some are meaningless—mere ornament. I think that the Skagits and Snohomish Indians, who roamed in the Cascade mountains, probably also made some of these. The spoons which accompany these dishes are carved somewhat similarly. A spoon which I obtained from a Twana Indian, but which came from a Quinaielt, had on its handle the head of a bird. A solitary Clallam bone shawl pin shows the heads of two birds at the head facing each other. . . .

so. That he said he would fix it up for me, if I wished. So he smothed the face, a very little, but some brass headed nails in the eyes, and nose, earrings in the ears, and but on a small body. See Frontispiece 37.

One canoe, formerly owned by a Twana, had on its head, a carved figure, supposed to be a monkey, in bas-relief. The joint of the fore-leg, being raised one and a quarter inches, and that of the hind leg two inches, but the middle of the body is in very

Fig 334. Carved man full size. Front view

Drawing of male wood carving

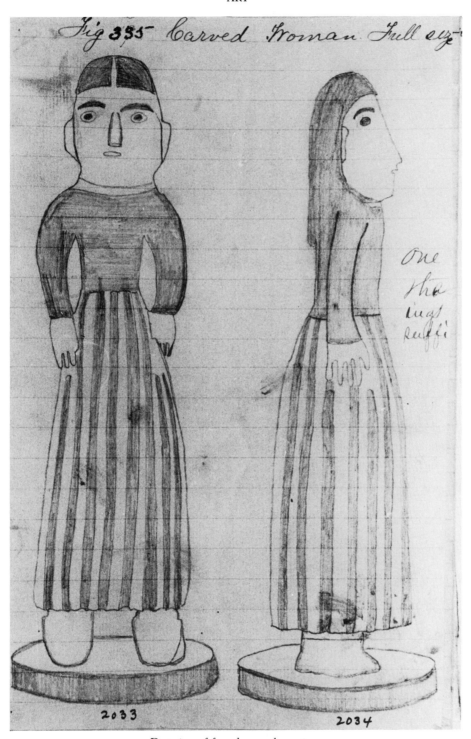

Drawing of female wood carving

Carving of a Clallam "in act of tamahnous"

Twana carving, partly natural

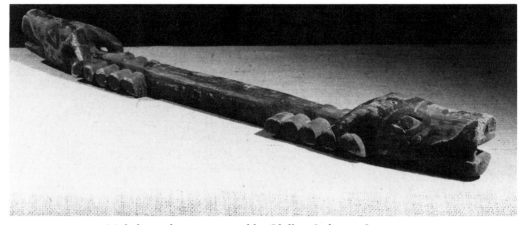

Makah wood carving owned by Clallam Indian at Jamestown
(Eells labels it as a tamahnous "handstick")

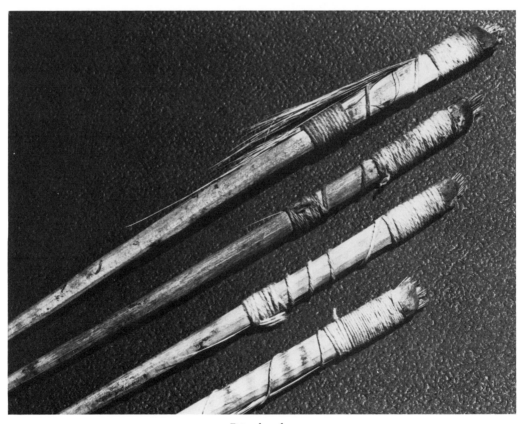

Paint brushes

Canoe head, Haida

Carving, wood body and metal wings

Carving on grease dish imported by Clallams from British Columbia

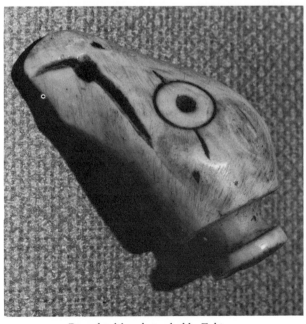

Bone bird head, probably Eskimo

On Metal

Their brass and iron shawl pin heads were often made in some artistic way. One has the figure of a bird on it, another that of two dogs facing each other. Those of others are meaningless. Their brass bracelets are also slightly ornamented. The silver bracelets, which a few of them obtain from the Makahs and British Columbia Indians, are very well ornamented with the head of the Thunderbird and other ornamentations.

The copper war club has also on its handle the head of the Thunderbird.

On Stone

A Clallam man carved for me for purely artistic purposes from a small piece of clay stone, an article about 4 inches long and ½ inch in diameter with a dog's face at one end and a man's face near the middle, and also a few other markings on it.

For a similar reason a Twana man carved out of similar material the body of an animal I am unable to name. The body is about 7 inches long, 1⅞ inches wide, and 1½ inches thick, with rather a straight neck. It has eyes, ears, and other marks on the body representing its shoulders and hips. Four wooden legs are inserted into four holes beneath. It has a tail of hair, a mane of red yarn, and a little white wool on its back.

At one time I found with a Clallam the same mentioned as above: a stone hammer, on which he had recently formed the head of an eagle, with also the figures of deer, fish, birds, and a dog. . . .

Clay stone carving, Clallam

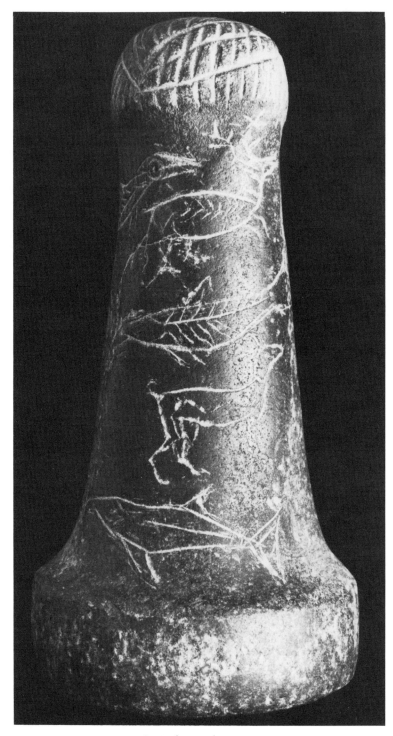

Incised stone hammer

On Paper

I have included a nondescript animal drawn by a Twana school boy. . . .

In 1879 I found with a Clallam man, Jim Quimmiak, at Clallam Bay, who had never been at school, an old book with over thirty drawings in it, some of which show good natural artistic ability. A number of these are inserted here.

In comparing the artistic work of the Twanas and Clallams, I am led to think that in basket and cloth weaving, the latter are the more skillful, and the Chehalis Indians excel the Twanas in this respect, both being excelled by the Quinaielt and Makahs on the coast. Both in carving and bead work the Clallams excel. This is not strange, as they have more intercourse with the skilled carvers of the northern tribes of British Columbia.[2]

Drawing by a Twana schoolboy, H. H. Robinson (1877)

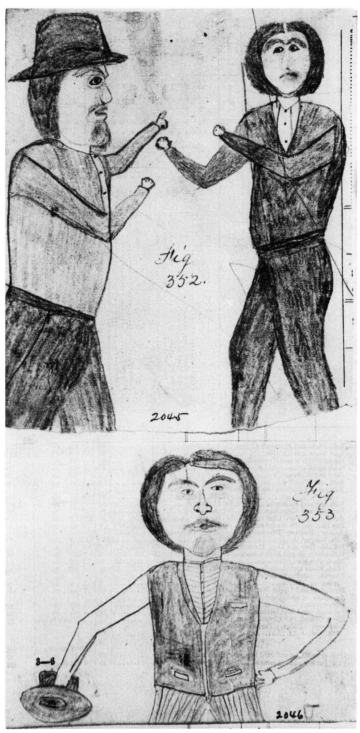

Samples of drawings by a Clallam, Jim Quimmiak

XVI

WRITING AND BOOKS

WRITING

The Indians had no system of writing before the whites came, nor have I ever seen any hieroglyphics in the region. The Clallam Indians have told me that on some rocks on the northern side of the Straits of Fuca in British Columbia, and, as I understand it, next to the water, are some drawings of deer, fish, and similar animals. I have never been able to visit them, nor can they tell me the meaning of them, if they have any. Southward, I have seen nothing of the kind until Patton's Valley in Washington County, Oregon, is reached, south of the Columbia river, far out of the range of these Indians.[1]

It has been found necessary to have all the schools in this region in English. It is the only practical plan, for two reasons. First, because of the large number of languages. Five belong to the Indians here described and there are five more spoken by those Indians who live on the coast: the Makah, Quillehute, Hoh, Quinaielt, and Lower Chehalis, besides the Cowlitz on the south. A population of about four thousand, with about five hundred and forty children, in school age, speak these eleven languages. The cost of reducing these languages to writing, of obtaining teachers in them, and of publishing books and papers in them, would plainly be so great as to prevent all schools. Second, nearly all the coming generation, whether or not the schools are taught in English, will learn to speak the language, even if they never go to school. Their contact with the whites now is so great that this will certainly be the case. I was a little surprised to find that at a game of baseball at Skokomish on July 4, 1885, in which about thirty persons were engaged, nearly all of whom were under thirty years, all talked English, with one or two exceptions, in their intercourse with each other. They represented the Twana, Nisqually, and Upper Chehalis languages. Even now more than one half of the four thousand Indians on the Sound are reported by their Agents as being able to talk English enough for ordinary intercourse.

These reasons have rendered it both wise and necessary for schools to be in English, though if circumstances were different, as among the Dakotas or in the Indian Territory, they might not apply.

Since the children have had the advantages of schools, they have written considerably, using the mails probably as much as white children of the same age. As the order in their languages is different from that in ours, it is very difficult for those who do not begin school until they are fifteen or eighteen years old to get our order or our spelling. Herewith I give some examples of the extremes in educations: letters which show the poor

243

side of those beginning to write and spell, and also one showing how well an Indian can do.

> I have write you a few lines. I tell you what have happen we have soon after you left John his child dead about 9 o'clock morning you left, he have little baby c h b (the chief) he been drunk and our teacher his punish him I want to know if you been tell Mr Eells about we want put out (the chief) all men his Dreary about-him all men said his, Dormitory n (and) I tell all men you displace hime all men said his very Disgrace now we all waiting if you letter come. all want get good acknoledge (knowl-edge or knowing) man and convert man soon you letter come and we convoke (as-semble) and we have employment (election) I am very glad if we have acknowledge man so he be able to encompass the drinking

> Now I be thinking about that Meloten (melodeon) I to know how be spell it I want to know the (way to play) I want to anybody to teach me. If you cannot found some-body here, Can I be go there learn that and I want like George have it book that little one the half dollar with.

> The Dezemper 15–85 Mr. B. Poltar (Butler) Please Lat (let) Nayalal hav the hors that yuo o (owe) me for that winchester for i hev but one from hem to Bay for the same. It has been so long now that i had (had) lat yu hiv the coun (gun) Bles (please) bay you the Balanz as soon as you wont it. [This was directed to Mr. Als (Eells).]

The report having come that a girl, absent from home at school, was sick, a letter of inquiry was sent asking if it were true. Her reply is noticeable for its repeating, and it is not the only letter which I have received which is peculiar in this respect, though all letters by no means repeat thus.

> I was very sorry to know that some Indians have been telling my father that I am sick, but you will find out that I am not sick at all. I am well and have not been sick for a long time. I am well all the time only last winter, but I have not been sick since last winter, so please tell father that I am well and happy, only sometimes I get lone-some for them. If I am sick I would write all at once and tell him, but as I am well I don't want him to feel uneasy about me. Dear Friend I feel bad for my father. I just know how he feels tell him that I am telling the truth that I am not sick. If I was really sick I would tell them that I am sick but I am sure that nothing is the matter with me. I am always ready to answer you when you write letters to me. My teacher told me to answer you right away and tell you that I am well. I was very much surprised to know that I was sick when I am not. I want my father to be sure of it that I am not sick, thats why I keep on saying that I am well. Only one girl from another Reservation was very sick, but now she is well so I suppose she is the one the Indians heard off. I know father is afraid I might die here when he heard I was sick. Everybody is well and I must close.

This one is a little singular for the big words in it. The writer has now outgrown this, and does well in his writing:

> I came home here last night about midnight. I found my parents in health. But I cannot say that all are well. Mrs. Tyee Charley is gone, no hopes are fresh of her

recovery. Quite a number of the Seabeck Indians are going over tonight to see her at Colcine Bay, as the patient desires to see her relatives before her anticipated departure to—Eternity. A few days ago a woman died in the same place, Colcine Bay, perhaps in the same part of the bay. Some suppositions from the relatives of the deceased that her husband put tamanamus to her and poisoned her. Such foolish faults are best to be unconcerned as they are not true. The young husband loved her with the truest of affection. They say that when he came to tell his brothers, that he could not speak a word when he sobbed, and as if his heart would break. Pretty soon the whole neighborhood were put to a great mourning, and when the mourning was over, the grief stricken husband wept, till he had no more power to weep. At nights often he would do the same. And why should he weep so, when he purposely caused the death of his wife. The friends of the deceased ought not to try to find such faults.

The Composition of an Indian Boy

A friend has written us as follows: "Some time ago, while on a visit to the Industrial School at Forest Grove, Oregon, the following composition was read by one of the boys from Puyallup. It being superior to anything in that line which I have heard from any of the Indians, I obtained a copy of it. Thinking that it might be worthy of publication and show what our Puget Sound boys are capable of, I sent it to you. . . .

The composition in full appears in the following:[2]

OUR DUTY AS STUDENTS

We were sent here by our parents to attend school in what they call a higher school than those on the reservations. We have not come here for pleasure and idleness, but for study and work, which we must accomplish in the best manner possible, because it is not for our personal benefit alone, but also for the Indian race.

We must make study a pleasure, and not a task, as much as we can.

There is a difference in this that may be noticed between the white people and most Indians, and that is this, that a white person is always eager to learn something new, while an Indian does not care about what there is around him that he does not know. I believe that this difference comes from the fact that a white man has always been learning and improving in learning from the things of nature, and that he is going higher and higher as time passes on, while an Indian has been constantly going backward in the past, and is still going down, though not as fast, just because he does not notice and learn from and about the little things which surround him.

You all know that the Indian question is very important to us who are Indians. Most of us know the importance of it and are trying to meet the demands of our ignorant people. We are representatives of the tribes to which we respectively belong. It is more important that Indian children should study hard than white children because they have their Indian parents and friends to benefit by their education. If we make this Indian school a failure by being lazy and indolent, it will be thought that Indians can never learn the ways of the white men, and hence cannot be educated like them. Many white men who do not like Indians say that an Indian can never learn the ways of the white men. If we are lazy and disobedient to our teachers, it will be so; but if we are diligent in our studies and industrious in our work, it will be far the better. It is necessary that we appreciate the great responsibility that is upon us while we are here; we cannot think of it too much; for if we do our duty here, it will decide the Indian question in our favor.

We must remember our parents, who sent us here, are ignorant of the benefit we come here for, and that it was very hard for them to let us come because they love us; and since they have let us come, they expect something that will be of great benefit to them when we go back. We must endeavor to meet their expectations, else they will not respect us nor care anything for us, and will not be willing to send any more of their children to this school or any other school. They will think that it wastes time for children to be in school when they ought to be at home helping them. We must bear in mind that most of us at least will never have another such opportunity as this to get what little education we can, and many a time will we regret that we did not study harder and improve our time more than we do. White people are fast coming over from Europe and from the Eastern States to the Pacific coast. It will not be long before this country is full of white people, and then it will be a thing of necessity for the Indian to be an equal of the white man in all things, so that he will not be cheated out of his land, his money or property.

There will be no more reservations, and an Indian will have to look after his own welfare. We have come here to learn to become as leaders, protectors, teachers and workers for our people, to guard them from the snares of bad white men. If we can only see the homes of the poorest of our people, after a long absence from them, and see the difference between the place in which we now live and that of the reservations, we would appreciate the necessity of our education far more than we do. Think of the dirt and filth in which most of our people live. This is what gives them their weak and ignorant minds, and consequently their poor judgment upon business affairs. They think that they can make more money by selling their land, which is not so. They do not think of the morrow, but only for the day and its pleasures. I have seen Indians who, when talked to kindly and in a persuasive manner by bad white men, yield to temptation and become slaves to some degrading and destructive habit, as whisky drinking, and lose their money, their property, and, in fact, everything else, besides their health, which is the worst of all. And why do they lose all this? It is because the white man has the advantage of him. He has all the education, while the Indian is ignorant of the harm that such a disgraceful and destructive habit does. Many of them are wicked and superstitious, and we ought to prepare to get them out of and above such things. All these things, caused by their ignorance, tend to destruction.

If God made us, and if we are fast going down to destruction and lessening in numbers by not obeying his laws, He has the power to bring us up again, if we obey his word. Most of us know that all this country was once owned by the Indians, before it was discovered by the white man, and that since the discovery the Indian has dwindled away, losing not only all the land, but almost his existence, which is far more precious to him than the riches of America.

This comes from the power of education over ignorance. The white man has now the possession of this whole country, and his knowledge and industry have given it to him. God created all mankind alike, and it is plain from this that an Indian can acquire as much knowledge and intellectual power as a white man or any other man of a different race can.

There is the negro, who was once as wild and as savage as any Indian is; and now after he has had the privileges of education, and associated with the white man, and learned from him the ways which lead to the success of life, he stands as his equal in knowledge and power. Why cannot the Indian do the same thing and reach as high a state of development as the negro can? It is partly because he is shut up on the reservations by himself, and kept like a prisoner, whereby he cannot see the real result of the white man's successes in life and civilization. How and why has he come to be shut up in these patches of land called reservations, when he was once himself the sole possessor of the whole land? It is because he has the bad habit of being lazy, and did not use the land in the way to get most benefit from it.

It now rests upon us who are here to do those things which are essential to success in life, and if we do it we can still save them from being blotted out as a nation from the face of the earth.

We go to school here at the expense of the Government, and we don't have to pay for our tuition, board, or anything else. This gives us the greatest advantages and privileges for learning how to be useful in the future.

White children do not have this advantage. They have to pay for their tuition, board, clothing, and everything else connected with going to school, and still they go with the utmost willingness and pay all this money, because they know that if they will not they will amount to nothing. We know that the good Christian man always has success and honor to follow his work, and that the bad man, although successful in some evil things, is not successful in good honest work. Take the whisky drinker for an example: as soon as he begins drinking, success is changed to failure for the rest of his life, as long as he does not quit drinking.

And now, which side has the Indian been on in the past, the right or the wrong side? I believe that he has been on the wrong side, partly because bad white men have taught him to be so, and partly because it is the easiest way for him to be. "If God be for us, who can be against us?" If we stand for the right, so much the better for the Indian race. God will always help us if we put our trust in Him; but if we stand on the wrong side, we are sure to go down. In order to be firm on the right side, we must have a good purpose, like Daniel had—a purpose for the right and not for the wrong; and if we trust in Him who is our Creator, we shall come out triumphant in the end.

I hope that you will each choose a good object to work for in your future. It will be for the benefit of your race as well as for yourself, and when you do choose such good purpose, remember that as long as you keep them you will be men and women among men and women.

We must always have the main object of this school fresh in our memory, and be attentive to the good and useful advice that is given us by our kind teachers and by friends who come to visit this school. It will be of great use to us in after lives and work.

It is necessary that we prepare in every way for this great work that is awaiting us. If we get proud, so that we do not want to go among our own people and help them in any and every way we can, we will do them no good and prove ourselves unworthy of our privileges. This we must remember, that even Jesus, the king and ruler of the universe, did not turn away from a leper, but healed him by touching his sores. There are many children on the reservations who need education in just such schools as this, and if we don't try as hard as we ought to, there are many of them that are brighter than we are and ought to be here in place of us who are lazy.

We need some of the white man's patriotism, love and respect for his country and fellow-men, in order to help our people with more earnestness and energy.

So you can now see, by what I have related to you, that there are some reasons why we should be very diligent in our studies and work. The secret of success in any undertaking is devotion. It seems to me we have the greatest reasons to be devoted to our work. Our very lives and those of our race depend upon our success. Our time is truly not our own. Let us beware how we use that which belongs to others. To succeed is life and light for us, and to send the rays of light to thousands of dark hearts. To fail is worse than destruction; it is eternal banishment from the presence of God, and the best way to save our race is by the word of God, the Bible and its teachings.

Samuel R. McGaw

The following is a letter or article, written by a Skokomish young man, Charles P. Waterman, for the *Weekly Argus* of Port Townsend.

Skokomish reservation. November 16, 1878

"Editor Argus: This piece is spoken by a boy sixteen years old. He can read and write, but just as his wishes are he wants me to write for him what he says. You will hear him as follows":

I am an Indian. I can read some, but I cannot say that I can read as well as a white man. I am very glad that white people learned me to read. If a number of boys should run a race, I would be the last one. I am not a good runner. You know how slow a snail goes, and I am almost as slow. If a horse and two snails ran a race, you know the horse can come ahead very far. If I and a snail ran a race for a mile, the snail would go half an inch, while I would go three quarters of a mile. White people say that the world is round like a bubble. I guess it is true. White people know a great deal. I cannot stand against a white man, and say that he (the white man) is not speaking the truth, when he says the world is round.

When I am on board a steamboat, it moves. I don't know how. And when one Indian gets ready to fight a great many white people, they take up old rusty guns, and load them, and fire against white people. I only a boy, am wiser than older Indians. I would not stand against white man with a rusty gun. And when they fight, they go behind rocks, and hide round like so many frightened rats, before cats—terrible eaters. Oh. I wished I was there when they go to fighting and I would tell them "Oh stop fighting, you will be swallowed up by the great eaters" (white people). And if they would not do as I please, I would tell them, "O you great fools, you are more foolish than monkeys, you are like little fleas biting an elephant leg, and then the big elephant got mad, and bit you: and you are gone, because you are small and have old rusty guns." I am a man too, but I would not fight. O, I would not fight, because I could not run fast, as I said before. If I was a big, tall man, my legs as tall as the fir trees, then I would fight. O, if every Indian think as I do, then peace and no war. If I would see a soldier, I would be like a dead man for fear. If they (soldiers) would march with swords and guns, I would run away. A monkey has no tumtum (mind). I always feel like laughing when I think of Indians trying to fight. Indians are like monkeys, don't know anything. If they go to war, they paint their faces in all kinds of colors, black or red. O gentlemen (whites) Indians are just like a show. Only I guess you always see a monkey. It always has a tail in a show. You see a monkey, and he does every ways, look around, scratch his face, just like Indians.

NEWSPAPERS

As Indians have become educated they have used the newspapers considerably. In 1874 John Palmer on the Skokomish reservation was taking the *Olympia Courier*, and before he died in 1881, he was taking five newspapers and magazines, both eastern and western. No others of the Twanas, I think, subscribed for any until 1877, when J. A. Atkins began to take the *Chicago Advance*, since which time a number of others have taken papers. The Clallams have done likewise, and the Puyallups have in general been in the advance in this respect.

PRINTING

As far as I know the Puyallups were the first to do any of this work. Before 1879 Peter C. Stanup of that tribe was setting type in the office of the *Tacoma Herald*, and occasionally furnished it with articles. The first which I saw of his was in 1878. In 1879 an Industrial Training school was established at Forest Grove, Oregon, for the benefit of all the tribes in Oregon and Washington. At that school a small paper was established in 1884, and the Puyallup boys in general took the lead in that work though other Indian boys also assisted.

At the Tulalip school the Snohomish children printed the *Youth's Companion*, also writing for it from 1881 to 1886. At the Puyallup reservation is also a printing press where the Indian pupils have done considerable printing.[3]

VOL. 4

XVII
LITERATURE

MYTHS

Thunder and Lightning

The general belief has been that these are caused by a great bird flapping its wings, and some point to trees that have been struck by lightning and say that the bird touched these trees and hence they were torn to pieces. Some say they have seen the bird, but others do not believe this. A fable by the Indians says that the Doswailopsh mountain had two wives: Mount Rainier was one, and a mountain near Hood's Canal was the other. Mount Rainier and this mountain quarrelled and Mount Rainier moved away, and now they always fight by thunder and lightning.[1]

The following in regard to this myth of the Thunderbird, by the writer, appeared in the *American Anthropologist* for October 1889, and although it had much which refers to other Indians than those on the Sound, yet is here inserted as connecting them in this respect with other Indians from Alaska to Central America and east to Maine.

THE THUNDER BIRD

By Rev. Myron Eells

Among the strange links which bind together the numerous tribes of Western America is the myth of the Thunder Bird. The general idea among the Indians is that thunder is caused by an immense bird, whose size darkens the heavens, whose body is the thunder cloud, the flapping of whose wings causes the thunder, and the bolts of fire, which it sends out of its mouth to kill the whale for its food, are the lightning. The Makahs and some other tribes, however, invest the animal with a twofold character, human and bird-like. According to them the being is supposed to be a gigantic Indian, named in the dialects of the various coast tribes Kakaitch, T'hlu-kluts, and Tu-Tutsh, the latter being the Nootkan name. He lives in the highest mountains and his food consists of whales. When he wants food he puts on a great garment, which is made of a bird's head, a pair of very large wings, and a feather covering for his body, and around his waist he ties the lightning fish, which slightly resembles the sea horse. This animal has a head as sharp as a knife, and a red tongue which makes the fire. He then flies forth, and when he sees a whale he darts the lightning fish into its body, which he then seizes and carries to his home. Occasionally, however, he strikes a tree and more seldom a man.

Authorities

For our knowledge of this bird we are indebted to Dr. W. H. Dall, in the Annual Report of the Bureau of Ethnology for 1881–'2; Oregon, by John Dunn; Mr. James Deans, in the American Antiquarian for 1885; Bancroft's Native Races of the Pacific; Mr. W. H. Holmes, in the Transactions of this Society for 1882–'3; especially to Mr. J. G. Swan, in his Makah Indians, Haida Indians, and Three Years' Residence in Washington Territory; and to Dr. S. R. Riggs, in his Gospel among the Dakotas.

Origin

The origin of the bird, according to Mr. Swan, as given by the Chehalis and Chinook Indians is as follows: "Ages ago an old man named Too-lux, or the south wind, while traveling north, met an old woman named Quoots-hooi, who was an ogress or giantess. He asked her for food, when she gave him a net, telling him that she had nothing to eat, and he must go and try to catch some fish. He accordingly dragged the net and succeeded in catching the grampus, or as the Indians called it, a little whale. This he was about to cut with his knife when the old woman cried out to him to take a sharp shell and not to cut the fish crossways, but split it down the back. Without giving heed to what she said, he cut the fish across the side and was about to take off a piece of blubber, but the fish immediately changed into an immense bird, that when flying completely obscured the sun, and the noise made by its wings shook the earth." They also add that this thunder bird flew to the north and lit on the top of the Saddleback Mountain near the Columbia river, where it laid a nest full of eggs. It was followed by the giantess, who found the eggs; whereupon she began to break and eat them, and from these mankind, or at least the Chehalis and Chinook tribes, were produced. The thunder bird, called Hahness by those Indians, came back and, finding its nest destroyed, went to Too-lux, the south wind, for redress, but neither of them could ever find the ogress, although they regularly went north every year.

The Cause of Thunder

As to the cause of thunder among these tribes, Mr. Swan says that when a young girl reaches womanhood she has to go through a process of purification which lasts a month. Among other customs at this time, if there is a southwest wind, with signs of rain, she must on no account, go out of doors, else the southwest wind is so offended that he will send the thunder bird, who then by shaking his wings causes the thunder, and from whose eyes go forth the flashes of lightning. As far as Mr. Swan knew, every thunder-storm which occurred while he lived at Shoalwater Bay, three years, was attributed by the Indians to this cause—that is, to some girl disobeying this law.

Superstitions

The Indians are very superstitious in regard to this bird, believing that if they possess any feather, bone, or other part of it, or bone of the lightning fish, it will be of supernatural advantage to them. A Makah, who had been very sick, was reduced to a skeleton, and it was believed could not recover, yet he managed to crawl one day, says Mr. Swan, to a brook near by, and while there he heard a rustling which so frightened him that he covered his face with his blanket. Peeping out he saw a raven near him, apparently trying to throw up something, and, according to the Indian, it did throw up a piece of bone about three inches long. The Indian secured this, believing it to be a bone of the thunder bird, and he was told by the Indian doctors that it was a medicine sent to him by his Tamahnous, or guardian spirit, to cure him. It was a fact that he did recover very quickly, perhaps through the effect of his imagining it to be such a bone and a strong medicine. It may also have been dropped there by the raven.

On one occasion, at a display of fire-works in Port Townsend, a number of rockets bursting showed fiery serpents. These the Indians believed belonged to the thunder bird, and offered large sums for pieces of the animal. They told Mr. Swan they would give two hundred dollars for a backbone of one.

A Quinaielt Indian once professed to have obtained a feather of one of these birds. He said he saw one of them light, and, creeping up softly, tied a buckskin string to one of its feathers, and fastened the other end to a stump. When the bird flew away it left the feather, which was forty fathoms long. No other Indian saw it, for he was careful to keep it hid, but the possession of it was not questioned by the rest, as he was very successful in catching sea otter. According to the Makahs, one of the principal homes of the bird is on a mountain back of Clyoquot, on Vancouver Island, where is a lake, and around it the Indians say are many bones of whales which the bird has killed.

Thunder-Bird Performance

Many of the Northwestern Indians have a performance in honor of this thunder bird, which is called the thunder-bird performance or "black tamahnous." It is said to have originated with the Nittinat Indians, according to the following legend as recorded by Mr. Swan: Two men had fallen in love with the same woman, but she would not give either the preference; whereupon they began to quarrel. But one of them, of more sense than the other, said: "Do not let us fight about that squaw. I will go and see the chief of the wolves and he will tell me what is to be done, but I cannot get to his house except by stratagem. Now they know we are at variance; so do you take me by the hair and drag me over these sharp rocks, which are covered with barnacles, and I shall bleed and pretend to be dead, and the wolves will come and carry me away to their house." This was done; but when the wolves were ready to eat him he jumped up and astonished them by his boldness. The chief wolf was so much pleased with his bravery that he taught the man the mysteries of the thunder-bird performance. This, the most savage of all the Indian ceremonies, spread among all the Indians on Puget Sound, as well as to the north, the latter being the most savage in the performance of the ceremonies. Among other things, the performers hoot like owls, howl like wolves, paint their bodies black, especially the face, from which fact, in whole or in part, comes the English name "black tamahnous"; scarify their arms, legs, and sometimes the body, so as to bleed profusely, in remembrance of its origin; they make much noise, by firing guns, pound on drums to represent thunder, flash torches of pitchwood about as a representation of lightning, and whistle sharply in imitation of wind.

The ceremonies, however, vary in different tribes, being much more savage and bloody in some than in others. Among the Makah five days are usually occupied in secret ceremonies, such as initiating candidates and other performances, before any public outdoor ceremonies take place. Among the Clallam the candidate for initiation is put into a kind of mesmeric sleep, which does not appear to be the case with the Makahs. Among the Clallam, however, the secret ceremonies are not always as long as among the Makahs, as the only time the writer ever witnessed the public exercises he was admitted very soon after they began, though there were secret ceremonies during the whole five days of the performance, in a house or behind a blanket. The affair closes with a general distribution of presents to the invited guests.

Traditions

Some traditions, especially of the Indians of British Columbia, make this thunder bird the Creator of man, if not of the world. Bancroft, in his *Native Races of the Pacific*, says that one tradition of the origin of the Ahts makes them the direct descendants of Quaw-te-aht (their Creator or deity) and an immense bird that he married, the Great Thunder Bird, "To-tooch," the flapping of whose wings shook the hills with thunder (too-tah) and whose forked tongue sent the lightning across the sky.

Another tradition about Mt. Edgecomb, near Sitka, says that Chethl—i.e., the thunder or big lightning, who can swallow a whale without difficulty—had a sister who climbed to the top of the mountain, and it opened and she fell through, leaving the great hole or crater open—as the world is a great flat plate, supported by a pillar which she guards from evil spirits. He now makes the thunder, and she hears him but never sees him.

The inland Tinne say that the world at first existed as a long ocean, frequented only by a great bird, the beating of whose wings was thunder and its glance lightning. It flew down and touched the water; whereupon the earth rose. It touched the earth and every living creature rose except the Tinne, who owe their origin to the Dog. It also gave to the Tinne a peculiar arrow, which they were to preserve with special care. They however failed to do so, but misappropriated the sacred shaft to common use; whereupon it flew away never to return, and the Golden Age of the Tinne was gone forever—an age when men lived until their throats were worn through with eating and their feet with walking.

Most of the natives of Alaska, except the Koniagas, believe in Yehl, the Raven, as their great Creator and the Creator of most things, and many traditions are told of him.

He is their great Deity, and he is also the author of thunder and lightning.

Figures

Representations of the thunder bird are made on various articles by the Indians, to encourage them in bravery and to insure the protection of that bird, or the like. These, when fully drawn, usually consist of a great bird, somewhat hideous, with a large fish near it, but often only the head and eyes are pictured.

Mr. J. Deane, in the *American Antiquarian* for November, 1885, gives a picture of one on the front of an Indian chief's house at Alert Bay, Vancouver's Island, B.C. It is standing on the skeleton of a killer whale, whose bones he is supposed to have picked. Long ago, when these whales were abundant, the Indians were afraid of them when out in their frail canoes. Knowing the thunder bird to be their enemy, the

Indians painted it on their houses, and even on their bodies, to secure its protection.

Dr. Dall, in the Annual Report of the Bureau of Ethnology for 1881–'2, gives an illustration of a mask of the bird form, obtained by Commodore Wilkes from the northwest coast of America, symbolical of the thunder bird. The brows and bill are black, and the caruncle over the eyebrows, and the tongue within it, are red, and it is trimmed with swan skin having the down attached. The same writer gives another illustration of one obtained by Mr. Swan from Bella Bella, B.C. The paintings on it are quite different from those on the previous ones. This form of mask is quite common, as they are used by the Indians in their black tamahnous ceremonies.

Mr. Swan, in his "Makah Indians," and also in his "Haida Indians", gives pictures of this bird. In the former work (p. 9) the bird is standing on the whale, with the lightning fish near by. On pages 69, 70, he gives illustrations of seven masks used in the thunder-bird performance, five of which represent the human face, and the other two the heads of birds. In some of these the eyes and lower jaw are movable, so that by means of a string the eyes are made to roll about and the jaws to clatter in a hideous manner. Most of these are made by the Clyoquot and Nittinat Indians, of British Columbia.

In the latter work Mr. Swan gives a representation of the thunder bird which was taken from the cape of a medicine man and which was brought from Sitka. The whale's head and lightning fish are here represented, but differing markedly from the other pictures referred to. Another picture is given, which was copied from the tattoo marks on a Haida Indian, and in this the thunder bird appears more in the form of a man, or half man and half bird, sitting down, but without the whale or lightning fish.

The writer has a stone war-club, also one of copper, and the handle of a third of bone. On the handles of all of these are the eyes of the thunder bird, to inspire the warrior with courage, and perhaps to protect him from the enemy. These clubs were obtained among the Clallam and Skokomish Indians. There is also on the Skokomish reservation a large stone, which weighs several tons, on which in bygone days have been made the eyes and nose of the thunder bird, the eyes being about six inches in diameter. The Indians formerly believed that when from any cause this stone was shaken it would cause rain. In his "Ten Years at Skokomish" (pp. 38–42) are given illustrations of three masks used by the Clallam Indians in the black tamahnous or thunder-bird performance, one of which represents the face of a bird, and another that of a hog. These were made by British Columbia Indians. They are generally painted quite fancifully. Sometimes the bird masks are three feet long, and made so that their mouth will open very wide. Two illustrations are also given of rattles used in these ceremonies, one of which, and by far the most common one used, is in the shape of a bird.

Extent of Belief in Thunder Bird

Mr. Swan says he has traced this belief from the Chinook Indians, at the mouth of the Columbia, to Sitka. Dr. Dall says it is known to extend as far north as Prince William's Sound, and Mr. E. W. Nelson declares that it exists among the Innuit on the shores of Behring Sea, and has proved his point by showing a carving of the bird from the Diomede Islands in Behring Strait. To the south, ancient Mexican mythology is said to have included a belief in such a creature. The Quichés of Guatemala, however, varied it so as to make Hurakan, the god of thunder, have a messenger bird, named Voc. The tradition of the inland Tinne, of British America, who live near the western shores of Hudson's Bay, two thousand miles from the Pacific coast, has been given. In the United States the tradition crosses the Rocky Mountains, for among the Dakotas, according to Mr. W. H. Holmes, the storm bird dwells in the upper air beyond human sight, and carries on its back a lake of fresh water. When it winks its eyes there is lightning, when it flaps its wings there is thunder, and when it shakes its plumage there is rain.

Dr. Riggs adds that this thunder god is a being of terrific proportions, in shape somewhat like a bird. As it flies, hid by the thick clouds, the lightnings flash forth and the thunder is its voice. There are four varieties, and they are male and female. One is black, with a long beak, and has four joints in each wing. Another is yellow, without any beak at all, and with wings like the first, but it has only six quills in each wing. The third is of a scarlet color, and has eight joints in each of its great wings. The fourth is blue and globular, with neither eyes nor ears. In place of the eyebrows are semi-circular lines of lightning, from beneath which project downward two chains of lightning, zigzagging and diverging as they descend. Two plumes of soft down serve it for wings. The home of this family of gods is at the western extremity of the earth, on the summit of a beautiful mound, which is on a high mountain. The dwelling opens toward the four cardinal points, and at each doorway is stationed a watcher— a butterfly at the east, a bear at the west, a reindeer at the north, and a beaver at the south. Each of these sentries is enveloped, except the head, in scarlet down, very soft and beautiful. These are gods of war, ever on the warpath. They are ruthless, cruel, and destructive, and a deadly enmity exists between them and the gods of the waters.

Thus we see that this singular belief, varied somewhat in different localities, yet based upon the same underlying idea, is widespread, and is found among tribes of very diverse languages.

Since writing the above I have found in DeSmets, *Oregon Missions* (New York, 1847, p. 352), that the Pottawotomie Indians say that "the thunder we hear is the voice of spirits, having the form of large birds, which Nanaboojoo has placed in the clouds. When they cry very loud, we burn some tobacco in our cabins to make them a smoke offering and appease them."[2]

In the *Transactions* of the Victoria Institute, vol. 21 (London 1888), Rev. S. D. Peet says, "Take for instance the bas-reliefs of the temple of the cross at Palenque, and see how nature worship expresses itself there. Here is the cross, with its four points of the compass, or the four winds with its arrow signifying the lightning, the thunder bird, surmounting it and before the cross, a priest offering a child, or the figure of a child, in sacrifice."

In the Annual Report of the Bureau of Ethnology for 1882–83 (pp. 188–91), Lt. G. Mallery gives several illustrations of the Thunderbird among the Dakotas.

In the Annual Report of the same Bureau for 1880–81 (p. 5), Mrs. Erminnie A. Smith speaks of the thunder god of the Iroquois as having wings and flying, though sometimes having the appearance of a man (see also, pp. 52–58).

Dr. F. Boas, in the *American Anthropologist* for October 1889 (p. 326), speaks of the Thunderbird among the Nanaimo Indians of British Columbia, and A. F. Chamberlain in the same magazine for January 1890 (pp. 51–54), has an article on the same subject, in which he speaks of the same belief among the Algonkian tribes; the Crees; the Hudson's Bay Indians; the Pottawotamies, quoting in regard to them from J. McLean's *Indians: Their Manners and Customs*; the Ottawas, quoting from E. F. Wilson's *Forest Children*; the Ojibeways, quoting from Peter Jones' history of that tribe; the Kississaquas of Ontario; the Passamaquody Indians, quoting from Leland's *Algonquin Legends of New England*; and the Tetons, Omahas and Ponkas, quoting from J. Owen Dorsey in the *Journal of American Folk Lore*, vol 2 (pp. 135, 136).

In the *American Anthropologist* for January 1894, F. H. Cushing speaks of the same among the Zunis of New Mexico (p. 112), and gives an illustration of the flint-plumed God of War and the thunderbolt, painted on a shield.

The Sun

The Twanas have the following two legends in regard to the origin of the sun.

First. A woman had a son, who ran away from home. After a little while she went after him but could not find him. Her people went after her, found her, and brought her back. They did not know what became of her son, until a short time afterward, they beheld him, having been changed into the real sun, coming up from the east. This is the origin of the sun.

Second. A woman having no husband had a son, who being left in the charge of its grandmother, who was blind, was stolen by two women, who carried him very far away, where they brought him up. He grew very fast and became their husband. His children were the trees, the cedar tree being the favorite one. His mother in the meantime sent messengers, the cougar, panther, and some birds, who went everywhere on the land searching for him, except to this place, where they could not go on account of a very difficult place in the road, which was liable to come together and crush whatever passed through. At last the bluejay made the attempt, and was almost killed, being caught by the head, nearly crushing it and thus causing the top-knot on it. It, however, found the son, a man grown, and induced him to leave his present home and return to his mother.

When they came to this difficult place in the road, he fixed it, and did good wherever he went. When his mother found that he was lost, at first she was very sorry and gathered his clothes together, pressed from them some water—urine—and wished it to become another boy. Being very good, her wish was granted. He was a little boy when his older brother returned. They were both somewhat like God, in that they could do what they wished. The older brother said to the younger one, "I will make you into the moon to rule the night, and I will be the sun to rule the day." The next day he arose in the heavens, but was so hot he killed the fish in the sea, causing the water to boil, and also the men on the land. Finding that this would not do, he retired, and his brother tried to be the sun, and succeeded as the sun is at present, while the other brother became the moon to rule the night.

The Clallams have the following tradition: A long time ago there was only one woman in the world, but no man. She made a man of gum and set him up and wished him to become alive and to be her husband. She went to sleep and life came to him. Being of gum, he was very sensitive to the heat of the sun, which was much hotter then than now. He worked when it was cool and rested in the shade when it was hot. He had some children. One day he went fishing and told him wife to look out for him if it became hot; but she went to sleep and did not do so, and the heat grew intense and melted him, and he died. His sons were very angry at the sun for this; one of them made a bow and very many arrows. He shot them up towards the sun and they formed a chain or rope on which the boys ascended and found a prairie land. They asked the geese, who could then talk, "Where is the man who killed my father?" and the geese pointed in one direction and said "Yonder."

The boys went in the direction indicated, and came to a house where two blind women lived, and they sat down. As one woman gave some food to her companion one of the boys took it. "Have you received your food?" said the first woman to the other. The latter replied "No," and both wondered what had become of it. Soon one of the boys said he had taken it and asked, "Where is the man who killed my father?" The woman replied, "Farther on," and gave them a very small basket in which were six salmon berries. The boys went on and soon found some swallows which could talk, and again they asked, "Where is the man who killed my father?" The swallows said, "In yonder house." The pair went to the house and found an old man piling pitch wood on a very hot fire, so hot it nearly roasted the boys, and this was what made it hot on the earth. They gave the old man the six salmon berries, which became very many and swelled within him and killed him. The fire then went down somewhat, and it has not been so hot on the earth since.

They supposed that the sun really rose and set, and had no idea that it remained stationary and that the world revolved, until the whites came.

The Clallams worshipped the sun, believing it to be Deity. In this respect they agreed with some tribes east of them, as the Spokanes, Blackfeet, and others; but I have never been able to detect any trace of sun-worship among the other tribes of the Sound, whom I have questioned on the subject.

Wind

This they supposed was caused by the breath of a great being, who blew with his mouth. In this they reasoned from analogy, as a man can cause a small wind with his mouth.

Cold

Cold, they supposed, was caused by our getting farther away from the sun in the winter. They supposed the sun to be much farther off when it is low than when it is high, that the cold regions are far away from the sun, hence that we are near these cold regions in the winter.

Eclipses

An eclipse of the sun—almost annular—occurred about 1875, which gave me an opportunity to learn some of their ideas about it. As near as I can learn, they formerly believed that a whale was eating the sun. At the time of the eclipse, several women and old persons told me that they stopped work, went home, and prayed in their minds to God. Many wished to know what I thought was the cause of it.

PROVERBS

Of the Clallams

Do not laugh at an old man, if you do, and he laughs at you, you will die.

Do not steal a woman in the day time or the sky or sun will see you and you will die, but you may steal her at night, if she is not another man's wife.

Of the Twanas

When anyone plays with you, you must never say naughty words to him.

Do not sit on a rock. If you do, you will not grow fast. (Not true.)[3]

Do not point at the rainbow; if you do, the finger which you raise for this purpose will become sore. (Not true.)

Honor your father and your mother.

Never see an old person going to carry water, without getting the bucket and going in their stead.

Never laugh at the aged. If you do, they will curse you; but if you do not, they will bless you.

When you hear a man telling his son to be good, go and listen, and do as he says. "As an example of this teaching," wrote a school boy to me, "I will relate the following. There were two boys, who were playmates. One said that his parents always talked bad to him, and he never felt happy. The other said that his parents always talked good to him, and he always felt happy. Afterwards the latter went near the house of the former, when his parents were talking to him. He listened to all that was said, kept the advice, and did as was said. He was a good boy, while the other was a bad one, and what the bad boy called a bad talk, was a good one." The same informant put the words "not true" in parentheses, at the close of two of the above proverbs.

FABLES

The pheasant and the raven. The raven had a trap and caught very many fishes, but would not give any to the pheasant. At last the pheasant went to hunt deer. While he was on his way a deer met him, driven by a man. The pheasant killed it, and when he was skinning it the man stood watching him and said, "Well, pheasant, you can shoot straight"; but the pheasant thought it was not so. So when the man saw that the pheasant was not proud, he said the latter would be able to carry the deer nearly home, only when he should almost reach his house it would become very heavy. And so it was; for when he was almost home it became so heavy that he could not carry it. He laid it down, and his wife came and helped him.

When the raven heard that the pheasant had killed a deer he sent his sons to carry some fishes to the pheasant, so that he might receive some meat in return; but when they were going into the pheasant's house the pheasant drove them out. Then the raven told his children to fight with the children of the pheasant, and they had a battle. The raven's children threw fishes at the pheasant's children, who, in return, threw the grease of the deer at the raven's children. The raven sat between the two armies, and when the little pheasants threw any grease the raven caught it and ate it. After a time the raven went to hunt deer. While he was travelling he met and shot a deer, driven by the same man the pheasant had met. While he was skinning it the man, acting as if he was surprised, said, "The raven can shoot straight." The raven was proud, and said, "I can shoot straight, because I am a raven." When the raven was about to carry the deer home, the man said that when he should nearly reach his house it would turn into something else. So, when the raven had almost got home, he dropped his game and went and told his wife where to find it. She went to the place where he had left the deer, but when she arrived she found it had all turned to rotten wood.

A woman and her husband. At one time there was a woman living at her father's house, and after a while a man came by night and took her for his wife, but soon afterwards he deserted her. After a time she took some of her father's slaves and went to the other side of the water to hunt for the man, but was unable to find him. So she started for home, but after having gone some distance she looked down on the bottom of the canoe and saw a man smiling at her. She knew it was her husband; he pulled her down, and the slaves saw her no more. Some time afterward she made a visit to her parents. At a second visit a child was born to her. On a third visit her face was covered with some kind of moss. During her second visit her parents wished to deceive the man, hence they took a slave with a face exactly like that of the married woman and started to carry her to the man, but a sea-gull cried out and said it was not the right woman, so they took the true wife and restored her to her husband. This man killed a great many fishes and sent them to his father-in-law. After a time the woman died and there was afterwards heard a voice crying, which was the woman's voice. When this woman's tribe go off to sea they always capsize. (Some Indians believe this to be true.)

A Quilceed Indian and a wolf. One day a woman espied a wolf swimming across Quil-ceed Bay. She told her husband, who, wishing to have the skin, went to kill the wolf, but his wife begged him not to do so. The man rowed out to the wolf and patted him on the head with his paddle. The wolf looked at him and threw his ears back as if he would beg for his life. At last they both reached the shore, when the wolf did not run away from the man, but stood on the shore and looked at him with his ears back. The man, then wishing to deceive the wolf, said, "I do not want to kill you but was afraid you might drown, so I came to help you across. Now, for a reward, I ask this: You must drive as many deer to me as you can." So the wolf went into the woods and drove home deer until the man's house was filled with meat. Every time the wolf came home he would drive home a deer.

The taming of two young wolves. There was once a great hunter (who the narrator said was his father's brother), who, at one time when out hunting, found two young wolves which he thought he might tame so that they would assist in hunting deer. He brought them home, and when they were partly grown he took them out. While they were going along they found the mother wolf, and as the man wished the cubs to grow fast, he took her, too. After that the hunter never failed to kill deer. "This," said the narrator, "only shows how animals can understand and act well to those who are kind to them."

Although there is something fabulous in the former of these last two stories, if not in both, they may show how the Indian dogs were first obtained by domesticating wolves.

Dentalia. They also say that a long time ago a man who lived at Union City, and was very successful in catching porpoises, had a brother who was his enemy, who lived up the river, and who tried to injure him but could not. This brother especially tried to injure him by seeking to prevent his catching porpoises, but could not. Failing in this, he made a wooden porpoise, put his tamahnous into it, and put it into the water, where he thought his brother would catch it. His brother at Union City found it, and, thinking that surely it was a porpoise, caught it; he found really that it was too strong for him and that he was caught by it, for it took him north under water to the unknown place where ducks live in summer, which is also inhabited by a race of pigmy men a foot or two high, between whom and the ducks there is war. He helped the pigmies, killed many ducks and ate some, whereupon the pigmies called him a cannibal and became enraged at him.

At last a whale caught him and brought him back nearly to Union City. He very much wished to be thrown out on dry land or in shallow water near the land. But his wish was not granted, for by some means the whale vomited him up in deep water, and he swam to land. This is the reason why the dentalia, the species of shell formerly used as money, are found in deep water, for they were vomited up with him. If his wish had been granted, and he was thrown on dry land or in shallow water, they would have been found there.

A dog. They have a tradition of a dog that was bad, which swam from Eneti to Union City and back nearly to the graveyard, a distance of about five miles, and was turned into a long rock, now lying there.

Serpents. The following I wrote for the *Seattle Post-Intelligencer* (July 18, 1885):

Among the Skokomish Indians of Puget Sound there is a superstitious fear of snakes. The tradition is that a long time ago they were not afraid of them, but that an Indian killed a large one, as it were, a chief among the snakes. Then all the small snakes attacked the man, fastened themselves on his nose, mouth, ears, eyes, and many other places, bit him and killed him. Hence now the Indians are afraid of them and will not kill them.

One day an old woman started from my house to go home, but, after going four or five rods, came back and said she was afraid to go, as there was a snake across the walk. I went with her and saw it. It was a small, harmless reptile, apparently half grown, about a foot long. Yet, although I was with her, she went a long distance around it. A strong man once told me that he was afraid to kill one. There are no venomous snakes in this region.

It is a singular fact that in various places in America the snake has been greatly feared or worshipped.

When Mexico was discovered, Montezuma at one time showed Cortez his gods. Among these was an idol which was covered with gold and jewels, and its body bound with gold serpents. In a collection of Mexican antiquities, which was taken to England by a Mr. Bullock, the cast of a terrible idol was shown, which consisted of a huge serpent coiled in an irritated position, with jaws extended, and gorging itself with a woman.

Like the Hindoos, they also kept live snakes as household gods in their private dwellings. Among the paintings of the Aztecs, found in Mexico, two have been preserved in which a figure is drawn smiting a serpent on the head. A similar but more expressive painting occurs in the Borgian collection, where a figure is represented as victoriously smiting the serpent's head, at the same time that the serpent is biting his heel.

A number of these Aztec images or idols, with serpents in various positions, are in the Smithsonian archaeological collections at Washington. Among the sculptures discovered in Guatemala are some which have serpents in connection with priests, prayers and sacrifices.

A strange mount had been found among the works of the ancient mound builders at Fort Ancient, in Ohio. It is in the shape of two large serpents, each three-quarters of a mile long. They are in the act of attacking each other. What form of government or system of priesthood devised them is unknown, but the fact remains that they are there, the relics of that ancient race.

Rev. W. H. Brett, in his mission work in Guiana, says that there is an inveterate hatred between the people there and the snakes, so that the people kill all the snakes they can, even the harmless ones.

When we go to the Old World, we find the same to be true. In the mythology of ancient Babylon the temple of Belus contained an image of Juno holding in her right hand the head of a serpent. In that of ancient Persia the god Mittras was always represented encircled by a serpent. In Java the ruins of temples were found by Sir S. Raffles adorned with serpent images. In Abyssinia the first king was said to be a serpent, and serpent worship prevailed there until the people were converted to Christianity. In ancient Britain serpents were held in peculiar reverence, and its image still remains on obelisks in the neighborhood of Aberdeen, Dundee and Perth. The story of St. Patrick banishing them from Ireland is well known.

But in India the most precise and singular forms of serpent mythology are preserved. Houses are built for and dedicated to them. They are religiously fed and tended, while the Cave of Elephants and other temples are sculptured with gods holding serpents in their hands. And Maurice, in his history of India, gives pictures copied from the originals, in which Krishna is enfolded by a serpent, which is biting his heel, and he is trampling on its head.

Ants. I was once telling a Clallam the story of the creation, and among other things told him that darkness covered the face of the earth. When I was done, he said that they had a tradition, that after the world was created, it was covered with darkness; that the ants, who then had well-proportioned bodies and waists, were sorry for this, and wished for light; but as it did not come, they girded themselves and danced before the Creator, hoping in this way to obtain more light, dancing being their old form of worship. Still light did not come. They were so anxious for light that they could not stop to eat, and as their stomachs became empty, they girded themselves more and more tightly, until they were reduced to their present form with small waists.

The flood. Many of the Indians on this coast have a tradition of a Deluge. The Twanas on Puget's Sound speak of it, and say that only good Indians were saved, though there were quite a number of them. It occurred because of a great rain, and all the country was overflowed. The Indians went in their canoes to the highest mountains near them, which is in the Olympic range; and as the waters rose above the top of it, they tied their canoes to the tops of the trees on it, so that they should not float away. Their ropes were made of the limbs of the cedar trees, just as they sometimes make them at the present time. The waters continued to rise, however, above the tops of the trees, until the whole length of their ropes was reached, and they supposed that they would be obliged to cut their ropes and drift away to some unknown place, when the waters began to recede. Some canoes, however, broke from their fastenings and drifted away to the west, where they say their descendants now live, a tribe who speak a language similar to that of the Twanas. This they also say accounts for the present small number of the tribe. In their language, this mountain is called by a name which means "Fastener," from the fact that they fastened their canoes to it at that time. They also speak of a pigeon which went out to view the dead. I have been told by one Indian that while this highest mountain was submerged, another one, which was not far distant from it and which was lower, was not wholly covered.

Whether any Indians to the southwest, south of the Columbia river, ever belonged to this tribe, it is difficult now to say. I doubt whether these languages show enough resemblance to warrant such a belief. Still, the Tillamook and Siletz Indians belong to the Salishan family.

The name of this highest peak, which was submerged, is E-latl, and the name of the lower one, which was not covered, is Du-hwe-hwa-kwud-bit in the Twana language. According to them the water was not level. They also report that the pigeon did not die, but after the flood went forth to view the dead.

Another Indian added the following. Dokibatl, a legendary hero, sent this flood to wash the earth about a hundred years ago. At first the people tied their canoes to a low mountain, but as the waters rose, the mountain took pity on them and rose also. They went to sleep and slept a hundred days, when the tamahnous of one man waked him up and bade them descend, as the flood had subsided. When they looked, they saw that the land was dry. When they came down, they saw a single pair of deer, a male and a female. Some said, "Let us kill them," but others said, "No, Dokibatl has sent them to us, and we ought to let them increase." They did so. The same is true of the bear, elk, and other animals.

The Clallams, whose country adjoins that of the Twanas, also have a tradition of a flood, but some of them believe that it is not very long ago, perhaps not more than three or four generations since. One old man says that his grandfather saw the man who was saved from the flood, and that he was a Clallam. Their Ararat, too, is a different mountain from that of the Twanas.

The Lummi Indians, who live very near the northern line of Washington Territory, also speak of a flood, but I have not learned any particulars in regard to it.

The Puyallup Indians, near Tacoma, say that the flood overflowed all the country except one high mound near Steilacoom, and this mound is called by the Indians, "The Old Land," because it was not overflowed.

"Do you see that high mountain over there," said an old Indian to a mountaineer, as they were riding across the Cascade Mountains about seventeen years ago. "I do," was the reply. "Do you see that grove to the right?" the Indian then said. "Yes," said the white man. "Well," said the Indian, "a long time ago there was a flood, and all the country was overflowed. There was an old man and his family on a boat or raft, and he floated about, and the wind blew him to that mountain, where he touched bottom. He stayed there some time, and then sent a crow to hunt for land, but it came back without finding any. After some time he sent the crow again, and this time it brought a leaf from that grove, and the old man was glad, for he knew that the water was going away."

I also add a few traditions I have gathered from other tribes this side of the Rocky Mountains.

The Yakima Indians also have their traditions, but at this time, writes Rev. J. H. Wilbur, their agent and missionary, it is impossible to tell what was their original tradition and what has been mixed with it from the early teachings of missionaries who were with them thirty or forty years ago.

When the earliest missionaries came among the Spokanes, Nez Peres, and Cayuses, who with the Yakimas live in the eastern part of the Territory, they found that those Indians had their tradition of a flood, and that one man and wife were saved on a raft. Each of those three tribes also, together with the Flathead tribes, has their separate Ararat in connection with this event.

The Makah Indians, who live at Neah Bay, the northwest corner of the Territory, next to the Pacific Ocean, and also the Chemakums and Quillehutes, whose original residence was near the same region, speak of a very high tide. According to their tradition, "A long time ago, but not at a very remote period, the waters of the Pacific flowed through what is now the swamp and prairie between Waatch village and Neah Bay, making an island of Cape Flattery. The water suddenly receded, leaving Neah Bay perfectly dry. It was four days reaching its lowest ebb, and then rose again without any waves or breakers till it had submerged the Cape, and in fact the whole country except the tops of the mountains at Clyoquot. The water on its rise became very warm, and as it came up to the houses, those who had canoes put their effects in them, and floated off with the current, which set very strongly to the north. Some drifted one way, some another; and when the waters assumed their accustomed level, a portion of the tribe found themselves beyond Nootka, where their descendants now reside, and are known by the same name as the Makahs in Classet, or Kwenaitchechat. Many canoes came down in the trees and were destroyed, and numerous lives were lost. The water was four days in gaining its accustomed level."[*]

It is the opinion of Hon. J. G. Swan that this was simply a rising of the tides, and has no reference to the Deluge of Noah. I suggest, however, that if they had preserved any tradition of the flood in their migrations, when they settled at Neah Bay, where nearly all of their floods, though smaller, were caused by the rising of the tide, that they would naturally, in a few generations, refer it to the same cause. The natives of the Sandwich Islands, where floods are caused in the same way, have a tradition of a great flood, but refer it to the rising of the tide.

The Indians of the Warm Spring reservation in Oregon, and of the Fort Hall reservation in Idaho, as far as I can learn, have no such tradition. It is possible, however, that they may have concealed it from their questioners, if they have one, as Indians do many of their traditions.

When these traditions are compared with those of other Indians in the eastern part of the United States, Mexico, and South America, as well as the traditions and records of the Eastern Hemisphere, it forms in many minds a very strong argument in favor both of the truth of the Bible account and also of the unity of the race.

Some have objected to these traditions, that perhaps they were not handed down from former ancestors, but were received from early traders and teachers; but for four reasons I cannot accept the objection: (1) because the first travelers have often learned this tradition; (2) they will even now often distinguish between the traditions of their ancestors and the teachings of the first whites who came here; (3) they have names for their Ararat, the great monument of the flood, as "Fastener" and "Old Land"; and (4) the Mexicans, when discovered, although they had no system of writing yet had a way of representing events by pictures, and this event was recorded among others.

Hence we must conclude that all the traditions had little or no foundation, which would be absurd; or that there were a large number of floods, which would be almost as absurd, for in that event the tradition of one flood in each tribe could not have been preserved so distinctly, especially when a bird of some kind and a branch of some tree are often mentioned in connection with it; or else that there was one great flood, so great that most of the descendants of those saved have preserved a tradition of it, and if so, all must have descended from the few who were saved.

[*]See "Indians of Cape Flattery," by J. G. Swan, published by the Smithsonian Institution.

ORATIONS

The following are by Twana men, showing their style, and ideas on certain subjects. The first are taken from the minutes of a council held with them by Commissioner F. R. Brunot, September 4, 1871.

By *Big Frank*, the present head chief:

> I am the only one who was at the treaty at Point-No-Point. I heard what Governor Stevens said, and thought it was good. I am like a white man, and think as the white man does. Governor Stevens said all the Indians would grow up and the President would make them good. He told them all the Indians would become as white men; that all their children would learn to read and write. I was glad to hear it. Governor Stevens told them, "I will go out and have the land surveyed, and it will be yours and your children's forever." I thought that very good. He said a doctor and carpenter and farmer would come. The chiefs thought that all was good, they thought the President was doing a kindness. I never spoke my mind to anyone. I talk to you, because you come from Washington. All the Agents talk differently. You talk as Governor Stevens did. I hear what you say. Every Agent who comes here, I don't know them. I thought all Governor Stevens said was very good. Perhaps the President thinks all the Indians are good, as they were to be under the treaty, but they are not. They are Indians still. I think there was plenty of money sent by the President, but I think much did not come here. Perhaps it gets scattered. I really think it does not come. When it comes it is in calico. But I know more is sent than gets here.

By *Spar*, the head chief at the time, since dead:

> When I came here I did not know much. I was here when the reservation was opened, and know what was done. When the Agents came, they never taught us anything, never said, "Go, and fix your places." All they think of is to steal; to sell the reservation cattle and reservation hay; to sell the fruit and get all they can; to go and log and sell them. That is all every Agent has done. They never advised us what to do, never helped us. After I had seen all this I was sorry. Did the President send men for this, to come and get what money they could out of the reservation and their pay? I know the Indians lose all their cattle. When they get the money, where does it go? When I asked about it, they say they will punish me. I thought the President did not send them for that. I got very poor and wanted to borrow the reservation team. You know what I have done. They refused me the use of the cattle.

By *Duke William*:

> I am glad to see you. All our folks are very poor. Our planting grounds, and logs, and apples, and hay are taken from us, and I felt sad, and wanted to go and see the President. I know I will not live long. I asked the Indians to give me the money, and I would go and see the President. I would have gone if you had not come here. Did the President send men as Agents to log and get all the benefits? That is what I wanted to go and ask the President.

268

By *Big John*, a sub-chief:

> You come to get the Indian's hearts. You ought to take time. You are the great chief and we want you to hear us. When we talked before, it was put down, and they said it would go to Washington. We do not know what became of it. We don't think the President saw it. We think it don't go far from here. I am a poor man. You are making all of these young men and women happy. I thought when a boy, that we should get all of the money promised. White men don't give things away. They don't take a shirt or blanket for lands. They get gold and silver. The Indians don't get money for their country.

The following were also by Twanas, some time after the preceding. A proposition was made to remove the tribe to the Puyallup reservation.

Tatum, a sub-chief, said:

> I am glad yet. My mind is glad yet. I am glad that Chief Jim and Big John's father selected this place. I know this land was given us in exchange for a large country that was once ours. I am still glad, and when any Indian comes along and tells me this land will be taken from me, I just take up my ax and chop down trees to clear land here. He tells us to increase our food and it will be all right. I do not want to carry my bones far away from that place, for God my father made me here, and my bones to decay here. I do not want to go to the Puyallup country, because I want my bones to lie here. I want the bones of all the young men to lie on this place, because I am afraid of that which is covered overflowing with rum, for I have truly seen that there is plenty of whiskey there, and that is why I will not go to Puyallup at hoppicking time again for there is no one who drinks at this place.

By *Big John*, an ex-sub-chief:

> You know I am not in authority now, but our head chief has asked me to talk, and that is why I stand up to talk about our land. I know, because I have been a chief many years, that this writing and talk will not amount to much, for many times we sent papers, but they always got lost. I have lifted my right hand to God many times, sending my words to Washington, but it has done no good. So it seems to me they were fooling me, and fooling God, too. The white men know we are nothing but Indians, and we are worthless, and our words are worthless, too. Why are some of these Indians made chiefs, and yet their words are as though they were low wretches, just above the ground? The letter, that we sent through the Agent, was written to get patents to our land, so that we might see where it is. How is it that white men will teach us about God, and to be good, and then when we lift our right hands to God, and send our words to Washington, they refuse to believe us, because we are Indians. All the old, the very old, were glad when they heard that we had sent the letter to Washington. And I am now confused in my mind because just when we sent our letter to Washington (about patents for our lands here) we got word that we are going to be moved away. I, as an Indian, do not want to leave the land which I have cleared, and go on to new land, and have to clear up again, for I have been working on my land a long time. A good many of us know our land, because we have worked on it, and eat from what we raise on it. All our animals, our horses, and cattle, live on our land.

I think a good many things. Sometimes I think our Agent's time is nearly out, and perhaps he is preparing his mind to throw us away to some other Agent. We went over to Puyallup, partly to pick hops, and partly to see how the Indians there were getting along, and we found them living in small huts, not like our houses, or even barns, but more like chicken coops, while we have houses, and are civilized. It is my mind and also the mind of all, that we will not go to Puyallup, because we have been there, and have seen how they live there. It is only when a white man sells his land, that he leaves it, because he knows that it costs a great deal to clear an acre, and a great deal more to clear two acres, and so on. It is the opinion of all our Indians, that if the whites should offer them ever so many million dollars for their land, they would not accept it, because we wish to stay here, and die here. If we shall be taken far away, what is to become of the house of prayer, that God has given us in which to worship him.

By *Curley*, an ex-sub-chief:

My heart has been crying for three days. I had pity in my heart for that poor woman there (pointing to an old woman). She told me about the news in the newspaper, and her heart was crying, and so she felt bad. I came to my mother, and she was crying, for she had heard the same message, and I felt bad for her. When we shall be taken to live far away, the old people will mourn for it. What man has seen the old and the young, and has written such a recommendation? Who is the man that has been trying to destroy the good work the Agent has been doing here? When my mother heard it she felt badly, and I felt worse. Our Agent ought to help us to hold our reservation, so as to stop the mourning of the old and the young. The Indians know me, the Agent knows me; I was bad, but I have changed: yet if I am driven away, my badness will return to me, and I will do something, and die soon. When I leave my house, I think of my house, and if I go far away I shall think of my home, and that is why I do not wish to be driven far away. Our tribe of Indians is but few and if we go to another country, we shall be run over, and treated like slaves, because we are few.

By *Duke William*:

Do take pity on the Indians. Do help them about their land. Don't treat them as you did other Indians far away. See how you did to Leschi at the time of the Klikitat (Yakima) war. You talked to him of his land, and he got mad very quick. It is not good that the people of this reservation should follow the example of those Indians. It is not good that you should split pitchwood and set the people on fire, as you did the Klikitats, and make war. Those who wish to move the Indians, let them set their countrymen on fire, not the Indians.

At a Council held October 30, 1878, at the Skokomish Agency, among the Twanas, a letter was read from the Commissioner of Indian Affairs, in which a request was made that they express their wishes respecting the transfer of the Indian Bureau to the War Department, whereupon the following speeches, among others, were made.

By *Dick Lewis*, head chief:

In what I say now, I only use my mouth to express the mind of all this tribe—the Skokomish Indians. Every man, woman and child feels as I shall now speak. Many years ago, our minds were in the dark. An army agent was here, and when he saw one of us have a house and barn and farm, and hay growing on it, he came and took it away, and said the hay was his. This is the way we were treated, and so all the people on the Skokomish reservation do not want a soldier for their Agent again. Our present Agent came here almost at the expiration of the treaty. We knew very little when he came, but we have learned and improved very fast since he came here. We now have good houses, chairs, bedsteads, tables, stoves, dishes, etc., and do not eat on the floor as we used to do. As we have improved so fast since he has been here, we are afraid, if we exchange him for a new Agent, we shall get in the dark again, and lose our minds. So if he is not tired, we wish he would stay, as we know him and he knows us, and helps to lead us in the light. He has come and taught us about God, and this is another reason we want him to stay with us. We do not wish to flatter him, but he really is a good man, and we tell the truth when we say so, and we ask that there will be no change. At Skokomish none of the Indians fight, so why should they send soldiers here. Send your soldiers where they are needed to fight wild Indians, but here we are all tame, and there is no need of soldiers, so do not send them here. If our Agent is not tired, let him stay with us.

By *Chehalis Jack*, a sub-chief:

We have had an Agent here ever since the treaty, but it was only when our present Agent came that we were taught the right way. When he came, he taught us, and treated us as Governor Stevens promised when he made the treaty. He told us this land, this water, this war was all ours. When our present Agent came, he encouraged us to work on our land, build good houses, and make farms. I then built me a good house, and have tables, dishes, lamps, trunks, stoves, and everything at hand as white men have. We do not want to lose this Agent. Let him stay until the treaty expires, and then leave. I never saw soldiers have large farms, and work on them. If soldiers come, they will teach what they know how to do—fight—not do all kinds of good work. I do not want soldiers to come and teach us how to fight, for we never kill white people. Why should we be treated so. We have never killed a single white man here. Why then should we be put under soldiers. Governor Stevens told us to take the Skokomish land and river, and live there until we all died, and only leave this land when we leave this world. If our Agent is not tired of us, let him stay until the treaty ends, but do not give us an Army Agent. I speak the wishes of all our people.

They had long been anxious for patents to their lands which have been assigned them on the reservation. This subject troubled them more than any other for about twelve years. The next two speeches, selected from many, were made with reference to this subject.

By *Jackman*, a sub-chief:

Today I want to talk a little with you. Yesterday we celebrated Christmas, Christ's birthday, the day his blood and bones came on earth, so that is his day. Yesterday he came on earth and he made both us and our land; and so it is that we want to stay here. God has made us and our land and we ought to be together. You, Mr. Eells, are our Agent, so it is good that you work for us, getting our patents for our lands. Now we want this paper to go to Washington, and have an answer returned immediately, so that we will get the answer before Spring. Washington is like our father, and he has made our minds tired by keeping us waiting so long, for we are very anxious for our patents to our lands. This, our land, is rightfully ours, as the old men, our fathers, never did sell it to Washington. This, our land, is a long way off from any town; no cars come here, and so it is good for us, and we want it very much. Neither does any steamer come here regularly. So we are as if a long way off from any town. This is all from me.

By *Chehalis Jack*, a sub-chief:

We know that you are our Agent, and we know that you are very tired with our talking all the time about our land. Your name is Mr. Eells, and Washington sent you here to take care of us, the Indians, and to try to get us patents, as you do today. But why is it that he does not hear you and us and send us patents for our land? At the first potlatch Governor Stevens made to the Indians at Point No Point, our fathers were asked where they wished to have their land. They took one whole day to consider, and talk it over; and they said "At Skokomish we will live, as that is a good place for us." This we have never forgotten, but all the time want to live and die at Skokomish. All of us have the same mind, wishing just that. So we do not wish to be moved to any other place, to Puyallup, to Chehalis, to Clallam, or to any other land, but here we wish to stay all the time at our homes. And now, Mr. Eells, please help all of us—your boys—in this room now, and if we get our patents, we will then all work earnestly on our lands and make it good and productive. This is all from me.

The following letter was written by a school boy about seventeen years old with reference to the same subject.

Skokomish Agency, W.T.
Jan. 5, 1879

R. B. Hayes, President of the United States

Respected Sir,

I am but an Indian boy, who has learned to read and write here, by the kindness and bounty of Government, and I ought not to take your time to read this letter, but my people have a great desire which they want granted, and have tried many ways, but in vain, and they thought you might help them. Many years ago the United States Government made a treaty with our people, and agreed to give us title to the reservation lands, if we would live on them, and be like white folks; and we are now very much like white folks, and all our friends are very anxious to have patents for their homes. Our chiefs send their talks to you, and hope you will be pleased to help them. Our Agent has written many times and sent their petitions to the Commissioner of Indian Affairs, but we do not see our patents yet, and he says he must not write to a higher office, so I thought I would write to you and perhaps you would listen. Our people are very anxious to have their houses secured to them as white people do, and then they will feel safe. Please tell some one to give us patents to our lands. With a great many good wishes for you sir. Very Respectfully Indeed.

"Simon Peter"

The following are a few out of many speeches taken down by me at Dungeness, July 1877, to carry to their Agent. They were made by Clallams.

By *Lord Jim Balch*, head chief:

I thank God that he has helped you to give me a good heart. God taught you, and so you have come to teach us. Truly we were bad formerly. Formerly we asked, "Where is our Agent?" Perhaps there was none (i.e., there was none to us, he took no notice of us). Hence, formerly we drank very much whiskey. We knew about the Agent at Skokomish only what the Port Gamble Indians told us. Formerly the Port Gamble Indians and Skokomish Indians alone received annuities from the Agent, and we only knew of him by hearsay. Formerly we heard that there was a Minister at Skokomish, but we knew nothing of what he said. No Minister came here when I was a boy, so we knew not what God thought was bad. Formerly we drank whiskey, probably because there was no Agent like Mr. Eells, who took care of us. So we all knew how to drink whiskey. I will not conceal our former wickedness. What does a child do? Always the same as his father. My father formerly drank whiskey. If my father had had any Agent like Mr. Eells, he would have done better, and then I would have done better also. By and by, as my children grow up, they will see that I am trying to be good, and they will become good. As you often come here, and the people do not improve very fast, it shows that formerly they were bad and hard. Now we are improving. So I thank you. I am done.

By *Cook House Billy*, the acting minister:

I thank God that he has given you instruction, so that you have been able to teach me. I acknowledge that formerly I drank whiskey. Now as you have come this time to see us, I intend to abandon all my evil ways. I will not say that I have always been good. God saw me do wrong, and perhaps Jesus put it down in his book. I am afraid to say that I did not do wrong formerly, for Jesus knows I did, and hence I will not conceal it. Formerly when I drank whiskey I may have told lies. Now I wish to stop this lying. Perhaps when I drank I stole, but when not drunk I did not steal. I think Jesus knows all about it, but now I wish to stop all this wicked conduct. I am afraid of hell for now I know about it. I know that when the wicked die, they go to hell; but if a person does no wrong he will go to God. What does one gain by drinking? Nothing but sorrow.

When formerly I worked for white men, I received one dollar a day, three dollars for three days, and then I paid it out for whiskey, at the rate of one dollar a bottle, and the whiskey quickly ate up all my money. So now I intend to stop drinking, and have a strong mind. When I drank I spent my money for liquor. I slept, I woke up, my money was gone. What did I have for my money? Now you may open your ears, when you get to Skokomish about my drinking. Heretofore, when you have come, I spoke not as I do now. You never talk bad when you come here, but always good, so I thank you for coming. It is as if you were in a bad place, and you were leading us in a good way. So I thank you. I am done.

These are amply sufficient to show these modes of illustration, their ideas on the subjects referred to their style, as well as can be after it is translated, and the amount of flattery, which they often intersperse with their speeches, for which considerable allowance must be made.

I have heard them speak on other subjects, on temperance and religion, but those orations have not been preserved. We do not get their real style, however, when they talk through an interpreter. They are natural orators, and their looks and gestures, which are numerous, speak eloquently.

XVIII
NAMES

As a rule the names of persons have no meaning. In 1880 I took the census of the Clallam tribe for the United States and among all their names I found only one or two exceptions. The name of one woman meant kind. I have repeatedly questioned persons in other tribes on the same subject, and have found the same rule elsewhere on the Sound—no meanings.[1]

As a rule the Indian names of places do have meanings, and I herewith give the meanings of as many as I have been able to learn. Before beginning I will, however, mention two points, which enter into a large number of names, the initial letter s, and the terminal syllable *bish* or *mish*.

INITIAL S

This letter begins quite a number of names, as Skokomish and Snohomish. It is, however, pronounced by the Indians so that when the names were first written, the "s" was separated from the main word by an apostrophe, thus, S'Kokomish, S'Nohomish, S'Klallam, S'Nanaimo, S'Hotlemamish, S'Komamish, S'Tailakoom. Probably others were pronounced in the same way, as many of the names begin with "s". As these names have been used by the whites, in some of them the "s" has been fully incorporated into the name, the apostrophe being dropped, as in Steilacoom, Skokomish, and Snohomish, while in others the "s" has been dropped, as in Clallam and Nanaimo.

The meaning of the letter I have been unable to learn. It has sometimes seemed to me that they use it, or drop it, without attaching any meaning to it. In conversation I have heard the Twanas speak of the Makah and Haida as S'Makah and S'Haida and Lillewaup as Slillewaup, and yet when I asked them what tribes they spoke of, they said Makah and Haida. In gathering common words I have often been puzzled, because in pronouncing them sometimes they would begin the word with an "s", and on pronouncing it a second time, they would leave off that letter. In these common words I have, after considerable study, come to the conclusion generally to drop the "s", as the more correct way.

On questioning one of the most intelligent, educated Twana Indians on this point, he said that there was a reason why it was used, but that he could not explain it to me in English.

TERMINAL *MISH* OR *BISH*

This termination ends a very large number of the names in the land occupied by the Twana, Chehalis, Nisqually, and Snohomish-speaking Indians. I have found the following: among the Twanas, Skokomish and Quilceedobish; among the Chehalis, Satsapish (Satsop), Ourlapish, and Staktamish; and among those speaking the Nisqually language, Snohomish, Skwaksnamish (Skwaksin), Duwamish, Samish, Samamish, Stillaguamish, Swinomish, Skywhamish, Sukwamish, Skykomish, Skwonamish, Sk'telmish, Kwehtl-mamish, Stolutswhamish, Skopahmish, St'kahmish, Puyalluphamish (Puyallup), T'kaw-kahmish, Squalliamish (Nisqually), Steilakumamish (Steilacoom), S'hotlmamish, Sa-hehwamish, Sawamish, Stehtsasamish, Nukwatsamish or Nookwachahamish (Nooksack), Stulakoomanamish, Skopamish, Sketehlmish, St'kamish, Stetlchasamish, S'slomamish, Smulkamish, Sekamish, Qunkwamish, N'kwachamish, Swodamish, N'Quientlmamish, Shomamish, and Cholbahahbish. I find not one name ending thus west of the Olympic mountains, none among the Clallams, and none east of the Cascade mountains, with the exception of Toppenish.

I am satisfied that it means "people," although it has taken me a long time to come to this conclusion. On the subject I have been able to obtain very little light from the Indians. One very intelligent Indian and one white man, well-versed in Indian affairs, gave me as their opinion that it meant much the same as it does in such words as Flemish, Scottish, English, and the like, but I have been unable to accept this, as Puget Sound is too far from Europe to allow me to believe this is the origin for this termination. The word for Indians, or people, in Twana is *Klo-wal-bish*; in the Upper Chehalis, it is *E-la-mish*; and in Lower Chehalis, *Klo-wal-bish*. It is hence very natural that in speaking of certain people, they should add the termination "bish" or "mish" to the name of the place where they live; for instance Kol-sid is the name of the bay in the Twana territory, and Kol-sid-o-bish that of the Indians living there. One thing only puzzles me, and that is that in the Nisqually language, which is spoken by far more Indians than the three languages above named combined, the word for people is *Ate-il-tul-bo*. This termination, however, may have been given to their names by the other tribes mentioned, or there may be some way of explaining this which I have not learned, as all of their languages are closely related.

MEANING OF PLACE NAMES

Names on Puget Sound

Neah Bay, Clallam county. This comes from the name of a Makah chief whose name was Neah, or rather, Dee-ah.

Makah or Makkah, Clallam county, means the people who live on a point of land projecting into the sea, or the "cape people."

Klasset is another name by other Indians for the same people, and means the same as Makah.

Clallam is the name of a county and comes from the Indian tribe of that name, which was originally written S'Klallam. It is said by the Clallam Indians to be a corruption of their own name for themselves. Nu-sklaim, meaning "strong people."

Judge J. G. Swan is of the opinion that it comes from the Makah name for them, meaning "clam people," *klolub*, a clam, and *aht*, a man. A Twana Indian says that it comes from their name for the tribe, Do-sklal-ob, meaning "the big, brave nation."

Se-quim, Clallam county, is a corruption of the Indian name for the same place, which is Suchekivailing.

Skokomish, Mason county, comes from the Indian name for themselves of the Indians living there, which was S'kaw-kaw'bish, which the Clallams call S'kaw-kaw-mish. It means "river people," for *kaw*, fresh water, the Skokomish river being the largest body of fresh water in that region.

Quilceed, Jefferson county, is a Twana name. The people there were called the Quil-ceedobish (Kwil-ci-do-bish), or "salt water people," in contrast with the Skokomish, or "fresh water people."

Du-hle-lip, at the extreme head of Hood Canal is said to mean "the head of the bay." The third band of the Twanas formerly lived there.

Twana is a corruption from Too-au-hu, the original name of the tribe, of which the Skokomish Indians were one band, and it is said by George Gibbs to be reported to mean "a portage," because a short portage across the head of Hood's canal will save a water trip around the peninsula by way of Port Gamble, but I have never been able to verify it, though I often inquired of the Indians. Another authority (Twana) says that the original name was Twa-dak-hu, or "hard language people," because it is the most difficult language in the region to learn.

Duk-a-boos, Mason county, is a Twana name, corrupted from the original one, Do-hi-a-boos, and means "a reddish face," because the bluff or mountain near that place has a reddish face or appearance.

Lilliwaup, Mason county, another Twana name, is said by a Twana to mean "an inlet," on account of the small bay there. *The West Shore* of Portland gives the meaning to be "falling water," from the beautiful falls there, on what authority I do not know, as I have never been able to verify it among the Indians.

Dewalto, Mason county, a Twana name, is from the Indian name Du-a-ta. It was thus named because in their mythology certain imaginary small sprites, or pigmies, used to live there, who used to make folks crazy if they once entered them. The name of these sprites, was *tub-ta-ba*, and that of their spirit world, Duata. This place was called by the same name because here, as it were, they came to the surface of the earth.

Ta-ho-ya is from two Twana words, *ta* meaning "that," and *ho-i*, "done," and thus means "that done," but why it was applied to that stream I cannot learn, but one person surmises that something especially notable was done there long ago.

Docewallops is more properly Doswailopsh. In Twana mythology, the mountain of that name was long ago a man, while Mount Solomon, opposite it, was his wife, and an apparently small but noticeable mountain far up in the valley between them was their child. Mount Tacoma was another wife of the same man, who lived at the same place, but the two women quarreled so badly that after a time the big woman, whose name was Tu-wah-hu, which is the Indian name for that mountain, picked up a basketful of the heads, tails, and parts of fish and left to find a more peaceable home.

She travelled up Hood's Canal and intended to stop at Skokomish, but the place was too small for her, so she went on, dropping, however, as she crossed the Skokomish river, a piece of silver salmon and a piece of hump-backed salmon into the stream; and this is the reason, they say, why these two kinds of salmon ascend only these two of all the streams in the region. She then went on until she reached the Nisqually, but that place was too small, so she moved on dropping a piece of silver salmon into the river, and hence, they say that kind of salmon ascend only that stream in that region. When she reached the place where Mount Tacoma now is she found room and settled down. About that time a mythological being called Do-ki-batl, or the Changer, came along and on account of their quarrels changed them all into mountains. The name of the man, Dos-wail-opsh, has been perpetuated in the name of the mountain and river there.

Chehalis, name of river, county, and town, is pronounced by the Indians Tse-ha-lis, and by some early writers was written Chickelis. It means "sand," and was given to the Indians about the river's mouth because of the sand there; and hence the early settlers gave the river and Upper Chehalis Indians the same name, though originally neither was called by this name by the Indians.

Wishkah, Chehalis county, is a corruption of the Chehalis name Hwishkahl, and means "stinking water."

The Wishkah river in these days is shunned by all Indians. Under no considerations can they be persuaded to go further up the stream than the Smith place, three miles from the mouth. Even when crossing from the Quiniault or Humptulips country to the Cy-nooche, they avoid crossing the Wishkah by going around to the north of its source. Their tradition is that many, many ages ago some great eagle captured an enormous whale on the sea coast and carried it to the headwaters of the river, and that the whale's decaying body poisoned the entire river, so that a great epidemic came and killed all the Indians living along the stream, and that the waters of the river are dangerous even unto this day. From this tradition the beautiful river has taken its unsavory name, which in the Indian tongue means "stinking waters."

Skookum Chuck, Thurston county, is from the Chinook Jargon, and means "strong or swift water." Skookum comes originally from the Chehalis word *sku-kum*, strong, and *chuck*, water, from the word *ti-tsuk*, in the old Chinook language, which in Nootka is *chauk*, and Clatsop, *ti-chukw*.

Tumwater, Thurston county, is a Chinook Jargon word meaning "waterfall." It originated from the English word "water," and "tum" by onomatopoeia, as the sound of the waterfall reminded people of that sound. So "tumtum," the word in the same language for heart, was given to it because of the noise of the beating of the heart, which reminded them of such sounds.

Tacoma. No name on Puget Sound has received such discussion as to its origin or meaning as this one. The name of the town or city was taken from that of the mountain. A very intelligent Puyallup Indian, Peter C. Stanup, whose reservation is near the foot of the mountain, told me that it means "the mountain," being pronounced by his people Ta-ko-ba, but that this was not the name by which the Indians originally called it, as their name was Tu-wak-hu, or Twa-hwauk. Mr. G. W. Travers, in his "Tacoma and Vicinity," gives the meaning as "near to Heaven," on what authority I do not know. To me this definition seems very doubtful, as the Indian idea of the land of happy spirits, before the coming of the whites, was not above the world, in the heavens, but below, in the earth. Mr. P. B. Van Trump, of Yelm, says:

> The first Indian I heard pronounce the name of the mountain was old Sluiskin, who guided General Stevens and myself to the snow-line, where we made the first ascent to the summit in 1870. Sluiskin's pronounciation, as near as I can represent it by letters, was Tah-ho-mah, and in his rendering of it there was, besides its music, an accent of awe and reverence, for Sluiskin was very imaginative and superstitious about Tahoma, believing that its hoary summit was the abode of a powerful spirit, who was the author of its eruptions and avalanches and who would visit dire vengeance on any mortal who would dare to invade (if that were possible) his dread abode. When Stevens and I were encamped at the foot of the snow-line we would often be awakened by the thunder of falling rocks or the deep thud of some avalanche. At such times Sluiskin would start from his blanket and repeat a dismal dirge-like song as though he would appease the mountain spirit.
>
> Mishell Henry, another old Indian guide to the two-named mountain, prides himself in giving its true name and its correct pronounciation. He has several times drilled me in pronouncing it, always smiling gravely and dignifiedly at my ineffectual attempts to give his deep chest notes. Henry was the first to mark out the present route to the snow-line, by which the tourist can now reach the snow-line and even ascend it for two miles without leaving the saddle. He guided our party (the Bayley party) in 1883, and himself ascended to the 8,000-foot level. Beyond that nothing could tempt him, for beyond (in his view) lay danger, folly, rashness; for even Henry, who was intelligent and much more of a philosopher than the rest of his tribe (Khikatals), associates the sublime summit of Tahoma with awe, danger, and mystery.
>
> Your correspondent gives the meaning of "Tacoma" as "the mountain," an interesting interpretation, considering the preeminence and grandeur of this noble peak. I have questioned the Indians as to their meaning for the word Tah-ho-mah. The answer of some showed their ignorance of the meaning. Others, with that reticence and suspicion peculiar to the savage mind, were stoically non-commital. One interpretation I have heard given is "nourishing breasts," the idea presumably being that the eternal snows of the twin summits have given origin to the streams and have occasioned the glacial deposits that have enriched the valleys, thus nourishing and sustaining vegetable life there just as through the ages the maternal breasts have nourished and sustained youthful human life.

Hon. H. W. Scott, the editor of the *Oregonian*, who lived on Puget Sound from 1854 to 1857, says that he knew hundreds of the Indians intimately and learned much of their language, yet he never in those days heard Tacoma or Tahoma spoken either by Indians or white persons, had never met anyone who had any knowledge of the name until after

Theodore Winthrop's book, *The Canoe and the Saddle*, appeared in 1862, and he is certain that the name was invented by Mr. Winthrop, and, being a euphonious and delightful name, is a credit to his genius. I cannot agree with Mr. Scott as to its origin, but believe it to be of Indian origin, as among the numerous tribes which live in sight of the great mountain and which speak various languages hundreds of words are used which Mr. Scott doubtless never learned or even heard in three years. Mr. M. W. Walker, who has lived much among the Indians on the east side of the Cascade mountains, is confident that the word originated among some of those Indians, probably the Tahamas, was originally Tah-ho-ma, and means "the gods."

In 1893 the Tacoma Academy of Sciences published a pamphlet of sixteen octavo pages prepared by Hon. J. Wickersham of that city, of which a second edition was printed the same year, enlarged to thirty-four pages, devoted solely to this name.[2]

In it Colonel B. F. Shaw, interpreter at the treaty of 1854, Commander of the Washington Volunteers in the Indian war of 1854–56, and a member of the State Senate in 1893, says that Tacoma is a Skagit word and means "plenty of food or nourishment," first applied to a "motherly woman" (*tacoma sladah*), then to her breasts as the source of nourishment, and lastly to the snow-capped mountains, from their resemblance to her breasts, whereupon it came rather to mean the "snow-capped mountains." Hon. J. G. Swan, quoting from Dr. W. T. Tolmie, John Flett, Judge Francis Henry, Hon. Edwin Eells, and Jacob Kershner agree in the main with the foregoing. Toma, Tacoma, Takob, and Tacobet are the different pronunciations given by the Puget Sound Indians to the name, and Ta-ho-ma is the Klikitat–Yakima name, which some of those Indians say means "a rumbling noise."

Seattle was the name of an Indian chief who was very friendly to the whites. As a rule, the names of Indians on Puget Sound have no more meaning than those of America. He pronounced the name Scachl.

Steilacoom was from the name of an Indian chief named Tail-a-koom.

Enumclaw means "a loud rattling noise." Years ago a band of Muckleshoot Indians were camped near the base of a promontory-shaped mountain, a few miles from the present site of the town of that name, when a very loud and rattling noise, like a terrible crash of thunder, was heard, which seemed to come from the interior of the mountain. The Indians were frightened away by the sound, thinking that evil spirits had their abode there. Afterwards they called the mountain Enumclaw, a name which still clings to the mountain. The Indians of today still regard the mountain with suspicion, and it is said that all that a deer needs to do when chased by the Indians, in order to save its life, is to steer its course towards Mount Enumclaw.

Kitsap comes from a chief of that name. The Indians, however, in pronouncing it, accent the last syllable very strongly, and pronounce the first as if the "i" were omitted, thus, Ktsap. The word is said to mean "brave," and "he was a very brave chief."

Squakson, Mason county, comes from a creek of that name at North Bay, Du-skwak-sin, meaning silent or alone, because it is the only creek of any importance in that region. When the treaty was made, an island was selected as the reservation for those

Indians, hence the name has been transferred to that island, but originally it belonged to the region near North Bay.

Tulalip, Snohomish county, means "a wide bay with a small mouth."

Stilaquamis means "river people."

Nooksack, Whatcom county, is the name of a tribe, but has no meaning.

Snohomish is the name of a tribe and style of union.

Snoqualmie is not of much account, but they are strong Indians.

Teekalet, the former name of Port Gamble, Kitsap county, means "the brightness of the noonday sun," because the sun at noon shines with peculiar splendor on Port Gamble bay.

La Push, Clallam county, is a Chinook Jargon word and means "mouth," meaning at that place the mouth of the river. It comes from the French "La Boos" [*bouche*].

Tatoosh, Clallam county, is also a Chinook Jargon word and means "milk" or "breast." It is originally from the Chippeway word *to-tosh*. Possibly, however, it may come from To-tooch, or Tu-tutsh, the Makah name of the Thunderbird.

Chemakum was the name of a small but brave tribe of Indians, which is now as a tribe extinct, who lived near a place bearing the same name. Its meaning I cannot learn.

Hoquiam, Chehalis county, means "hungry woods," because long ago there were very many dead trees near its head, and the Indians said they died from hunger.

Kaisalmis, Chehalis county, means "gravelly."

Oyhut, Chehalis county, means "road" in the Chinook Jargon. I presume it was given to the place because there is a short road from Gray's Harbor to the Pacific Ocean.

Other Names in Washington

These are here inserted for the information given, though not belonging to Puget Sound.

Cathlamet, Wahkiakum county, is written Cathlamah by Lewis and Clark and was the name of a tribe of Indians as well as a stream. It evidently comes from the Indian word *calamet*, meaning "stone," and is believed to have been given to the river because of the fact that it has a stony bed along its whole course.

Kalama is believed to be a corruption of the above word, *calamet*—"stone."

La Camas, Clarke county, is the Chinook Jargon name for an esculent root. It comes from the French, *la*, and the Nootka, *chamass*, which Jewett says means "fruit, sweet, pleasant to taste."

Walla Walla, written Wolla Wollah by Lewis and Clark, is a Nez Perce and Cayuse word, the root of which is *walatsa*, which means "running"; hence "running water." Two meanings of it are given, one being "a small stream running into a large one"—that is, the Walla Walla river emptying into the Columbia; another is "ripple after ripple," "fall after fall." These meanings were given the writer by Mr. P. B. Whitman and Dr. W. C. McKay, who have lived among the Indians most of the time for over forty-five years, and speak the Walla Walla language as fluently as they do the English. The Walla Walla *Union*, however, of November 29, 1890, says:

> There has always been dispute as to the origin and meaning of the name Walla Walla, most people clinging to the idea that it is an Indian term meaning many waters. In a recent number of *St. Nicholas*, Joaquin Miller gives a fresh interpretation of the origin and meaning of Walla Walla, which is at once probable and beautiful. He says, "The lover of pretty names will easily trace this Walla Walla back to its French settlers' 'Voila! Voila!'
>
> "No man can look down from the environment of mountains on this sweet valley, with its beautiful city in the center, whose many flashing little rivers run together and make it forever green and glorious to see, without instinctively crying out, Voila! Voila! It is another Damascus, only it is broader of girth and far, far more beautiful."

For our own knowledge and gratification we interviewed a proficient French scholar as to the pronounciation and meaning of "Voila! Voila!" He uttered a sound that was as near like the common pronounciation of Walla Walla as it seemed possible to come without uttering those words, and explained that the French word means "there," and is used as the words "see there," "look there" are used in English, as the means of attracting other persons to something beautiful, attractive, or noticeable, seen for the first time.

I, however, sincerely doubt the French derivation of the name, as Lewis and Clark, who came in 1805, before the French did, and who were the first whites to cross the continent and enter the Walla Walla country, called the tribe the Wolla Wollahs.

Wallula means the same as Walla Walla, but is in the Walla Walla language.

Almota, Whitman county, is a corruption of the Nez Perce word *aliamotin* and means "torch-light fishery."

Alpowa, Garfield county, is a Nez Perce word and means "the mouth of Spring creek." The Indian name of the creek is *alpaha*, which means "spring creek," and was so given because of the numerous springs there.

Pataha is a Nez Perce word and means "brush creek," from *paton*, "brush," because formerly the brushes were very thick on it.

Asotin is from the Nez Perce word *hashotin*, which means "eel creek," from the abundance of eels in it.

Yellow Hawk's creek, Walla Walla county, comes from a Cayuse Indian chief of that name, whose Indian name was Petumromusmus, which meant "yellow hawk," or "eagle."

Taxsas, Whitman county, is a Nez Perce word, which means "moss-covered rock."

Siwash, Stevens county, is the Chinook Jargon word for Indian, and is a corruption of the French word *sauvage*, for "savage."

Kumtux, Whitman county, is a Chinook Jargon word meaning "to know" or "understand." The Nootka word is *kommetak*, the Clayoquot word *kemitak*, and the Tokwaht word *kumituks*.

Chewelah is a corruption of the word *cha-we-lah*, which is the name of a small striped snake. It was applied to that place either because the snake abounded there or because of the serpentine appearance of the stream.

Conconully is a corrupted Indian name meaning "cloudy," but was applied to the lower branch of the Salmon river. The proper Indian name for the valley where Conconully lies is Sklow Ouliman, which means "money hole," on account of the number of beavers caught there in early days when beaver skins were money to the Indians.

Okanogan, spelled Oakinacken by Alexander Ross, Okinaken by G. Franchere, Oakinagan by W. Irving, and Okinakane by Dr. George Gibbs, is the name of a county, signifying "rendezvous." It was given to the head of the Okanogan river, where it takes its source in the lake of the same name. It is here that Indians from various parts of the state and British America often met for their annual potlatch, and to lay in their supply of fish and game.

Osoyos is from the Calispel word *sooyos*, and signified "a narrow place" or "the narrows." When it came to naming the lake, an Irishman who was present suggested that "O" be prefixed in honor of his native country, which was done.

Spokane has some reference to the sun. Ross Cox says that in 1812 he met there the head chief of the Spokane tribe, whose name was Il-lim-spokanee, which he says means "son of the sun." *Il-li-mi-hum*, however, in that language means "chief," while *skok-salt* means "son." *Illim* is evidently a contraction of *illimihum*, and I think that the name, as given by Ross Cox, means "chief of the sun people"; not probably the name of the chief, but his title.

Names Given by Capt. Vancouver

The following names on Puget Sound were given by Capt. Vancouver on his visit to and exploration of the Sound in 1792:

New Dungeness, from its resemblance to Dungeness in the British Channel;

Mount Baker, as a compliment to the third lieutenant of Vancouver's expedition;

Port Discovery, after the name of his ship;

Puget Sound, from his lieutenant of that name;

Port Townsend was named Port Townshend in honor of the noble English marquis of that name;

Mount Rainier, after his friend Rear Admiral Rainier;

Marrowstone Point, because the clay there seemed to be such a rich species of marrowstone;

Oak Cove, from the few oak trees found there;

Foulweather bluff, from the change of weather experienced in its neighborhood;

Hazel point, on Hood's canal, from the hazel bushes or trees as he calls them, found there;

Hood's canal, or channel, as he named it, after Right Honorable Lord Hood;

Port Orchard, from the gentleman of his expedition of that name who discovered it;

Vashon island, after his friend, Captain Vashon, of the British Navy;

Restoration point, because he celebrated the memorable event of the restoration whilst at anchor there;

Penn's cove after a particular friend of that name;

Gulf of Georgia and New Georgia, in honor of the king of England at that time;

Port Gardner, after Vice-Admiral Sir Alan Gardner;

Point Wilson, in honor of Captain George Wilson, of the English navy;

Cypress island, from the abundance of upright cypress trees found there;

Whidbey island, because Mr. Whidbey of Vancouver's expedition first circumnavigated it;

Strawberry bay, from the many excellent strawberries found there;

Point Grey, after his friend, Captain George Grey, of the British navy.

Vancouver also gave the following names to the respective places, but does not give the reason why: Admiralty inlet, Point Partridge, Deception pass, Point Susan, Possession sound, and Bellingham bay.

Lieutenant Broughton, of Vancouver's expedition, also gave a large number of names to places on the Columbia river:

Mount Coffin, because there were a number of Indian canoes, containing dead bodies, at that place;

Oak Point, from several oak trees there, one of which was thirteen feet in girth;

Young's river, after Sir George Young of the royal navy;

Mount Hood, in honor of Right Honorable Lord Hood, the same person after whom Vancouver had named Hood's channel, or canal.

The following additional names he also gave, but many of them seem now to be lost: Swaine's river, Baker's island, Point Sheriff, River Poole, Point Warrior, Knight's river, Rushleigh river, Call's river, Arry's island, River Mannings, Bellevue point, Menzie's island, Barring's river, Johnstone island, Parting point, Friendly Reach river, Whidbey's river, and Chinook point.

Other English Names

Mount Olympus was first discovered by Pérez, a Spaniard, in 1774, and named Mount Rosalia.

He also discovered Cape Flattery, and named it Martínez, but in 1778 Capt. Cook named it Flattery, because of the encouraging state of affairs in his voyage up to that point.

Destruction Island was first discovered in 1775 by the Spaniard, Hecea [Heceta], and named Isla de Dolores, (Isle of Sorrows), because seven of his crew were killed there by the Indians. It was afterward named Destruction Island by an English captain, who lost a boat's crew there in a similar manner.

Cape Disappointment and Deception Bay were so named in 1788 by Lieutenant Meares, an Englishman, though he was then in command of a Portuguese vessel, because he did not find the river San Roque of Hecea.

Quimper Peninsula comes from Lieutenant Quimper, a Spaniard, who came to the region in 1790. He also named the Canal de Lopez de Haro.

Elisa, another Spaniard, in 1791, named the San Juan Archipelago, Guemes Island,

Tejeda (Texada), and Port Los Angelos, or the Port of the Angels. He also left the names Rosario and Hidalgo, though he gave to them other places than those which bear them now.

Indian Names in Oregon

The meaning of the following names in Oregon and Idaho are also here inserted for preservation.

Sauvie's island, Multnomah county, obtains its name from a man of that name, who lived on it for a long time. It was originally called Wappatoo island, Lewis and Clark being the first writers who gave it that name. Wappatoo is the name of an esculent root, which was much used by the Indians, and which grew there in abundance.

Wasco means a basin, from the basin-like rocks which have been worn at the Dalles by the water. The dishes of the Indians made from the horns of the mountain goat were called by the same name. There is an Indian tradition about a man and his wife, between whom there was trouble, whereupon the woman left him and their child. Thereupon, in his sadness, it is said that he went there and hammered out the basins in the rocks; though they were really made by the water.

Umatilla is from the Indian word *u-a-tal-la*, which means "the sand blew bare in heaps," because the wind blows the sand there so that it is bare in places, while by the sides of these places, it is in heaps and ridges. It is written U-till-a by H. H. Spalding, Umatilla by W. Irving, Umatallow by A. Ross, and Youmalolam by Lewis and Clark.

Siskiyou is a Chinook Jargon word, originally from the Cree language, and means "bob-tailed horse." It was applied to the mountains between Oregon and California because, in 1828, Mr. A. R. McLeod of the Hudson's Bay Company, while crossing the mountains with a pack-train, was overtaken by a snow storm in which he lost most of his horses, including one noted bob-tailed race horse. Hence his Canadian followers named the place the "Pass of the Siskiyou," a name which afterwards extended to the whole range and adjoining district.

Willamette. The discussion in Oregon several years ago showed quite plainly that the proper name was Wallamet, and that it was of Indian origin. There is a tradition that some of the Indians of the Wallamet valley were separated from the Nez Perce Indians, and Mr. P. B. Whitman says that after he had learned to talk the Nez Perce language, he found himself able to talk with the Tualatin Indians of the Wallamet with very little difficulty. Hence, he believes that the root of the word Wallamet is the same as that of Walla Walla and Wallula, and to be the Nez Perce word *walatsa*, which means "running," and when applied to water means "running water." According to Mrs. F. F. Victor, in the language of the Indians west of the Cascades, *whah* means "water" and *wah*, "to spell."

According to Mr. S. A. Clarke, formerly the Indians on both sides of the Wallamet, all of them being Calapooias [Callapooyas], had many a war, but sometimes wiser counsels prevailed and they settled their difficulties in a peaceful way, or when they were completely worried out by their battles, they met for a treaty of peace. When they did so they met on the banks of the great river and made up their differences, and hence the name Wallamet means "river of peace."

Chemawa, Marion county, according to R. H. Lee, means "our old home."

Chemeketa, the Indian name of Salem, and the present name of a prominent hotel there, means the same as Chemawa, according to S. A. Clarke, but according to H. Lang, author of a history of the Wallamet river, it means "gravelly."

Multnomah was originally the name of an Indian village on Sauvie's island, and was given as a name to the Wallamet river by Lewis and Clark, as they supposed that it was the name of the river instead of that of the village.

Long Tom, the name of a stream in the Willamette valley, is a corruption of the word Lung-tum-ler, the Indian name of the stream.

Scappoose was the name of a creek, near where the town now is, and means "pebbly creek."

Other Names in Oregon

John Days river was named after John Day, a Virginian and noted hunter of Astor's expedition, who came across the continent in 1810–11 with W. P. Hunt, one of the partners of that company. Before he reached Astoria he suffered terribly from starvation and was found in a starving condition near the mouth of that river. He subsequently became deranged and died at Astoria.

Malheur is of French origin and was given to that river by the Canadians of the Hudson's Bay Company. It means "the ill-fortune river."

La Coquille, Coos county, is also of French origin, and means "the shell."

Rickreall, Polk county, is a corruption of *La Creole* (French) meaning "the Creole."

Luckiamute is a corruption of *La Camas*—"the camas."

Jump-off-Joe, the name of a stream in southern Oregon received its name from the trapper McLeod, who led the first white expedition overland to California in 1832. They camped one night on this stream, but Joe McLoughlin, who was out hunting, did not come in till after dark, and not knowing that the camp was on a bluff, he stepped over the edge of it in the darkness and fell quite a distance below. He received injuries that could not be cured and died in a few years, but from the circumstance the creek received its name.

Rogue river was so called because of the wickedness of the Indians of that part of the country, who, when the caravans of the Hudson's Bay Company were on their way to and from California, often attacked them, stealing mules and goods, and killing men and mules. Hence they were called *Coquins* in French and Rogues in English.

Names in Idaho

Idaho means "gem of the mountains." It is Indian.

Pend d'Oreille is of French origin and means "the hanging from the ear." It was given by the Hudson's Bay Company to those Indians because they wore long ear pendants.

Coeur d'Alêne is likewise of French origin, signified "the heart of an awl," and was also given by the Hudson's Bay Company to that tribe, as they were sharpers in trade so that the traders said among themselves, "Look out, they will pierce you."

Nez Perce is also French and means "pierced nose," though why it was given to that tribe has been a question, as none of the tribe except their slaves pierced their noses and wore the *haiqua* or dentaleum shell, their old money and ornaments, in them. Possibly, however, this peculiarity in the slaves attracted the attention of the early voyagers and gave them their name. So the Flatheads did not flatten their heads. Others say that Nez Perce was given to them as a name because their country was mountainous and ridged like a nose, though that would not account for the word "pierced," while the country of the Flatheads was more level and flat. Still others say these names were thus given because in the sign language, which these Indians use, the sign for the Nez Perce tribe is made in front of the face with one finger, while the sign for the Flatheads is made by striking the forehead flatly with the open palm of the hand. This is reasonable if these signs were not invented after the tribes were thus named by the whites. The Nez Perces were called Chopunnish by Lewis and Clark. The Flatheads were called Les Tetes Plates (Flatheads) by the Canadians.

Lapwai, Nez Perce county, is a Nez Perce word and means "the dividing line between two countries," that is between the lower and upper Nez Perces. It is from *lapit*, two, and *waitish*, country or land.

Koos-koos-ka was a name given by Lewis and Clark to the Clearwater river, and is said to have originated through the following mistake. When the Indians there were asked about the rivers, they pointed to that stream and said "*koos-koots-ka*," meaning "small water or stream," then pointing to the Columbia, they said "*ma-kus-koots*," meaning "large waters," thus meaning, this is the small stream, but there is the great river, but the travelers mistook their meaning and supposed that the *koos-koots-ke*, or *koos-koos-ke*, as it was afterwards written, was the name of that stream.

The Payette river was named after a gentleman of that name in the Hudson's Bay Company.

Fort Hall was built by Capt. N. J. Wyeth, and named after one of his partners.

The Bitterroot mountains obtain their name from a small bitter root, eaten by the Indians, found in them. I do not know what kind it is.

XIX

DOMESTIC LIFE

MARRIAGE

Money answers to a multitude of things, and money and property have purchased many a wife on Puget Sound. When a young man formerly went around picking flowers, and carrying them along, it is said that it was a sign that he wished to get married. Gibbs says that on the small prairies it is not unusual to find human figures rudely carved on trees. These are said to have been cut by young men in want of wives, as a sort of intimation that they were on the market as purchasers. I have never seen or heard of such figures.[1]

When an Indian wishes for a wife, it is a rule that he seek for her within a certain circle of his relations, or a certain gens or clan. So said an Indian of perhaps forty or forty-five years to me. He did so, and was refused; and then said he was at liberty to seek one where he pleased. He was a Skokomish Indian. He went to Squakson and found a girl of perhaps fourteen, and married her. Her father consented, and though she did not, yet she had to submit, for she was bought and paid for. (An order from the U.S. Indian Department has prohibited this in the future.) Usually a man's relations help him to pay for her, although this often does not take place until some time after they have begun to live together. The price varies from one to three or four hundred dollars.

Marriage is by no means confined to persons within the same tribe, for most of the tribes of the Sound are thus connected with all the surrounding tribes. For instance, the Skokomish Indians are intermarried with the following tribes: the Clallams, Squaksons, Chehalis, Nisquallies, Puyallups, Chemakums, Port Madisons, Snohomish, Samish, Duwamish, Skagit, Victorias, Skewhamish, Klikitats and Snoqualmies. Out of 242 Indians in the tribe in 1880, there were only 20 full-blooded Skokomish Indians, and they were called full bloods when not at least one-fourth of some other blood. The Clallams have the blood of eighteen other tribes in their veins; a few having the blood of four different tribes. Two hundred and ninety out of 485 are full-blooded Clallams.

The following are the figures in regard to the Skokomish or Twana Indians: 64 were intermingled with the Clallams, 52 with the Squaksons, 43 with the Chehalis, 24 with the whites, 20 with the Nisquallies, 19 with the Snohomish, 16 with the Port Madisons, 11 with the Puyallups, 9 with the Chemakums, 6 with the Samish, 7 with the Duwamish, 2 with the Skagit, and one each with the Victoria, Klikitat, Skewhamish, and Snoqualmie tribes or bands.

Of the Clallams, 30 are mixed with the Cowichans, 29 with the Makahs, 27 with the Twanas or Skokomish Indians, 23 with the Victoria Indians, 19 with the Quillehutes, 15 with the Chemakums, 10 with the Samish tribe, 9 with the Skagits, 10 with the Nanai-mos, 5 with the Snohomish, 3 each with the Port Madison, Lummi, Nootka, and Clay-oquot Indians, and 1 each with the Nittinat, Soke, Bellingham Bay, and Puyallup tribes, while 14 are part white. Their ancestry was traced back only to the grandparents of the older ones.

Gibbs says that generally they seek wives in other tribes than their own, perhaps from policy or an indistinct idea of propriety. It seems to be a matter of pride to say, "I am half Snoqualmie–half Klikitat." With chiefs this is almost always the case. I once saw a Nit-tinat woman who had just been married to a Clallam. When they were first married he could not talk Nittinat, and she could talk neither Clallam nor Chinook. Their married life must have been under difficulties. When marriages take place between persons of different tribes, usually the woman goes to the tribe of the man, though there are some exceptions.

Marriage with Indians generally takes place much earlier than with whites, boys of fourteen and girls a year or two younger being married. Sometimes such young persons were married together; but usually, to prevent the union of two such young folks, a girl was married to a man of considerable years and a boy to a woman old enough to be his mother, with the calculation that, if they did not suit each other, they could separate when they were older and seek other companions, so that they would be more evenly mated.

The ceremonies at the weddings vary; sometimes, as with whites, being very elaborate, and sometimes less so. The most formal I ever witnessed was in June 1881, on the Sko-komish reservation; the parties being a Skokomish man and a Chehalis woman, who had been informally married two or three months previous. The Chehalis Indians had come the week before, and were camped near a mile from the agency. When I went to the place, about 1 P.M., the Skokomish Indians were feasting. The Chehalis Indians were camped a few rods distant, all of their tents being open except the one containing the bride. After the feast was over the Chehalis Indians sang for a short time, while pounding on sticks for an accompaniment.

After a time the bride was brought into the crowd of Chehalis Indians, and when we saw her, she was covered with many blankets and quilts that we could not see her person. Her friends then unrolled two bolts of calico and stretched them on the ground to the Skokomish Indians, foremost among whom the groom was sitting. This was for a carpet on which the bride was to walk, the ground not being suitable for this purpose. Next they put some plates on the calico, and her friends, surrounding her, began to dance toward the groom. She was held up by two women and walked on one line of calico; the plates being taken up just before she stepped where they were and the calico being taken up as soon as she had passed. When about half way to the groom, her friends stopped in their march, but remained dancing, while she, supported by the two women, went to the Skokomish Indians, where she sat down by the side of the groom on the ground. She was then uncovered, and among other things on her were strings of beads and four breast gorgets of dentalia shells, of different shapes; in one of these there being four rows and fifty shells in a row, each row being separated by a few beads.

A large number of gifts were now brought by her friends and placed on her head, but were immediately pulled down behind her or by her side. These consisted of calico, cloth, dresses, shawls and the like. Two horses were also led along as presents. Shortly after, a Chehalis Indian in a loud voice gave her a new name. Then the Chehalis Indians went to her (at first three at a time) and carried back some of the presents, but not all, to be afterward distributed among her Skokomish friends. The dentalia shell (their ancient money) and some other things remained with her. After this there was an exchange of presents until it became tiresome to me; and, having been told that the main ceremonies were over, I left, after being there about three hours. About four hundred dollars, in money and articles, were paid for the girl, though much of it was returned. Much of the giving of presents means that other presents of like value are to be given in return. Oftentimes there is much gambling, feasting, and horse-racing at the time of these gatherings, though they have no real connection with the marriage ceremony.

Miss S. A. Beatty, in the *Californian* for November 1882, describes a similar wedding, only more elaborate. She says,

> For some weeks previous small squads of Indians, on their sorry looking horses had been coming in, always accompanied by one or more precious race horses, wrapped in the inevitable pink and yellow bed-quilt. A little way behind, was sure to be a wagon with supplies. Sometimes a white covered emigrant wagon, drawn by the time honored old oxen, slowly wended its way across the little prairie. And still they came, from Cowlitz, Nesqually, Puyallup, Squaxon, Skokomish, Tullalup, Quinault, and the towns near, and the bustle increased until a general din prevailed.
>
> Tents were set in the edge of the woods, convenient to water, and if one kept at a safe smelling distance, the scene was quite Arcadian: the blue smoke curling up among the young firs, horses grazing, dogs lying in the sun, lazily eyeing little copper-colored papooses tumbling about on the short grass.
>
> In the mornings all was quiet until eleven or twelve o'clock, when the lordly Indian came yawning out of his tent, sauntered around to see what his neighbors had for breakfast, finally reaching the boarding school where he would like very much to borrow a little tea, sugar, or coffee—sometimes all three—then back again to his kettle of fish or dried clams.
>
> In the afternoon racing was predominant, the race-track being a central road, crossing the prairie, about half a mile long. One of the ugliest horses I ever saw, a black and white blotched affair, seemed to win in most of the races. In answer to our questions, they always said that "the betting wasn't heavy, only some old clothes, blankets, guns, and a few horses." Once in a while a man had to borrow his own clothes to wear until he won others or begged from the whites.
>
> As the day darkened, supper-time came, and a great clatter of kettles and pans was heard among the tents, the women and old women screaming and laughing as they made preparation for the meal of the day. All sat around the campfires jabbering, their gutteral tones strangely intermingling with the bursts of laughter, as they watched and turned the roasting salmon, which forms a part of every meal.
>
> Every night we could hear the singing and the beating of gambling sticks, and we went out one evening to see them play. This gambling was kept up until two or three o'clock in the morning, and some of the Indians grew very much excited, although it would puzzle an outsider to see any cause for excitement.

Meantime, in some of the tents and houses the women and a few men were engaged in dancing. A number of women stood on a long board raised an inch from the ground, so as to spring slightly, their shawls cast aside, or wrapped tightly around them and tied in a knot behind, their eyes cast down, hands hanging by their sides, and feet close together. Facing them, or at one side, the men formed themselves in an irregular kind of line, some standing, some sitting, a number with sticks and bones in their hands, preparatory to helping in the music. Presently there sprung out into the open space an old man, fantastically adorned with ribbons, feathers, and red blanket, in his hand an old tin pan and string of large, flat shells. He commenced a most doleful minor, occasionally introducing lively passages, and danced up and down and around the circle, throwing himself into all possible positions, shaking his shells and beating his pan.

Soon the women began to dance up and down, lifting their feet a few inches from the board, holding the rest of the body perfectly immovable, then joined in the singing. Then the men struck in with their bones and voices, soon ending together with a loud groan on a high pitch, descending to their lowest tones. The whole thing was strange and weird beyond expression, and was kept up all night without change, except in the soloist. Sometimes an old woman takes the place of honor. In one of the tents we found an old woman leading, holding in her hand a saucepan, or rather what was left of one, the handle and all but an inch or two of the bottom being entirely gone.

One day was a sample of all the rest; and soon we began to ask when the wedding was to be, but evasive answers were given; some didn't know, some didn't care to know, and it was put off from day to day, until our patience was nearly exhausted. Finally, one morning, after two weeks' preparation, they sent word that they were all ready, the wedding was to be right away—"Boston folks must come now." So we hurried on our hats and followed the messenger.

Soon we heard the beating of tin cans and the blowing of horns, and looking in the direction indicated, saw a large procession coming towards the middle of the ground, where the principal crowd had gathered around the groom. It came slowly onward, headed by several horsemen in flying colors, with small flags and bits of evergreen fastened to the horses' heads. Behind was a large wagon, in which the bride was seated, surrounded by her household goods and a few women in holiday dress. This enviable personage was a young maiden of ten or twelve years, a daughter of Cowlitz Jim. The groom had reached the advanced age of fourteen, and went by the classic name of John Smith; his father was well known as Captain John Smith.

The procession came within a few yards of the others and stopped. Then the chief rode out on his horse between the two crowds, and delivered a long harangue to both parties, wheeling on his horse, to turn to one, then to the other. As it was in Indian, we couldn't understand much of it, but it seemed to be in reference to the duties of the young couple. A great jabbering ensued on both sides, and much running to and fro of Captain John Smith and friends and Cowlitz Jim and friends. Soon all went back to their places, and two squaws of the bride's party brought some bolts of calico and spread it in a straight line from the bride to the groom, making a carpeted path. Two others had a lot of calico over their arms, cut into pieces a yard and a yard and a half long; these they strewed on either side of the calico path. Two others had strings of beads which they threw along with the pieces of cloth. Then they told the Boston folks to help themselves; it was a free potlatch. Several neighbors had come over to witness the ceremony, so we all pitched in with much laughing, scrambling after the pretty pieces of calico and long strings of beads. After we had made our grab, they distributed more things—apples, beads, dishes, pipes, calico, and clothing—and told us we must not take anything, this was the Indian potlatch; so we stood still, looking on at the fun.

While the last potlatch was going on, the bride was taken out of the wagon, and a more comical-looking sight we never saw; perfect shouts of laughter went up from our party. After being dressed in all her finery, two or three gay quilts had been thrown over her head, completely enveloping her, so that we could see neither face, hands, nor feet. Two clutchmen took hold of her, one on either side, and led her along the calico trail, Cowlitz Jim and a few relations following. Slowly they came, the two fathers halloing some gibberish at the top of their voices. Then they set her by the boy, who had been blindfolded, with their backs to one another. One of the principal women, who had been flourishing around in white, suddenly blossomed out in a red dress, sat down by the bride, and took off, one at a time, three quilts, five striped and four plain shawls, and seven dresses, leaving only a dingy, tattered, dark calico. On her head were headdresses of the long trumpet shaped shells (dentalium) used as Indian money; around her throat were necklaces of the same; also of beads by the quantity, some of them being larger than a robin's egg. She also had around her waist an apron made of Indian money, and glass beads, and according to the value of the money, worth perhaps a thousand dollars. In her ears were several earrings, her fingers were loaded with rings; and her arms from the wrist to above the elbow, were covered with brass and silver bracelets; some not going clear round, were clinched into the flesh. Over an hour was occupied in taking off her jewelry and superfluous clothing.

Then they commenced on the boy. First he was made to kneel, and one of the chiefs put fifteen or twenty dollars on his head, this caused a most outrageous jabber and wrangle. While they were so engaged, one of the younger Indians stole slyly up and snatched the money. We fully expected a big fight, but everybody broke out into the heartiest laughing. It seemed to be the joke of the day, and we thought they never would stop and go on with the ceremony. But presently an old woman gave some more money, then Captain John Smith threw a string of beads around the boy's neck, and took the handkerchief from his eyes. One of the young Indians rushed up and made him sit down; another caught hold of his boots and pulled them off; still another grasped the legs of his overalls and pulled them off, and so on until he had on but a simple suit, like unto his bride.

The young man and wife were then set side by side, so that they could look at one another, if so inclined, but the boy was angry, and would not vouchsafe so much as a single glance at his bride. He did not want to be married, and if his wife's happiness depended on his good behavior, she would evidently have a sorry time. Fortunately she did not seem to be concerned either way.

The bride and the groom being disposed of, the business of the day commenced, the handing over to the rightful owner the purchase money and the things. A good part of the crowd ran back and forth trying to make a trade. Old clothes were traded, given to the bride, or carried back again. Quilts and blankets performed the same journey, horses were brought out, inspected, and made to show their good qualities on the race track. A general hubbub ensued for several hours. When we left, the two fathers were still shouting their claims at the top of their voices. The afternoon closed with a big race, nearly all the horses on the prairie taking part, and dancing and gambling made hideous the night. The next morning by noon all had gone.

Generally, however, the ceremony was not so elaborate, oftentimes there being no ceremony, and sometimes when there was a ceremony, it took place some time, perhaps a year, after the parties had begun to live together.

At one time a Twana woman was bought and married to a Twana man, with whom she lived about two years, when he died. His relations then claimed the right to keep her with them, not even allowing her to return to her brothers to live, and they also claimed the right to marry her again to whomsoever they would. It required a little firmness on the part of those in authority to prevent this. Once bought, always bought.

The following in regard to the Makah Indians on the subject is here inserted as of interest, by way of comparison. Judge J. G. Swan, in his "Indians of Cape Flattery," gives an account of a rejected suitor, the parties being the relatives of chiefs.

> In going to the house where the bride lived, the ceremonies consisted of the representation of a whaling scene. Eight men carried on their shoulders a canoe in which were three men. Another man, covered with a blanket, crawled on the ground to represent the whale. At times a man in the canoe would throw his harpoon toward the whale, taking care not to hit him. After arriving at the house, the harpoon was thrown with such force against the door, a single plank, as to split it—Cupid's dart knocking, in their way. The door was not opened, when guns and blankets were piled beside it, and a similar knock was made, but all to no purpose, and the parties returned home. An acceptable suitor came afterward from the Nittinats. Before landing, a speech was made, stating why they had come and how much they were willing to pay. Having landed, they formed a blanket procession. It was headed by a medicine man who was gaudily dressed, with face painted red, a bunch of eagle's feathers in his hair, a wooden rattle in one hand and a bunch of scallop shells in the other, with which he kept tune to a song. Next to him was another Indian with a blanket on his shoulder, while he held a corner of another blanket, the other corner of which was held by a third Indian, who was followed by another in a similar way, and in this manner eighty-four blankets were carried to the door of the bride's house, which at this time was open, showing that the lover was accepted. But the blankets were not enough, so the party returned to their canoes, and in a similar way brought as many more. But the parents of the girl were in no haste, and the marriage was deferred for a week; the time being spent in speechmaking, dancing and the like. At last the parents yielded, and the maiden was carried off in triumph.

In general, he says, the groom receives back what he has paid, which he takes home with him, and which he distributes to his friends; the fact being that what is said to be paid for a wife is what the groom is willing to give to assembled friends. The same is true of other tribes, the bride herself receiving quite a share.

Polygamy. This was allowed, and common, among the more important Indians. There is hardly any of it now left. I have never known any man to have more than three wives, and only one to have that many. At first the authorities gave orders to prevent any more plural marriages, but at last about 1885, there came an order for all who had more than one wife to put away all but one. In two cases on the Skokomish reservation, it required some locking up of some of the parties concerned to enforce this, but it was at last accomplished.

Gibbs adds, "The more wives a man possesses, the richer he is. The accession of a new wife in a lodge very naturally produces jealousy and discord, and the first often returns in dudgeon to her friends, to be reclaimed by her husband when he chooses, perhaps after propitiating her by some presents. The first wife nearly always retains a sort of predominance in the lodge, and the man, at least after his appetite for a subsequent one is satisfied, usually lives with her."

CHILDREN

At the birth of children, the woman sometimes attends to herself, but is generally assisted by some of her female friends. A few women become somewhat well known as *accoucheurs*, being superior to the common woman in this respect. As the people have become more civilized, labour has become more difficult. In a few instances I have known it to cause the death of the mother and also of the child, though this is not common. Formerly after the birth of the child, the mother was kept secluded as unclean, for about a week, and for a long time, she was not allowed to touch fish, flesh, fowl or game, or the gun, fishing apparatus, or anything by means of which they secured the game, as they feared it would bring ill luck.

Infanticide. I have never known of this or heard of it except in the case of twins. Gibbs speaks of it—then less common than formerly—as a proof of want of affection between parents and children.

Abortion is sometimes practiced; more commonly, it is said, by means of some medicine which they have.

Twins

Twins among the Indians of Puget Sound are very uncommon; but in former times, when any did appear, they had an exceedingly hard time, as the Indians were superstitiously afraid of them. During the past eighteen years, I have known of but one pair among the Twana Indians, and one pair among the Clallams. The Twanas were well taken care of, as the parents had always lived on the reservation where the Indian Agent had previously had a pair; and so they had had an opportunity of seeing the white customs in regard to them. These parents had also been educated in school, and were quite civilized. To all intents and purposes they were white, and so nothing was done about them except that there was some talk about the former customs in regard to them.

But the pair among the Clallams did not fare so well. Their parents were old-fashioned Indians, were surrounded by old-fashioned Indians, were about eighty miles from the reservation, and they had never had a home on it. The home of their parents was in Port Discovery, but they were at Neah Bay, catching seals, about eighty miles from home at the time the twins were born. Immediately the Neah Bay Indians became afraid of them, and quickly drove them and their parents away, as they were afraid that the twins would scare all the fish away from their waters. Accordingly, the parents returned to Port Discovery on a steamer, though the Indians were quite unwilling to have them go in that way, fearing that they would frighten all the fish away; and earnestly wished them to walk the entire distance, over mountains and through the forests or on the beach, although there was neither beach nor road much of the way.

When they reached home, some of the old Indians of their own tribe were very much afraid. They threatened to kill one of the twins, so that the father did not dare to leave home. Hence he could not go off and work and earn food; neither would they allow him to fish near his home, although the fish at that time were very abundant there, for fear that all the fish would leave. Hence the man was greatly troubled to get food enough for his family to keep them from starving. They told him to live on clams. They would not go near his house if it could be avoided, and, if they had to pass it, would make quite a detour around.

It is said that long ago, when such an event occurred, the other Indians drove the fortunate or unfortunate mother into the woods with the twins—the father going also if he wished—and there they had to live alone, and they were not to return as long as both twins were alive; one must be disposed of in some way. If any friends pitied them enough to furnish them with food, it was carried to some place where the parents were not present, and then, when the carrier had retired, the parents could take it to their lonely home.

Other tribes on the Pacific coast had somewhat similar customs, while others honored the twins greatly, according to the reports of the British Association for the Advancement of Science, which speak of them in British Columbia, and Power's "Tribes of California," which speaks of them in that state.

Cradling

A considerable number have adopted cradles on rockers, similar to those among the poorer classes of the whites; still the old way of caring for infants is quite common, especially among the Clallams. For this they sometimes hollow out a piece of thick cedar board, which is a little longer and a little wider than the child, to the depth of about an inch, and sometimes they use a plain board, which is not hollowed out. In either case they place on the board beaten cedar bark, on which they lay the child, who is covered with cloth and tied to the board with strings, which pass through holes in it. The arms and feet are thus tied so firmly that the child cannot move them, and in fact can move hardly anything except its head. Sometimes another board is placed in a slanting direction so as to elevate the head and another so as to elevate the feet.

Occasionally a cap or bonnet, woven from cedar bark, split, is placed over the head and face of the child by the Clallams to protect them from the smoke and dirt. These are usually imported from the Makahs.

One method of rocking the baby is to take a green pole about six feet long and not far from two inches in diameter, tapering toward the upper end, fastening the larger end in the ground or in the floor, in a slanting direction, then suspending the child from the upper end; and then when it cries, to keep the pole springing and the child swinging by means of a string. Often the mother's toe does this, while her hands are busy at other work. Another way is to attach some ropes to the joists of the room, or to some of its posts, fasten a blanket to these ropes, place the child and its bed in the blanket, and swing it with a string attached to the rope.

The practice of flattening the head, which is done while the child is fastened in this bed, has been spoken of in Chapter III.

Sometimes, it is said, a board was carved in the shape of a rough-looking face, and when a child cried severely, a parent put this mask over his or her own face and sang a song (no. 10, Chapter XIV) to frighten the child so that it should stop crying. I have one of these masks, which was made for me by a Clallam. The hideousness of the carved face ought to have been effective. I have never seen this operation performed or heard of it elsewhere except among the Clallams.

Baby Rattles

The only time I ever saw a rattle to amuse the babies with was at Squakson. It is made of small slits of wood woven together so as to make a closed basket about 3 by 3 inches, and 2 thick, with a handle about 2½ inches long somewhat after the style of American rubber rattles. I incline to the opinion that formerly they did not have such but made this in imitation of our style. Stones and pieces of tin are put inside to make it rattle.

Carrying Children

When travelling on foot, the children are generally carried in the well-known method, placing the child on the back of the mother, and wrapping a shawl around both mother and child.

On horseback they are carried much as white people. I have never seen or heard of them being carried on the Sound as they are commonly carried by the Indians east of the Cascade mountains, by tying a strong string or rope to the board on which the child is fastened, and then hanging it to the horn of the saddle, thus letting the child hang down by the shoulders of the horse.

Nursing

The children are often nursed until they are much older than is common with white children—sometimes even until they are three years old, or perhaps older.

Clallam baby cradle, cedar bark head rest

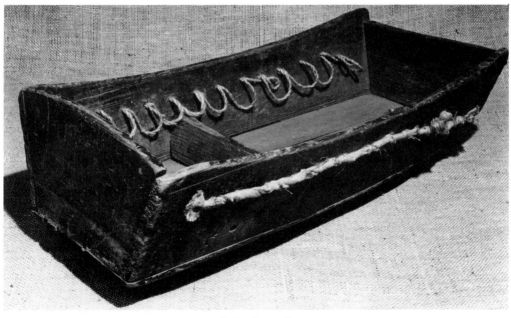

Infant's cradle

Models of Indian cradles, Makah

Detail of cradle

"Baby frightener," Clallam

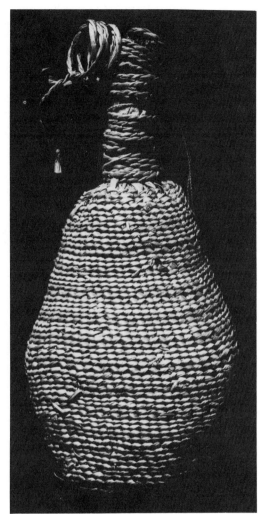

Baby rattles, Twana

Naming Children

Usually they are not named at as early an age as with the whites, but when one, two, or three years old. Formerly, when the name was given, a feast was made and presents given to the guests, but I have not learned of any such event since I have been among them. After careful inquiry I have not been able to learn that their names mean anything. They say that their names are like those of white people, that perhaps long ago, when the names first originated they meant something, but if this is so it was so long ago that they have entirely forgotten the meaning. Gibbs says that some but not all of their names have a meaning, as Squashum, the name of a sub-chief of the Snoqualmies, meant "smoke" or "fog." I have not found it so.

An Indian may change his name once or several times during his life; sometimes he does so when one of the same name dies, as it is not good etiquette to pronounce the name of the recently dead. Two or three years after death the name of the deceased may be mentioned; and with the Clallams, at least, a person may take the name of his departed father, grandfather, or other direct paternal ancestor. Often when this is done, the person thus changing the name makes a feast and gives presents. The grandfather's name is especially preferred.

Nearly all the men, women, and children have "Boston" names, which they have received in various ways. Some of these are a combination of Indian and American names and constructed utterly regardless of taste, as Squakson Bill, Old Shell, Mr. Axe, Mr. Stone, Stuttering Dick, and Chubby. Others aim a little higher, but just high enough to make them ridiculous, as Dr. Bob, Mrs. Bob, and Sally Bob; Tyee Charley, Mrs. Tyee Charley, his wife, and Julia Tyee Charley, his daughter. Others have been content to be simply like Americans, as John Robinson and Joseph Spar. Others still have aspired to as great names as America or Great Britain could give. Such as General Grant, Horace Greeley, Benjamin Butler, Robert Burns, Patrick Henry, and Andrew Johnson. We have had on the Skokomish reservation both Simon Peter and Andrew Peter, his brother, not sons of Zebedee, but of Old Peter himself.

I once stood at a grave yard at Port Townsend, at the head of a row of graves with an Indian, who rather surprised me by saying, "Here lies General Scott, General Gaines, and General Taylor." The man who for many years was the prominent head chief of the Clallams, rejoiced in the name of Duke of York, and those of his two wives, Jenny Lind and Queen Victoria. I had the honor of performing the marriage ceremony of his son, the Prince of Wales, and to find that, on account of his name, it was telegraphed all over the world among the Associate Press dispatches. Often, however, it has been sadly corrupted by the other Indians, either through ignorance or inability to pronounce it correctly, to Patch-o-wels. The successor of the Duke of York was Lord Jim Balch, but his successor was only Cook House Billy. We have also had Duke William, Duke of Wellington, and Lord John, whose son curiously was named John Lord.

These old English royal names were given when the Hudson's Bay Company held sway here. Afterwards, when loggers and mill men settled in the region, who were known to the Indians and often to many whites only by the names of Jack, John, Pat, Bob, Jim, or Bill, the Indians were satisfied when they obtained similar ones. Often so many obtained the same name that some other one, descriptive, had to be joined with it, so that we have had Little Billy, Big Bill, Sore-eyed Bill, and Squakson Bill; Big John, Carpenter John, Tenas (little) John, and Doctor John; Tenas Charley, Doctor Charley, and Tyee Charley. Of late years, however, I have made it my practice when it could be done— when I legally married the older ones, or when they obtained their first legal papers, or when the children enter school—to give them such names that they would not be ashamed of them.

WOMEN

Formerly when a girl reached womanhood, a puberty dance was given. On reaching Jamestown among the Clallams in December 1878, I found that on the night previous to my arrival there had been such a dance. All of the Indians within six miles, about 125 in number, had been invited to it. It was too late to see the performance, but I was told that it consisted of singing, feasting, and tamahnous in connection with the dancing. I have not known of such a dance among the Twanas since I have been among them.

The standing of the women in the family and society is inferior to that of the white women, though by no means do they become as near like slaves, as some Indian women in the interior of the continent are reported to be. At one council, I knew of one woman who spoke and was listened to as if her opinion were well worth hearing.

Gibbs, in his *Tribes of Western Washington and Northwestern Oregon*, says that "the condition of the woman is that of slavery under any circumstances. She is the property of her father, of her nearest relative, or of her tribe until she becomes that of her husband." While on Puget Sound she is bought when she becomes a wife, yet I have never seen anything that led me to believe that the word "slave" could properly be applied to her. His statement may refer to other tribes than those on the Sound, or to those on the Sound long ago.

The women soon grow old and early in life begin to have a wrinkled and aged appearance.

Squaw's lecture. Mr. George E. Barnes in an article in the *Seattle Post-Intelligencer*, speaks of one curious practice among the Indians on the Sound in early days, which he calls the squaw's lecture. At stated periods it was delivered exclusively to the Indian women. He says,

> An important member of the tribe, the big chief or the medicine man, would select a promontory or island remote from the mainland, perhaps in the vicinity of Port Ludlow, and paddle himself there, solitary and alone, on a fine day. Soon all the squaws would be seen following him, paddling vigorously toward the common point. No bucks were among them; they all remained on the mainland. The preacher, instructor, exhorter, or whatever he was, often stood in the water up to his knees for a full hour or more while he delivered his discourse; but the Indian maidens and squaws gathered as close around him as their canoes would permit, so as to catch every word that fell from his lips. Savonarola was never more in earnest than this dusky preacher; his face and action showed he realized the importance of his work. He was supposed to be instructing the women as to their proper duties in their savage life; but whatever he said, they were eager to hear it all. There was no noise save the occasional chafing of one canoe against another as they moved with the slight swell of the water. It was an exciting spectacle to see the dusky women, when the service was over, start in an emulative race for the mainland, their dark sinewy arms plying the flashing paddle as the light canoe cut swiftly the placid waters of the Sound, until with laughing banter the prows touched the shore and they rejoined the bucks, who were idly awaiting them.

Too grateful for the blessing lent,
Of simple tastes and mind content.[2]

IMMORALITIES

Unchastity was very common, especially before people were married. Unlawful connection with another man's wife was not very common, as the injured husband generally felt too greatly wronged to allow such acts to go unpunished. Still, he would bear much more in this respect than white people do. There are cases on the Skokomish reservation to illustrate this. One man is caring for his son by another Indian woman than his wife, at his home, and as far as I know his wife never made any serious disturbance because of his unfaithfulness. Another man is caring for two children of his wife, born since their legal marriage, whose fathers are white men, and I have never known of any serious trouble between the man and his wife because of this.

Such intercourse with unmarried girls was hardly forbidden, and it brought no disgrace if not accompanied with childbirth, which they took care to prevent. In fact when the Indian Agent first began to punish such acts among the Twana school children under his care, the older Indians were opposed to any severe punishment, for they said that their parents never told them that it was very wrong.

DIVORCE

This was very common and easily obtained. Very few men or women went through life without one or more divorces, nor did it lower their social standing. If a man put away his wife, he generally gave her a present, but if she left him, he did not give her anything.

INDUSTRIES

The business of the women was to cook, get berries, roots, and sprouts, dig clams, clean the fish, dry the berries, clams, and fish, make the mats and baskets, spin yarn, and make the old-fashioned blankets and cloths and some of the ornaments. Since the introduction of white industries, they have been accustomed to do much the same work in the house as the white women. Basket-making, mat-making, gathering berries, and digging clams, spinning yarn and knitting socks, sewing, washing for whites, and digging potatoes for the whites, as well as the general duties of housekeeping are their principal industries now. Socks, washing, berries, and potato digging are their principal sources of money-revenue.

The men's business was to hunt, fish, make canoes, planks, build houses, and take care of the horses. They still do these things, except making planks. They also do much work at farming. Many of them work in saw-mills, and a large number are loggers, preferring

Indians in the hop fields, Skokomish

this business to farming, even when they have good land, if they can only make it pay. Canoeing for whites has been quite a business with Clallams, until lately. Steamers have ploughed their waters so often and regularly as to almost entirely destroy the business. Hop-picking on the White river, Puyallup, and Duwamish river bottoms has for ten or twelve years been a great business for all the Sound Indians in September, as well as for more northern Indians and those east of the Cascades and west of the Olympic mountains. They have made money very fast in the short season of the business. For the last two or three years white pickers have begun, however, to crowd greatly on this source of revenue as the times have grown harder. A dozen years ago they had almost the monopoly of the business and those who have kept sober and attended to their business have held their own with the whites to the present times. Many growers prefer them as they are more willing to live out-doors, begin early, and complain less than most whites.

Logging has been for twenty-five years a very prominent business among them, as they sell the logs to the different saw-mills on the Sound. After the road is built, they cut the timber. As they wish to cut the trees much higher than they can when they stand on the

Frank Allen and Billy Thompson, Skokomish Indians on chopping boards

ground, they cut notches in the tree, and insert therein a plank, about 4 or 5 feet long, and 6 or 8 inches wide, with the end ironed, on which they stand and cut with an ax. When the tree has fallen, they measure it with a pole, saw it with a cross-cut saw, and take off a part of the bark, so that it will slide easily. This is done with an ax, or a heavy iron made for the purpose, about 3 feet long, widened and sharpened at the end. They then haul the logs to the water with three yoke of oxen. For a whip they use a small stick about 5 or 6 feet long, with a small brad in the end, with which they punch the cattle. They use American yokes and chains. When the saws are dull, they file and set them with American files and saw-sets. When the boom is full, a steamer from the mill comes for it and tows it to the mill. The money being received, they first pay the necessary expenses of running the camp, including the provisions, and divide the rest among themselves according to the amount of work done by each.

They mess together, some of their wives generally cooking for the camp. Their logging roads are expensive. Of necessity in hauling long logs there cannot be short turns in them, they must be tolerably level, and also must go through heavy timber. Large trees must be cut down, large logs cut out of the way, roots dug out, holes filled up, and small banks dug down. This is done with axes, saws, spades, and shovels. Then skids, about a foot in diameter and 8 feet long, are placed across the road, at intervals of about 10 feet, on which the logs are hauled. Where it is very muddy, especially over the salt-water marsh, corduroy road and bridge are made. On one road there is more than 1,000 feet of this work. The skids are kept constantly oiled with dog-fish oil, so that the logs may slide easily. This is much after the customs of the whites, except that they divide the profits instead of paying the hands. Whenever they have tried the latter plan, they have failed financially.

The census of 1880 gave the following figures in regard to the industries of the Twanas and Clallams. Of the Twanas, 43 were farmers, 4 carpenters, 2 blacksmiths, 4 laborers, 7 hunters, 20 fish men, 21 lumbermen, 1 interpreter, 1 policeman, 6 medicine men, 7 washerwomen, 6 women basket and mat makers, and 1 assistant matron.

Of the Clallams, 34 were laborers in the saw-mills, who represent 102 persons, 19 are farmers representing 68 persons, 23 day laborers, 79 fishermen, 17 sealers, 14 canoe men, 6 canoe makers, 7 hunters, 3 policemen under commission from Government, and 6 others under appointment from the chiefs; 13 are medicine men and 4, medicine women, 1 carpenter, 2 wood choppers, 1 is apprenticed to a farmer and 1 apprenticed in the blacksmith shop. Of the women, 40 report themselves as mat and basket makers, and 9 as washerwomen.

CONVERSATIONS

Common conversation is about whatever concerns them. As they could not read, to us it would often seem trivial. As they have learned more, they have talked about more important subjects, yet as a general thing the weather, hunting, fishing, horses, cattle, school, government, quarrels, games, religion, traditions, myths, and the deeds of ancestors, are the principal subjects.

CUSTOMS

Sleeping customs. They all slept in the same room on their bed-platforms or on the ground.

Customs when about to build a house, to go on a hunting or fishing expedition, to make a journey, or to engage in any new pursuit. Formerly, as now, when about to build a house, they did nothing special, as their houses were so small and often removed, that it was an event of no great importance; but when about to go on a hunting or fishing expedition, to make a journey, or engage in anything special, they would tamahnous, their way of invoking the presence of the Great Spirit, so that they might be successful. They do very little of this now.

Etiquette. In travelling, if they camp near acquaintances, they will not go in to the house or stay in it unless first invited. They are very hospitable to friends. There was not much form in salutation; only a word or two, and sometimes shaking of hands, which they have learned from Americans. Visitors are not questioned much. Their hosts waited until they were ready to tell the news.

XX

POTLATCHES

A PECULIAR CUSTOM WITH THE INDIANS in this region is the potlatch, which takes its name from the Chinook word, meaning "to give," as the most prominent feature in it is the distribution of gifts.[1] I have never heard of this custom existing farther south than the Columbia river or farther east than the Cascade mountains, but on the west it extends to the Pacific Ocean, and on the north into Alaska, a rich chief there having in 1877 made one at which four thousand Indians are said to have been present. It seems to be chiefly confined to those Indians who live near the salt water, as it would be difficult for those who have to travel on horseback to carry the amount of articles which they have need of on such occasions.

AGE AND ORIGIN

How old the custom is no one seems to know. A part of the ruins of a very old potlatch house were found while digging below Port Gamble.

The origin is enveloped in mystery since it runs back farther than the memory of the oldest inhabitant. It is certain that the giving of one makes the giver a great man among the other Indians. I infer that one or the other or both of the following reasons may have been the cause of them.

It may have been that the chiefs, in order to gain and keep the good will of the people, gathered them together and made presents to them. Gradually other tribes were invited, on account of relationship or friendship, and the compliment was returned. Other persons, not chiefs, but who wished to become such, or at least to become prominent persons, followed the example, until it has grown to its present size, so that often nearly all the surrounding tribes are invited, and almost every person of any prominence, both of the men and women, feel bound to have a share in giving one, at least once in a lifetime. They have grown so large, however, that seldom does even the richest person feel able to give one, hence they combine together, sometimes twenty or thirty being concerned in the same one.

Or, it may have been that the common small feasts, which often take place among them, have occasionally grown larger, until they have become a potlatch. In fact, there is hardly a dividing line between the two: the small feast at times being quite large, and having connected with it the distribution of presents, and the potlatch being at times quite small, only a few from the nearer villages and of the same tribe being invited.

FREQUENCY

They are not at all regular in their occurrence, but the same region usually has one every year or two. The same person is not often engaged in giving one more than once in fifteen or twenty years, and perhaps only once during life. Sometimes, however, there are exceptions to this. Persons will sometimes save everything they can get for years, living in the poorest way and being clothed very scantily, while they have trunks filled with goods, and a large amount of money stored away. When the potlatch is over, the same person will sometimes begin to save again in like manner for the same purpose.

The Twana or Skokomish Indians have given three potlatches within fifteen years, different members of the tribe being engaged in the different ones; and during eight years a part or all of the tribe have been invited to eight others, given by four of the neighboring tribes, and some or all of them attended all these except one. They do not often go more than a hundred miles to attend them. They last from about a week to three weeks, and are usually held in the fall or winter, as several hundred Indians can hardly afford to spend that amount of time—and a week or so more needed in getting ready, going, and returning home—during the summer when work can be had, and the money which comes with it.

At present their glory is departing in this region. Many of the younger people, who have been in contact with the whites for the past twenty-five years, have become ashamed to go through many of the practices, which were formerly the most savage and the most interesting; they have invented nothing new to take their places, so that the last one which I attended was called very dry by the chief. They are likewise slowly learning that their money can be of more use to them in some other way than to give it away. Probably to the north, where their civilization is less rapid, they will last some time longer.

In the distribution, all the invited ones do not receive equal amounts, but special friends, the young and strong, and those who expect soon to make a potlatch generally receive the most, in order that their favor may be gained, so that when they shall make one they will be liberal to those making the present one; but the old and those not expected to make one do not receive very much, as, according to their ideas, it would be a poor investment to give to such persons. Sometimes, indeed, instead of calling it a gift, they call it a paying back for money once received. This has been especially the case when they have been urged to cease the practice; they have replied, that as they have received money at such times, it would be much like stealing it were they not to make a potlatch and return it.

It has been my fortune to be present a good share of the time at four of these festivals, in order to watch over the Indians, prevent drunkenness, and see that they did nothing improper, according to their ideas of impropriety. One of these was on the Skokomish reservation in the fall of 1876. It was the largest and longest of any, about twelve hundred persons being present, and it lasted three weeks. The next was at Jamestown, in Clallam county, in February 1878; the next at Skokomish in the fall of the same year; and the last at Squakson Island, in the fall of 1880. The distribution of gifts is about the last thing done, the previous time being spent in religious ceremonies and social intercourse, including feasting, while side shows are the procuring of wives, and gambling, the latter being very prominent.

Besides these they have attended several others. For about five years, I kept a list of those to which some of the Twanas or Clallams were invited. I have not done so since that time because at the close of the five years, the Indians had become so civilized that the potlatches became less frequent. During the last fourteen years I am not aware that any of the Twanas, Clallams, Nisquallies, Squaksons, Puyallups, Port Madisons, or Upper Chehalis Indians have given a potlatch, with one exception, and very few of them have attended one given by other Indians. During the five years from 1874 to 1879, I knew of the Twanas attending seven given by themselves, the Clallams, Squaksons, and Upper Chehalis Indians; and I knew of the Clallams attending six among themselves, the Twanas, and Sooke Indians of British Columbia, but undoubtedly they attended more as they are more addicted to them, and live so far away that some of them probably attended some when I did not know of it.

POTLATCH NO. 1

This was given by several Twanas on the Skokomish reservation in October 1876. For many years they had been preparing for it. Old women went in rags, while filling trunks with calico to give away at this time. Of these boxes of dry goods some had been deposited in my hands for more than a year. In the winter of 1874–75, they began the erection of the house, working only a day or two at it now and then; but in the summer following, the leader of the affair died and nothing more was done until the spring of 1876, when others took hold of it and half finished it. They set the time for the potlatch in August, but because they were not ready, deferred it for one month and then for another. Two or three weeks previous to the event they again went to work at the house and finished it. It was by no means large enough for all who were present, but mat houses, tents, and other temporary shelters were put up around it by various persons.

The Invitations

About the 14th of October, they sent runners to the various surrounding tribes to invite them to come. Each one who takes part in the potlatch first decides whom he wishes to invite. He then prepares tickets of invitation. These are about the size of a lead pencil, and from three to six inches long, which he entrusts to a runner. When all engaged in the potlatch have done so, the messengers start. Occasionally only one or two messengers carry the invitations from all the givers, but usually there are from three to eight, sometimes one messenger carrying the tickets of only one giver.

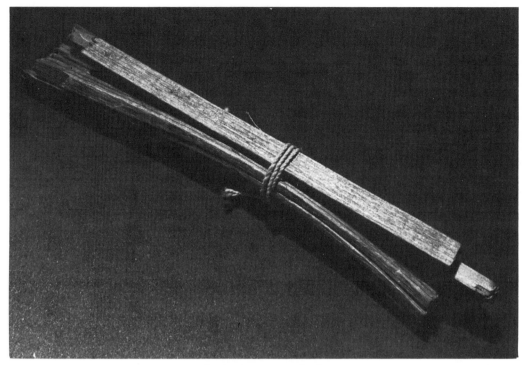

Invitation to a potlatch

Twice I have been present where these invitations have been received, and they were certainly very cool receptions. At one time the man whom they wished to invite was not at home, but his two wives were. The messengers stood about a rod from the house, when one of them said a few words and threw a small stick or card of invitation towards the house into the grass. Other messengers who came with him gave him four or five more, which were also thrown into the grass where they were left. Other Indians who chanced to be present did not seem to take much interest in the event and the messengers departed. This was on the Skokomish reservation at the house of Mountain Man, and the messengers were Squakson Indians.

At another time I was sitting in the house of Chubby at Jamestown, a Clallam Indian, talking with him, when six or eight messengers from British Columbia entered. Chubby sat near the fire with his back towards the door. When the messengers came in, he did not get up or even turn around. They ranged themselves in a row behind him, each one made his speech of invitation and threw his ticket on the floor toward Chubby, who answered with a grunt each time, and then they went out. Chubby hardly looked toward the messengers, his children soon broke up the tickets for playthings, and he seemed to take the affair as coolly as if a child of four years had entered the house.

The invited usually start only a day or two after they receive the invitations. Once, however, at least, I knew them to start before these were received. I was going with some Indians on a steamer from Jamestown to Clallam Bay. Among them was a messenger to invite the Clallam Bay Indians to a potlatch at Sequim. When we reached Port Angeles, which is about twenty-five or thirty miles from Sequim, and nearly forty from Clallam Bay, we met the Clallam Bay Indians already thus far on their way to the potlatch. These were closely related, and I suppose knew they were to be invited.

The Reception

At the Skokomish potlatch of 1876, the first installment of guests, about a hundred Chehalis Indians, arrived on the 29th of October. They came in wagons and on horse-back to within about four miles of the house—as near as they could because of water. Here they were met by a leader of the potlatch, and after considerable speech-making they camped for the night. The next day the Twanas sent six large canoes to take them to the house. At noon they rowed past the agency, one mile from camp, abreast, singing a solo and chorus, accompanied by drumming on two drums and pounding on canoes. After passing the agency they broke line and so went on for a mile or more until they came in sight of the potlatch house, when they again formed abreast and rowed to the house in alignment with their music. At landing there was more ceremony, for the visitors had brought many presents. Each present was held by the donor while he made a speech, after which he gave it to a Twana, who replied to the speech, when the gift was handed to the one for whom it was intended.

These presents consisted of calico, blankets, two beeves, dried meat, and money (sixty dollars having been counted as coming from one canoe), and seemed to be given to the prominent Twanas. The Chehalis then landed and went to one part of the house assigned them, where they took lodgings. The whole performance occupied three hours and was longer than that of any other tribe.

Two days afterwards the Clallams came in sight and when about three miles away a member of the Twanas went into a canoe to meet them and learn their wishes about landing, this being the common custom. They learned, however, that while the Clallams were coming, a child had been killed by the caving of a bank. The child had some relations among the Twanas, who immediately began a mourning. The Clallams stopped on the beach at a Twana burying-ground, a mile from the potlatch house, where they left the corpse in a box on a log, covered with mats and blankets, as they intended to take it home with them on their return. Here a canoe-load of the Twana relations of the child came, and there was mourning again, but it did not last very long, and after it was done the Clallams entered their canoes, went a half mile farther and camped, most of the afternoon having been thus consumed.

The next morning they all came abreast close to the shore near the house in about fifteen canoes, singing and dancing and pounding on drums, canoes, and boards. It was intended that this should be the grand reception, as the Clallams were about the best musicians and performers on the Sound, but a strong wind arose so that it was hardly possible for the canoes to remain long near the water's edge. While they were in front of the house they sang solos and choruses, some of them holding guns and paddles in their hands and jumping up and down. One had a rattle. Some had on cedar bark bands, which had eagles' and hawks' feathers and wings in them. The faces of the majority were painted—many black, a few red. After a few minutes of this performance the Twanas replied to them from the beach in a somewhat similar way. Some of the faces of the Twanas were blackened a little, but not as much as those of the Clallams, and they had neither rattles, headbands, guns, or paddles.

Thus, the salutation and reply were kept up for about half an hour, when the Clallams landed with no further ceremony and went to their quarters in the house.

The ceremonies of landing were a slight part of the black tamahnous and the only performance of the kind during the potlatch, and this was the only reception in which the Twanas replied to the songs of their guests.

It was intended that this should have been a much grander performance, much longer on the water, and also when disembarking, as the Clallams are among the best performers on the Sound at such times, but before they were ready to land a strong wind arose, which made the water so rough that the canoes could not remain long at the water's edge.

Other tribes kept coming every day or two for two weeks, and the reception was much like that already described. Generally, they were met two or three miles before reaching their destination by some of the Twanas, who learned their wishes about landing and directed preparations to be made accordingly; and commonly they brought some presents of cloth, food, and money, and danced and sang, but a few landed without any ceremony. When they had all arrived, it was estimated that there were from a thousand to twelve hundred present, comprising, besides those already mentioned, Squaksons, Nisqually, and Port Madison Indians, and a few from the Snohomish, Lummi, and Puyallup reservations.

They who lived farthest off had come a distance of about 150 or 175 miles, but these had relations by marriage among the givers of the potlatch.

Entertainment

Dancing. Generally the evenings were occupied with dancing of some kind, either serious or comic. Frequently, one whole evening was allotted to the dancing of one tribe. These dances were accompanied with drumming, singing, and clapping of hands. In dancing they jumped up and down, sometimes joining hands in a circle, and sometimes each one dancing singly, jumping the whole length of the house. At times the men alone danced, and again the women joined them, generally having a part of the circle to themselves. Once almost all joined in the dance, having green branches in their hands. On this occasion they danced at one time without progression, and at another time they moved around from one end of the house to the other.

The Clallams gave one dance, difficult to describe, in which men only participated. In this a leader, painted, with eagle wings and feathers dangling from his head, and arrayed in a long blanket, played very curious antics with contortions of his neck, hands, and entire body; while the rest stood near him, jumping up and down to their music, and afterwards, all dressed in striped shawls and blankets, danced the whole length of the floor with many absurd maneuvers. I think this was a war dance. One dance was said to be in memory of a deceased child, after which presents were made by friends of the child to some of the Twanas. Thus almost every evening was occupied from the time of the arrival of the first until the close of the affair, a period of three weeks.

Gambling. There was more or less gambling during the day-time and occasionally at night, but few, comparatively, being engaged in it at any one time. Sometimes the gambling was accompanied by music. Once it was said there was a bet on a game of $200 in money, together with several horses and guns, but the parties played until six o'clock in the morning and then stopped, neither party winning.

Generally they gambled with disks, but sometimes with the pairs of bones or cards already described. There are said to be professional gamblers among them who visit such gatherings, without an invitation, in order to ply their avocation.

Tamahnous. There was much of tamahnous in connection with the dancing, and one evening was wholly occupied in a tamahnous over a sick woman and child. There was some of this in the day-time also.

Feasting

The Twanas, from their own resources or from the presents which they received, were expected to feed their guests most of the time. Sometimes they gave the food to the visitors, who cooked it for themselves, but once or twice a day commonly they both cooked and distributed the food. When this was done, they seated their guests in the middle of the house in two rows on mats. When the meal consisted of boiled rice, wheat, or fish, it was placed before them in large kettles, from which they helped themselves with their native ladles; but when it consisted of berries and crackers, bread, apples, potatoes, and dry food, it was placed in troughs, made of 6-inch boards, 8 or 10 feet long and three-sided. Sometimes, when the meal was over, two persons would stand, one at each end of a long row of eaters, holding tightly before their faces a piece of calico on which all would wipe their mouths. They then arose and departed.

The Potlatch Proper

The potlatch or distribution of gifts took place in the day-time, two days after all had arrived. The women first gave away their things, and afterwards the men did the same. The gifts of the women were chiefly new calico, with a few dresses and a little money. Each giver gathered those to whom she wished to make presents in two rows facing each other, in the middle of the house; next she placed her trunks at one end of the rows, took out the pieces, laid them in a pile or two, counting them over; then, taking one or two things at a time, she carried one to each woman. Each piece contained, commonly, between 5 and 9 yards. Occasionally two or three women combined together and gave at the same time, if they were not very wealthy, but the richer ones gave each by herself. About thirty women thus distributed their gifts. Often several gave to the same person; though every woman present did not receive gifts, only those who were preferred. Three of the more prominent women gave about one hundred pieces each, and I am not aware that any woman gave to more than this number of persons. If all averaged half as much, they gave away nearly 10,000 yards, and this was the best estimate I was able to make of it.

Several years afterwards one woman gave me the names of eighteen women who gave away at this potlatch 2,090 pieces of calico. These pieces varied in length from 5 to 10 yards. At an average of 7½ yards, this would amount to 15,675 yards. If the other twelve gave in the same proportion, the whole amount would have been 26,123 yards instead of 10,000. Besides this, some gave blankets, shawls, dresses, and money, varying in value from five to thirty dollars. The number of pieces of calico given varied in number from 70 to 200, most of them giving from 100 to 140.

This occupied about two days and a half. A day and a half was then consumed by the men, who gave money chiefly, but occasionally blankets and a few guns. The recipients were arranged much as with the women, but were all men, and the distribution was conducted in much the same style. There were ten male donors, each of whom gave, generally, from $1 to $2 to each of his friends, so that most of the latter received from $2 to $10 each; some got more, and one who was expected to make a large potlatch in a year or two received $40. They gave on an average a little over $300 each, and the whole sums given away amounted to about $3,300. A few of the donors borrowed some of this money from their friends with considerable ceremony, promising to repay. One Indian who received a nice beaded cloak and some other articles put them on a fire, where they were consumed, in memory, it was stated, of a deceased child.

Leaving

The distribution of gifts was the last scene, for then the visitors put their things in their canoes and left with very little ceremony, as quickly as possible, and in three weeks from the first arrival the house was deserted by the visitors. It is considered by them a breach of etiquette to remain in the house any longer than absolutely necessary after the gifts are distributed. A few of the Twanas remained in the house, using it as a dwelling, for a month or two, after which it was deserted for nearly two years, and some things about it suffered to go to ruin. This whole affair occurred three miles from my residence. I was not able to be there all the time, but was present a few evenings and a part of nearly every day and gathered what information I could from others who were there in my absence.

POTLATCH NO. 2

Another potlatch took place at Jamestown in Clallam county, and was given from February 2 to February 10, 1878, by a part of the Indians of that place. The house was built for a large dwelling a year or two before—the potlatch, however, being in contemplation—and was about 32 by 84 feet. It was by no means large enough to hold all of the Indians who attended, but in the village there were about a dozen dwellings in which some of the visitors were received. The beds and seats of this potlatch house were much the same as that of the Twanas, but the shelves overhead for the storing of articles were differently arranged. Instead of being all around the house over the beds, they were along the side walls, with one shelf across the middle of the house. The two at the ends were used chiefly for storing articles belonging to the visitors, and the central one was for storing food, which included sixty sea biscuits and a few half barrels of sugar, brought by the guests and presented to their hosts. In one corner a blanket was fastened up, evidently to make a screen for a dressing-room. I was present nearly all of the time, having been requested by the Twana and Clallam chiefs and the Indian agent to go, in order to oversee the festivities and prevent any conduct that might tend to produce a disturbance. Hence I went with the Twanas, and had a somewhat different view from the one I had occupied at the previous potlatch.

The invitation was received at Skokomish January 26. The messengers remained the next day and then returned. The Twana Indians prepared to go as soon as they could and on the 30th we started. The account of this trip has been given in Chapter XI, "Travelling by Water." We arrived at Dungeness on the evening of February 2. The morrow being Sunday, I induced them to land at once, instead of postponing it until next day as is usually their custom when reaching a potlatch place in the evening. A canoe came to meet us, and there was a little conference in regard to the landing, and then this canoe returned, and I went with it, as the Twanas preferred that I should not be with them during their landing ceremonies.

After I landed, singing began in good earnest, the Twanas pounding on their canoes, beating their drums, and singing loudly, with faces painted red for a time; and then the Clallams on the beach replied in a somewhat similar way. The Twanas stood up in their canoes, which were held together abreast. This was kept up for a half hour or an hour, when they came to shore, and the Twanas made some presents to their hosts, generally to some of their especial friends, or to the givers of the potlatch, in order to get their good will, so as to receive much from them when they should give their presents.

About ten canoes from Sook, in British Columbia, had arrived that morning, with perhaps 125 Indians; 25 persons from Port Discovery, the same number from Port Townsend, and 40 from Sequim had arrived during the day; 60 from Port Gamble had also arrived within a day or two.

That evening was given to the Twanas, who sang and danced the black tamahnous. In the dance each remained in one place, and, to keep time to the music, jumped up and down a little or bent the knees. Their faces were also blacked in various ways. In fact, from this time for five days the faces of most of the Indians present, men, women, and children, were blacked more or less, some during the whole time. The paint was laid on in diverse patterns of stripes and spots, and some were wholly in black, others in red or black.

The next day being Sunday, most of them attended divine service; but they were too much excited to give up the whole day to rest, so in the afternoon a number of the women assembled in one of the large dwelling houses in the village, sat down on mats in two long rows, facing each other, and pounded with small sticks (1½ or 2 feet long) on larger sticks and boards in front of them, and sang for some time.

There was a second performance in another house afterwards by the women, in which they sang much as before, only they were accompanied with the drum, and were seated in a large circle. Within this circle two women and four girls danced. These six dancers, being graduated in size, arranged themselves accordingly, from the tallest to a child about eight years old. Their shawls were pinned behind their backs so as to cover their hands, which were extended about a foot and a half from their bodies, and they danced around a circle 8 or 10 feet in diameter.

The evening was given to the Sook Indians in the potlatch house. For a time they danced in one end of the house in a manner similar to that of the Twanas the previous evening, but with more jumping, and their singing was more varied and quite wavy. After a time two of them stripped to the waist and, with their drawers rolled above their knees, ran forward the whole length of the house, striking at everything and everybody within their reach, their arms constantly swinging around them; sometimes they went down on all fours, and, having snuffed the ground, rose again. Around the waist of each was tied a rope which extended back 6 or 8 feet, and was held by another Indian, who frequently jerked it, sometimes throwing the tied man to the ground.

Another dancer had a hideous mask on his face and a blanket on his shoulders, but his actions were not so fierce as those of the other two. He often sat down. When these were done, other Sook men came, shaking rattles, beating drums, singing, and going back and forth in the house and scattering the people who were standing around. This performance was kept up until late at night.

Monday forenoon was spent at a feast, to which men only were bidden. Beef and potatoes were cooked thus: A large number of stones were placed in a fire out of doors, and when hot the food was placed on them, covered with small dry bushes and mats, and so kept until it was cooked. At this feast the Indians did not eat in the main potlatch house, but at the residence of one who helped to give the potlatch, and who was the sole giver of this particular feast. The Indians all ate around the house on the platform made for beds, and the long troughs for food were placed in front of them on the same platform. Most of these troughs or plates were similar to those used in the Twana potlatch already described, but some were dug out of wood, were 5 to 6 feet long, 2 or 3 inches deep, and about 10 inches wide. There was one which was dug out roughly, about 24 feet long and the same width as the others. Whatever food was not eaten was carried away, and after the feast was over crackers were given the guests on purpose to be carried off.

For napkins they used small bundles of beaten cedar bark about 2 feet long, which are very desirable, as in these feasts they eat with their hands. As soon as the meal was finished there was to be some kind of performance by the medicine men, and no other persons were allowed to remain. In the afternoon, as I returned from my dinner, I saw a masked Indian, the same I suppose that was masked the night before, and three others similar to the two half-naked men of the previous night, dancing backward and forward for a distance of about 100 yards on the beach in front of the houses. The masked dancer went through some performances not fit to be described. Their dance consisted chiefly in running around with ropes encircling them, held by others, as on the previous night. This dance continued until about 2 P.M., when they danced off into the woods, followed by forty or fifty of their friends, with the singing, etc. They all formed a large circle as they moved off, and did not return until five o'clock, when they reached the beach a quarter of a mile from where they left it. Some three of them, apparently tired out, were each jerked up by six men wrapped in blankets and carried into the potlatch house. One walked in supported by attendants. I have inquired frequently the meaning of this ceremony, and could get only the answer, "It is their tamahnous." I infer it was an initiatory custom with the black tamahnous. Some of them, I heard, were starved a part or all of the time.

One young Clallam half-breed, it was said, was told that he would be obliged to go through some such initiatory ordeal at this potlatch, and he declared he would rather run away and hide until it was over, but the Port Discovery Indians took him some time before the festival, guarded him closely, and compelled him to submit. I suppose this was true, as he was not seen anywhere until the ceremony was over. While these scenes were being enacted the women met and sang in their usual way, and when I asked why they did so I was told that they were tamahnousing in order to get strong minds towards the men.

Towards evening the Indians of Elkwa, Pisht, and Clallam Bay arrived, and landed with considerable ceremony, dancing, drumming, rattling, singing, and making presents. The presents were generally a blanket or a few dollars to each one making the potlatch. One man gave the head potlatches eight or ten small sticks about 3 feet long, a promise, it was said, that he would, after reaching the house, give his host $150 in money. There were also a few more large presents given to the same man, which were kept, and returned to the givers at the close of the potlatch, so that the presenting was a mere form.

Many of them had the down of ducks on their heads, and blankets. Before they reached the house a few Elkwa Indians, who had previously arrived, ran along the beach and entered the Elkwa canoes, so as to land with their own people. This was the last arrival. Some were invited from Victoria, but did not come. Those present were, as near as I could estimate: Twanas, from Skokomish, 90 miles distant, 8 canoes, 75 persons; Sook Indians, from British Columbia, from 40 to 75 miles away, 10 canoes, 125 persons; from Sequim, 6 miles, 40 persons; from Port Townsend, 25 miles, 25 persons; from Port Gamble, 40 miles, 5 canoes, 60 persons; at Dungeness, 100 persons. Total: 425.

The evening was given to the Elkwas, and their performances were similar to those described. On Tuesday I was not present, but was informed that gambling and the giving away of calico were the principal features of the day.

On Wednesday forenoon the Indian who was to give the feast, Tenas Joe, made his potlatch in his own house, and in the afternoon there was a dance given by four girls, graduated in height. These were fed by two old men. Some handkerchiefs and other articles were burned on a fire in memory of the wife of Tenas Joe, deceased. In the evening the Clallams danced their war dance, which was rather pretty and was said to be an imitation of the Makah dance. There were nearly twenty-five dancers, mostly men, who were dressed in American style, except that they had no shoes and wore parti-colored shawls and blankets thrown around them. One man carried an open umbrella. Their heads were bound with head-bands of cedar bark or kerchiefs, in which were long white or gray feathers generally tipped with red. Much feathery down was sprinkled over them. They had hollow wooden rattles and tails and wings of hawks or eagles in their hands. Their faces were blacked in various ways. With the music of the drum and singing they jumped around in a space 20 feet in diameter, throwing their arms wildly about, now up, now nearly to the ground, with movements quick as those of a cat near a very hot fire. That evening six of the principal potlatches gave me $7.50 to pay for my board while watching over them.

About 11 A.M. Thursday, the finale of the black tamahnous began. First, five men came out of the potlatch house to an open space in front of it. They were stripped to the waist, with no pantaloons on, but with drawers rolled up above their knees, and with shawls thrown over their shoulders. Each wore a head-dress consisting of a band, from which hung a large number of strips of cloths of various colors, but mostly red, about an inch wide and 12 or 15 inches long. So many of these strips hung in front that it was impossible to catch a glimpse of the face. Their legs were painted with stripes of red, and wet with water to imitate blood. They jumped around in many ways, high and low, sometimes running and clapping their hands, while the other Indians accompanied them with the usual chanting and black tamahnous music. After a few moments they ran back into the house. Then about as many more came out in much the same garb as those seen on Sabbath evening and Monday afternoon, with ropes around their waists held by others. These had cut themselves slightly under their tongues and chins, so that the blood ran down their arms and breasts a little, and their faces were so black that it was impossible for me to recognize them, although well acquainted with some of them. They jumped around much as the previous set had done, and then went back to the house. Then the first set again came and performed in the same way as before, and ere they returned the second set were out again, but some of them were not held this time by the ropes.

Such actions as these were kept up for nearly three quarters of an hour, when one set ran off up the beach for 200 or 300 yards, accompanied by their friends, both men and women, and soon the other set followed in a similar manner. I judged from appearances that I was not wanted, so did not go. They remained there about two hours, while I went to dinner, and the performers, it was said, were washed by the others. After this they came back. The first set were in front, surrounded by their friends, who kept up the usual noise. They ran towards the water as they advanced and then away from it a few rods, so that they moved along the beach very slowly.

After them the second set came in a similar way and three women had by this time become so excited that they also danced as the men did, but in their usual dress. After them came a third company, following one boy. He had on a shirt and pair of pantaloons, rolled up above his knees, and on his head a band with a very long feather standing up in it. He walked into the water knee deep, bowed his head until he dipped the tip of his feather in the water, then he walked slowly away from the water for about two rods, then went into the water again as before, and so advanced along the beach very slowly towards the house. This was said to represent a crane, and is called the crane tamahnous. I understood that this boy, who was about fourteen years old and was a Clallam, was being initiated into this kind of tamahnous. When each company came near the house each dancer was seized by two or three persons and hurried, half running and half carried, into the potlatch house. Two or three times I asked them what this was intended to teach and could only get the answer, "It is their tamahnous." So I could only look on and gather most of my information in this way. As these are the rites of a secret society it is not strange that the members do not explain them to the uninitiated.

After all went into the house two companies were formed, one at each end, and there was a strife to see which should conquer; but the house was so crowded it was impossible to see what had become of the dancers. A new dance was now performed. In this a number of men, taking hold of each other's hands, formed a circle about 12 feet in diameter and ran around a pole which was set in the ground. Outside of this circle was another running in an opposite direction, and outside the second was a third going in the same direction as the first.

There was no confusion and they kept good time to the usual noises. After this they formed sides to push against one another, each endeavoring to push the other from his position. There was not room inside for any one who did not wish to be pushed, so I stepped outside. The fun continued about two minutes and ended in a hearty laugh, which closed the scene for the afternoon.

In the evening all dancing was carried on in one-half of the house. A large fire was built in the center of that half. At the end of the house I saw four of the heads adorned with head-dresses of cloth strips which I had seen during the day. I suppose they belonged to the first set of dancers. Their bodies lay prone underneath the bed platform. Each one, held down by a single man, kept his head constantly moving from side to side, and one groaned most of the time. They evidently struggled to rise, and during the evening one did get up, and it required two or three men to put him down again. Most of the company were seated around the side walls. Soon one man of the company arose, took a hollow wooden rattle, said a few words, and walked around the fire, frequently making some motion towards the men who were held down. Having gone around the fire once or twice, he shook the rattle towards some one, whereupon ten or fifteen men jumped up, ran around, threw their arms wildly about them, bent down almost to the ground, and went through various antics; at times two or three would catch hold of each other and jump up and down together; then one or two would seize the one with the rattle with feigned violence and exertion, feigned, I suppose, because only once during the evening did I see him brought to the ground, while he seemed to make little effort to stand up. This would occupy about five minutes, during which the music ceased not, when all would return to their seats, and the leaders would lay down the rattle. Then another would take the rattle, and the performance would be repeated, and this was kept up for an hour or more.

After this was done, two of those nearly naked arose and danced the whole length of the house and back again, held with the ropes around their waists as before, and accompanied by others; then they were taken out with a great shout and, as I supposed, released. This done, a company of a half dozen men took one of those who had been held down and slowly carried him outside where with a whoop he was let go; after him three others were taken out and released in a similar manner, the whole act being accompanied with the usual music. That ended the black tamahnous scene as far as I know.

By the next day nearly all the black paint was washed from their faces, and I saw but very little more of it during the potlatch. As far as I have learned the northern tribes on the Sound practice this black tamahnous in a more savage manner than their brethren of the south, and I am told that in British Columbia it is marked by still greater severity.

Friday forenoon was occupied by Dick Locks and his father in potlatching money in the potlatch house, for the residence of the former was five miles away, and he was a relation of the head potlatcher. In the afternoon Port Discovery John gave sea biscuit to the men, twenty-five to each. In the evening fifteen or twenty Clallam young men came dancing into the house where I was sitting. For a time they stood in a row and danced backward and forward the length of the house; but at last they stood at one end, dancing to the usual noises, except that of the hollow wooden rattle, for this instrument was laid aside when the black tamahnous ceased. One Indian put on a shawl, took another sort of rattle made by the Clyoquot Indians, and danced in front of the rest shaking his rattle, jumping up and down and around and squatting. While this was in progress a small company of Twana young men were dancing in the doorway and on the outside, mostly out of my sight, but there was evidently some rivalry between the two companies. There was considerable merriment in these dances.

Saturday forenoon, Port Discovery John, son-in-law to the principal potlatcher, gave away his money and blankets. It was the first time I had witnessed all the ceremonies connected with the donation. He first arranged all the men around the house on the bed-platform, and then, with five or six friends, spent some time in counting his money. Next, twelve or fifteen women came to serve as a choir, and sat down on mats near the money. Then came four girls, arranged according to size (as before described) with faces painted completely red, hair covered with down, hands extended as on the previous Sunday, under shawls or blankets pinned behind them, who danced the whole length of the house and back a few times, the tallest going first, led by an old man—"Old Slaze"—and followed by one still older. The choir sang, accompanied with a drum.

These ceremonies occupied about fifteen minutes, after which the potlatch began. The giver told a man, who acted as crier, the name of the person to whom the money or article was to be given; the crier then took the gift, heralded forth the amount of the same, with the name of the receiver, and carried it to the latter. Previous to this, however, certain amounts, varying from $20 to $50, tied up, were given to several persons, which I was told was to pay them for certain articles brought, or was money which they had brought and was now returned to them. These things occupied all the forenoon, and in the afternoon Old Slaze gave about twenty-five sea-crackers to each man. The next day being the Sabbath, I was with them but a very short time. The ceremonies, I was told, were about as those of the preceding day. This ended the affair, and after it, all left as soon as possible.

They left about noon, but the greater part of them went only five or six miles away, as they were reduced to sea-biscuit and sugar, which was very dry, and they wished to go where they could get clams and fish. The Twanas only remained with me until next morning, when we left.

The amounts given by the men, as near as I could learn, were as follows:

Wednesday: Money, $100; one beef, $30; one gun, $8; total $138.

Thursday: Money, $170; one canoe, $20; twenty blankets, $40; total $230.

Friday: Money, $270; one gun, $10; twenty-seven blankets, $54; total $334.

Saturday: Money, $430; twenty-five blankets, $50; total, $480.

Sunday: Money, $420; twenty blankets, $40; total $460.

Total: Money, $1,390; blankets, $184; miscellaneous, $68; whole amount, $1,542.

One hundred dollars of Old Slaze's money belonged to his wife, but they combined together.

The men present received various sums, generally about $10 each, but some received as much as $30. Besides this, seventeen women gave to the other women calico at different times from Monday until Friday, each piece containing generally 5 yards, but varying from 4 to 9 yards. A rough estimate made the whole of this amount to 5,000 yards. There was only one case each of drunkenness and quarrelling that came to my knowledge.

During most of the time there was a large amount of gambling among the men, and some among the women, with disks and bones.

POTLATCH NO. 3

This took place in the same house as number 1, and was given by the Twana Indians in the fall of 1878. The chief potlatcher, Old Sam, lived at Seabeck, 30 miles distant, but he preferred to come to the house at Skokomish to make his gifts. He and a few of his friends took up his abode in the house about a week before the invitations were sent out. This time was spent in repairing the house and giving feasts to the other Twanas. The following account was written for the press at the time by Puyallup Indian Peter C. Stanup for the *Tacoma Herald*.

Editor, *Tacoma Herald:*

An Indian Potlatch

Although this is not much news to your readers, I ask you to be kind to insert the following concerning the Skokomish Potlatch, which will give your readers some idea of how the Indians do when they make Potlatch.

About the first of October, the Skokomish Indians, or Potlatch company, send their couriers all over Puget Sound and along the Pacific shores about the Quinaults and invite all they can get to come to their Potlatch. On the 15th of October the first canoes left their homes for the Potlatch. The first day the Indians arrive at the Potlatch was on the 22d of October, and continued till the 28th. These Indians are the Skokomish, Squaxin, Chehalis, Waneuchee, Quinaults, Nisqually, Puyallup, Port Madison, Muckleshoot, Tulalip, Clallam, Samish, Steklow, Swinomish and Victorians. On arrival of each tribe, they always presented the Potlatch company with blankets, money, guns and all kinds of provisions, so as to make sure for getting their share of the Potlatch money.

Every night almost all of the different tribes would be singing and dancing, while various kinds of gambling would be going on, and many piles of gold and silver were to be seen and guns and blankets were gambled for.

Meals two times every day were served by the company, free of charge, to everybody. These provisions consisted of flour, pilot bread, sugar, tea, coffee, venison, ducks, huckleberries, potatoes, Indian potatoes, lakamas, dried clams, dried salmon, salmon and apples.

Sheriff Watman, of the Skokomish, wrestled with Bill Posper, of the Seabeck. The latter threw the former; but the Sheriff's brother got mad and attempted to raise a row; but the crowd was too much for them, and so they did not fight. Watman and his brother left for their home, and old Sam, the head of the Potlatch company, on learning that the Watman brothers had gone home, he (old Sam) immediately sent for them to come back and Potlatch one horse, blankets and money to pay for their trouble.

The Potlatch company commenced its Potlatch with the women Potlatch. There must have been given away four or five thousand yards of calico, dresses, shawls, baskets, beads and crockery, from the 28th of October to Nov. 1. The men's Potlatch, commencing the 31st of October and ending Nov. 4, consisted of horses, guns, blankets, clothing and money. The following are the names of the Potlatchmen and amounts of money each and all distributed to their friends.

Sam Chamats	$2,000
Tyee Charlie, 3 guns 70 blks	700
Jim	400
Mowitchman	360
Durley, 34 blankets	300
Slokum	270
Bateese	230
Bill, 10 blankets	160
Duke	100
Skokomish George	70

Am't: 3 guns, 113 blks, and $4,500

Clallam and Quinault women presented the other women with cedar bark mats, fancy made, various kinds of baskets, Indian spoons (large), straw for getting mats, beads, Indian long beads, earrings, dresses, shawls and salmon.

War dance by the Clallams was given on the 30th which represented a crowd all ready to go to war. All have their war uniforms on them, and Black to-man-a-woos, with various kinds of Indian-made false faces.

The Potlatch house is 273 × 33 feet.

Number of canoes presented, 100, and 5 boats; wigwams and tents, 40; and one little shantie used as a jail in the Potlatch. There was no whiskey to be known all throughout the time of the Potlatch. Church every Sunday by the Rev. M. Eells, at the Potlatch house, to which the Christian Indians would always be very attentive.

Leaving the Agency for the Potlatch, we found the distributing of the money going on, and on the same day (Nov. 4) Indians left for home. Some of those who made Potlatch before, made $50 from the Potlatch and the lowest was $4. Indians left Potlatch for the Reserve and camped all night, and there the Skokomish Indians did all they could to comfort them at their camps.

P. C. Stanup

POTLATCH NO. 4

This took place at the Squakson reservation in November 1880. I was present the whole time, a week, going at the same time as the Twana Indians. Most of the Indians from the other places arrived before I did, but the Snohomish and Samish Indians did not arrive until the next day. When all had arrived there were about seven hundred, from the following tribes: Chehalis, Twana, Nisqually, Puyallup, Squakson, Port Madison, Samish, and Snohomish.

The house was about 50 feet by 185. Many camped outside. The main thing which took place at this potlatch, different from the others already described, was the "removal of their dead," an account of which is in Chapter XXI. There was no black tamahnous in connection with it, and not as much red tamahnous as with some others. In addition to their native gambling, cards, chuckaluck, monte, and a new game played on a wheel with a regular gambler who had a partner, and which was a regular swindle, were introduced by Indians and half-breeds. A trader, a white man, was present, who found that prize boxes of candy, crackers, and cookies went off faster than anything else. The whole affair, however, was pronounced very dull, the younger and middle-aged being so civilized that they were ashamed to enter into the old Indian ceremonies with zest, and they had nothing new to introduce.

The distribution of the gifts by the women began on Monday and closed on Wednesday. They did not, however, it was said, give away very much calico, probably from 2,000 to 4,000 yards. Thursday and Friday the men gave away their money. Six men and one woman thus distributed $1,400, varying in amounts from $70 to $470 each, the woman's gift being $125. For distributing this the men were arranged in the house as in Potlatch number 2. A part left Friday afternoon, and the rest, who were detained by the tide, went the next morning.

At one potlatch at Port Gamble it was said that five men gave away $2,000 each. It may have been an exaggeration, but the amount was large, and every man, woman, and child who could go was present.

In December 1879, Doctor John of Jamestown, a Clallam, made a potlatch, but did not invite any but Clallams to it, and not all of them, those of Clallam Bay being left out. About $200 in money and $100 in blankets and other articles were given away.

FOURTH OF JULY

Of late years the celebration of this day has largely taken the place of the potlatch. In doing this they usually differ from the white man's celebration. They spend nearly a week at it, feasting, visiting, horse racing, and the like. One man is at the head of it, and bears the brunt of the expense, assisted, however, by some others. There is at times a distribution of gifts, though not always. A few years ago, Old Patsy was at the head of a celebration of that day at Hadlock, and it was heralded abroad in the newspapers and described as a potlatch. It undoubtedly did combine both. The following is an account of it.

Mason Co. Journal, July 17, 1891

POTLATCH AT PORT HADLOCK

Patsy's potlatch goes on record as one of the most generous and joyous distributions that has warmed the heart of the Puget Sound Indians for many a day. From Judge Wickersham, who was among the spectators, some interesting facts are learned. It took place at Port Hadlock, six miles south of Port Townsend, beginning on Friday last. There were 500 Indians, full fifty canoes loaded, coming from Quilayute, twenty miles south of Cape Flattery, and from the cape itself, Snohomish, Tulalip, Lummi, Skokomish and Port Madison. They were very largely old Indians. Patsy, whose Indian name is Shupald, is a Squaxin by birth, his home having been on the head of North bay. He is now 60 or 65 years old, pretty well preserved, as is also his squaw. His potlatch amounted to about $2,000, made by working in the mill where he has been employed for some twenty years. The potlatch is based upon the theory that it is wrong to hoard, and by distributing his wealth among his friends and relatives the Indian wins a great name among his fellows. So Patsy, having accumulated a comfortable "pile,"

MADE A POTLATCH

and called his neighbors in. Invitations to these affairs are simple. A small stick about four inches long is sent out, and when the guests receive that they know that they are wanted and are expected to come. The messenger carrying the stick tells them when to come, and few miss it. Patsy made a big feast for all his friends, which opened the festivities on Friday, the 3d. That night the Snohomish Indians held a big dance— the usual Indian dance. It was kept up all night. Everybody attended. A big house 50 by 150 has been built by Patsy. It had a floor and a platform three feet high and four feet wide around the inside. Upon and under this platform were stored their effects, while as many as could bunked on the platform, the rest going outside in tents, of which there were thirty or forty.

On Saturday night the Clallams had a big dance. It was a great pow-wow. They congregated just outside on the grass, probably to the number of 100 or 125 bucks and squaws, all decorated with fir boughs tied around their waists and over their heads. Their faces were painted black. After dancing a while the old medicine man took a position at the door and permitted the others to pass in after a long ceremony. The squaws formed on one side in a lane and the bucks took the balance of the floor. There were three principal personages in the dance, first the medicine man, with his big drum and his peculiar antics and jumps; second, the master of ceremonies, who announced the songs; then, the leading singer. All sang, and there was a marked difference in the variety of the songs. At first there was a great deal of memory of the dead, their chiefs, etc., most of lauding the Clallams and what great deeds they had performed. The dance lasted all night.

Patsy's potlatch house with guests

The Klootchman First

Sunday morning began the potlatch. The klootchman's potlatch came first. They began by bringing out the great bolts of calico and blankets that Patsy had brought, piling up a pile five or six feet high in the middle of the floor. "Mrs. Patsy" superintended this feminine distribution though Patsy sat near by smilingly enjoying the scene. The calico was unrolled and cut in pieces of sufficient length and a committee then went around with Patsy's wife and gave to each klootchman her new gown.

After the distribution of the dresses came the chickamin (money) potlatch. Patsy and his wife together with their sons and two or three friends gathered in the center of the hall and began to lay out silver dollars and halves. Then they talked over the distribution until the decision was reached, the amounts ranging from $2 to $10 apiece and aggregating $800.

The Potlatch broke up on Sunday night, and everybody went away singing the praises of Patsy.

Judge Wickersham was fortunate enough to get about a hundred pictures with his kodak, showing a great variety of scenes. He has also a picture of Patsy and a crayon sketch of the old chief himself, who by this sacrifice of his property has established for himself an enviable home among the tribe—*Tacoma Globe*

VOL. 5

XXI

FUNERAL CUSTOMS

BURIAL

Their sepulchers, as far as I can learn, represent five different ages, which have, to some extent, co-existed.[1]

In the ground. There are places where skeletons and parts of them have been plowed up or still remain in the ground, and near together in such a way as to give ground for the belief that formerly Indians were buried in the ground and not in regular cemeteries. Such deposits exist at Doswailopsh and Hoodsport, among the Twanas, and at Dungeness and Port Angeles, among the Clallams. These graves were made so long ago that the Indians of the present day profess to have no knowledge of the occupants, but believe them to have been their ancestors. They care so little, however, about the remains that thirty-five years ago the land containing bones at Doswailopsh was taken by a white man, and they were told to remove the dead before all traces of the graves were obliterated, but no one went there to do so, nor were they angry when the underbrush of the cemetery was burned and the ground plowed and levelled. No care was ever taken to learn particulars in regard to these skeletons or graves, but I understand that the graves were not deep. It is possible, however, that they were buried according to the second, or canoe, method; that they fell to the ground; and that in the course of a long, long time, earth and leaves have made a soil over them.

In canoe. The most common method, as far as the earliest whites have observed, was to bury in canoes. The body was wrapped in mats, blankets, or cloth, and placed in a large canoe. Sometimes it was first placed in a box, and then in a canoe, over which a smaller canoe was placed, upside down, to protect the corpse. The canoe was then elevated, perhaps into the forks of two trees, or else on a frame built for the purpose, and left for a year or more. After this sometimes the body was taken down and buried in the ground, but this latter custom I am satisfied was not universal. It may be, too, that this was the reason for the ceremonies described under the first form. While there may at times have been special places as cemeteries, and probably were, this was not always so, but often the body was elevated near where the death occurred. The Skokomish valley, I am told was once full of such sepulchral canoes.

What the burial ceremonies at that time were, or what they placed around the dead, I am not accurately informed, but I have been told that they did not take as much care of their dead as they do now. Probably some useful articles were left near the corpse, as such have been found at these places. An old resident has informed me that the Clallams

331

always buried their dead in a sitting posture, and I am satisfied that the Twanas often bent theirs up, so that the knees nearly touched the chin, else they could not have put them in boxes where I have seen them.

Vancouver says, in 1792, that among the Clallams of Port Discovery, he saw many skeletons in canoes, while children's skeletons were in baskets that hung from high trees, and that with the children's skeletons were boxes filled with a paste made from the fern root. Some skeletons were in holes, lightly covered, while many bones were on the beach. He also mentions seeing in the same place a cleared space recently burned over, in which the skulls and bones of a number of persons lay among the ashes.

Dr. Gibbs believes from this that some great epidemic had recently passed over the place, and that probably they had burned a house in which many persons had died to prevent the spread of the disease.

At Penn Cove, Mr. Whidbey, one of Vancouver's officers, saw "several sepulchers formed exactly like a sentry box. Some of them were open, and contained the skeletons of many young children tied up in baskets. The smaller bones of adults were also noticed, but not one of the limb bones was found." These had probably been buried elsewhere. Except this account, no one has spoken of a cemetery devoted to infants.

Gibbs says that "in case of chiefs or men of note much pomp was used in the burial ceremonies. The canoes were of great size and value, the war or state canoes of the deceased. Among the Chinook and Chehalis the tamahnous board of the owner was placed near him. The Puget Sound Indians do not make these tamahnous boards, * but they sometimes constructed effigies of their chiefs resembling the person as nearly as possible, dressed in his usual costume, and wearing the articles of which he was fond. One of these representing the Skagit chief Sneestum stood very conspicuously upon a high bank on the eastern side of Whidbey island."

A. B. Rabbeson in the *Tacoma Ledger* of May 23, 1886, says of the Nisqually Indians in 1846, "Another custom they had was that upon the death of a man having slaves and horses they would kill the slaves and horses, excepting the favorite slave, whom they would bind upon the body of the dead man and place both in a canoe, which would be placed on high poles, and thus the poor wretch was left to starve to death—consigned to a living tomb. These practices we also determined should cease and the Indians be compelled to bury their dead."

The following is an account of a modern burial of this kind which I witnessed in October 1877: The deceased was about thirty-five years of age and was a widow. Her father took charge, and being an old man there was more of the old Indian style than I ever saw before. She died about nine o'clock in the morning and at three o'clock in the afternoon I was invited to go to the house and hold a religious service. When I arrived she had been placed in a Hudson's Bay Company box, which was only about 3½ feet long, 1¾ wide, and 1½ high. She was much emaciated when she died or they could hardly have put her in the box, even by doubling her so that her knees nearly touched

*The Twanas do, for I have seen them. See Chapter XXIII.

332

her chin. A fire was still burning where many of her things had been consumed according to their custom. Her mother was singing a mourning song, others joining in it at times, often saying, "My daughter, my daughter, why did you die?" About thirty persons were present and all out of doors, the coffin box being under an old shed. I held a funeral service and returned home, having been invited to go to the grave the next day.

About nine o'clock the next morning they called for me and we went in a canoe three miles to the cemetery, two other canoes having preceded us, one carrying the corpse. Sometime previous a medicine man had asked the deceased to become his wife, but she had refused, and he had said if she did refuse he would kill her by his "tamahnous." This, her friends believed, was the cause of her death, and they compelled him to give the canoe (25 feet long and worth $30) in which she was buried. Four boards of old Indian make, about a foot wide and 7½ feet long, used as posts, were secured in the ground to the depth of a foot and a half.

Before being erected, a hole was cut in each post 2 feet from the upper end, and 5 inches square, in which cross-pieces were placed for the canoe to rest on. As each hole was cut, and the board laid aside until the rest were ready, a handful of green leaves was placed over it which was allowed to remain until the post was ready to set up, when the leaves were thrown aside. Leaves were not, however, put on the last board, for as soon as the hole in it was cut, they were ready to set all of them in their places. Two other boxes, which I presume contained many articles belonging to the deceased, or brought by her friends, were placed in the canoe, together with the coffin box, and the whole was elevated to its position and braced. Over the central part of the canoe a roof of boards covered with white cloth, so as to more than cover all the boxes, was placed, and holes cut in the canoe so as to render it valueless for travelling. On the two posts nearest the water the head-board and foot-board of her bedstead (American make) were nailed, and on each of these a dress was fastened. I then said a few words to them and pronounced the benediction, when all went down from the hill to the beach except her father, mother, and brother, who remained for ten or fifteen minutes mourning and pounding on the canoe.

It was now half past 1 P.M., and a little food was given to all, there being twelve men and three women present, after which the father and mother of the departed made presents to all. One man received a gun, two persons a blanket each, and the rest $1.50 each. After this four men made short speeches in their native language, which I did not understand.

They said she was buried in this way because she was a prominent woman, and that in about nine months a potlatch would take place very near where she was buried, and that each tribe should come, a few of their prominent men would be sent to the grave with presents, after which she would be put under ground. The predicted potlatch took place about thirteen months afterwards, but she remained in the canoe long after it was finished; but she was taken down two or three years after the burial, so quietly that I did not know it. See figure in the Annual Report of the Bureau of Ethnology for 1879–80, page 172.

Scaffold burial. About forty years ago, gold mines were discovered on the Fraser river in British Columbia, and, boats being scarce in this region, unprincipled white men stole many of the canoes in which the dead had been placed and emptied them of their contents. This incensed the Indians and also caused a change in their mode of burial. They collected their dead in cemeteries, and because enough trees could not be obtained in such places which were suitable for canoes, they built scaffolds for them; but instead of using canoes generally, they made boxes, and elevated them on a frame, and when they did use canoes, they cut holes in them so as to render them useless for any other purpose.

The ruins of one such grave yard were about two miles from the reservation, when I first came here, though the dead had been removed previous to that time. These ruins have since been destroyed. The dead were generally in boxes, which were probably covered in some way to protect them from the weather. Sometimes the boxes were placed near the ground, and articles were hung on posts and uppercross pieces. Sometimes the coffin boxes were elevated a few feet. Several such burials have taken place since I came here, but all were afterwards put under ground. One was that of an infant and was covered with cloth. Again and again times were set to put these under ground with ceremony, but it was not done at these times and when it was done I never knew.

Another set of Twana coffins was enclosed with a small house, which was entirely covered with red and white cloth. There was a window in the house, through which could be seen the coffins covered with a red shawl. Six coffins were placed in this house, one after another, it having been a kind of family vault. Some were laid on the ground,

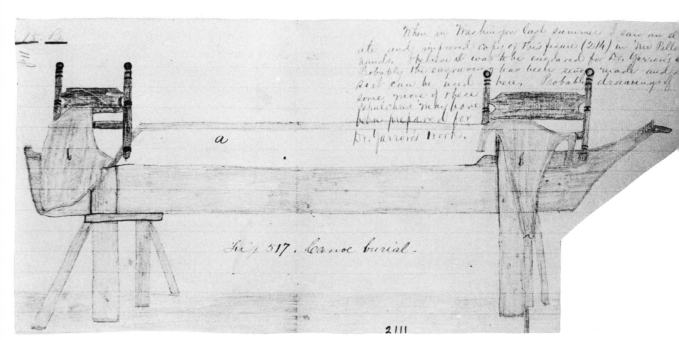

Canoe burial

and others immediately on them. They were there in 1874, and I know not how long previously. In 1878 they were put under ground.

Another Twana grave house of different shape had in it two coffins, one resting on the ground, and the other on it, barely covered with earth. Around such graves, clothes, flags, and similar articles were placed often on poles.

Sometimes these grave enclosures were in the shape of a small house, sometimes merely like the roof of a house; sometimes they were covered or partially covered with cloth or blankets; and sometimes they had nothing of the kind on the boards of which they were made. Sometimes no articles were placed near them; but often lying near by on the ground or perhaps on a shelf built for the purpose were dishes, lamps, tin pails, a tub, beads, clothes, canoes, and similar articles, generally broken so as to be useless to thieves, but not always so. Some are surrounded by a good paling fence, and some are not. I once saw dishes containing water at Port Gamble in which were floating small

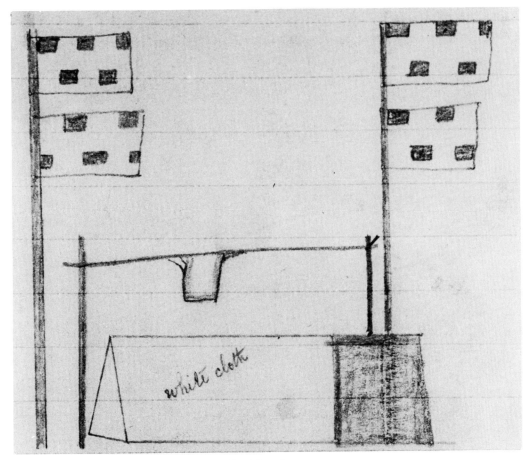

Burial enclosure

Twana cemetery, 1877; from a stereoptican photograph

American rubber toys. Sometimes these houses are painted, but generally they are not. Sometimes the coffin rests on the ground, sometimes it is raised a little, and sometimes the house is made so closely that I could not see how the coffin was placed.

In the ground with Indian accessories. As the Indians have come more in contact with the whites, they have learned to bury in the ground, and this is the common method at present. Usually they obtain a chief coffin of American style, put the body in it, and with it a number of articles, chiefly cloth or clothes and keepsake articles, which the deceased valued highly, and occasionally money. I have heard of a Clallam chief who was buried with a $20-piece in each hand, and another in his mouth. As a rule, however, money is too valuable for them to use much of it for this purpose, and besides, the temptation is too great for some one to rob the grave, as unprincipled white men have occasionally done. An Indian I think has never been known to do such a thing, partly from superstitious fear, I presume.

The body, when I have seen it put in the coffin, is generally wrapped and tied hand and foot, face and head; cloth, either white cotton or calico, is laid in the coffin, and the body put in on the cloth, in such a way that the cloth comes around the sides, and across the body; more is put over, partly folded and partly jammed in until the coffin is full. I have also often seen other things, usually the old clothes of the deceased, thrown into the grave and buried. Sometimes I have seen them carried off into the woods and left, a few rods from the grave. Sometimes a house, similar to those already described, is built over the grave, and sometimes only a picket fence, and at times the grave is left

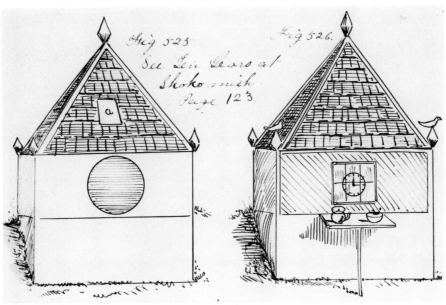

Burial enclosure

entirely unprotected. Occasionally where there is no protection several poles are erected on which cloth and various articles are hung.

I here give an account of an interment of this class, at which I was present in August 1877. The deceased was a Twana boy about eleven years old. When I first saw the body, it was tied up in a quilt, and probably a few articles were tied up with it. It was then put in the coffin and nothing else was put in but the boy's hat. At noon we left the agency for the cemetery, three miles distant, in a canoe. Only five persons went, a medicine man and his wife, two male friends, and the father. The mother did not go. The number who go to the grave depends not on the mode of burial, but on other circumstances. The father was bareheaded all day. When he left the agency he gave his hat to his wife. She sat on the bank and mourned while the woman in the canoe replied. While on the way, too, sometimes this woman would mourn, and the father would stop paddling and mourn also. (For these songs, see Chapter XIV, mourning songs.)

When we reached the landing, the father, who had acted as one of the pallbearers all day, assisted in carrying the body up the hill to the cemetery, and then returned to the beach, and mourned while the rest dug the grave. They intended to bury him in the same grave with a cousin of his, and immediately on the latter, but some one else had left a child on that grave above ground; so it was left undisturbed, and the new grave was dug by the side of the old one. During most of the time, the father of the boy and the wife of the medicine man remained on the beach, where they built a fire, on which I think a mat was burned. When we left, the fire was still burning. When the grave was ready all came to it, the body was put in, a pair of the boy's pantaloons were laid on the coffin, and the grave was filled up. Over this grave, and that of the cousin, adjoining, a shed was built, over which a quilt was nailed. On our return, there was some more mourning by the father and the woman.

On December 22, 1881, a woman on the Skokomish reservation, aged about twenty-four, and her daughter aged five, died of consumption. They were put into one coffin and buried the next day on a scaffold-aerial burial near their home. Her husband at this time, Rufus Willard, gave away nearly all his household effects, dishes, chairs, and the like. He had no other children left. The mother of the woman, Jane Henry, and the father-in-law and mother-in-law lived on the reservation, but her father lived at Port Madison, eighty miles distant. When he and his friends, who were Catholics, heard of it, they were dissatisfied with the mode of burial, and wrote to that effect. Nothing, however, was done, except to talk, until February 13, 1882, when about half a dozen of the Port Madison Indians came. After feasting, giving of presents, and one or two days of talking and council, a decision was reached. Some were in favor of taking the child out of the coffin, it was said, and burying her in another place, but most were opposed to it, and the Agent vetoed it. It was decided to take them to the grave yard at Eneti, three miles distant, where a brother-in-law of the woman, his wife, and a child of the woman were buried, and there to bury them in the ground. This was done February 17.

On reaching the place about noon, the coffin was opened, the child taken out, new blankets wrapped around her, more money put with her, more cloth put in with the woman, the child put back, and the coffin nailed up. They were quite offensive at this time. There was much mourning. When they were put in the ground, the outside box was first put in, then the coffin, and they were well covered with boards. I then held a short religious service. Then each of the men present threw on a shovelful of dirt. This was a custom adopted by the Indians within a year, but from whom they copied it I have not learned. Two men then did the rest of the work. A little dirt was then put in, enough to cover the coffin in the shape of a mound of a grave. Over this two wide boards were placed like a roof, on which white cloth and blankets were spread. Two more boards were then put up in the same way, a mat was put over them, and the grave was filled up.

All then went down to the beach one or two hundred yards, where there was a fire, for there was snow on the ground. The maternal relatives of the deceased then gave $25 or $30 away, also a few blankets, to the men present, most of whom received a dollar each. The first gifts were to the Port Madison Indians, the next to the two men, who had dug the grave, and lastly to the other men present. A few remarks preceded these gifts. Then the husband and his relatives gave a dollar each to about ten persons. Two or three guns were also given. The mother and mother-in-law gave some cloth to some of the women present. Thus the affair ended. There were forty or forty-five persons present, seven or eight of whom were women. The Indians felt very badly about these deaths because two persons, a mother and child, died the same day, a thing they say unknown to them.

Civilized burial. Of late years the Twanas, Puyallups, Upper Chehalis, Port Madison, Snohomish, most of the Clallams, and of the other tribes, have adopted the American custom of burial, placing no gifts around the grave, or articles of any kind, building a paling fence around the grave, or else a good fence around the cemetery, and sometimes obtaining gravestones and even expensive monuments. The Puyallups are further advanced in this respect than the other tribes. In 1878 the Twanas began a new cemetery, all the graves of which are after the style of the whites. Many, however, who bury thus, still cling to the custom of placing some articles in the coffin.

OTHER FUNERAL CEREMONIES

Occasionally, those attending a funeral are expected to bring some present to be placed in the coffin, or around the grave, as a token of respect for the dead. The only gifts I have seen thus brought were pieces of cloth by women. Sometimes some absent themselves from funerals because of this custom.

For several years after I came here in 1874, very few presents were distributed at the grave. After a time this custom began to be revived among the Twanas, and has often been observed by them, even when burying in the civilized style. Usually the present has consisted of a half a dollar or a dollar to each man and a half a dollar, and perhaps some calico, to each woman present, but sometimes a gun or a horse worth from $20 to $50 has been given to several men present. Sometimes one was to divide his large gift with others, and sometimes he was to keep it entire. The medicine men are usually included among these prominent persons. Occasionally presents are sent to women, who are unable to be present, but whose husbands are at the funeral. Sometimes these presents are made at the grave, after the burial, and sometimes they go to some house not far distant, and there the gifts are bestowed, and a feast is given. I have known $100 or $150 to be given away at such times so that it becomes a small potlatch, though usually the amounts are much smaller.

They give two reasons for this practice. One is that these articles are a remembrance of the deceased, and the other that they are to pay the friends for attending the funeral, for if they should not do so, hardly anyone would attend. Once I knew these presents to be given at the house before going to the grave, as the way was long and muddy. If the recipients lose relatives, they are expected to return these presents if they are able.

The reason that they formerly placed articles around the grave was that they believed that, as the articles decayed, they were taken by the attending spirits to the abode of the dead, particle by particle, and there put together again for the use of the deceased. They also believed that the body was carried to the same place in a similar manner.

Besides the articles previously mentioned, guns, canoes, Indian money, and other valued articles were put in or near the grave, generally being first broken if left exposed.

In some Twana grave houses for a long time were three rude images of a man. They were placed inside some windows, so as to be plainly visible from without. The faces were nearly the diameter of those of an ordinary man, but the body was smaller than that of a person, only about three feet long. Each one was surmounted with a cap or hat, and dressed with clothes. None had a nose, mouth, eyes, ears, or arms. Two of them were in the grave of a chief.

It is said that in and around the grave of a Clallam chief, who died many years ago, $500 worth of articles were placed.

On some graves these articles were formerly renewed every few years, with considerable ceremony oftentimes, the frequency of the renewal depending on the number and wealth of the relatives living, the esteem in which they held the deceased, and the power which the old belief had over them.

I have never known of their placing food near a grave, except the above instance related by Vancouver, page 3. Dr. Gibbs says the same.

They generally bury much sooner after death than the whites, about as soon as they can after obtaining the coffin. They have sometimes been so much in haste as to ask the government carpenter to make the coffin before death had actually taken place, and in one or two instances they actually began making the grave clothes for a person, while alive, who recovered.

Twice, however, I have seen notable exceptions to this haste. A Twana child died in January 1878. It was raining so hard that the parents did not feel inclined to take it to the grave immediately. The relations of the parents were preparing to go to a potlatch the next day, and they urged the parents to go with them, so as to forget their grief. They did so first putting the child in a box, and then placing it in an old unoccupied house, where it was left. They returned in twenty days; afterwards when the father found it convenient, he made another box, put the first one into it, and buried it, more than five weeks after it died.

In March 1879, a woman died at Quilceed. She was the wife of a Twana, though she had not long before come from Olympia. About three weeks after her death, she was brought to the Skokomish reservation, forty miles, on her way to Olympia, thirty miles further, for burial. The coffin was not made until she reached Skokomish. She had previously been wrapped in cloth and placed in a rude box. Before she was put in the coffin at Skokomish, this box was broken to pieces, most of the cloth was taken off, much of it quite roughly; her head was untied, considerable money was put into her mouth, and then tied up again. After this she was put in the coffin, with shoes and a large amount of blankets and calico. By this time she had been dead so long that she was very offensive. After this she was taken in a wagon to Olympia and buried.

Usually they handle the dead quite carefully, but there are exceptions to it, as in the instance just mentioned. In September 1879, a Chehalis boy died at Skokomish, where he and his parents had relations, and where they had wintered for two or three previous winters, and where they had been since the July before the death. Still they wished to bury him near their old home. They had no wagon. As soon as he was dead, they bound him up very roughly in a quilt, tied him across a horse with his head and feet hanging down loosely on each side—barbarously—and thus with two friends, they started for Chehalis.

SUPERSTITIONS ABOUT DEATH

In March 1880 quite an excitement occurred at Skokomish, and as it is the only instance of the kind of which I have known I will here relate it. Dr. Charley had three wives. There was some jealousy between the middle one, who was originally from Snohomish, and the youngest, a Twana woman. A child of the family had died the previous winter, and the Snohomish woman had cut off some hair from the youngest wife, while the latter was asleep, and hid it with the child, and thus it was buried. She believed, as all of the Indians believe, that when such a thing is done, the one whose hair is thus buried, will soon die. From some unguarded remark of this Snohomish woman the fact leaked out. Then all was excitement. She tried to deny it, but the Indians determined to investigate it, and with the Agency physician, Dr. J. M. Givens, they went to the grave and opened it. The Snohomish woman also went; and while the others were digging she also dug and clawed with her hands, so as to get it first, but she was not quick enough. The others got it first. When Dr. Givens asked her why she did so, she said she wished to kill the other woman. The other Indians tried her for the act, and banished her to her old home in Snohomish, with the expectation that her relations would return with her after a time and pay damages, when she would be returned to her old position as wife of Dr. Charley. This, however, they never did. Although she returned on account of a child or two of hers in school, yet she was never restored as his wife, and after the death of these children, she left Skokomish permanently.

Formerly they were very superstitious about going near the dead, and hence it was difficult to induce them to attend Christian services at a funeral. They feared that the evil spirit which killed the deceased was hovering around, and would enter and kill the living also. They were more especially afraid to have children approach a corpse, as they believed them to be more likely to be killed by the evil spirit than a grown person.

They also had a superstitious fear about the buildings in which a death occurred, as they believed that the spirit which killed the deceased still remained in the house, and might attack any who might live there. For this reason they often built a house of mats near by into which they removed a sick person just before death, so that it should be torn down after the death, when the spirit would leave. If a person died in a good permanent house, too good to be torn down, the survivors would desert the house, and perhaps tear off the roof, nor would they return to live in it for from one to three years. As they have become more civilized I have noticed some singular changes in these superstitions. One has been that the living must not pass out the door through which the dead was carried out. Hence, in one case, when a Twana child died in a good house, I saw the dead carried out of the window, the family afterwards living in the house. At another time a dead person had been carried out through the only door in the house, the door was taken down, and removed to the other end of the house, and the old doorway was permanently closed, the family continuing to live in the house. Then as the Indians learned that the whites had disinfectant medicines, they have believed such to be a sufficient remedy for the evil spirits, and have obtained carbolic acid to scatter around in the house, although the disease of which the deceased died might not have been in the least degree contagious.

It is not good etiquette to pronounce the Indian name of the dead for a year or two, though they have no such feeling in regard to the English or "Boston" name. Whether this is a superstitious fear or not I am not certain. If it is they will not acknowledge it. I have asked a number of the least superstitious and more communicative among the Twanas and Clallams about this, and they all say that it is not because of a superstitious fear, but simply because it makes them feel very badly to be thus reminded of their dead, as if a needle were put into their hearts. It was, however, once said that the reason was that when the name was pronounced the dead person turned over in the grave, and Old Seattle or his relations objected very seriously to having that city called by his name, for fear that it would be pronounced very often, and so he would be continually turning and never have any rest. In after years, however, they take the names of their deceased ancestors, especially grandfathers.

MOURNING OBSERVANCES

They have no regular periods for mourning, but continue it after a funeral, sometimes on every day for weeks or even months. This is not usual, however. Sometimes only for a few days do they mourn, and sometimes they skip long intervals. Women, especially the older ones, are the most apt to continue this mourning, which they do by going outside of their houses, perhaps by the river bank or beach, and there sitting and singing the mourning song. If they meet an esteemed friend whom they have not met since the death, or see an article which belonged to the deceased, which they have not seen for a long time, or visit the grave (which is not often done), they break forth anew into demonstrations of grief. This is true even for three or four months after the death. The degree of mourning depends largely on the esteem in which the deceased was held. Sometimes when the loss is felt to be very severe, the mourners cut off their hair. Only in one or two instances, however, have I seen this done. Occasionally, too, at large gatherings afterwards, as at potlatches, they burn valuable articles, as cloaks, in memory of the deceased. Gibbs gives the following as a stereotyped formula for these times of mourning by the Nisqually-speaking tribes, and others often use the same sentiment in their own language. *Ah'Seahb, Shedda budda ah-ta-bud. A-de-dah.* "Ah chief, my child dead. Alas."

Among the lower Chehalis Indians in 1853, according to Swan's *Three Years' Residence in Washington Territory*, while the corpse remained in the house, not a word was spoken, except in a whisper, nor did they begin mourning until the funeral was over. Every day at sunrise and sunset for thirty days the mourning chant was repeated by the relatives, when the days of mourning were ended. This may have been the case with the Sound Indians, before the innovations of the whites caused them to change, but I have not seen such customs as to the whispering, time of beginning mourning (which is here before the funeral, or even sometimes before death), or period of mourning, in twenty years, either among the Twanas or Clallams.

In one instance I heard the death chant sung before death. A young woman was very sick, about a mile from the Skokomish Agency. She was with some distant relatives and it became evident to all that she would die if she remained there. Her only chance of life seemed to be to remove her to the Agency, where her brother was, and where the Government physician could watch her more closely. This was done, and yet when her relatives saw her carried away from the house, they felt so sure that she would die that they began to sing the death song. It was about the only time I ever heard it, when I felt like telling them they must stop, as I feared it would have an unfavorable effect on the sick person. She afterwards recovered.

Removing the Dead

It was quite common to remove the dead to some more favorable place, when they buried above ground. At least I have seen it several times among the Twanas and once among the Squaksons. I have also heard of it among other tribes. Sometimes the reason has been to put those under the ground, sometimes to take those in a cemetery off a reservation to one on it, and sometimes to gather the remains of a family or of relations into one place.

The following are accounts of such removals. In March 1878, two Twana children, related to one another, died almost at the same time—one was the child of a medicine man. All of the tribe, it is said, were invited to the funeral; and all the men and women told me they were going, but I found that their word "all" meant very much the same as it does in the Bible, the larger share. About two thirds of the men and women went who were then at home—fifty—and not a child. A large number of those who remained at home did so to take care of the children, but not all. As a general thing the most important persons went. The intention was that as these two children should be buried, their deceased relatives would be moved and put with them, in one common grave.

As they went to the cemetery, about four miles distant, in canoes, there was much lamentation on the way. When they arrived at the cemetery the medicine man tore down an enclosure where two of his children had been buried with four other children, relations. Another medicine man, belonging to the same clan, also tore down an enclosure where the bodies of two of his children were placed along with those of two others, their relations. Two of these corpses were above ground and two below. The coffins beneath the ground could not be taken up, but the clothes around the bodies were so well preserved there was no difficulty in removing them. One of the coffins made for one of the children just deceased was large enough to contain two bodies, so another body, long previously deceased, was put with it. Other rude boxes were made of such capacity as to admit of twelve children being put into eight of the boxes and coffins, most of the old coffins being broken open and the bodies taken out. In one case it was found impossible to jam two of the bundled bodies in the same coffin, whereupon the cloth which was wrapped around one was roughly torn off, a little calico wrapped around the skeleton, and then it was put in with ease. The corpse originally in this coffin was lying with its knees near its chin, but all were not so, as some had been laid out straight.

A large grave was dug near by, about 12 feet long and 5 feet wide and 4 feet deep, lined with mats; and all the boxes and coffins were placed in it, completely covering the bottom of the grave. Several of these boxes were wrapped with many thicknesses of calico; while quilts, blankets, shawls, and a few fancy articles of bead work and a few small boxes were placed in the coffins with the bodies. All the coffins were next covered with several layers of calico, blankets, mats, and cedar boards to the depth of about 8 inches. An old man then made some remarks, followed by a speech from the child's father, and when this was concluded the grave was filled with earth, a little new calico having been thrown in with the dirt.

Next, all gathered on the beach, a fire was built on which two or three pieces of cloth were burned; a few men made presents to the fathers of the children just deceased; some calico was given by the women to the mothers; and the two fathers, with another medicine man, presented small sums of money to all the men present, each one giving at least one dollar to every man. The two wives of the medicine man, whose child had died, the mother of the other deceased child, the wife of the other medicine man whose children were moved, and an old woman, a relative of the bereaved families, each gave about five yards of calico to every woman present. As the old boxes and coffins were opened, the bodies were often handled quite roughly. Only a few persons handled them, and they were chiefly medicine men. During all the time there was considerable crying and mourning by the relatives.

In November 1880, I was present for a week at a potlatch at the Squakson reservation.

When it was about half done, a day was selected to fix up their graves, about a half a mile from the potlatch house. Persons were selected from the different tribes to do this work, three of them being Twanas. In all there were about twenty-five men and fifteen women, mainly middle-aged or old ones. Most of the time the women and a few of the men mourned, saying, "My child, my child." Especially was this the case when a new grave was opened. A small house was built about 21 feet × 5, and 5 high. Then several enclosures, where the dead had lain, were torn down, and the dead were carried to the new house. All of these coffins were above ground, some being on the ground, and some on them, till in some instances the small houses were as full as they would hold.

Some were in coffins, one being a very good one with many silver-plated ornaments on it; some were in long boxes; and some in trunks. The trunks I presume all held the remains of the dead, most children probably, as I saw several of them opened, but it is possible that a few may have contained nothing but articles given to the dead, for some were not opened. Sixteen coffins and long boxes, nine trunks, and two or three bundles of bones were removed to the new house. All were placed on the floor, for there was a floor to it, or else placed on each other, until in some places they reached the roof. Each end was thus filled, while the middle was not, that space evidently being left for future dead.

Some of the boxes, coffins, and trunks were moved as they were, a part being wrapped with cloth, others partly covered, while some had nothing around them. Some again were wrapped with new cloth, shawls and quilts; some were opened and new cloth and articles put around the bones, and the bones and cloth were all put back again; others were taken out of the trunks. Though all the trunks were in a good state of preservation, only mouldy, the old trunks were thrown aside, and the bones, with new articles wrapped around them, were put in new boxes or trunks. Only two or three were served in this manner. I could not see whether the bundles of bones, which were taken to the house, were taken out of the old houses in blankets, or whether they were taken out of boxes, as I could only be in one place at once; but when they were put in the new house, they were wrapped in blankets.

They were careful to put the heads of those in the coffins and long boxes either east or west. I could not tell which, but they would sometimes put them one way, talk awhile, and then change them. The length of the house was east and west. The short boxes and trunks were put in any way with no particularity, except to have them closely packed. Some loose blankets were stowed in among the coffins, and others were spread over a number of them. There was talk of some persons going back the next day and putting the bundles of loose bones, which were left in blankets, into boxes, but I think it was not done, as the house was at last nailed up very closely, and a quilt was nailed on the outside, so that it was impossible to look inside. Then the canoes all came away. So did I, but a few persons evidently stayed, as in the early part of the evening, from the potlatch house, I saw a fire on the beach, near the house.

A few years after this, a potlatch was held among the Snohomish Indians, the prominent object of which I was told was to fix up their graves.

Cemeteries

In nearly every case, their old cemeteries, which I have seen, were near the beach, not a great distance from their dwellings. They fronted to the water. The graves were arranged very irregularly. This was probably done for convenience sake, as, with only canoes to carry their dead, it was not easy to take them far back. Lately, as they have obtained wagons, new cemeteries, some distance from the water, have been made, at least among the Twanas, Clallams, and Puyallups. They are well cared for except in one instance as far as I have seen—at Sequim among the Clallams. This one is on a sand spit, where the wind is continually shifting the sand, undermining the grave houses, and uncovering the bones, so that it looks sadly neglected, although recently used.

XXII

GOVERNMENT

AND POLITICAL ECONOMY

RULERS

The influence of the whites has been so great upon this part of Indian customs, that it is about as difficult to discover accurately their ancient habits in regard to government, as in regard to any other customs.[1] In reference to other customs, the moral influence of the whites has had its effect only so far as the Indians were willing to adopt our habits; and enough of the old has remained to help me to trace back the customs to the time when they had only their old habits. But in regard to this branch, the United States Government has stepped in with its Agents, soldiers, and power, and has said, "you shall and you shall not do so and so," until almost every vestige of ancient government is deeply buried in the past.

I have never found anything that answered to the gens of eastern Indians. Dr. Gibbs said the same forty years ago. If there was any such thing, civilization and the reservation system long since exterminated it. The only thing that has reminded me of it was when Big John's wife died, and he wished for a new one, he said that he must seek her in a certain circle. He did so and was refused. Then he said he could go wherever he wished for one. He obtained a Squakson woman.

There is nothing that might be called caste, unless the slaves were such. The classes of people were chiefs, sub-chiefs, head men, medicine men and women, common people, and slaves.[2]

Formerly, most of the tribes had head chiefs, with sub-chiefs over the various bands. Dr. Gibbs mentions several of these head chiefs, but his account was written after the treaties were made, and as he says, consequent changes had taken place. Patkanim was then made head chief over the Snohomish Indians, although previously he had only been head chief over the Snoqualmie band of that tribe.

Formerly, I am told, there was no head chief over the Twanas, but each band—the Skokomish, Duhlelip, and Quilceed—was governed entirely by a chief of its own, and these sometimes carried on a petty warfare with each other. The same may have been the case with other tribes. Even where there were head chiefs they often had but little influence, except with their own bands, though there were exceptional cases. Among the Dakotas, Blackfeet, Nez Perces, Klikitats, and similar tribes where war was very common, it was but natural that these wars should hold the tribe together under one head chief whose influence was great. But I hear of very few stories of great wars among the Indians of Puget Sound, hence naturally, as it were, the tribes almost fell to pieces.

Theoretically, this chieftainship was hereditary, though there were exceptions. Seattle ruled his mother's not his father's tribe. This was sometimes the case with others, the reason seeming to be that the father dying when the son was young, the boy was carried back by his mother to her tribe, and brought up among them. According to Dr. Gibbs, if an eldest son of a chief was too stupid or bad, he was sometimes set aside for the next; and if he was too young when his father died, his father's brother took the place.

In their councils all were allowed to speak and even prominent women sometimes took part. A woman, Sally, even ruled the Chehalis Indians at least from 1841, Captain Wilkes' time, to 1855, that of Dr. Gibbs. Those who were wealthy or those who had given potlatches were also quite influential. The advice of medicine men, too, was especially taken in consideration, and oftentimes they actually but quietly ruled the chiefs.

I have not been able to learn of any special class of braves or war chiefs. The chiefs in time of peace, still had charge in time of wars.

After the United States sent Agents among them, these had almost supreme authority, being the supreme court when the Indians could not settle their own cases, and often making and unmaking chiefs. Generally, however, they have not found it practicable to introduce such reforms as the abolition of gambling, or tamahnous, until at least a respectable minority of the people favored them. In 1874, the hereditary chieftainship had been abolished. In fact, it probably slowly died soon after the treaties were made in 1854–55. Among the Twanas and Clallams, at least, the office was in 1874 elective, and held during good behavior, or until the chief should resign. The Agent appointed those who were elected. In time, however, there were two grave difficulties connected with this method. One was that the chiefs would decide in court in favor of the rich and most numerous, as their office depended on it, leaving out of view justice; the other was that sometimes some of the most worthless persons were elected chiefs. To obviate this, the government appointed Judges under pay, so that they should not depend on the people for fees or favor, and these worked in connection with the chiefs. But these Judges with government back of them soon came to have more influence than the chiefs, and the latter office died a natural death. The chiefs were to make the laws and the Judges to decide the cases in court. For a number of years before the chiefs were dropped, they were changed so often that no one obtained much celebrity. The reason for these changes was that if the chiefs did well—imprisoned, and fined heavily, and enforced the laws—so many of the people became dissatisfied that they demanded a change, and if the agent did not grant their desire readily, they made it so hot for the chiefs that they resigned; and if the chiefs did not enforce the laws well so as to please the people, the Agent was dissatisfied and discharged the chiefs.

The Judges held their office, until after the Indians became citizens, when it was found that if they imprisoned any one, a writ of habeas corpus could be obtained for them, and so they could go out. Then the Judgeship was abolished, and now only policemen remain under pay of government, who have very little power but whose main duty is to gather the children into the schools, when the parents are willing to have them go.[3] They are really paid for their time thus spent. Often the most influential person who can be had is obtained for this purpose, so that he may be able to induce the parents to allow the children to go to school.

TRIALS AND PUNISHMENTS

These were usually conducted in the presence of all the people, and often nearly all the Indians would be heard before the affair was settled, if it was of much importance. In cases of murder, life for life was the law, but money and property were generally accepted instead; and, in fact, plenty of time was given the murderer and his friends to give this property before the murderer's life was taken. Dr. Gibbs says that in 1855 ten blankets were usually sufficient for a common person's life. Of late years this has greatly increased, so that from $200 to $600 has been required. For twenty years, however, murders have been very seldom committed among the Indians on the Sound, so that there has been hardly any example of the enforcement of the law. There is no torture among them now, nor has been, except when captives tried to run away or were contrary, when they cut the soles of their feet.

Under the rule of the Agents and Judges, imprisonment and fine were the common modes of punishment, usually a week's imprisonment or $20 fine was a heavy punishment, but in a few instances six months in jail was given on the Skokomish reservation. A number of the Clallams of Dungeness have been transported to the Skokomish reservation and kept there for several months, and in one case, a Twana, a very bad Indian, was turned over to the military authorities at Port Townsend, where he was kept in the guard house and at hard work for six months. Drunkenness, debts, and immoralities, with a few cases of theft, have constituted the large share of cases which came under consideration when courts were held on the reservations.

SLAVERY

This existed all over the Sound, most of the slaves having been taken in war. When the treaties were made, one article stipulated that this should be abolished, and hence there has been very little of it since I have lived among the Indians. One Twana had three slaves twenty years ago, who remained with him because they preferred to do so, and were treated about as any other person would have been. One was a girl, and the old folks apparently thought as much of her as they would have done had she been their own child. It was, indeed, a common remark that she ruled them. Twelve or fourteen years ago two left, and have since been married, and the other stayed with his master until he died about four years ago when he was about sixty years old.

Dr. Gibbs says that some of the Indians told Col. M. T. Simmons that the first slave was made as follows: at a feast a man criticized the cooking; the Indians deemed it an insult, and deliberated on a punishment; some wished to kill him, but it was decided to make him a slave, so that he might always serve the man whom he had insulted. He also added that the people were often made slaves when they were unable to pay their debts. Dr. Gibbs also says that in 1855 they probably constituted one tenth of the population, and the system was the cause of much trouble among them, both in trying to procure more, and in attempting to recover those who had escaped. When a master died, a part at least of his slaves were killed. The children of slaves were always disgraced, even if they were half free. Even within six years one girl was refused as the wife of a man, because some of his relations remembered that some of her ancestors were slaves.

PROPERTY AND COMMUNAL POSSESSIONS

Except in case of land, property was individual and not communal. Each one's rights were respected. Portions of land and water belonged to tribes or bands, who, however, were not always very particular about preventing others from fishing or gathering berries or roots there, if there was no hostility between the two tribes.

Other property was individual. Even a man and his wife had their individual property, and no one has a right to demand a wife's baskets and mats for her husband's debts. I once saw an eastern paper speak of potlatches as evidence of the existence of communal property, but I do not understand it to be so. The idea is to make a present of what by right belongs to one person, so as to make himself a great name, or for friendship as whites do, only on a larger scale. The receiver claims no right to say how much he shall get. The giver has the whole right of keeping all he has, or of giving to whomsoever, whenever, and as much as he pleases. Still the potlatch idea has been so imbedded in their natures, that a man who has been to potlatches and received considerable at them (and all have), would feel so mean, and be called so mean by public opinion, that if he had considerable property and could make a potlatch, that he would feel impelled to do so.

When a person, too, accumulates considerable property, his poorer friends will come and live off of him, or borrow of him, so that very few remained long much richer than their fellow Indians. This fact has been noticeable with those who have worked for government. They have often had a good salary, and might have laid up considerable and put themselves in good circumstances, and sometimes tried to do so, as white people, but often their friends have lived off of them, or borrowed their money in such a way that it would not be returned in a *very* long time, and so they have found themselves with but little laid up for the future.

Inheritance

At the death of a man, all of his property that was not destroyed at his funeral was divided among his relatives. His wife and minor children seldom received much of it.

Sometimes, indeed, it has taken a firm hand by the Agent to prevent his relatives from taking everything from a wife who had no children. One reason, I presume, of this was that she was bought and owned by him, yet not as his slave, and yet was not his equal. Sometimes they divided their property among their relatives before death, and sometimes it was not divided until after the decease.

WARS

In declaring war after all efforts at peace had failed, they consulted together in a council where all who wished could speak, and then did as the chiefs said. Then they would tamahnous in order to be successful, painting themselves black and red, and making themselves as hideous as possible. Gibbs says that most of their battles which were witnessed by early settlers consisted chiefly in howling at night, and firing their guns, beyond bullet range in the day.* This does not, however, apply to their wars with the whites, which will soon be described, or their wars with the Chemakums. These, it is said, were bad neighbors and troublesome to all, and their power was first broken by the Makahs. Afterwards they were worsted in a great fight with the Snohomish Indians, and late in the forties, they were attacked by the Sukwamish Indians, under Seattle, and their fort destroyed.

When a truce takes place, one man, who is favorably known, is sent to the opposite party to arrange the terms of peace; and if a treaty is made, then sometimes they prepare a feast, to which the principal men on both sides are invited, and of which they partake together. In their later truces, they used the white flag, or something white as a sign of the truce.

NOTED INDIANS

Herewith I give sketches of some of the more noted Indians on the Sound. The earlier ones were chiefs; the later ones could not be so, but have obtained their notoriety from their ability. For most of those about Leschi, Quiemuth, Kitsap, and Patkanim, I am indebted to the *History of the Pacific Northwest, Oregon and Washington*, by Hon. Elwood Evans.[4]

Leschi, Quiemuth, and their associates. Leschi, chief of the Nisquallies, his brother Quiemuth, and Klowowit, chiefs of the White river and Green river bands; Nelson, a White river Indian; Stehi, a Nisqually; Kanaskut, a Klikitat; and Kitsap, were the leading hostile chiefs in the war of 1855–56 on the Sound.

Contributions to North American Ethnology, vol. 2, p. 191.

Leschi was the great leader. In December 1854, he and Quiemuth first come into notice in connection with the treaty, which was made by Governor I. I. Stevens at Medicine creek, with the Nisqually, Puyallup, Squakson, Steilacoom, and other associated bands. Quiemuth was the first to sign it, and Leschi the third. Nevertheless, in the fall of 1855, dissatisfied with it, they organized a war, which was the most severe of any on the Sound, and in fact the only one. It was carried on mainly at Seattle and in the White river, Puyallup, and Nisqually valleys.

Leschi, says Governor Evans, and his brother Quiemuth "were natural leaders, born orators, consummate strategists, fertile in resource, and of brilliant audacity, they gave strengths to the malcontents, and transformed a mere outbreak into a protracted war."

After the Indians on the Sound were conquered, Leschi and the other chiefs fled across the Cascades, where they and the other Indians surrendered to Major Garnett of the Ninth Infantry. Governor Stevens had announced his readiness to receive and provide for such hostiles as would come in, and disavow further hostilities, but excepted from amnesty Leschi, Quiemuth, Nelson, Kitsap, and Stehi, as instigators in the hostilities and participators in the massacres on the Sound. They, however, surrendered themselves and were brought to the Sound for trial. Leschi was found guilty and hung. The other chiefs mentioned were tried and acquitted.

Kanaskut was the leader of a band which fired the volley by which Lt. W. A. Slaughter was killed at the junction of White and Green rivers. In turn, he was killed at Lemmon's prairie, near Elhi. He was stealthily approaching the camp of Lieutenant Colonel Casey, in order to kill him, when he was discovered and shot through the spine by Private Kehl, then on picket duty. He was still so strong that it required two men to handle him. He gave orders for his men to fire on the soldiers, which were understood by one of them, when Corporal Shaughnessy finished him by a shot through the head.

Quiemuth. On October 20, 1855, Quiemuth visited Secretary Mason, then acting governor at Olympia, soon after hostilities had begun, and assured Mason again and again of his friendship. Mason told him to get his brother Leschi and their families and come to Olympia where he would give them food and shelter. This Quiemuth agreed to do, but failed to keep his promise, for when he met Leschi they went to the hostiles at Puyallup. As they did not come the next day, according to promise, Mason sent Charles Eaton and twelve men to go and invite the chiefs to come to Olympia. They crossed the Puyallup river, when they learned that about two hundred Indians had collected farther on. This, Eaton said, meant war, and they must not go on. Two men, McAllister and Connell, did not believe it and said they would go on and have a friendly talk; but they were soon killed—James McAllister, it is said, being killed treacherously by Quiemuth. The rest of the whites were soon besieged in a house near by, but defended themselves so that the Indians at last drew off.

Quiemuth, after the war closed, went east of the Cascades, but grew tired of the war and separated from Leschi. Stories here conflict. Evans in his history says that he was taken there and delivered with the other chiefs to Governor Stevens. James Longmire, in a Pioneer story in the *Tacoma Ledger*, August 22, 1892, says that after the separation, he came to Ozha, a Frenchman on the Nisqually river, and asked to see Longmire. Ozha took him to Longmire and said he wished to surrender to Governor Stevens, if Longmire would take him there. He did so, with a few friends in the night, and delivered him to the Governor in Olympia. The rest of the night Longmire stayed there and went to sleep, but it had been told that he was there and a company of eighteen or twenty persons gathered and Longmire was awakened to find Quiemuth falling and dying with a pistol shot and stab to the heart (Nov. 7, 1856). It was believed that a son-in-law of the McAllister whom Quiemuth had murdered killed him, and he was tried for it but acquitted. Governor Stevens was very angry when he found that the chief, then under his protection, was killed in his office. He was to his brother what the Prophet was to Tecumseh.

Kitsap. This Indian, after whom Kitsap county had been named, was both the chief of a band that lived on the peninsula adjoining Port Madison, and also a great Medicine Man. It is said that his name signified "brave," it being one of the very few personal names of Sound Indians which means anything.

During the Indian war of 1855–56, he joined the enemy, doing his utmost to drive out the whites; at that time he commanded the Klikitats. It may be mentioned that Lieutenant Slaughter was killed during this war near the town of that name in King County. At various times during the war Chief Kitsap received serious wounds, which he himself successfully treated. Subsequently, he boasted that he was invulnerable to the attempt of white men and Indians alike and, of course, many of the tribes believed him. With other hostiles he was driven east of the Cascades and finally taken captive. Many delivered themselves up to the military and were pardoned, but the government demanded that Leschi, the leading chief, Kitsap, and a few of the moving spirits should be surrendered to the civil authorities for trial, and it was done. But while imprisoned in the guard house at Steilacoom awaiting trial, he made good his escape, and for two or three years remained at liberty. In January 1859 he was recaptured by the United States troops, put on trial at Olympia, and acquitted.

During confinement at Fort Steilacoom, he was taken sick, when some red-colored medicine was administered to him, which effected a cure. He now thought he had made a wonderful discovery in medicine craft. Soon after his release and return to his people, three of his warriors fell ill, to whom he gave some "red medicine"—a mixture of red paint and water—which drove them to the happy hunting ground in a few hours. Their relatives, believing the dose to have been administered intentionally according to Indian custom, watched their opportunity for revenge. In April 1860, while under the influence of liquor, two of them shot him and then cut his corpse to pieces. Thus ingloriously ended the career of Chief Kitsap.

In 1857, the county which now bears the name of Kitsap was organized. This was after the termination of the war with the Indians, but previous to the trial of Chief Kitsap. The legislature named the new county "Slaughter," in honor of the dead Lieutenant. Shortly afterwards, however, the people of the county were privileged to choose a name, and strange to say, repudiated the name of the American hero, selecting that of the Chief, who had commanded the band which slew him.

Patkanim. He was one of the first of the Indian chiefs to come into notice, first, as being somewhat hostile, but afterwards as being a firm friend of the whites. He was first a chief of the Snoqualmie band, but when the treaty was made, he was made head chief of the whole Snohomish tribe by Governor Stevens, and he was the ruling spirit among the Indians north of Seattle.

In 1848, at a great assembly of Indians at Whidbey Island, at which about eight thousand were present, they held a war dance, and two thousand participated in it. These were mainly Snohomish, Clallam, and Duwamish Indians. Patkanim was the first speaker, and he advocated driving out the Hudson's Bay Company. John Taylor, another chief, followed, and he wished to include the Americans. Grayhead, or Snohodentah, opposed this, as he said that the Americans were his protectors from the Snohomish and Snoqualmie Indians, who fought his people and made slaves of them. The Duwamish chief said that he lived between the two nations, and would protect the Tumwater Indians, but Grayhead preferred one American with his rifle to all the Duwamish Indians. A plan was then laid to kill Capt. A. B. Rabbeson and Mr. T. Glasgow, who were present, but warned by Mr. Glasgow's woman, they escaped.

The next year, with about a hundred Snoqualmies, Patkanim went to Fort Nisqually. Trouble began, first about a Nisqually man, who had married a Snoqualmie woman, but it culminated in a fracas with the Hudson's Bay Company and Americans, in which an American, L. C. Wallace, was killed, and another one, Lewis, slightly wounded. It was believed that the Indians went there with the intention of attacking the Fort, but a blunder of one of the guards of the Company seems to have precipitated matters. Patkanim was at the time inside the Fort and apparently friendly, but aided by the other Indians he escaped. Wallace and Lewis were outside the Fort. Sometime afterwards Sub-Agent J. Q. Thornton offered Patkanim eighty blankets if he would bring in the offenders. Six were brought in and tried. Four were acquitted, but two—Cuisass, a brother of Patkanim, and Quallawowt—were found guilty and executed in the presence of a very large number of the Indians. Even after this Patkanim was friendly to the Americans.

In 1855, just before the beginning of the Indian war, he warned A. A. Denny of Seattle of danger, with so much sincerity that Mr. Denny believed him, although Acting Governor Mason and others would not. Result proved the warning to be true. If Governor Mason had acted in accordance with it, many lives would have been saved. At first many whites would not believe that he was friendly, although he professed to be so, but his subsequent acts proved that he was. Whether it was out of love for the Americans, or hatred to the hostile Indians, or from his wisdom to see that in the end it was the only safe course, cannot now be told.

During the war Governor Stevens employed him to enlist some Indian scouts. He did so, bringing with him fifty-seven Snohomish and Snoqualmie Indians on the fourth of February, 1856. On the eighth, he surrounded and captured a camp of seventeen Indians at the Snoqualmie falls without firing a gun. Three of these were Klikitats: the rest belonged to Patkanim's tribe. Two of the Klikitats he hung and beheaded. The other one told him where the various camps of the enemy were, agreed to guide him to Leschi's camp, and did so. On the 17th, he attacked Leschi on White river. He intended to have surprised Leschi, but the barking of a dog betrayed him. He and Leschi then met, but their conference was fruitless and he attacked Leschi, who was fortified by being in a log house. After a desperate fight, he drove Leschi out and across the river, and killed eight of his men, one of whom was a chief. The fight lasted ten hours, when Patkanim's ammunition gave out, and he withdrew. As trophies he secured only two heads.

He lived to a great age, but was at last overcome by that great enemy of the Indian (and white man), whiskey. He has been honored by having his portrait placed in the *History of the Pacific Northwest, Oregon and Washington*, one of two such chiefs on the Sound.

Duke of York, or T'chitz-a-ma-hun, appears to have been the hereditary chief of the Clallams.[5] As early as 1854 he was appointed as such officially by Governor Stevens, through Indian Agent M. T. Simmons. He continued to hold his office until 1876, when he was superseded by Lord Jim Balch, but he retained the position of superannuated chief, until his death. Soon after the coming of the whites he went to San Francisco on a sailing vessel. The practical knowledge which he gained at this time was of great service to his subjects and the whites afterwards, as he learned of the power and numbers of the whites, and of the great folly of any conflict with them.

Sometime after his return, the Clallam Indians of Port Townsend headed by King George, a brother of the Duke, became greatly enraged at the whites there, who were very few in number, and planned to destroy them all. They could easily have done so, and the whites knew it. But the Duke of York stood between the surging mass of Indians and the few whites, and held his people back by his eloquence as he told them of the power of the whites and how they could come and destroy the whole Clallam tribe should they kill the few Americans there. At last he succeeded and the old residents of that place have ever remembered with great gratitude this act of his, the saving of their lives, and treated him accordingly.

He was very polite in his manners. This he had evidently learned at San Francisco, on shipboard, and from his intercourse with the officers of the army about Port Townsend. He felt greatly honored in being allowed to represent his people in shaking hands with President Hayes, when he visited Port Townsend. He has also been honored in having his portrait placed in the *History of the Pacific Northwest, Oregon and Washington*; and also with his two wives, Jenny Lind and Queen Victoria, in Nordhoff's *Oregon and California*. His two sons are respectively named Prince of Wales and Charles Swan. An older brother died many years ago, and among the Duke's papers, which he left, was the following about that one: "Port Townsend. W.T. 23rd Feb. 1857. This may certify that at the request of his Royal Highness, Duke of York, I have named his son and heir, after the hero of Nicaragua, and his name shall henceforth be called General Walker S. Mc-Curdy."[6] But this son died, greatly to his father's grief, as he expected him to succeed to the chieftainship, and he lies buried on the Skokomish reservation.

In June 1888, the Duke of York died at Port Townsend, and was buried in the Masonic cemetery at that place, being followed to the grave by a large concourse of whites and Indians. His friends, chiefly whites, have erected a stone monument to his memory.

During the last thirty years, there has been no Indian war on the Sound, and so no chief has had an opportunity to distinguish himself in war. Only in the arts of peace and progress in civilization has there been any opportunity to become noted, and although but few of their names have been widely spread abroad, on this account, still there are some who might at least have honorable mention.

Lord Jim Balch. He was the successor of the Duke of York as head chief of the Clallams. He was the founder of the colony at Jamestown near Dungeness the most successful settlement and the only one of a farming nature among the Clallams. It was named in honor of him by Agent E. Eells and John F. Palmer.

Until about 1873 he could get drunk and fight as well as any Indian, and his band about Dungeness at last became so bad that the settlers near there petitioned the Agent to remove them to Skokomish, a punishment they feared more than any other except being sent to the soldiers at Fort Townsend. This so aroused them that about fifteen of the leading Indians put their money together, amounting to $500, and bought 210 acres on the water front. This was divided in strips so as to give nearly all a piece of the water front, with the rest running back. Balch gave more than any other one for the purchase of this in 1873. Although there has been some drinking there since that time, yet a great change took place. He was noted for years for his enmity to drunkenness and for the punishments which he visited upon the drinking ones, not excepting even the medicine men, who threatened to kill him by their incantations for it. His later life was not quite so firm.

He also took a firm stand against potlatches, not going even six miles to attend one given by members of his own tribe. For a time he would have nothing to do with the Indian doctors in case of sickness. And although in this respect as in the case of temperance he became weaker in his later years, yet the village there, the school since 1878, a day school, and the church since 1882, over which he exercised a fatherly interest though he was never a member of it, all are monuments of his perseverance in the arts of peace and civilization. He died of consumption.

Major B. Hallam of the Snohomish reservation was educated by the Catholics, was interpreter for a long time, also chief of police, and the leader of the tribe for years. He was tall, straight and well built, and did much to help his people. But at last, largely because of trouble with his wife he went to drinking after he had become a citizen, and one night in 1893 or 1894, when drunk, lay down on the railroad track, was run over and killed.

Henry Alexis, of Port Madison, was educated at the Catholic school, and ever clung to his religion. He was a priest, school teacher, interpreter, and leader of that tribe for many years until his death of consumption.

Sitwell, of the Puyallups, died in 1886. He was the last of their chiefs during the war and was friendly at that time. The following from the *Tacoma Ledger* is properly inserted here.

A DYING CHIEF

Old Sitwell of the Puyallups upon his Deathbed

Just up from the ferry landing of the Puyallup river on the reservation, sitting back from the road in a garden of weeds and wild flowers is the little cabin of Sitwell, chief of the Puyallups. He is dying. The conditions surrounding the old man in the last hours of his life, chief of the tribe though he be, are not such as to cheer him back from the grave—were he other than an Indian.

Two beds are in the room—rude bunks—and three chairs. Two little square windows look out upon the weeds. On one of the beds is stretched the old, grizzled, gray haired chief, moaning and whining in his distress. A woman lies beside him pressing her one hand upon his breast and occasionally wiping away the great drops of perspiration that break out upon his low forehead and withered cheeks. Another big, hardfeatured woman sits at the foot of the bed rocking her body back and forth. Both of these are speechless, answering any questions only with a dismal shake of the head. Sitting upon the other bed and reaching on the floor, their heads against the wall and their bare feet to the center of the room are men and women—old and young—quiet, speechless, ready to attend to the wants of the dying man, or waiting for the coming of the great spirit. On the otherwise unpapered and unplastered walls are tacked a number of brilliantly illuminated pictures—the Virgin Mary, the Burning Heart and the portrait of Rutherford B. Hayes.

The chief has been sick for more than a month past, but a short time ago seemed on a fair way to recover, but suffered a backset and now the Indians who may be met on the streets of the city or lingering about the old man's house, answer when you ask them as to his health, "The chief is dying." The age of the old man is variously estimated at from 70 to 110 years. Having no records, it is impossible for anybody to tell positively, and so, like the old negro slaves, they come to be accredited with fabulous years. Sitwell is chief of the Puyallups by birth. Since, through the laws of the United States the Indians have been given the right to choose their chiefs by election he was displaced, being superseded by Chief Coates, but the latter abused his authority and got drunk too much to suit the tribe and they returned some months ago, by use of ballot, to the old man, whom all the people seem to think highly of. Coates, at the recent election, to use a highly civilized phrase, was "snowed under."

Sitwell is a small squarely built man; like all of his tribe has a quite intelligent face and kindly expression. He has always been well disposed towards the whites and was one of the friendly chiefs in the memorable outbreak and massacre of '55 and '56. He is the last of the three chiefs, Sitwell, Salatat, and Chilly Whilton, who ruled the Puyallups at that time.

A *Ledger* reporter inquired of an English-speaking Indian yesterday what would follow the death of Chief Sitwell.

"Oh! big funeral—big time—all Indians go there," was the reply.

"And then what?"

"Elect new chief—Chief Dick."

Chief Dick is he of the plug hat, red rosette and streamers in the Fourth of July celebration and popularly known as General Spot. Chief Sitwell is a convert to the Roman Catholic faith, and when he dies will be buried with its rites.

Jim Shipman of the Nisquallies was chief, judge, Presbyterian minister, and leader in civilization for many years among his tribe previous to his death, which was of consumption in 1889 or 1890.

Jim Walker has long been known as the efficient head of the Indians on the Chehalis reservation, as chief, judge, policeman, and very successful in bringing children into school, whose parents did not want to send them there.

John Palmer was born near Port Townsend, about 1847, and belonged to the now

John F. Palmer

Peter C. Stanup

extinct tribe of the Chemakums. His father and many of his relations died when he was quite young, through intemperance, which made him a bitter opponent of drinking. When about two years old he went to live with the family of Mr. James Seavey, with whom he went to San Francisco, where he remained for a year or two. Most of the time until 1863 or 1864 he spent on a sailing vessel near the mouth of the Amour river, where he learned to speak Russian. The captain's wife took quite an interest in him, and taught him to read in English.

He returned to Puget Sound and served under Government as interpreter at Neah Bay until about 1868, when he went to the Skokomish Reservation, where he was interpreter and sub-chief most of the time until his death February 2, 1881. He understood four Indian languages, besides English and Russian, namely Nisqually, Clallam, Twana, and Chinook Jargon. He had a library worth fifty dollars and took several papers both Western and Eastern. He was the first by a year or two of the Indians to unite with the church there. He was very firm on two points, against intemperance, and the Indian tamahnous. On this latter point he was with one exception ten or fifteen years ahead of any member of his adopted tribe. It was often said of him that he was more of a white man than an Indian. His influence was very strong in favor of civilization. He was accidentally killed while working in the saw-mill at Seabeck by being knocked off a platform in such a way that his head struck on some sharp cornered slabs and refuse lumber, about two feet below.

Peter C. Stanup was born about 1857 and was a member of the Puyallup tribe. His earliest education was obtained with school there, and when a young man he began setting type in the office of the *Tacoma Herald*. When the Indian Industrial School was established at Forest Grove in Oregon about 1878, he was among the first attendants. After his return home, he became interpreter, especially for the Presbyterian clergyman, Rev. M. G. Mann; and after studying, he was licensed to preach by the Presbytery. This continued for several years, though after a time he left the work.

He went to Washington, D.C., to assist his Agent, Hon. E. Eells, in defending himself against some charges which had been brought against him. In 1893, he again went to Washington to secure some legislation he wished in regard to the Puyallup reservation.[7] But intemperance proved to be too great an enemy for him. He became an acknowledged leader in his tribe in their relations with the whites and government. He became quite rich also, and was wined and dined until this enemy overcame him. In May 1893, while intoxicated, he was drowned in the Puyallup river. He had read law, and had he lived, would probably have been soon admitted to the bar.

The following is from the *Tacoma Ledger* of May 23, 1893, just after his death:

> Although not a chief nor of a chieftain's ancestry, Peter Stanup was a natural leader among the Puyallups, as his father had been before him. He was born in either 1857 or 1858, and up to 1875 lived on the reservation among his people.
>
> He was naturally bright and of a self-reliant nature. His parents were Roman Catholics, but he adopted the Presbyterian faith.
>
> While yet a lad he exhibited a desire to acquire an education, and from missionaries learned to read, write and cipher. In 1875 he went to Olympia, intending to learn the

printing trade. He secured a position as devil on the Olympia *Daily Echo*, and quickly picked up the business. At the time he was a devout member of the Presbyterian church, and was the butt of many practical jokes, which he, with native cleverness, always managed to turn upon the jokers. He remained there about four months, receiving small wages. When the paper was removed to this city and started as the *Herald*, Peter came along, and was employed as a printer.

He then conceived the idea of securing a better education, and went to the Indian School at Forest Grove, Or. Upon completing the course he studied for the Presbyterian ministry, and was ordained. He returned to the Puyallup reservation, and for several years preached to his people, doing a great deal of good. His example and the prominence which he had obtained served as a spur to many of the younger generation, and the general enlightenment that at present exists among the Puyallups is largely traceable to his influence.

During the past ten or twelve years Peter had become engaged in many land speculating enterprises. He was possessed of great business ability, and in negotiating land deals between Indians and whites, and by good investments he had amassed a fortune valued at $50,000, most of which is invested in lands.

About ten years ago he married Annie Kahim, a pretty and attractive Indian woman, who had received an excellent common school education, and who, like Peter, was considered remarkably bright. Their married life has been marred by the death of four of their children. Except for these griefs they have been a very happy couple. The two children now living are both girls. One is 2 years old and is very ill. The other is about 8 months old. The Stanup residence is a neat frame structure on the banks of the Puyallup, and is on a well cultivated and valuable farm.

In 1888 Peter began writing an Indian romance but abandoned it. He wrote a number of excellent articles at various times on subjects pertaining to the customs and habits of Puget Sound Indians. He was an excellent talker and speaker, and took a great interest in political affairs. He was a member of the last two Republican conventions. . . .[8]

XXIII

RELIGION:

Objects of Reverence and Worship

THE PRACTICAL PART OF THEIR RELIGION is a compound of shamanism and spiritualism, called in the Chinook Jargon *ta-mah-no-us*, a word which has been locally adopted into English, as it is very expressive, meaning a combination of ideas for which we have no equivalent in English except by the use of one or more sentences. It is derived from a word in the old Chinook language, *it-a-mah-na-was*. In general, it means anything supernatural either among good or bad spirits, between the Supreme Being on one side, and Satan on the other. Hence, both a good and bad tamahnous are spoken of.[1]

The word is used as a noun, adjective, and verb. As a noun, tamahnous is the spirit or supernatural being in the other world, which has an influence over man, as his guardian spirit or the spirit which makes him sick or kills him; also the act of invoking the good ones and driving away the bad ones, so that a great tamahnous is often spoken of, meaning a great gathering of people who are performing their incantations. As an adjective, it qualifies and defines certain persons and things, so that a tamahnous man is one who, by his incantations, can influence the spirits—a medicine man; a tamahnous stick, or stone, or painting, is one in which the spirits are believed to dwell, or which is sometimes used in performing their incantations. It is likewise a verb, and "to tamahnous" is to perform the incantations necessary to influence these spirits. In some cases it is done mainly by the medicine men, but in others by any one.

OBJECTS OF WORSHIP

Objects of reverence and worship consist of the Supreme Being, Dokibatl, angelic spirits, Satan and demons, tamahnous sticks, stones, drawings, and the like, idols, and the sun.

The Supreme Being

It has puzzled me considerably to satisfy myself whether or not these Indians had an idea of a Great Spirit, previous to the coming of the whites—some such Being as the

Indians on the Atlantic coast are generally believed to have had an idea of; yet I am tolerably well satisfied that they had some such idea, but if so, it was a dim one, and of not much practical value to them.

In the next section will be given an account of what might properly be called an incarnation, a great being called Dokibatl, who came to the earth long after the creation of the world; and some say that the world was created by him, long before he came to the world, while others think that it was created by a Supreme Being other than him. If the ideas of the latter class were held before the coming of the whites, then they had a dim idea of a Great Spirit. I am also told that they had a dim idea of a Great Being who created the sun, long before they knew of Dokibatl, but that they never speak his name. Judge Swan, in his "Indians of Cape Flattery," says that "the Makah Indians have an idea of such a being, but likewise never speak his name." It is certain, however, that when the Indians learned of the Supreme Being of the whites, they had no native name which was applicable, and so he was given a name which in all the languages means the "Above Chief," namely, Saghalie Tyee in Chinook Jargon, Wis Sowul-lus in Twana, Shuk Si-ab in Nisqually, Tsitsl Si-am in Clallam, and Klokut Als in Upper Chehalis.

Dokibatl[2]

Whether or not the Indians received their ideas of a Supreme Being from the whites is a little uncertain, but one thing is certain, and that is, that they did not get their ideas of this personage from that source. They are as full of their *traditions* about him, as they are of their *practice* of their incantations, and these two things stand very plainly in their religion. He is called Do-ki-batl, or Do-ki-badl, by the Twanas, Do-kwi-batl by the Nisquallies and Skagits, and Nu-ki-matl by the Clallams, the difference in the name by the latter tribe being accounted for from the fact that it is much more nasal than the other languages, the same difference being seen in other words common to the several languages.

The Clallams say the Being was a woman, but most other tribes say a man. The ideas about him are confused. One of the Clallams, a tribe which worshipped the sun, says that this being was the Sun incarnate, while many of the Twanas say that he was the original creator of the sun, moon, man, woman, beasts, birds, and all things. I have never been able to learn that this latter tribe worshipped the sun. He seems to have held the same rank as the I-ka-nam with the Chinooks, A-mo-te-kin of the Flatheads, and Ti-me-hu of the Spokanes.

According to one Indian, he made the moon before he did the sun, to rule the day. It was made in the night, but when it rose in the morning it shone so hot that it caused the water to boil and killed the fish. It also by its heat killed many land animals and did much damage generally. Hence, he made the sun as it now is to rule the day, and condemned the moon to shine in the night.

One Indian told me that he made man out of the ground and a woman out of his rib, and gave them a good land, telling them to eat all the fruit except one kind of berries;

but the woman, tempted by Skwai-il, the King of Evil, ate of those berries. When Do-kibatl came he said, "Have you been eating of those berries?" She said, "No." He replied, "Yes, I know you have." On account of this her children became Indians, ignorant, fool-ish, and dark-skinned. The man, however, did not eat of the berries, and to his children were given letters, the knowledge of books, and a white skin. A part of this story is so much like that in the Bible as to make me strongly of the opinion that it is the early teachings which they had from whites, mixed partly with their old myths. How did they know there were such beings as whites with letters and books so as to study out a cause for the difference, much before the whites came?[3] My informant, a Twana, however, said that he knew the Bible history and that this was native, though somewhat similar. How-ever, he is not the most truthful Indian in the tribe (Robert Burns alias Sko Bob).

The Clallams, too, have a tradition that the first man was made from the earth. But, while their ideas of his first work are somewhat confused, their belief of his second com-ing is quite clear, and nearly all of these tribes agree as to what he did. He changed things very decidedly; hence his name, which means "Changer." At that time some of the In-dians hardly knew where he came from, but they think he came from the south or southwest, where the sky comes down to meet the world, and that he was last heard of to the north, in British Columbia.

A long time after the creation, say the Indians, the world became bad and the people became bad and foolish, whereupon Dokibatl determined to come here and rectify af-fairs—to punish the world and to change the foolish into something else.

According to them, the animals had been first made as men, but they were foolish. If a person stubbed his toe and fell down, he died. The hummingbird tried to fight the rain. None had any houses, or knew how to build them.

At one time they had a potlatch. The skate fish was an old man and stood in the door, whereupon the rest knocked him down and tread upon him, until his fat spread out, all around, when they, foolish things, ate and grossed themselves with it until nothing re-mained. On account of these and similar acts, Dokibatl changed a large number of these persons into animals as ducks, fish, sharks, skate-fish, and the like. Five persons were changed into the Northwind. He also taught those who were left a number of useful arts, as the making of the houses, the catching of fish, and the like.

According to the Skokomish Indians, one man, knowing that he was coming, sat down with his bone knife and began to whet it, saying, "I will kill him when he shall come." Soon he came, but was so much like common men that the man did not know him. Dokibatl said, "What are you doing?" "Nothing special," was the reply. Again the same question was asked, with the same reply. Then Dokibatl said, "I know what you have said; you want to kill me. Let me take your knife." It was given to him, and he thrust it into the man's ankle, behind, which made the man jump, and he continued to jump, was changed into another form, jumping on all fours, and this was the origin of the deer. As he plunged the knife in the ankle to the handle he left it there, where it still remains, having become the fetlock.

Another man was acting similarly with his knife when Dokibatl took it and thrust it into him, and he became a beaver, the knife becoming its tail.

Another man was pounding against a cedar tree with his head, trying to break it down, so foolish was he. Dokibatl asked him what he was doing, and he told, whereupon the Changer told him that he had better go away. He did so, and as he ran, wings, a strong head, and long bill came to him, so that he could bore holes in trees, and this is the origin of the woodpecker.

He found another man out in the rain, not knowing enough to get under shelter, and trying to keep off the rain by swinging his arms and hands around. He was changed into the hummingbird, and the arms are still swinging.

Another man was performing his incantations, or tamahnous, with his hair tied up in a knot on his head. He was changed into a bluejay, the knot still remaining.

A boy knew that Dokibatl was coming, and was afraid that he might be changed, though he did not wish to be, so he ran away, carrying with him a water box or Indian pail with water in it. As he was running some wings came to him to help him get away fast; he began to fly and became a turtle dove. The shaking of the water made a noise something like that when *pu-pu-pu* is said very fast, and this became the noise of the bird as it begins to fly. When it first found itself changing it began to cry *hum-o, hum-o*, a noise which was changed into its present mourning sound. This word is the name of the bird in the Clallam language. In Twana it is *sub-bep*, in Nisqually *hub-boh*, and in Chamakum *hum-o*. It is one of the very few words which connects the Chemakum with the other languages.

Other men had painted themselves in various ways, and when they were changed, their colors partially remained, and this was the origin of the colors of the birds.

Near the mouth of the Skokomish river he found some men fighting, and he changed them into stones, which now lie there on the beach, a very large one having been an officer in the battle.

As he walked across the land near the mouth of the Skokomish river, he slipped, whereupon he cursed it, and it became the marsh now there.

As he walked down Hood's Canal, on the west side, he found two canoes turned over, their owners being away fishing. These he changed into two long stones, now lying there.

In crossing a small stream he again slipped, and hence cursed it, on account of which no fish go up that stream.

A short distance south of the mouth of the Lilliwaup river are two places in the rock, about two feet long, which look somewhat like large foot tracks deeply made in the stone. These the Indians believe to be the foot tracks of Dokibatl. They are between high and low tide, and were evidently washed out by the water.

On the opposite side of the Canal, about three miles below the mouth of the Dewutts, is a large stone of very hard conglomerate, about thirteen feet high and five or six feet in diameter, tolerably regular in its rounded shape. This was a woman previous to the coming of the Changer, who they say changed it to its present form. Its Twana name is A-tak-tcin. It is plainly a part of a land slide from the adjoining bluff.

At Squakson he found one man crying. He was changed into a stone; the tears on his face being lines, which are said to be still visible on it.

He found some Indians in the water trying to catch fish in a very rude way. He asked them what they wished. They replied that they wished to catch fish. Then he taught them how to make a fish trap or weir across the river, such as they now use. He asked what kind of fish they wanted, and when a silver salmon came, asked if that was the kind. An affirmative answer having been given, he said, "Do not kill it, but wait until it has deposited its eggs, so that there may be a large number of them." They did so. Then a salmon trout came, and a similar conversation took place about it.

About five miles below Skokomish, on the east side of the Canal, is a bank of red earth, which the Indians used for red paint before the coming of the whites. This was formerly the Klikitat Indians, while the bank on the opposite side of the Canal was the Skokomish Indians. They engaged in a great game of gambling in which the Klikitats won. Dokibatl changed them into land, and after that the present race of Skokomish Indians obtained their paint there for painting themselves red when they gamble, so that they may also win.

Between Seabeck and Port Gamble are three spits. These were formerly three brothers named Tsay-o-witl, but Dokibatl changed them into their present condition.

He found the Indians gambling with their disks, and told them it was not good. He took their disks of wood and threw them into the water, but they came back to the Indians; he threw them next into the fire, but they came out; he threw them away as far as he could, but again they came back. Thus he threw them away five times, and every time they returned; and so at last he allowed them to keep these for sport, as they had conquered him—the only thing which did. I will add, however, that this story was told me when I was trying to influence them to stop gambling, and my interpreter afterwards told me that he was partly of the opinion that they had made up the story for the occasion, as he had never heard it before. I have, however, heard it more than once since. Some of these disks they say were changed into a shell fish which is circular and has a star on its back.

The Doswailopsh mountain was a man, and Mount Solomon, opposite it, and Mount Rainier were his wives. These wives quarreled. Mount Rainier left and went to its present location, and all were afterwards changed to their present condition.

Protection island, below Port Townsend, was, some time previous to his coming, a part of the mainland. It was a woman and the wife of the rest of the mainland, which was a man. For some reason he became vexed at her and kicked her away, and when Dokibatl came, he changed them both into land.

The mountain back of Freshwater bay, nine miles west of Port Angeles, was a woman, the large rock at the west end of the bay was her daughter, and Mount Baker was her husband. The woman was bad and abused her husband shamefully. He bore it for a long time, but at last took all of his things into a canoe and went across the Straits. When Dokibatl came, he changed them into what they now are.

Thus he went to all lands, gave to each tribe their language, and to some tribes special kinds of food: to some fish, to some crows, and to one tribe beyond the Klikitats snakes. So say the Skokomish Indians, and that distant tribe is so far away that it cannot be disproven.

The Nootkas and other Indians of British Columbia have a tradition of a similar being.

The Nootkas say that he came to their country from Puget Sound. The Nanaimo Indians speak of him as a great wanderer and call his name Qals. The Comox name him Hums-no-otl. The Skquamish call him Quais, the Cowichans L'kungen, and the Kwakiutl, Kanakila, but all speak of similar traditions in regard to him.

The Nootkas, according to Bancroft in *Native Races of America*, volume 3, 151, say that he was an old man, and that his canoe, paddles, and everything else he had were of copper. He taught the people many things, that he came from above and that they should all die, but after death should rise and live above. On account of this they became angry and killed him. Their descendants, however, reaped great benefit from this crime, for they have had copper ever since. Huge images, carved in wood, still stand in their houses, which represent the form of the old man, and help them to remember him.

Whether or not this whole story about Dokibatl is a dim tradition about the coming of Christ or not I have never been able to satisfy myself. I only record it as I have learned it from the Indians. But it is certain that as they first learned of the coming of our Savior they connected the two together. For a long time I never heard his true name, but was told that it was the Son of God, and ever since I have learned it, they often call him Jesus.

One Skokomish Indian says of Dokibatl that he came first to create, second to change or make the world new, and that, when it shall become old, he will come a third time to make it over again. It is very plain that the tradition about his second coming as a Changer was not received from the whites; but about his third coming, and perhaps about his first, I have not been so positive. Still, my informant said about that: "We know your teaching, but this which I tell you is different; we received it from our ancestors."

The Pueblo Indians and Mexicans have a somewhat similar tradition about their god, Montezuma, at least as far as relates to his coming to this earth. Says Prof. L. H. Morgan: "In this supernatural person, who was once among them in bodily human form, and who left them with a promise that he would return again at a future day, may be recognized the Hiawatha of Longfellow's poem, the Ha-yo-went-ho of the Iroquois. It is a ramification of a widespread legend in the tribes of the American aborigines, of a personal human being with supernatural powers, an instructor in the arts of life, an example of the highest virtues, beneficent, wise, and immortal."[4]

Other writers speak of a similar tradition among the Aztecs, Peruvians, Zunis, the Karoks, Hupas, Pomos, Maidus, and Pimas of California.

Angelic Spirits

They believe angelic spirits to be constantly around. Every man and nearly every woman formerly was thought to have one which was called his or her tamahnous. Such a spirit was supposed to guard the man or woman who often communed with it in the dark, when alone in the woods, and by various incantations, invoked its aid in time of need. These angels were the most useful deities they had, and the practice of invoking their aid was the most practical part of their religion.

One Indian to whom I was once speaking on the sinfulness of worshipping more than one Deity, as they did with their multitude of spirits, replied that they did not worship their tamahnous spirits, but only asked them to intercede before the Deity for the people. This idea may be original with them, but it is not improbable that it was derived from the Roman Catholic faith in praying to saints, taught them by the priests, who were among them forty years ago.

Demons

They firmly believe in the presence and power of malignant spirits, and much of their tamahnous is to conquer them or to gain their favor and aid. The main idea of sickness is founded on this belief, that it is caused by these spirits, and the practice of their medicine men is to counteract them. The chief of these demons, according to the Twanas, is Skwai-il, who resides below, but in another place from the disembodied human spirits. Often a parent tells a child, "You must not steal or do wrong; if you do, Skwai-il will see you and take you to his dwelling-place."

The Sun

An old Clallam man informed me that before the coming of the whites they knew nothing about God, but worshipped the sun as their God and they prayed to it daily, saying, "Sun, take care of me," and they gave food to it at noon. Another Clallam told me that they also believed the sky to be supreme, and that it was a common saying of the old ones to their children, "You must not do wrong or the sky will see you." Such ideas come to the surface but very little in their intercourse with the whites, yet I think my informant spoke the truth, and I quote the following from Swan's "Indians of Cape Flattery" in corroboration: "Every night we wash and rub ourselves with cedar and every morning talk to the great chief or his representative, the sun, whose name is Kle-se-kark-tl"; while the following note is added by Mr. Gibbs: "Among the western Selish [Salish] or Flathead tribes of the Sound I have not detected any direct worship of the sun, though he forms one of their mythological characters. He is by them represented as the younger brother of the moon." According to Father Mengarini, he is, however, the principal object of worship among the Flatheads of the Rocky Mountains or Selish proper, as well as by the Blackfeet. Among both tribes he was supposed to be the creation of a superior being.

Inanimate Objects

They believe that these spirits, both good and bad, may dwell at times in certain sticks or stones, hence these sticks and posts become objects of reverence or fear. The sticks are generally reverenced at all times, for, although the spirit dwells there only a small portion of the time, yet after it has been given to the spirit by its earthly owner that spirit is supposed to always watch over it and be angry with any one who treats it disrespectfully.

Some of these are posts which support the potlatch houses, and some support the houses in which people dwell, though when this is the case the houses have usually been used as potlatch houses. Generally they are of cedar, from 1½ to 2½ feet wide, and from 8 to 10 feet long. . . .

Some such posts supported the ridge pole of an old potlatch house at Port Angeles, reaching from the ground to the cone of the roof. They were from 21 to 24 inches wide, and about 18 feet long. The side posts of the same house, which then remained, were similar in size to those at Sequim, but were not painted. They were simply carved, without much artistic effect. Another side post was said to have had the figure of a man carved on it, the full length of the post, but when I saw it, it had been cut down, and only a part of the feet remained.

Others are sometimes placed on the cross beams of the potlatch houses to support the ridge pole. These were taken from such posts in the potlatch house of Skokomish, which was built in 1875–76. Some were unveiled with considerable ceremony. They were owned by separate individuals. Some were not painted any, some a little, and some quite well, with figures of a bear and man, a man's face and heart. The unveiling of these two was done several days after the potlatch began, though unfortunately I was not present to see it done. The rest were not veiled to begin with. While the owners and people were quite superstitious about allowing any one to desecrate them, for fear that the spirits which sometimes dwelt in them would become angry, yet they were very careless about protecting them.

Several years after they were made and placed in position in 1881, a heavy snow crushed the house, and the posts were scattered around promiscuously in the ruins. A few of their owners removed theirs to their dwellings, but others did not take care of theirs, but allowed them to be knocked around, until they were knocked into the water of Hood Canal and floated away. They seemingly acted on the principle that while it was wrong for a person to abuse them, yet when the elements abused them, the spirits must take care of them, or they would not be cared for. After some years, however, they lost their fear of them, and I was allowed to take a few of the poorer ones which remained, though at that time the paint had all been washed off.

To show how much the people were afraid to molest these, I will relate the two following incidents: A half-breed boy of fourteen or fifteen years was telling a lady how much afraid some of the people were to touch these sticks and stones when the lady said to him, "You would not be afraid to touch them, would you?" "I, I don't know," he replied slowly. Here he was, brought up mainly among whites, in school ever since he had been old enough to go, and yet really afraid to touch them.

The cross beams on which these, which support the ridge pole in the potlatch houses, rest, are also believed to be sacred, although they are neither carved nor painted. If any person knocks one of these down so that it falls on the ground, it is said to make the

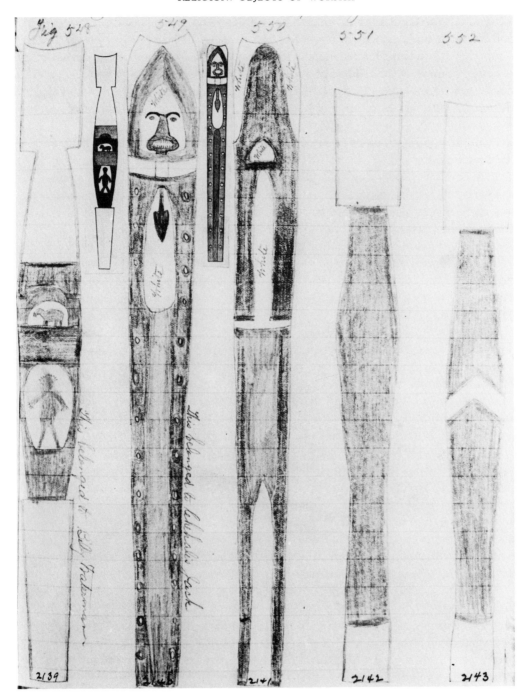

Tamahnous posts

spirit which dwells in them so angry that he may send sickness upon the whole tribe. The following incident will illustrate this.

About 1875, when I had been among these Indians only a year or two, as I wished to obtain something of the kind for my collection, I asked one Indian, who was so civilized that he cared nothing about these things, whether I would be likely to find anything that would suit me at an old communal house four miles distant, which had been deserted for years and of which nothing remained but the posts and beams. He said that he thought I could. Accordingly I went there, and finding that all of the boards of the house had been removed, as well as some of the posts and cross beams, and I supposed that all had been removed for which the Indians cared. Some of the posts were slightly painted in an uninteresting way. There was, however, one post which had a large heart carved on it. It was about 8 feet high and 2 wide. This I cut down, and supposing that all had been removed which was of value, I put it in my boat and started for home.

On my way home I began to think that perhaps it would have been best first to have asked the chiefs about it. Stopping to see one of the younger Indians, I told him about it, and he seemed to think nothing of it. But on rowing up to another house, an old man came to me and on seeing it, said, "The devil has got you now!" He then told me how afraid the people were to have such things treated in that way, and also told me the owner's name. I told him the circumstance of my getting it, and that I did not intend to do anything wrong. He was satisfied of that, but still was afraid. As he was related to the owner, who was then about twenty-five miles away, I offered to leave it with him until the owner's return, but he said that he did not dare to have it about the house. Seeing one or two others, I explained to them about it, and brought it home. One of these told me that when the large beam, which was supported by the post, fell, it made the spirit very angry, and that it would probably send some sickness upon the people.

When the owner returned I talked with him about it, and offered to return it, but he said no. I then offered to pay for it, but he again said no, that if I had gone to him before getting it, and he had sold it to me, the Indians would have thought it very bad, but as it was cut off above ground, it could not be helped, and he appeared good-natured. I, however, gave him a sack of flour and some sugar, as a peace offering, and he has ever since been quite friendly to me. About two years afterward, there was considerable sickness among the Indians, and some deaths among the children, and one Indian hinted to me that I had caused the sickness by making that spirit angry.

I still keep it. Occasionally the Indians speak about it, but their ideas on the subject have changed greatly within the last four years, and they have, apparently, long since ceased to have any anxiety about it. Seven or eight years afterwards, as I was moving it, an Indian came along and offered to help me. I asked him if he was not afraid of it. He said no, and picked up one end and carried it to where I wished to place it.

When the next house was crushed by the snow and the posts lay scattered on the ground, I wished much to get hold of some of them, but judging from my first experience, concluded I had better be careful. So at first I simply made drawings of them. But two years ago, knowing that the ideas of the Indians on the subject were changing, I ventured to ask the owner, who told me plainly that he cared nothing about them, and that I

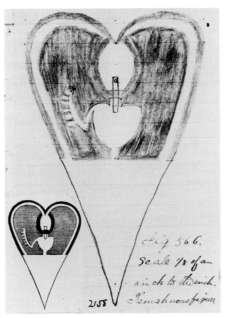

Tamahnous figure

Tamahnous powder charges; left is made of a sea lion tooth. Left and center are Quinaielt

might go and get them if I wished. So I obtained four, which are about 8 feet long, and at the same time I knew that an Indian cut up one of the sacred beams for rails.

A rather curious representation I saw at a potlatch house at Squakson in 1880. It was made from a board carved in the shape of a heart, about 24 inches wide by 56 long. A part of it was painted blue, a part red, and the rest white. It had a handle of glass from some pitcher fastened to it. It was nailed on to one of the side posts of the house, and was the only tamahnous figure on it. It was said by the Indian to be really what gave away the articles at the potlatch.

Occasionally these tamahnous representations are on the door of the owner's house. The idea was that the tamahnous would guard the house and its inmates, protect the owner while asleep, or assist him while hunting.

Another kind of tamahnous sticks were about 7 to 10 feet long, round, 2 or 3 inches in diameter at each end, and about an inch more in the middle. They were painted very simply, black on one side, and red on the other. They went in pairs, and I obtained two pair for the Chicago Exposition of Twana Indians. They were originally very valuable, and a man would give a horse to some person for making him or her a pair: although the real trouble of making a pair was not worth much over fifty or seventy-five cents. The value consisted in the tamahnous which dwelled in it. When a person tamahnoused, the owners held these in their hands, and the spirits were said to make them dance, so that no one could hold them still. At Skokomish they were not kept in the house when not used, but in the woods. Long ago I was never permitted to see them, but in 1892, when I obtained these, I was conducted a mile from the owner's house—a woman—and found them in a hollow tree. The other pair was kept by a tree nearer home. The owners by that time had abandoned for years their faith in them, and so were willing to part with them, and yet hardly dared to allow me to tell the other Indians that they had been so sacreligious. I saw some in a house where they were kept, at Quinault, in 1892, with the head and face of a man at the top, and heard that similar ones had been used at Skokomish, but when the Indian looked for them in the woods, he found that they had been burned by a fire which had swept the woods.

I have also heard that long ago, both Twanas and Clallams had large blocks on which they would place their hands, and thus put their tamahnous into them, and they would dance, somewhat after the white style of table tipping by the spirit rappings.

Hon. C. Hale, at one time was Superintendent of Indian Affairs for Washington Territory. He was a Spiritualist. His son Henry was not, but sometimes told his father that his religion and that of the Indians was about the same, only the Indians were further advanced in it than the whites.

Idols[5]

"Are there any idols among the Indians here?" was the question which was asked me by a visitor. I had not been here long before I became satisfied that the principle of idolatry was here. The sticks and stones just described contained the principle of idolatry, yet they were of such a shape that they could not properly be called idols. I had been here four years before I saw what could be called by this name. As I visited them at one of their religious gatherings, in 1878, I saw it. It was about 4 feet long, roughly carved, with the face and body of a man, but with no legs or feet, the lower part being set into the ground, and around this they performed their incantations. The eyes were silver quarter dollars nailed to it, and at the time it had no clothes on, except a necktie of red cloth, white cloth, and beaten cedar bark. It is said to have been made by the father of a very old man, and is kept secreted in the woods when not wanted. I saw it several times after they were done with their performance, and the Indians willingly allowed me to make a drawing of it. It has since been carried off to the woods again.

The Indians say that although it was made by the father of the old man—recently deceased—who owned it, yet that it is hundreds of years old, such imperfect ideas do they have of chronology; also that the reason it does not decay is because its tamahnous preserves it. (It is of cedar, and consequently would not decay quickly.) They report that at one time it was left near a tree, but that when they went to get it again, it was a little distance away, and they profess to believe that its tamahnous had such power that it walked that distance. Its forehead at its base is in bas-relief, ¾ of an inch; its nose ⅝; and its chin ¾. For a description of the ceremony in connection with it, see Chapter XXV, "Tamahnous for lost spirits."

The Twana Indians also say that long ago, they had another similar image, which the owner kept hid in the woods. A great freshet, they say, came and flooded the land where it was. The owner's tamahnous told him of this, and also told him that the idol had climbed a tree to get away from the water. He accordingly sent a man to get it, but told him not to look for it on the ground where the idol had been left, but to look up in a certain tree. Sure enough, when he reached the place, he found it in the tree, and singing with a great buzzing noise, and by reason of this noise, the person hunting for it found out exactly where it was.

I have been told by the Twana Indians that the Clallams of Port Discovery had large idols, 10 or 12 feet long, which they worshipped long ago, which they kept in the woods, but which are now nearly decayed.

Mr. M. Huntoon, formerly of Elwha, told me that at one time he found on his farm a small wooden idol, but that not valuing it, it was lost. It may have been an idol, and yet it may have been a carved work, such as are described in Chapter XV. I have seen such among the Clallams which were imported from the Makahs as playthings.

Mr. J. G. Collins, of Whatcom, near the Lummi reservation, has written me that he has a stone image, about 5½ inches long, which has a human face and a bird's body. It has a small mortar in its back that will hold two thirds as much as an egg. It may, however, be a mere work of art.

A Twana school boy, A. P. Peterson, drew for me, following his father's directions, two pictures of such images, each of which had the face and body of a man; one having arms, the other without them, but neither of them having feet or legs. The boy wrote in connection, "All kinds of images are made when they are tamahnousing. The man is not to serve the tamahnous, but the tamahnous the man I am told."

Two images somewhat similar have been found in the woods near The Dalles of the Skokomish or Skokomish falls, and are now owned by W. F. Putnam of Lake Cushman, near the head of the river. They are 4 or 5 feet long, a foot and a half or two wide, and several inches thick. They were evidently old idols, hid in the woods so long ago that they are a little decayed.

The Twana Indians have the following tradition. A long time ago a man made an image of a man, into which his guardian spirit entered and over which it had considerable power, even to make it dance. Two young men, however, did not believe this, and made sport of it. At one time, when many people were assembled in the house where it was, these young men were told that if they did not believe it could dance they might take hold of it and hold it still. But when they did so it began to dance, and soon, instead of their holding it still, it made them dance with it, one holding to an arm on each side of it. Nor could they stop it, or even let go, but after dancing for a time in the house, it took them outside and started toward the salt water. The people, afraid that something would happen, followed, trying to stop it, but could not do so. It danced to the water and into it, and made a plunge head foremost, when all three were changed into the fish called the skate, which still lives in the water.

The following from the *Tacoma Ledger* of 1892 or 1893, I think also bears on this subject.

> Executive Commissioner G. V. Calhoun, of the Washington world's fair commission, yesterday wired the acceptance by the commission of an object for exhibition at Chicago that is quite unique. It is a stone totem. The totems of Alaska, so far as known, are wooden and the present specimen must have been the product of quite an advanced civilization, as it is made of granite, and was at one stage of its existence very highly polished. It was found in Sumas valley nearly thirty years ago by E. G. Ward. It is four feet and a half high and one foot and a half across the top. The sculptured part is in the form of a crouching or stooping man with a mouth like a frog. The vertebrae are all marked down the back. There is, contrary to what is usually the case in totem-poles, but the one figure on it, the rest of the stone being plain. The stone weighs 600 pounds and is to be loaned to the commission, the owner reserving the right to sell. Several state antiquarians think that the relic should not be allowed to leave the state, at least permanently.

At Quinaielt both in 1892 and 1893 I saw in the house of an Indian doctor, a large image curiously carved and painted, partly man, and partly whale, which was said to be a tamahnous to assist in catching whales. It was 6 or 8 feet long, about 2 or 3 wide, and 6 or 8 inches thick. A photographer has thus far tried in vain to take a picture of it, the owner being unwilling.

In connection with the idol are tamahnous sticks, held in the hand, which are used in the ceremonies and which are believed to have spirits in them. Their use will be described in the ceremonies in connection with that idol. A similar one I found lying on a Clallam grave at Elwha.

Tamahnous Spirits

Tamahnous water. It was believed that formerly the Clallam Indians of Elkwa possessed a mysterious power over all other Indians; that if they wished to call a person a long distance off—20, 30, or 50 miles away—they simply, talking low, called him and he came; that if they talked thus about a person, his heart was in a complete whirl, and that if they talked ill and wished to do evil to any one thus distant, his eyes were made to whirl and the evil wish came to pass. The cause assigned for this was as follows: Far up in the mountains at the head of the Elkwa river are basins in the rocks; one of these, they say, is nearly full of black water and it is always as full whether the weather is wet or dry. In this water, which is thought to be tamahnous, the Elkwa Indians washed their hands and arms and thus, it was believed, gained their great power.

Marsh tamahnous. When persons are out picking berries or wandering through swamps, they sometimes see a phantom, will o'the wisp. This they believe to be a marsh tamahnous, an exceedingly powerful evil spirit, and that the person who sees it will soon die, unless there is a great tamahnous to counteract it.

Stick Siwash. They believe that there is in the woods a great man or giant, thought by some to be as large as a tree: hence his name, which means a "tree Indian." They believe that he will carry off women and children when they are out in the woods alone, or when two or three of them even are together. He has never been known to attack men.

Water monster. They also believe that there is a great water animal, which has overturned canoes, and eaten up people, but which cannot be killed. I have noticed that they seem to think it dwells at places where naturally the navigation for canoes is more than ordinarily dangerous, as at Port Wilson, near Port Townsend, where the tide rips are very bad, and at a dangerous place near Duckaboos, on Hood Canal. When passing these places in canoes, I have often been told to keep still and not say a word for fear of arousing the monster, and have also been told how he has sucked under whole canoes at these places. All kept as still as they could also.

375

XXIV
RELIGION:
Implements of Worship,
Ecclesiastical Organization,
Beliefs and Dreams

IMPLEMENTS OF WORSHIP

These implements consist of hand sticks, head bands, drums, rattles, and masks.

Hand sticks. In the tamahnous around the idol, which has just been described, hand sticks are used, which are held in the hand. They were about 4 feet long, and from ⅔ of an inch to 1½ inches in diameter; the wider ones, however, being flattened. Some of these were painted red, one had in addition a little blue paint, and some were not painted. A band of cedar bark was wound around each one not far from a foot from the upper end in a place cut for it. They were sharpened at the lower end, and when not in actual use, were stuck in the ground around the image. One of them was carved in such a way that it seemed as if the first part, a foot long, entered, wedge-like, into the rest, and this was said to represent a shark's tongue.

These, unlike the idol, had been recently made for the occasion, and each one was owned by a single individual, though I thought that sometimes the same one was used by others than the owner. When in use they were held in the hand, being grasped about the middle, when not in use their head bands were hung on them. I once saw a broken one on the grave of a Clallam chief at Echola, and these are all I have seen during the twenty years I have been here. I suppose they keep them concealed in the woods. When fifteen years ago I asked an old Indian, who was quite an adept at making articles and had gladly made many for me, to make one of these for me, he declined, for he said that if he did, the rest of the Indians would be angry with him. They were not intended for profane hands, though they readily granted me the privilege of making drawings of them. They are not as superstitious now about them.

A carved stick of wood was found on the Skokomish reservation, which has been the subject of much discussion. It is 8 inches long, and 1½ to 2 inches in diameter. It seems to have the carving of the head and tail of a fish on it. Some have supposed that it was a

Tamahnous hand sticks

Tamahnous hand sticks

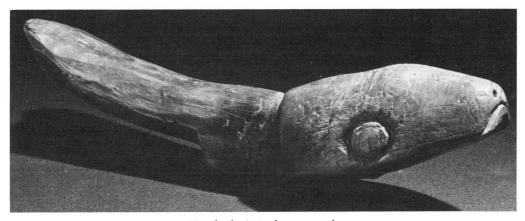

Hand adze/tamahnous article?

part of the handle of a hand adze. Others believe it to have been held in the hand, while tamahnousing. It is of yew wood, and was found while making a logging road about 8 feet from the face, and about the same distance from the top of a bank.

Head bands. During the same ceremony as that in which the hand sticks were used, and also in many other forms of tamahnous, a head band is used. They are usually of beaten cedar bark, about an inch in diameter, with one or more feathers in it. Eagle feathers are preferred for this purpose, but hawk feathers, and those of other large birds are used.

A somewhat similar head band was made for me, which had the head and bill of a red-headed woodpecker in front, the wing feathers of the same bird at the sides, and the tail feathers behind.

I have also seen one head band of black bear skin and one of cloth. In black tamahnous these bands are generally colored black, and the ends of the feathers are tipped black, but in other kinds of tamahnous they remain their natural color.

Drums. These with the Twanas, and usually with most of the upper Sound Indians, have a square or rectangular head, the sides of which are from a foot to two or more feet in length. They are made of skin, usually deer skin, stretched over a wooden frame. Each drum has only one head. On the reverse side two leather thongs or straps are crossed at right angles to form a handle. By this they are held with one hand while the drum stick

Cedar tamahnous head band, Twana

Cedar tamahnous head band, Clallam

Twana drum

is held in the other. They are only from 3 to 6 inches deep, and vary in tone according to size, as much as our snare and bass drum.

The Clallams usually make their drums with a round head, but similar in all other respects to the Twana drum. I have seen the round drums at Quinaielt, one of which was covered with the skin of a sea lion, which I secured for the Chicago Exposition. Those two, however, are the only ones I think which I ever saw with painted heads. All others have had no paint on them. Occasionally the Clallams use the rectangular ones, and the Twanas the round ones, but not often.

I have a Twana one, which was used by a medicine man when doctoring a sick child. The child died and the drum was broken through the head and thrown away as no good. These drums are used on nearly all religious occasions in black and red tamahnous, in doctoring the sick, and in gambling, in fact whenever the help of the Spirits is invoked.

Rattles. These are of several different kinds. One variety is made of deer hoofs. These are often strung in quite large bunches. I have also seen blank rifle shells mixed with them. These rattles are held in the hands or fastened to the waist or other parts of the body, while tamahnousing. I do not know that they are ever used in tamahnous for the sick, or in the black tamahnous.

The Indians believe that a spirit or tamahnous dwells in and protects these. One woman who became a Christian said that she did not know what to do with hers. She wanted to get rid of them, but did not know how to do so, without making the tamahnous angry, for while she had given up the old religion, she still had a superstitious fear: she believed that a spirit dwelt in them, but not one which she wished to guard her; but rather an evil spirit, whom she was afraid to offend; and yet she believed that the less she had to do with him the better. She said that she had kept them in her trunk, but that the tamahnous often kept her head in a whirl and gave her bad dreams. If she should give them to her friends, she was afraid the evil spirit would treat them likewise. She was afraid to throw them away lest the tamahnous should be angry and take some revenge. So she was in a quandary. She wanted me to take them, thinking I could manage them, and I did so.

The Clallams also have rattles made of the scallop shells, which are found in their waters. I have never seen them used by the Indians of the upper Sound, although they could easily procure them of the Clallams. A hole is made near the hinge of each shell, and a number of them are strung on a small stick about the size of a lead pencil, but much longer, 20 or 25 inches long, which is bent in a circular form and serves for a handle. These are shaken edgewise, so that the edge cuts through the air. If they should be shaken sideways they are liable to be broken by striking against each other, and if they should be thus broken the person holding them would die shortly, according to their belief. I have one bunch of very small shells, but similar in shape to the large scallop shells which I found among the Clallams strung on a string and used as playthings by their children.

The black tamahnous rattle is somewhat in the shape of a bird, but hollow, and is used in the black tamahnous ceremonies. In making one, two pieces of wood are hollowed out, nearly the shape of the bird's body, the neck and head are carved on one end, and a

Twana deer hoof rattles

Clallam shell rattle

handle is made in the place of the tail. Shot or small stones are placed inside, and the two pieces are fastened together with strings, which pass through holes in the sides. Bark is wrapped around the handle. The back part is painted black, the underside a very dark red. They are shaken with a kind of circular movement, being held in one hand. Usually the whole is 12 or 14 inches long, and 4 in diameter. I have one, however, which is 10 inches long with the body only 2½ inches in diameter. They were considered very sacred.

Those of the same shape were also made which were not painted black, but some other color or no color, and these were not so sacred. I have one with two heads, side by side, painted dark red on the back, and green on the under side. It is 12½ inches long, and the body is 2 by 3 inches in diameter, being somewhat flattened.

Others are constructed on the same principle, but of an entirely different shape. I have one which is rectangular, 5¼ by 6½ inches, and an inch thick, with a hole cut through it at one end for a handle. It is mostly painted yellow, but has a face on each side, which is red below the eyes on one side and below the mouth on the other, but with no paint further up on the face. The face on one side is 3 by 3½ inches, and on the other 4 by 4. In making it, a piece of cedar of the required size is split in two. Each side is hollowed a little, small stones are put in, and the whole is fastened together with pegs, so well that when painted, it is difficult to see where it was split. It is called the tyee (chief) rattle. I have never seen them in use, but understand they were used at great festivals to call the people together early in the morning.

Others constructed on the same principle, that is, hollow, and with stones inside, are occasionally imported from the Haidas and Clyoquots of British Columbia, who are expert carvers. These are painted various colors, and though not black, were used in the black tamahnous ceremonies. One such, which I saw at the potlatch at Dungeness in

Black tamahnous rattle

Clallam rattle

Black tamahnous rattle

Clallam rattle

Clallam "tyee" rattle

1878, was in the shape of a bird, and had on its back the carving of a bear eating a man's head.

Another was somewhat quadrilateral in shape with a fantail and a handle on the side opposite the tail. It was painted on both sides quite elaborately with the eyes and face of a Thunderbird, but I was only able to get hold of it long enough to make an outline drawing of it. It had an orifice, with teeth in it which could be opened and shut, so that the tail could be taken out, and put in again. The Clallam name is Il-skai, which means "tail."

Masks. These were and are still used by the Clallams in their black tamahnous ceremonies. I have never seen them used by the Twanas, though formerly they were used a little by them, having been introduced by the former tribe. The Twana name is nearly the same as that of the Clallams, and was adopted from the latter.

Often they are made in the shape of a man's face, with more or less blue, red, and black paint on them, much as they would paint their faces at times. These will cover the whole face. The nostrils are openings through which the person can see. One was a poor one, and was painted with charcoal. The nose was a separate piece of wood nailed on, 2¾ inches high at the nostrils.

Others are made in the shape of the head of a bird or wolf. These only cover the upper part of the face for 5 or 6 inches below the upper part of the forehead, and the person sees beneath them. They extend out in front for 12 or 14 inches, and have painted on them the bill of the bird or the nose and teeth of the wolf. White, red, and blue paint are put on other places quite fancifully, while hair or feathers rise on the upper edge to represent the hair and feathers in the animal. Another kind opens like a bird's mouth and shuts again with a hinge, operated by a string. I once saw one of this kind on a Clallam grave. It was a bird mask, about 5 inches high, but extending out in front 20 inches, and painted black and red.

A Clallam chief told me that he had a large mask that opened and shut out each side of the face to an angle of 180 degrees, and then closed again. It extended in front 2 or 3 feet, was painted both inside and out, and was made by the Nittinats of British Columbia.

The best masks by far come from the Makah Indians, and the Haidas and some other British Columbia tribes. I have seen but very few made either by Clallams or Twanas. I have one made by a Twana, which is a wolf mask. It is 5 inches high, 9 wide, and 21 long. The sides are painted with streaks of black and red. A part of the upper surface is adorned with feathers and curled hemp, from a rope to represent hair. Its workmanship, however, is very poor.

Clallam mask

Twana masks

Indian masks, drum, and dancing robe

These three styles seem to prevail: that representing the human face in honor of the performer, a man; that representing a bird, in honor of the Thunderbird; and that representing the wolf, in honor of the wolf, who taught man the mysteries of the Thunderbird performance.

Other implements. After I had been among the Indians for about eighteen years a woman on the Skokomish reservation but who was a native of Snohomish, furnished me with twenty-three articles, all of which were somewhat similar. She told me that they were used in tamahnous, but how I have not been able satisfactorily to learn: I am satisfied that some of them were held in the hand, others were perhaps fastened to the

Tamahnous articles of hair

clothes, or made into a head band. I cannot tell. They are from 3 to 7 inches long, ¼ to ½ an inch in diameter at the upper end, and are made of human hair gathered in small bunches, and wound at one end, so as to fasten the hair together. They are wound with string, ribbons, and strings of beads. Some have pink and red feathers with the hair. A few have small pieces of iron, an inch or two long in the upper end, covered with ribbon, tape or beads. The fastenings at the upper end extend from ½ inch to 2½ inches in length. Mrs. T. Webb, who was on the Skokomish reservation about 1864, as daughter to the Agent, thinks she saw something similar used by an Indian when she was here, when he was being initiated into the Black society. He sat for days and much of the time seemed to be winding something similar to these around, and then rewound it.

In their black tamahnous ceremonies they often hold in one hand a sharpened stick 7 or 8 inches long, and ½ or ¾ of an inch in diameter, with which they strike wildly as they run around. Cloth is tied around the upper end for a handle.

In 1892 I obtained from a Quinaielt Indian a piece of skin nearly covered with beads, for the Chicago Exposition. It was doubled and so long that it would go over one shoulder, under the other arm, and reach nearly to the feet, with a tail at the lower end. It was 5 or 6 inches wide, and was called the otter tamahnous. It was in the shape of an otter. It was beautifully covered with bead work, and was said to be the last piece of a complete suit, used for this purpose, which they said came originally from the Yakima or Klikitat Indians.

HOLY PLACES

As far as I have been able to learn these Indians have not, and never have had, any public places of a sacred character, as areas, sacred mounds, temples, or sacrificial implements, unless their potlatch houses might be called such. Yet as they often live in these both before and after their potlatches, they can hardly be called sacred.

In this connection, however, I give the following, which was related to me many years ago by Mr. Tudor, then engineer of the steamer *Favorite*. He said that on the Skykomish river, on the eastern side of the Sound, there are three small prairies, and on one of them is what was evidently an altar, made of cobble stones, some of them being about the size of a man's hand, and some being smaller. The altar was about 12 by 16 feet, and 8 feet high, with a pillar in the center, which is much higher. Surrounding this is a circle, 30 or 40 feet in diameter, made by digging a trench and throwing up the earth. I did not learn the height of this, but have the impression that it was a foot or two high. There is a supposition that the tamahnous man or some privileged class only were allowed inside this circle.

I have never seen or heard of anything similar at any other place on the Sound, though it is possible that there may be back in the mountains. The Twanas say that formerly they went far back in the mountains for some of their religious ceremonies, which lasted for several weeks. They then washed themselves, fasted, built large fires, and went without sleep, but they have never hinted to me of anything like an altar of stones.

ECCLESIASTICAL ORGANIZATION

As far as their worship is concerned, there are no priests or special classes of persons for this object. Each man or woman had a tamahnous, with whom he or she held intercourse in secret, and whose aid they invoked in their public tamahnous. This was to assist them in their worship, gambling, to obtain fair wind, and all favors. Their medicine men, whom they generally fear very much, at these times seem to have had very little if any more influence than common persons.

Medicine men are numerous, and are feared because of the power they are supposed to have with spirits. They demand large fees, and sometimes in advance, for healing the sick. If the medicine man does not consider the amount offered sufficient, he will do nothing until enough is given to satisfy him; but if he fails to heal he gets nothing, and sometimes has to pay the relations of the deceased for his failure. He also receives pay for other work he is supposed to do, such as making a person sick at the request of an enemy. After the wife of a white man near here had died, an Indian said to me, "See your style of doctoring is very bad by the side of ours. That man has lost his wife, and money too, while with us, if a man should lose his wife, he would not lose his money."

At times when a medicine man fails to cure, his life is in danger. This can, however, generally be averted by the payment of considerable money and property. Formerly these men were occasionally shot, when the friends of the deceased believed them to be the cause of the death. After the treaty was made, the Indian Agent prohibited death as a punishment for this. Then some of the Indians complained bitterly because while the doctors were allowed to kill the people with their tamahnous, the people were not allowed to kill them in return, the only way they had of protecting themselves against the doctors.

Besides curing the sick, these doctors were often in demand to make persons sick, and even to kill them, for which they also received large pay. For instance, if a man was angry with another, he gave the medicine man a large amount, so as to induce him to kill his enemy by means of his tamahnous. The doctor was not limited as to time when he should do this, but could take any favorable opportunity within a year or two.

Since my residence here, this calling has been confined to the men among the Twanas, but in 1880 I found four women doctors among the Clallams, and I once saw one medicine woman performing among the Squaksons.

Rain makers. There are no rain makers; but at Eneti there is on the Skokomish reservation an irregular basaltic rock about 3 feet 4 inches in diameter and 1½ feet high. On one side there has been hammered a face, said to be the face of the Thunderbird, which could also cause storms. The two eyes are about 6 inches in diameter and the nose about 9 inches long. It is said to have been made a long time ago by a man who felt very badly and went and sat on the rock and with another stone hammered out the eyes and nose. For a long time they believed that if the rock was shaken it would cause rain, because the shaking of it made the Thunderbird angry. They have now lost faith in it, so much so that about eighteen years ago they formed a boom of logs around it, many of which struck it. The season was stormy and many of the older Indians said, "No wonder, as the rock is shaken all of the time." It is on the beach facing the water where it is flooded at high tide, and the impression is being gradually worn away by the waves.

As I was digging in an Indian garden one day, I found an oblong stone, somewhat flattened at the top and bottom, 2¾ inches long, 2 wide, and 1½ thick. The Indian noticed it very quickly, and said that it came from Quilceed Bay, and that formerly, when such were brought toward the reservation, they caused rain. It is evidently a hard clay stone, with considerable sand in its composition.

There are near Clifton, at the head of Hood Canal, a large number of excellent clay stones, and it is said that such stones were also believed formerly to bring rain in a similar way.

Rain stones from Skokomish

People who understand animals. I have been told of an old Clallam woman, so old that she cannot see because of her age, who is said to understand what dogs say, and that other old persons do the same; also that Skookum Charley, a Clallam medicine man, recently deceased, understood what the crows say.

BELIEFS

Future existence. Their belief was that the next world was neither above nor below, but somewhere within the earth. The good all went to one place, and the bad to another, where Skwai-il, the leader of the evil spirits, dwelt; but their ideas were so indefinite in regard to the division between the good and bad, that very few at death were called bad. Nearly all dead Indians were good Indians. More will be said about this in Chapter XXV, in describing the tamahnous for lost souls.

Transmigration. They believed that some wicked and foolish persons were turned into animals or stone. (See Chapter XXIII, "Dokibatl.") Also that spirits from the other world would come into this, are born and so live again. (See "Tamahnous for lost spirits," Chapter XXV.)

Omens

When the Indians see something very unusual, they generally think something bad will happen. For instance, if they find a fish very different from any they have ever seen, or a white squirrel, or find a frog cut open and laid on a rock, or anything very unusual, they think something bad will occur, as a great storm, or that some one will die. If it does not occur for a year and then comes to pass, they believe that the omen is fulfilled. To go near a dead person, especially for children to do so, is an omen that they will die soon.

Dreams

They have great faith in dreams, and my opinion has often been asked in regard to them, why we have them, and whether a revelation does come through them. Many of their visions of the other world, of their communications with their deceased friends, and of the spirits of living persons who have strayed there, occur in dreams. In Chapter XXVII will be given an account of the Shaker religion, a new one. This is largely founded on dreams and visions.

The following story of a dream was told me by the medicine man who dreamt it: A child of his died and he felt very sorry about it, crying much of the time. One night he went to sleep and dreamed that some one came to him, similar to the picture of an angel which I had shown him, and took him off to the other world, leading him at first by the fingernails. They went till they came to where the roads forked, one going up towards the good land and the other downwards. He was led in the lower one where there was no fire and where it was very dark. A tree or stick stood between the two roads, and his leader jumped on it and thence to the upper road and laughed at him, saying he could not jump so, but if he did try he could not get into the good road and go to his child. He, however, made the attempt, and in two jumps reached the upper road, and they went up until they came to a house, at which his leader knocked. They were admitted, but there was no one in the house, save an old man, who told them that the child was farther on.

They proceeded until they came to a prairie where was excellent grass and some sheep, which were very lean and did not eat. Next they came to a barren land where there were some fat sheep, and again to a good grass country with lean sheep. After a time they reached a hill where there were some children and persons singing, and his leader told him that his child was among them, but that he must not go over the hill and see the child. The spirit then gave the dreamer some maple leaves and huckleberry leaves, telling him that the maple leaves would be a girl and the others a boy, as children for him. He was also told that he must not cry for his child as he now knew that it was safe, and that he must not cry for other friends, as his wife or mother, if they should die; but if he felt very sad he might cry for three days.

393

The man says that since that time, when a friend of his has died, he only mourns for three days. His leader also told him that this world would come to an end in three years.

Visions

Visions have also been common. Their tamahnous was obtained in visions when faint, as will be related in the next chapter, and the new religion mentioned above is full of them.

XXV

RELIGION:

Tamahnous, or Sacred Rites

IN GENERAL, TAMAHNOUS MAY BE DIVIDED into three parts: the red tamahnous, black tamahnous, and tamahnous for the sick. In the first, the people paint their faces red; in the second, black; and in the third, the rites are controlled by the medicine men, with usually no paint.[1]

RED TAMAHNOUS

This is so called because all who take part usually paint their faces red. All who have a tamahnous take part in it, and even children who are too young to have a tamahnous are not excluded from it. It was the common form of worship. The object was to gain from their tamahnous what they wished, as the Christian prays for various things. Thus, we have tamahnous for the living, for wind, to assist in gambling, for lost spirits, and propitiatory tamahnous.

Finding Tamahnous

The first thing for a young man to do by way of sacred rites was to find his tamahnous. In order to do this I am told that a father would send his son into the woods or mountains a long ways from home, where he was not allowed to eat for a period of from ten to thirteen days, though he was required to bathe often, and keep up a good fire. They say that such fasting would kill a man under ordinary circumstances, but that his tamahnous keeps him alive, though he has not yet seen or found it. At last his tamahnous reveals itself to him in the shape ordinarily of a bird or beast, which ever afterwards is sacred to him. The women also have their tamahnous, which they find in much the same way.

Judge Swan says that among the Lower Chehalis Indians, the fast continues from three to seven days; that during the time he must neither eat nor sleep, but may drink water, and that what he sees may be animals or trees or fog intermingled, but which appears quite different because of a disordered imagination, caused by his long fast. He also adds that those who are strong enough to continue the fast for a long time, see a medicine tamahnous, and become Indian doctors, but that those who cannot endure such fasts, see only a tamahnous of an inferior grade.[*]

According to the same writer in his "Indians of Cape Flattery," the animals most likely to come around at such a time are owls, wolves, minks or mice, during the night; or eagles, crows, ravens, bluejays, elk, deer, or seals in the day-time. These are all considered tamahnous animals, some possessing a more powerful influence than others. As an Indian could scarcely be in the woods several days and nights without seeing some of these, he is generally successful in obtaining a manifestation. They do not, however, imagine that the animal which they see is their Guardian Spirit, but only the form in which he shows himself.

To the above animals the Twanas add the grizzly bear, black bear, panther, woodpecker, and hawk as tamahnous animals. In regard to the owl, they are quite superstitious when it hoots, for they believe it has come from the spirit land, where it often lives.

A. P. Peterson, a Twana school boy, wrote for me the following.

> A person, especially a boy, cannot get a tamahnous, unless he swims frequently, keeps clean, and goes off without clothes, far from home. He must not eat much, and then if he keeps clean, soon after he gets away from home, he will find his tamahnous. Boys often go to the mountains without clothes, but with fire. When he gets up in the mountains, he makes a big fire, so as to make those who send him sure that he has got up there. Whenever he finds his tamahnous, he goes home, and goes to sleep without a word. If he should tell about it then, the tamahnous would not like it and would go off.

The story of Big John's grandfather. When he was a young man, he was sent by his father to find his tamahnous, but could not find it. Again and again he was sent, but with the same result. At one time he stayed eighteen days with nothing to eat or drink and at one time his throat was so dry, that it about stuck together. Again his father drove him off, and he went down Hood Canal along the beach, but found nothing. He then came back, and on his return, saw three young men who had eaten some poison, lying dead on the beach. Accordingly, he turned back, and as he went along, he saw a sunfish, and remembering that he had heard that one young man had found his tamahnous by eating the whole of a sunfish, except the heart, he concluded to do the same. Hence he went to work, and when he had eaten all around it, except the heart, he fell down dead, that is, his spirit left his body. His spirit was taken by the sunfish, a long way off, through a region of darkness. At last he saw a gleam of light, as it were, between two clouds. There he saw a woman singing, and although he could not hear her, as she was so far off, yet he could hear the echo of her singing behind him. She brought his spirit back to his body, and thus he obtained his tamahnous. It was very strong.

[*]*Three Years' Residence in Washington Territory*, chapter 10.

Afterwards when the men met and talked about their tamahnous, he told about his. Sometimes he would tell about his fog tamahnous, and the next day, there would be a very, very heavy fog; or he would tell about his ice tamahnous, and there would be severe cold and ice, when the elk would come toward the salt water, and the people would go and kill them.

Using Tamahnous

When a person has obtained his tamahnous, he invokes its aid, as his guardian spirit, on the same principle that a Christian or Mohammedan prays to his God, that is, to obtain help and protection and success. This is often done when he is alone in the woods, or it may be when he is with a large number of persons, all of whom desire the same thing.

The fifth month, Sta-ko-lit, was so named because it was the month for tamahnous. Then it is said, they went far off into the mountains, washed themselves frequently, remained half naked, built a large fire 100 feet long and 20 feet wide, remaining about seven days without sleep, and tamahnousing. Returning home they slept much.

Tamahnous for wind. In Chapter XI, I have related how I travelled with about seventy-five Twana Indians from Skokomish to Dungeness. The morning we left the Duke of York's place near Port Townsend, they had a tamahnous for wind. This was done before starting and consisted of singing to their tamahnous and halloaing, while the drum, which is a tamahnous instrument, was brought and beaten in time to their singing.

At other times, while travelling in their canoes and they wished for fair wind, they would whistle, sing a little, strike on the water with the blade of their paddles, so as to spatter the water forward, while others kept time by pounding on the canoes with the handles of their paddles.

Tamahnous for gambling. A more common form of invoking the aid of these spirits is the gambling with the round disks. It is never used in any other kind of gambling. This has been described in Chapter XIII in the account of gambling.

Crazy tamahnous. Another way in which this crops out, I have been inclined to call crazy tamahnous. I do not fully understand, but am satisfied that the crazy feeling is caused by the effect of the imagination. It is said that a bad tamahnous attacks a person, who becomes crazy, and then there must be a regular work of tamahnous so as to drive out the bad spirit. The following are the facts as I have obtained them, a Twana school boy, A. P. Peterson, having given me most of them.

> I have often seen my mother when she acted crazily, and it was said that she became so because she had a bad tamahnous. When persons almost die, they will talk very foolishly against themselves, and it is said that the tamahnous make them do so.
>
> I was standing by the river one night looking at the canoe of our school teacher, which floated down and was caught on a snag, and I was thinking how I could catch it. I looked down and saw another canoe, a little ways off, and I thought that is what they call ghosts. To be sure, I thought again, it is a canoe. I looked very sharp at it

and saw the folks and paddles moving, coming up the river. I thought I would ask them to help me get the teacher's canoe, but to my surprise, they disappeared, and I could not see them again. When I saw it first it was not going down the river but coming up towards me. This is what the Indians call·ghosts or spirits, and when a man sees one he afterwards becomes crazy. So I thought, let me see if I shall become crazy, for I do not believe in such things as God has taught me better. [Item. He did not become crazy.] Another school boy also saw a canoe as he went to Union City. He saw it, but as he looked, it began to disappear, until he could see nothing, but the man's head. Another young man, not in school, saw a large canoe, with both Clallams and Twanas in it [in a similar way], and he became crazy.

A white man who formerly lived near Skokomish and had a Twana woman for his wife, Charles Bates, a man of limited education, once told me that from his observation he was satisfied, that when a bad tamahnous gets hold of an individual, he cannot eat, or if he does he is compelled to vomit up the food. He said that he had often seen his wife in that condition, and was satisfied that she feigned nothing, but that he believed that it was the bad tamahnous which caused the trouble. At such times, he said, she acted in a crazy manner, and it was useless for her to try to eat, until her friends tamahnoused with her and drove away the evil spirit, after which she recovered her usual health.

There is nothing in these statements which cannot, I believe, be explained by the laws of the imagination, but the Indian has never studied mental philosophy, and so knows nothing of those laws, but attributes all to tamahnous.

Tamahnous for the living. This seems to be allied somewhat to the former, and possibly also the propitiatory tamahnous, though differing from the former in that the candidate selects the time when he is to be sick. He calculates in advance the time when he is to be sick—tamahnous sick it is called—and the tamahnous is to take place, sometimes laying plans about it for a year or two, and even building a house for it, which afterwards is sometimes torn down, or used as a barn or shed. They say that their tamahnous tells them beforehand when this is to take place. It usually occurs in the winter when there is little else to do, and so is sometimes called "winter tamahnous."

When the time has come previously determined upon, and the house, firewood, food for all who are to be present, and all things are ready, the candidate or candidates starve themselves until they are nearly sick, when all their friends gather at the house and have a grand tamahnous to cure him. Several days are usually spent in performing the incantations, and in feasting. The night is spent in the tamahnous and the day time in fasting and sleeping.

During the tamahnous, the candidate sings a kind of solo, and his friends respond with a chorus, keeping time with the drum. Some of the ceremonies are very severe, as the candidate shakes his head very much, and fasts, so that one woman, a Twana, was made so sick, the strain on her nervous system having been so great, that she did not recover her usual health for years. I do not fully understand the object of it all. I have been told that an evil tamahnous possessed the person and the object was to drive it out. I have also been told that the entire affair was to secure the good will of the tamahnous of the candidate, and so was a propitiatory affair. At one time it became rather proverbial among the more intelligent Twanas to say, when a person was said to be sick, "a tamahnous sick, I guess," with such a slur as to show that there was nothing dangerous about it.

Propitiatory tamahnous. This is allied to the former. In December 1876, I spent a night with the Clallam Indians at Sequim in order to teach them. When I arrived at the place, I found that they were about to have a tamahnous. As they did not think they could well defer it, they proposed that they should first tamahnous, and that afterwards, later in the evening, I should hold my services.

They began with a feast of something like a mush in kettles, after which all, about thirty-five in number seated themselves around the fire. An old man then stood in the circle and sang a solo, and all joined in the chorus, pounding on sticks at the same time, while one man beat the drum. The man danced alone some, while his wife made presents to the others of bowls, baskets, and bundles of mat grass. He then sat down, and she, wearing a red blanket, took his place dancing back and forth, with a small stick in her hand, moving it like a wand, moving her hands, face, nose, chin, legs, and feet in an indescribable manner; but when her face, painted red, was turned a quarter of the way around and elevated to an angle of 45 degrees, her eyes still more turned and elevated, her hand with the wand above and in front of her face, she looked more like the typical witch or veritable old hag of old stories than I had ever seen. Her solo was very short, and the accompanying chorus was long and both were repeated many times.

Then another woman took her place and acted much like her. Next an old man, a sub-chief Inapoo, danced and sang, holding in his hand a large bundle of deer hoof rattles in which were mingled a few metallic cartridge egg shells. A medicine man, Dr. Bill, went at it next. He soon became so hoarse, though he was a strong man, that his solo was a growl. He puffed and puffed until he was exhausted. He, as well as those who followed him, used the rattles. Other women followed, one of whom danced, or rather jumped very hard, within two or three feet of a fire, which was so hot that my face was uncomfortably warm, though ten or twelve feet away.

Thus, three men and five women performed; the whole besides the feast occupying about an hour and a quarter. After all was done, I held a religious service, at which among other things I told them that all people were sinners. In replying, the sub-chief told me that he was not a sinner, as he had just tamahnoused, and so his heart was clean.

It has often been more difficult for me to learn the principles and reasons of a tamahnous than to get an opportunity to observe the ceremonies, but I have reason to believe that this one was performed in order to cleanse their hearts from the evil which they had done, which would offend their tamahnous. Such ceremonies have been very common during the long winter nights.

At a court which I attended in February 1878, convened at Jamestown, to consider the case of divorce between a Clallam man at Sequim and his wife, a British Columbia woman, she accused him of cutting her with glass on her arms and body. He replied that she was tamahnousing, and broke a bottle to get a piece of glass for this purpose, as it was her way of tamahnousing, that she asked him to cut her thus, that he did so very lightly, and as he had only scratched her a very little, she took the glass and cut herself quite deeply. This was accepted by the Chief and other Indians as true, and the divorce was not granted. I have not been able to account for this act of self torture of hers, except that it was intended to propitiate her tamahnous.

At each of two times when I have visited Dungeness I have found quite intelligent Clallam Indians, who had been in school some, though then married, one a young man, the other a young woman, just beginning a tamahnous—Howard Chubby and Mrs. Nancy Howell. The parents of both were great believers in the superstition. Both persons declared that they wished to have nothing to do with the tamahnous, and had resisted it all they could for some time, but that it took such a hold of them, that they could resist it no longer, else they believed they would die. So they had a tamahnous, which lasted one or two weeks. They always afterwards felt that they had taken a step backward in civilization from which they could not recover.

A somewhat similar affair occurred in the boarding school at Skokomish in 1891, but with different results, as it could be controlled by the teacher. The subject was a girl sixteen or seventeen years old, the daughter of a medicine man. She was some sick, and slightly out of her head, but in a few days medicine cured her. She, however, declared she was tamahnous sick, and acted strangely at times. She held up a pillow, said it was herself, and that herself was her father, and the two would talk with each other. It was noticed, however, that when anyone but the superintendent, whom she feared, was around, she acted in this manner, but when he came in she calmed down and acted as quietly as any one, or went to sleep, with no sign of illness which the physician could detect. Accordingly, he prepared a dose of assafoetida and castor oil, with seidlitz powder, or something like them, to make it effervesce in her stomach, so that she would continue to taste it, and gave it to her. One dose cured her. She never wanted another for her tamahnous sick, or showed any symptoms of the disease while in school. A strange incident in the affair was the fact that she said she hated her father because he had been trying to kill her with his tamahnous, and she has treated him as if she hated him to this time. Possibly these last two cases belong to the crazy tamahnous, or that for the living.

The Spirit Land tamahnous, or tamahnous for lost spirits. The Indians believe that in the Spirit Land, people live and die as they do in this world, and when they die in that land they come back into this world, are born again and live.

Sometimes the people of the Spirit Land come up into this world and get the spirits of their relatives, so that they may soon die, and so the sooner join them. After this the person whose spirit has been taken wastes away or dies suddenly. If by any means it is discovered that this has been done, and there are those who profess to do it, then they attempt to get the spirit back by a tamahnous, and if it is done the person will live. Sometimes a person who is believed to have intercourse with the other world persuades one who is in the best of health that he has visited the Spirit Land and seen the spirit of his dupe there, and the latter is thus frightened into having a tamahnous. Again, when some credulous individual has been ailing a little for a long time, but not sufficiently to feel that he needs to employ a medicine man, one of the arrang humbugs takes a fancied journey to the land of shades to search for the lost soul of the invalid, the discovery of which he soon announces, and once more there must be a tamahnous. Frequently in the winter when time hangs heavily on their hands and they are at a loss for amusements, these soul searchers pretend that they have received tidings of a number of errant spirits and they get up a general spirit hunt.

In January 1878, a tamahnous of the last kind took place among the Twanas, and I learned the following facts concerning it from one white man and some school boys who were present:

The performance is carried on mostly in the night, as it is said that day-time with us is night-time in the spirit world, and vice versa. The breaking of the ground is an important part of the ceremony. The surface of the earth is often actually broken, in order, they say, that the spirits of those who are performing can descend into the other world. When, as they pretend, the descent is accomplished, they represent pantomimically that they travel along a road, cross at least one stream, and travel on until they come to a place where the spirits dwell. Men only act the part of travellers in the nether world, though women and children are present at the tamahnous.

When they are supposed to cross the stream, they actually set up some boards on opposite sides of a beam in the house, which was about 10 feet from the ground thus $\bigwedge$ to represent the bridge. They crawled up the board on one side, and down on the other. If in going down a man should slip, they believe he will die within a year. Formerly it is said they thought that this was true, but some years before the tamahnous here described, it is said that a man did slip on such an occasion, and as he died within a year, they became convinced of the truth of this belief.

Only eight men went through the journey in 1878, but nearly all the rest of the tribe were present, pounded on sticks, and sang their tamahnous songs to the accompaniment of the drum. Having discovered what underground spirits had possession of the spirits of the people of this world, they surprised and fought them. (Just then a very great noise was kept up by all present to represent the battle.) Those from this world conquered, and on one evening professed to recover and bring back to this world the spirits of three persons, which they pretended to roll up in cloth like a great doll, and work over for some time, after which they seemed to give them to their real owners. When they put the spirit of one man on him, he sang his tamahnous song; and when a medicine man received his, he cried very much.

While performing these ceremonies, they used the hand sticks already described, wore the head band, and danced around the idol. The house in which this took place was built the previous season for this purpose, and was similar to the large dwelling-house, and was used for that purpose soon afterwards, and still later for a store house. It has lately been torn down. I am told that when they are professing to fight with the underground spirits and to conquer them, they break through the sides of the house, which are not very strong, and run outside accompanied by all the spectators. At times they also profess to bring berries from the other world, and if so, the bushes in this world will bear abundantly the next season, but if they do not they will be scarce.

BLACK TAMAHNOUS

This is a secret religious society, whose rites were by far the most savage of any practiced by the Indians. When going through the ceremonies they always painted their faces more or less black, hence the name. The strips are about the width of a finger. I have, however, seen them painted all conceivable patterns, spot, spots, stripe, stripes, and a part or the whole of the face wholly black.

Hon. J. G. Swan in his "Indians of Cape Flattery" says that it originated among the Nittinat Indians near Barclay Sound in British Columbia. From them it came south. The ceremonies among the Makahs, as described by Judge Swan, were very savage and bloody, far more so than I have seen among the Clallams, though from all accounts it was formerly more savage among the latter tribe than it has been since I have been among them. The Clallams introduced it among the Twanas and other tribes up the Sound, among whom the rites were less severe than they were among the Clallams. A Clallam recently told me that the Clallams, Twanas, Port Madisons, White River Indians, and a part of the Lummis practiced it, but not the Snohomish Indians, Skagits, Nanaimos, nor all of the Lummis.

The origin of it, according to Judge Swan, is ascribed to the following legend. Two men fell in love with one woman, and at last came to a quarrel, but one of them said, "Do not let us fight about that squaw, I will go and see the chief of the wolves about it, and he will tell me what is to be done. In order, however, to get to his abode, I must use strategem. They know that we are at variances, so you take me, and drag me over these sharp rocks which are covered with barnacles, and I shall bleed and pretend to be dead, and the wolves will come, and carry me off to their home."

This was done, and lacerated and bleeding he was left on the beach. The wolves came, and supposing him to be dead, took him to the lodge of their chief, but when they were ready to eat him, he jumped up and astonished them by his bravery. The chief wolf was so much pleased with this that he taught them the mysteries of the Thunderbird performance, and the black tamahnous was the result. The cutting on the arms, legs, and bodies of the Indians is to represent the cutting of the founder of the ceremony by the stones.[*] (See "Thunder-Bird performance," Chapter XVII.)

Both men and women were initiated into the Society. The ceremony of initiation, as I understand, varied somewhat with different tribes. Since I have been among the Twanas, there has been very little of it among them. As early resident of the reservation, Mrs. Thomas Webb, who saw the ceremonies nearly thirty years ago, has told me that the candidate was starved for a long time (one man saying that he did not eat anything for eight days) and that he was closely watched. Occasionally the candidate was let out and pursued by two or three others with all their might, and sometimes he himself pur-

---

[*] "Indians of Cape Flattery," pp. 66, 67.

Robe used in tamahnous, obtained at Jamestown, Clallam County, Washington, from Cook House Billy; made by his wife

sued others, and if he gave out in the race or other exercises, he was not considered worthy to become a member. If he did not, he was taken back to the tent and watched and starved, and the same scene repeated every day or two. At last he was brought out perfectly rigid, and taken by several men and thrown up as high as they could into the air, sometimes eight feet, and caught, and this was continued until he apparently came to consciousness and screamed. There was also very much cutting of the body and limbs, quite deep, so that the candidate became quite bloody, but he did not seem to take any notice of it. After these ceremonies, he would sometimes sit, in his house or lodge, looking like an idiot, for two or three months, and speak to no one, not even to a husband or wife, but simply wind something on a stick and unwind it again day after day.

The only time I ever witnessed the ceremonies of the Society to any extent was at a potlatch near Dungeness given by the Clallams in February 1878. A full account of what I saw is given in the chapter on potlatches (Chapter XX).

I am told that formerly the candidate was starved so that he would tear a living dog to

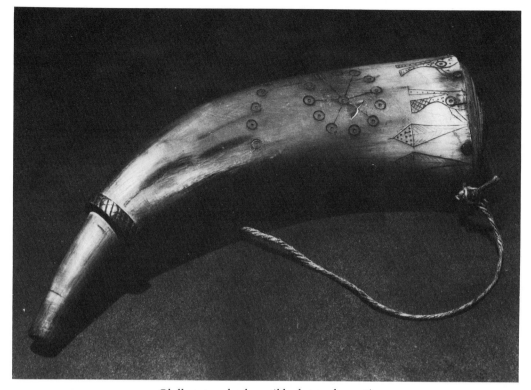

Clallam powder horn (black tamahnous?)

pieces with his teeth, but this was omitted when I was present, and has been for many years. The whole affair which I saw was carried on with perfect soberness, except the push, as much as nearly as we would show in our religious ceremonies, although there was one indecent thing done, not fit to be mentioned. Some days there were twenty-five whites present, nor did the Indians care, so long as the whites did not laugh. It is said that formerly two slaves laughed at the performances, whereupon they were immediately torn into pieces and eaten. If this is so, it is the only case of cannibalism I have ever heard of among the Indians on the Sound. This instance, however, if so is not strange, as among some of the Tsimpshean Indians of British Columbia they often tore dogs to pieces and bit pieces out of living persons in some of their savage orgies. Even among the Makahs the noise was often greater, guns being fired off to imitate thunder, and gashes were cut in their arms and legs and on their bodies 5 or 6 inches long, and from ⅛ to ¼ of an inch deep.

The only representation among the Indians I have ever been able to obtain which refers to the black tamahnous was on a powderhorn. The carved figures at the larger end are said to be black tamahnous, and to represent a wolf's head, though I can see no special resemblance.

OTHER SACRED RITES

Purification. When a young man went forth to obtain his tamahnous, he washed himself much, as already described, this washing being very essential. A Clallam medicine man, Dr. John, told me that the children who wished to become strong medicine men were accustomed to bathe daily, both summer and winter, in the river or salt water, remaining there for a long time, sometimes, he said, for hours, supposing that thereby they would gain the favor of their tamahnous. He said that he did so when young. There is some philosophy in this, for with their mode of living—in the smoke, grease, and dirt—bathing was essential to cleanliness, and so to health, and only a strong, healthy man could endure the ceremonies of initiation into some forms of tamahnous.

Sacrifice. Formerly, I am told, when they went to a new land to live for any length of time, they would build a fire, and burn thereon some fish, good mats, or something else valuable which had been made with the hand, except clothes, which they said they gave to the land to gain its favor. Even now in some of their tamahnous, they do something similar. When I spoke to them first about the sacrifices of the Bible, I found that they had enough such ideas, so that I could build upon them, and they could easily understand it.

Dancing. This was a common mode of worship, and has often been spoken of in the descriptions of tamahnous; but the sexes did not often join hands in it, but in separate groups, or singly, the men and women simply jumped up and down, keeping time with their singing, rattles, and drums.

Prayer. Occasional prayer was offered I am told to the Great Spirit, when they worshipped him. They also prayed often, especially when alone, to their tamahnous. I have learned of one Clallam and one Twana prayer. Each asked for protection, acknowledging the weakness of man, and the power of the Great Creator.

VOL. 6

XXVI

RELIGION:

Tamahnous over the Sick

THIS KIND OF TAMAHNOUS HAS MORE POWER over the Indian mind than any other. The others have reference in a general way to religion, and are partly practiced to while away the time in the winter, or to call people together for a social time; but this has reference to their lives. It is material, intensely practical. Hence, the order in which they have abandoned their tamahnous has been, first, the black tamahnous, as the most savage and least reasonable; second, the red tamahnous, which embodied the main part of their religion; and lastly, the tamahnous over the sick, which while it contained some elements of religion, also contains much superstition.

THE MEDICINE MAN

The medicine man is the foundation of this kind of tamahnous. Without him there would be none of it; still the counterpart is that without the superstitious desire for his services among the common people, there would be no call for him, and hence there would be none.

How an Indian becomes a medicine man I have not fully learned. I can only state what I do know. The exercises are very severe, and consist of daily bathing for a long time, among other things. Judge Swan says, in his *Three Years' Residence in Washington Territory*, that among the Indians about the mouth of the Chehalis river, the rites are somewhat similar to those practiced by a common person when obtaining his tamahnous, but much more severe. One young man who obtained a common tamahnous, told the Judge that he was not able to continue the fasts and other rites long enough to see the medicine tamahnous, and so saw only one of an inferior grade. Had he been able to continue the rites, he said, he would have become a medicine man. Only one or two Indians have become doctors among the Twanas since I came among them. I never learned anything about the rites they went through, or that they went through any. I only knew that they began practicing the cure of the sick, and that one at least of them began this long after he had procured his own tamahnous.

The following in regard to them was written by an educated Twana Indian, A. P.

Peterson, whose brother-in-law is an Indian doctor, though the writer has never obtained a common tamahnous.

These medicine men were well fitted to be at the head of their people, and were well known among all the tribes of Puget Sound. They were respectable, according to Indian etiquette, working earnestly for the welfare of their people, giving feasts, and the like. They were good hunters, good fishermen, good husbands, and good fathers, and were loved and feared by their people.

This tamahnous is not obtainable by anyone who wants it, but in order to get it, a young man must go through a very severe training. He must always have a clean body, good habits, and a good character, and must be obedient not only to his parents, but to all his relatives. He must love and seek advice, and be kind to the aged, and never laugh at their infirmities. He must be an early riser, and not wait for breakfast, and never under any circumstances ask for anything to eat. And yet the tamahnous does not come to him gradually during this process of training. A young man may have a good character, be obedient and respectable, have a clean person, and have all the characteristics at home, without going anywhere away from home, and yet have no tamahnous. No, he must go through a training much more severe than this. He must not take a fine day for swimming (only), but during a rain or hail storm, a snow or thunder storm, were the days when the Indian boys had to go and swim, nor was it in front of the Indian houses by the side of the canoes, but they must run, yes actually run along the beach, running now and then into the water, and plunging in all over, returning again in the same way. He carried too a bunch of yew wood branches, with which he rubbed himself from head to foot, and after he was through rubbing himself, he did not throw it carelessly away, but put it under a pile of stones for future use. The further a young man thus went to swim the better it was. They say the water has fine needles. It will pierce the flesh five times, and then it will be all past, for the body will then be so numb, that it will not feel the cold. Thus, they say that it has expended its last needle on the flesh to try the young man, but is at last conquered.

During the severest part of the winter, when the water was all frozen over, the man or woman who was training the young person, would go into the water and make a hole in the ice, where the water was about four feet deep and stick a pole into it. Then the young man or woman who was being trained, was ordered to go into the water by that pole, and to stay there until ordered out. At first the water would pierce like a needle, but after a while the person would feel perfectly warm, having conquered the five needles of cold. So on, the process of training was kept up, with one object in view—tamahnous. At last it would come all in one day about as follows: As the young man would go along the beach, walking and swimming now and then, all at once he would find a stream of water flowing from the woods. Out of this stream animals of every kind would come, snakes, frogs, fishes, and water animals of the smaller kind. Then with great presence of mind, which he had acquired by his severe training, he would get right in the midst of the stream, letting all the vile reptiles pass by him, until the very last one would come, which was the real tamahnous. As he would come down he would have his mouth wide open. If he should catch the first, second or anyone but the last, he would not be a good tamahnous man, but would kill many people, but if he should catch the last it would be his good tamahnous. In size it was like a fawn, it was spotted, and had a red mouth. The young man would then put his arms around it, and kiss it, and then lose all consciousness, and next he would wake up in the tamahnous land. He was then shown the name of the tamahnous, and also was shown a tamahnous in the act of curing a sick person. If he was taken just where this was done, he was able to cure any disease of the same nature, but if he was only shown this at a distance, he would not cure in every instance. He was also shown all about tamahnous, and the songs he was to sing, after which he was taken back and regained his consciousness. But this was not enough. He had to have two or three experiences of this kind before he was admitted into the list of tamahnous men. After this he would get more tamahnous, but smaller ones, including dancing or red, black, and spirit land tamahnous. Then he was in every since [sic] a tamahnous man. Still while he was young it was law that he must keep his tamahnous a secret, nor could he practice it until he was about middle age, for it was not believed to be a wise thing for a young man to tamahnous, though he could do so at any time.

At another time the same young man added the following, which is fabulous, but which was told him by the older Indians.

> There have also been a great many boys, who in order to get their tamahnous, according to Indian story, were brave enough to go to Hood's canal, with a rock and sink themselves in order to get a tamahnous.
> A boy went down with a stout stick and when he had almost reached the bottom, a shark met him, in order to kill him, with his big mouth wide open. The boy not much afraid, took the stick and put it into the monster's mouth crosswise, and the shark was killed. Another shark came and was killed the same way. At last the king of sharks, who had sent the others, met him, and the boy killed him. Afterwards the boy died, and his body went up, and was washed on to the beach, while his spirit remained in the bottom of the canal, the tamahnous, which he had just found, taking care of his spirit and showing him all things. After that the spirit went back to the body, and he became alive, and went home, and went to bed.
> The tamahnous which are found there are said to be good ones. I have heard their songs and they were very good. Sometimes I fell as if I would cry, when I hear them. When a person is hunting his tamahnous on the beach and finds a stream of water with animals in it, if he should catch the first, second, third or any one but the last, he would not be a good tamahnous man, but a bad one, who would kill many people. The last one only is a good tamahnous. If he finds the tamahnous like a fawn, and jumps after it, and throws his arms around its neck, it will make a big noise and open its mouth; then the boy puts his hand into its mouth and so kills it. That is his tamahnous.

Cause of Sickness

A wicked medicine man can, as they believe, in an invisible manner shoot a stone, ball, or poison into the heart of a person to make him sick. They believe this so firmly that they say when the heart of one who died was opened, the stone or bone has been found in it. He is also supposed to be able to send a woodpecker, squirrel, bear, or any treacherous animal to the heart of his enemy to eat his heart, plague him, make him sick, or kill him.

If a person is vexed with another his usual way to punish him with sickness is to hire a medicine man to send a bad tamahnous into his enemy. The medicine man bides his time, and may wait even a year for this. Such persons are believed to be able to do this even when far away. At one time there was trouble between a Twana man and his wife, who was from Port Gamble, fifty miles away. She left him and returned to her relations. He followed her, lived with her for a time, and earnestly wished her to return home with him, but she would not do so, nor would her relations help him much as they believed him to be to blame. At last he returned to Skokomish alone, but threatened to make some of the Port Gamble Indians sick. Six or eight months afterwards there was considerable sickness among them, which they fully believed to have been sent by a Twana medicine man, hired for the purpose by the disaffected husband, and they earnestly asked me to urge the Indian Agent to put a stop to it by punishing the suspected ones.

But medicine men are not the only ones who are believed to be able to make others sick, although they are the most powerful. Others can at times do the same. A school boy at one time wrote to his father, that his brother went to church and sat beside an Indian, Curley, who was not a medicine man, though he was an influential Indian. When this brother came out of church, his neck was ailing. "If my brother dies," said the writer, "I will bring the man near whom he sat in court, and make him pay several hundred dollars." He did not, however, die.

In general, although they believe a medicine man can send sickness fifty or one hundred miles, yet they are much more afraid, if they come in close contact to such. As a rule most of the Twana medicine men have not attended church much; and when I have asked them the reason why, I have been told that the other Indians have been afraid to have them go where they would be in so close contact with them.

One of the intelligent, educated young Twanas, Charles P. Waterman, whose father was a medicine man, but who died when Charles was very young, told me that while he did not believe in this idea of a doctor being able to send a bad tamahnous into another person, yet he had learned from his father that while the medicine men said they could do so, really that they had a subtle kind of poison, which they secretly rubbed on the person whom they wished to make sick when convenient, and afterwards pretended to shoot the tamahnous into the person. Hence, he said, the person became sick. This fact, he said, was not generally known, as the medicine men kept it secret; nor would he have known of it had it not been that his father was a medicine man. Consequently, he said, he was careful not to allow a medicine man to touch him; otherwise he did not fear them. My own thoughts are that while actual poison may have been used in some extreme cases, so that the medicine men may keep their hold on the people, yet that it is very uncommon, else it would in time become commonly known, and whites would have learned ere this what this poison might be.

I am satisfied, however, that when a person becomes sick, who perhaps has been threatened, or even who may not have been threatened, even though the sickness may be light, yet that he believes it has been sent into him by a medicine man, and that this effect of the imagination greatly increases the sickness; and so the person can hardly be cured without another medicine man to assist, and this faith in this Indian doctor greatly helps to cure him.

Curing the Sick

In curing the sick the good medicine man tries to find out from the sickness what kind of a tamahnous has been sent into the individual, and in what manner, whether in the shape of an animal, stone, or other wise, and from where it has been sent; then by means of his incantations he tries to draw it out. In this work he is the leader, but is usually assisted by some of the common people, both men and women, from a half a dozen to twenty or more in number. These take small sticks in their hands, about a foot and a half long, and a half an inch or an inch in diameter, and pound on the floor, or on large sticks or rails in front of them. I have never learned that these sticks are considered sacred. They are split out of any common stick for that occasion, are very rough, and are thrown away when the persons are done using them. One person beats the drum, and all sing an accompaniment to the noise, at least a chorus. In the mean time the medicine man sings a solo, and places his hands on some part of the body and draws forth, or says he does, the evil spirit, and when he says he has it he holds it between his hands, invisible, and blows it up or takes it to another man who throws a stone at it and kills it, or drowns it in water in a vessel nearby. When the sick person is not cured, they say there are several spirits, but sometimes the person dies before they are all drawn out or else the opposing medicine man is stronger than he and so he can now draw them all out. Sometimes he says that the good spirit of the invalid, the life-sustaining principle, is gone, having been taken away and he tries to find where it has gone, get it, and restore it.

The first time I ever saw an Indian doctor perform over a sick person was in October 1876. The patient was a woman of perhaps fifty years. As I went to the house a prominent Indian came out and told me that although they had sent to the agency physician for medicine, yet they were not certain where she was sick. At times she could not see, she would know almost nothing, and could not tell where she was sick, and they were tamahnousing to find out what was the difficulty, and when they had learned this they would send and obtain the right kind of medicine. They say that they often do tamahnous, first in order to learn what is the difficulty and afterwards to cure.

Having asked permission, I went in and took my seat, as directed, behind the doctor, so that he was between me and the patient. The house was about twenty feet square, a summer house, built on the gravelly beach of the Skokomish River. There were about fifteen persons in the house, both men and women, all of whom while the doctor was performing beat with small sticks on larger ones and sang in regular time. I was in one corner of the house, the patient (female) in the opposite corner facing me, sitting up and held by another woman. There were two fires near the middle, and the doctor was between them on his knees on the gravel. He was stripped to the waist, having only pantaloons and boots on, and faced the woman, having his hair tied in a knot over his forehead. He had a small tub of water near the woman. As he began he almost lay down on the gravel and sang and kept swinging his head up and down, constantly singing, while the other Indians joined in the singing for about twelve minutes, when he began to vomit violently over himself and the ground. (I presume this act was not in the program as it is the only time I have ever seen it in connection with this tamahnous but it was not strange, as so much swinging of the head, close to the fire, would have affected almost any one in the same way. Only strong men can endure such work and all the Indian doctors are among the strongest of the people.)

Then came a rest of a few minutes, when he rested and washed himself off. But soon all began again, when he worked up to the woman and, as near as I could see placed his mouth on her chest or shoulders and sucked very strongly and then blew out of his mouth with all his force, making a great noise, sometimes blowing into the water in the tub, and sometimes blowing into the air, always remaining on his knees. This was kept up about fifteen minutes longer, when I left during another respite. But this was neither the beginning nor end of the tamahnous. Sometimes they kept it up for most of the day and night or longer. The agency physician said she had disease of the brain, but at no time was very dangerously ill. He afterwards attended her very faithfully, and the Indians tamahnoused as faithfully, and she recovered.

The following account was given me by a school boy in regard to his brother:

> When I was at the Indian doctor's house they tamahnoused over my brother, for that is the reason my parents went to his house. First he learned what was the kind of sickness. The doctor took it and soon after that my brother, about nine or ten years old, became stiff and while I sat I heard my father say that his breath was gone. I went out, for I did not wish to see my brother lying dead before me; when I came back he was breathing just a little but his eyes were closed; the doctor was taking care of his breath with his tamahnous and waiting for more persons to come, so that there should be enough to beat on the sticks when he should tamahnous so as to learn the kind of sickness. Then he went on and saw that there was another kind of sickness besides the one he had taken out and it went over my brother and almost immediately killed him. The doctor took it and travelled (in his spirit) with another kind of tamahnous to see where my brother's spirit was; he found it at Humhummi (15 miles distant), where my parents and brother had camped in a recent journey. So my brother became better after a hard tamahnous.
>
> With this picture [opposite] you will see how the doctor fixed both kinds of sickness which he took out. It shows the first sickness which he extracted. It has tails, which when they come close to the sick person make him or her more sick. Number 1 shows the way it goes when it kills a person, and stays in the house. Number three is the second one which was hanging over my brother. Number 5 is another sickness which is in my brother.
>
> There is a class of persons which we can not see; they are poor looking persons; they take young people from these and other Indians; when they take a certain person that person always gets crazy. Another brother of mine heard their dog barking; the people thought it was from some white people, but there was no white man near and they knew it belonged to these people.

I once witnessed a performance which I have been inclined to call a *silent tamahnous*. I was camped with five canoes of Indians one night in February, 1878, one of our number being a medicine man; after supper some water was poured into a bowl not far from a woman who had complained of being much ill, though she was often ailing a little; she

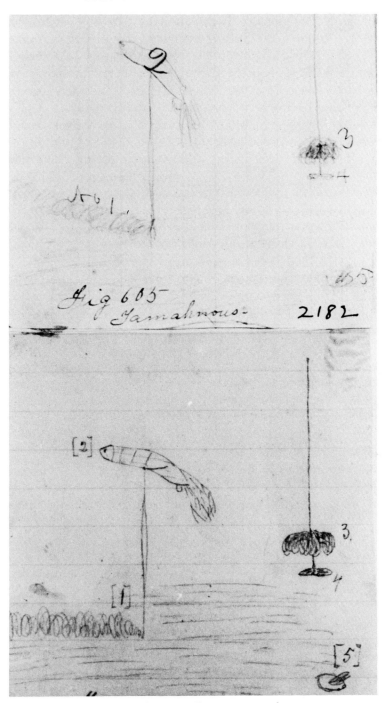

Schoolboy drawings illustrating tamahnous

was sitting perhaps ten feet from me. The doctor went to the bowl but no one else seemed to take notice of it; the woman's husband went away. Another woman lay unconcerned in the camp, it being a half-circle mat house, and other Indians were about, but they did not come near; there was no noise or singing, or pounding on sticks or drumming; the doctor put his hands in the water, warmed them a little, and then placed them on the woman's side, her dress having been opened and partly taken down for the purpose, and he acted as if he were trying to draw out something. This was done a second time, when he plunged them into water, placed his mouth next to them and blew suddenly and powerfully a few times; this was done two or three times, when he left, the performance being ended.

Should white persons be treated in the way an Indian doctor treats his patients, it seems as if in most cases they would be killed. It is almost bad enough to make a well person sick. But it is a fact that in many cases the Indians recover. Enough get well to make them have a strong faith in the medicine man, and enough die to make them believe that another medicine man, and a bad one, has great power.

In some diseases, as rheumatism and others of that class, very little harm or good can be done by this tamahnous. In others, it is positively injurious, as in brain diseases, measles, whooping cough, and the like. The Indians acknowledge this fact. In the fall of 1877 the typhoid fever was among the Twanas, and they were very careful about tamahnousing over it, saying that it was a white man's disease, and they could do but little with it. The noise and excitement are too much for the patient. In measles and whooping cough they have also learned by awful experience, that the plunging of the hands of the medicine man into cold water and then on to the patient is very fatal. In the spring of 1878 the measles prevailed among the Twana children. At first the parents were quite careful, and obeyed the orders of the agency physician; but when the children began to recover, and were nearly out of danger, they tamahnoused over them, apparently in order to get the credit of curing them, but the undressing and application of cold water were too severe for many of the little ones, and they died; several children of the medicine men being among them. The Clallams at Dungeness went through a similar experience a few years later.

Causes of Recovery

When the patient recovers, I think it is due to one or more of four causes.

1. He would have got well anyway, tamahnous or no tamahnous.

2. There may be a kind of mesmeric power in the medicine man, which affects the patient favorably. A Christian lady, at one time on the Skokomish reservation, Mrs. John R. Walker, once told me how she had been able to cure some kinds of sickness by passing her hands over the patient; but she added that she had become afraid to do it, as the pain seemed to come from the sick person into her fingers so severely that she could not bear it. She was a very nervous person. Dr. W. F. Tolmie, a physician long in connection

with the Hudson's Bay Company, and for many years in charge of Fort Nisqually, told me that after seeing the tamahnous of these medicine men on the Sound for years, he went back to London, where he had an opportunity of witnessing some of the curiosities of mesmerism. Returning to the Sound, he told the Indians to go on with their mode of doctoring, for he was not certain but what there was enough mesmeric power in their doctors to be of value, in the absence of regularly educated physicians. Hon. J. G. Swan is of the same opinion.

3. It is possible that occasionally the medicine men suck blood from their patients, and that there is actual medical practice on the same principle as cupping. I have been able to suck blood from my own arm, and presume that Indian doctors can do the same, though I have never seen it done. I have heard them speak of it in such a way as led me to believe it might be sometimes done. In 1880 a Twana man, Big Bill, wished to unite with our church. He was an invalid, and made request that he might be allowed to employ an Indian doctor to suck blood from him, an act which he said relieved him. I have heard others speak of the same.

4. I am satisfied that some of the cures are attributable to the confidence which the Indians have in the medicine men. As a man can be scared to death, so faith may cure him. When they are taken sick, severely, so, they believe that some bad tamahnous has hold of them, that hence no white man's medicine can cure them, and that no one but a medicine man can expel the tamahnous, and hence after his performances they sometimes recover. It is the power of the mind over the body.

In 1883 one Twana woman declared to me that she had given up all tamahnous and intended to live as a Christian. At that time her lungs were diseased, and she was slowly going with consumption in its first stages. Not long after this she failed rapidly. The agency physician gave her up, and said that it was useless for him to do anything more for her. Her white and Indian friends also believed she would soon die. She sent for me and asked earnestly that notwithstanding her previous declarations, she might be allowed to tamahnous two or three times. I saw from her talk that her mind was much troubled and in a flutter from fear, and while I believed she would soon die, I did not think a tamahnous would hurt her; I advised her not to get an Indian doctor, but also told her that if she should do so, I should not be angry with her. She employed one, and to the surprise of her white friends, was up and around in a few days, and lived about a year and a half after this before consumption finally carried her off. Fear of a bad tamahnous was quickly killing her, and the removal of that fear by the tamahnousing of a doctor relieved her.

In 1885 a Twana man sent for the agency physician because he was sick. At the same time he was employing a medicine man. After watching the case for several days, the physician could not find that the man had any disease which medicine could cure. He was, however, satisfied that the man was very much afraid that a bad tamahnous had hold of him. A good look at the man's face and eyes showed to me that the man was terribly frightened. After employing Indian doctors for a time he recovered. I have, at other times, seen when a person has a slight sickness which medicine can cure, if he has been told before this that some one was planning to send a bad tamahnous into him, or if when he is sick, some one says the same, medicine does not make the person well. It cures the disease of the body, so that no physician can find any sickness left, but still the person does not get well and up. Fear keeps him sick and only a tamahnous cures him.

In my book, *Ten Years at Skokomish*, pages 43–51, I have given other instances of this kind, even more marked. In my opinion they could be plainly accounted for on the principles of mental philosophy, but the Indians had never studied that science, and so cannot account for the cause and cure, as a white person can. From it, I take the following.

Chehalis Jack is one of the most intelligent and civilized of the older, uneducated Indians. He has been one of those most ready to adopt the customs and beliefs of the whites; has stood by the agent and missionary in their efforts to civilize and Christianize his people, when very few other Indians have done so; and was one of the first of the older Indians to unite with the church. He was a sub-chief, and tried to induce his people to adopt civilized customs, setting them an example by building by far the best house erected by the Indians on the Skokomish reservation. He was told by some who opposed civilization, that because of this some enemy would send a bad tamahnous into him and make him sick.

In July 1881 he was taken sick, evidently with the rheumatism, or something of the kind, and the threats which he had heard (although he would not believe them when well) now began to prey upon his mind, as he afterward said. Yet for six weeks he lived at his home, a mile from the agency, and would have nothing to do with an Indian doctor. The agency physician attended him and his rheumatism seemed to leave him, but he did not get well and strong. At last the physician said that he did not believe any physician could find what was the matter with him. After six weeks thus spent, by the advice of some friends he tried some Indian doctors on the reservation, but some in whom he had little confidence. He grew worse. He left the reservation for other Indian doctors, twenty miles away, who said they could cure him, but he did not recover. He came back home, and imported another Indian doctor from a hundred miles distant, but was not cured.

We were afraid he would die, and it was plain to several whites that he was simply being frightened to death. I had long talks with him on the subject, but could not convince him of the truth of it. He said "tamahnous is true, tamahnous is true. You and your brother have told us it is not, but now I have experienced it, and it keeps me sick." During the winter the agency physician resigned and another one took his place in March 1883. Jack immediately sent for him, but failed to recover. By the advice of white friends, who thought they knew what was the matter with him, he gave up his Indian doctor and tried patent medicines for a time, but to no purpose. He left his home and moved directly to the agency, being very near us, having no Indian doctor. Thus the summer passed away, and fall came.

Intelligent persons had sometimes said that if he could be made to do something, his strength would return to him, and he would find that he was not sick. He had fourteen cords of wood cut on the banks of the Skokomish river. There was no help that he could obtain to bring the wood to his house, except a boy and an old man. He was much afraid

418

that the rains would come, the river rise and carry off the wood. He left the Agency, returned to his home, and had to help in getting his wood. About the same time he employed another Indian doctor in whom he seemed to have considerable confidence, and between the fact of his being obliged to work, and his confidence in the Indian doctor, he recovered. It was the effect of the influence of the mind over the body. The principles of mental philosophy could account for it all, but he was not versed in those principles, and so thoroughly believes that a bad tamahnous was in him, and that Old Cush, the Indian doctor, drew it out.

Ellen Gray was a school girl, about 16 years of age, and had been in the boarding school for several years, nearly ever since she had been old enough to attend, but her parents were quite superstitious. One Friday evening she went home, to remain until the Sabbath; but on Saturday, the first of January 1881, she was taken sick and the nature of her sickness was such that in a few days she became delirious.* Her parents and friends made her believe that a bad tamahnous had been put into her, and no one but an Indian doctor could cure her. They tamahnoused over her some. The Agency physician, Dr. Givens, was not called until the sixth of January, when he left some medicine for her, but it is said that it was not given to her. Hence she got no better, and her friends declared that the white doctor was killing her. The Agent and teacher did not like the way the affair was being maneuvered, took charge of her, moved her to a decent house near by, and placed white watchers with her, so that the proper medicines should be given and no Indian doctor brought in.

The Indians were, however, determined if possible to tamahnous and declared that if it were not allowed, she would die, at three A.M. They kept talking about it, and she apparently believed it and said she would have tamahnous, but it was prevented, and before the time set for her death, she was cured of her real sickness. (Her menses returned.) But she was not well. Still, the next day she was in such a condition that it was thought safe to move her in a boat to the boarding house, where she could be more easily cared for. The Indians were enraged, and said that she would die before landing, but she did not. Watchers were kept by her constantly, but the Indians were allowed to see her. They talked to her, however, so much about her having a bad tamahnous, that all except her parents were forbidden to see her. They also were forbidden to talk on that subject, and evidently obeyed. But the effect on her imagination had been so great that for a time she often acted strangely. She seldom said anything; she would often spurt out the medicine when given her as far as she could; said she saw the tamahnous; pulled her mother's hair; bit her mother's finger so that it bled; seemed peculiarly vexed at her; moaned most of the time, but sometimes screamed very loudly; and even bit a spoon off.

Sometimes she talked rationally and sometimes she did not. But by the fifteenth she was considerably better, walked around with help, and sat up when told to do so, but did not seem to take any interest in anything. Everything possible was done to interest her

---

*It was suppression of menses.

419

and occupy her attention and she continued to grow better for three or four days more, so that the watchers were dispensed with, except that her parents slept in the room with her. But one night she threw off the clothes, took cold, and would not make any effort to cough and clear her throat and on the twenty-second she died, actually choking to death. It was a tolerably clear case of death from imagination, easily accounted for on the principles of mental philosophy, but the Indians had never studied it, and still believe that a bad tamahnous killed her.

Charles Waterman, an intelligent young Twana man, once told me how he had been sick and cured by a medicine man. He ascribed his cure to the confidence he had in him. He said that the medicine man came and spoke encouragingly to him, and said that he would soon cure him, while going through the incantations. After the medicine man had done so, he felt a little better, and each time he did so he felt a little better, and thus his heart grew strong and at last he recovered.

In their tamahnous over their infants, however, who are not old enough to have such confidence, I have noticed that they have by no means been as successful as with older persons. In fact, the medicine men have been as unfortunate in this respect as almost any one, several of them having lost from half a dozen to ten children notwithstanding all their powers.

Mr. John Flett, late of the Puyallup reservation, who has spent a great share of his life with the Indians on this northwest coast, both in connection with the Hudson's Bay Company and our government, and has seen very much of their tamahnous, told me several years ago, that he had never seen but two cases in which he could reasonably account for all the phenomena produced, and the recovery. These two, he said, might possibly have been accounted for by some other person, but from his data he could not do so.

One of these was as follows. He saw a medicine man suck the breast of an invalid, and then plunge his hands into a vessel of water and blow into it, whereupon it became very thick and green, so that it might have been cut with a knife, somewhat like a curd. The sick man recovered. This was on the Puyallup reservation.

Mr. Flett said that he was once present in Oregon when a medicine man pretended to draw forth a bad spirit from a sick person. He showed the extracted object to the people, holding it between his fingers and it grew alternately larger and smaller as they looked at it. But Mr. Flett afterwards discovered that it was a small piece of a round rush, about a third of an inch in diameter, and a half an inch or so long, which he had secretly drawn from his own mouth, where it had been moistened. He showed it as a bad tamahnous, pressing it between his fingers to reduce its size, while its own elasticity caused it to expand when released. In like manner they sometimes show small stones which these doctors draw from their mouths but which they pretend to draw forth from their patients.

I have sometimes asked these Indians why their tamahnous does not affect white persons. In fact, the Superintendent of Indian Affairs for this Territory about twenty-five years ago, offered their medicine men a hundred dollars, either to make him sick or to kill any of his horses by their tamahnous, but they could not do so. They say that a white man's heart is hard like a stone, so that the invisible stone which they shoot cannot affect it, while the Indian's heart is soft like mud, and thus is easily affected. They also say that a cause of this is that the Indian swims very much, and often times has his clothes off while at home, and so his heart is susceptible to the influence of the tamahnous, while the white man's customs are different, and so his heart is different.

I have known of one or two white men who were illiterate, and who had lived much with the Indians, who when sick had been tamahnoused over by Indian doctors and recovered and who hence avowed their faith in the tamahnous. On the other hand, they have been so angry with some Indians who had become considerably civilized and disavowed their belief in such tamahnous, who were not affected by it. Jimmy Talikus, a Clallam of Elwha, enraged the doctors by his government as a sub-chief and policeman. They tried their tamahnous on him, and he dared them to do it but he was not made sick by it. It is said that a medicine man was walking along with a friend, when he saw John Palmer, a civilized Twana, some distance off. The medicine man said, now I will try my tamahnous on him and see what it will do. He did so, and watched the invisible shot go straight towards him, until it was very near him, when it took a sudden sheer off and went to one side. They professed to believe that his heart had become hard like a white man's and so rejected the tamahnous.

I have never known the Indians or their medicine men to be as angry with any other Indians as they have been with their Agent Eells and some of his employees at times, and if they could have killed them by the use of secret poison in any way, they would have done it. This makes me disbelieve the poison theory.

Sometimes when a person is tamahnous sick through the effect of the imagination, they will say many things against those who are trying to cure them. The reason they do so, according to Indian belief, is that their tamahnous is the one that speaks. One woman sick in this way, pointing at the face of a person who was trying to cure her, said, "You can never take me out with your little tamahnous." Then all at once she said, "Here comes the old man of whom I am afraid." The old man, a doctor, did come. Such a tamahnous-sick is said to be caused by his master going into a person, and causing him or her to die talking or laughing at the grief of his or her friends. When the person dies in this way, the death is sure to be revenged by the relatives.

IMPLEMENTS OF TAMAHNOUS

The only one I have ever learned of which is used in curing the sick is the drum, already described. In British America, Dakota, and New Mexico I have read that the doctors have small medicine sacks, or images, which are an assistant in the work. But I have never seen any such on the Sound or been able to learn that they were used. At Quinaielt, too, I found small images of men, called the medicine men's doctors, which the latter used by shaking them in the face of, or over the sick person. These were usually about a foot or a foot and a half long, and rather slim. Sometimes a few deer-hoof rattles were fastened to such. They were very chary of them so that the Agency physician had never been able to obtain one. I, however, obtained two or three for the Chicago Expo-

Haida "doctor" shown singing

sition, and a few months afterwards obtained one for that physician. But I have never learned that such images are used among the Sound Indians. The Quinaielt doctors charged about two dollars each for theirs.

STOPPING TAMAHNOUS

To stop the Indian doctors from performing over the sick was one of the most difficult things the Indian Agent ever tried to do among the Indians. About 1871 or 1872 Agent E. Eells had orders to do this from the Superintendent of Indian Affairs for Washington Territory, but it was simply impossible. The Indians would hide away, or leave the reservation, or doctor at night to cure the sick in their way, and not an Indian would dare to testify to the fact. Again in 1883, he had similar orders from the Indian department of Washington City, but still did not believe the time had come when it was possible. Other kinds of tamahnous were largely to while away the time.

Not until 1885 did the Agent believe the time had come. By this time a respectable minority of the leading Indians said that they had given it up and wanted to have nothing more to do with it, even if they should die. They still believed there was something in it, but thought that that something was the devil, and that the less they had to do with him, the better. So the Agent ordered this work of the medicine men to be stopped. He lived eighty miles away on the Puyallup reservation, but there was a school teacher at Skokomish when this order was promulgated, who was chief of police; also a farmer, physician, and two Indian policemen.

Not long after this time the wife of one of the chiefs, Mrs. Mary Adams, was taken sick. They called the reservation physician and two Indian doctors as she grew worse. One of these Indian doctors had for years ruled the reservation whenever he wished to do so—Tenas Charley. He had never been a chief, but he had ruled the chiefs. If he told them to do anything, they were afraid to do differently for fear that he would kill them or their children by his tamahnous. Even when a case came before the Agent, although he could not frighten him, yet he could and often did keep the witnesses from testifying in court, and so he had at times managed the Agent. This man was the leading Indian doctor hired at this time, and he was paid a horse for his services. The sick woman recovered, as the Indian doctors expected she would, after they had tamahnoused over her, and as the government physician expected she would do, after taking his medicine. The Indians did not try much to hide the fact that they had broken the law, but seemed determined to fight it out. I was first told of it very secretly. Afterwards the Indians seemed to smell that I knew it, and talked with me about it considerably, and I learned much more about it, which was not to be kept a secret. After they got into trouble about it, they tried exceedingly to find out who told me first, but they never did. They asked me, and guessed and guessed, but never hit. Had they found out, he would have caught very severe treatment from some of the others.

When the Agent came to the reservation he held a court over it. He told them that for fourteen years he had talked to them about the foolishness of this practice and tried to reason with them, but that he should do this no longer. He should simply enforce the order. He said he did not make this new law, and never had made such a one, but that Government had done so, and told him to see that it was obeyed. He fined the principal medicine man the horse which he had received, and said the horse should be for the use of the police.

This angered Tenas Charley, also Billy Adams, Mary's husband. Soon after, the latter resigned as chief, thus saying virtually to the Agent, "I will no longer help you."

A Geo. Dick, said Tenas Charley, and Dick Lewis, the head chief, rose and resigned, although he was one of those who had said he would not employ an Indian doctor in sickness, professing to disbelieve in it. This showed how much he was still afraid of these doctors. Thus the Indian court was going to pieces, and the Agent saw that no Indian would be bold enough to sustain and help him in this contest, much as they might secretly wish him to conquer.

As court adjourned at dark, and the Agent was going out, Tenas Charley shook his fist in the Agent's face, saying in Chinook Jargon, *Cultus kopa nika kopa mika* ("I do not care anything for you"). He also added that he would never stop his tamahnous. It now became clear that it was to be decided who was to rule, the Agent or Tenas Charley, for although the latter had ruled many a time, he had always done it in such a way as not to have an open conflict with the Agent.

After supper the Agent went to the school teacher, B. F. Lauglin, and told him as chief of police to arrest that man, and bring him in. He waited until the next morning, and then took the farmer, G. W. Coates, a heavy six-footer, and the two Indian policemen, and went to Tenas Charley's house, a mile from the Agency.

It was a little late, and a good many Indians had gathered there, so that the room was quite full of them. Some sympathized with Tenas Charley, and the rest were afraid of him, so that they would not help in his arrest, even by advising him to submit. The Indian policemen, too, were afraid to take him by force for fear that sometime he would kill them, their wives, or their children by his tamahnous. As far as they dared to go was to tell him that the Agent wanted him and then if he was willing to go, all right, they would go along with him, but this was all they would do. The teacher, too, was evidently a little afraid and put Mr. Coates, his brother-in-law, ahead to do the work.

As they went in, Tenas Charley was lying in bed partly covered up, and Mr. Coates afterwards said he did not know him very well and did not see exactly where he was, and so while he was a little slow and did not at once pounce on Tenas Charley with his handcuffs, Tenas Charley drew a knife, jumped from his bed across the room to his guns, and said he would shoot any one who should try to take him. The whole police force, afraid that others might help him, retreated, leaving Tenas Charley victor, in possession of the field, and reported to the Agent.

The Agent was a little non-plussed. In nearly fourteen years' experience with them, he had never had an Indian act so: for while one or two had run away to avoid arrest, and others had been slow in their movements when arrested, none had ever shown fight before. "I did not think those white men would show the white feather," he said, as Mr. Coates had been among the roughs of California, and professed to be as brave as any body.[2]

He, however, wrote out a proclamation, and sent it to the Indians, in which he said that the law would be enforced even if he had to bring soldiers from Fort Townsend, seventy miles distant to do it; that Tenas Charley was in open rebellion against the United States; and that if any other Indians should help him, they would be as liable to punishment as he was.

This led most of them to quietly desert him, as the soldiers had never been brought to their reservation for such a purpose and they felt that it would give them all a bad name if this should be done. So most of the Indians came to the Agency to talk about it.

But Tenas Charley said that he would fight before he would deliver himself up, and if the soldiers should come, he and his friends would burn all the houses, and kill all the whites they could in the region, then flee to the mountains and hide; and although they might be killed at last, they would have their revenge by doing plenty of damage at first.

The Agent, however, sent for Mary Adams, who had been in school many years, and could read, write, and talk English quite well, and told her all the consequences if Tenas Charley should continue to resist. As her father, Jackman, was a sub-chief and very prominent, she was in a position to have some influence, and the Agent advised her to use it, so as to induce Tenas Charley to surrender. He also talked with some of the leading men about it, who were of the better class, and who had determined to abandon the tamahnous over the sick.

Had this affair not taken place, the Agent had intended to leave the reservation on that afternoon, and in order to do so, he had to ferry his horse across the Skokomish river at high tide, as the Agency was near its mouth. He ferried his horse across about noon, and went on with his preparations for leaving, as if nothing had happened, and this led some of the Indians to think he was going for the soldiers. The better Indians, considerably frightened, then went and reasoned with Tenas Charley as best they could, and told him what punishment the Agent would inflict upon him, should he surrender, but that it would be better than to fight. So after dinner he came down and delivered himself up. He was put in jail for ten days, and fined forty dollars. It did him good, for he learned not to oppose the government, and became in many ways a better Indian.

I am not aware that on any other reservation there was any special opposition to the enforcement of the law. They quietly submitted or left the reservation when they wished the services of an Indian doctor, for no attempt was made to enforce it off of the reservations. Since the Indians have become citizens, especially during the past two years, a good share of those on the Puyallup reservations have returned to tamahnous over their sick.

XXVII

RELIGION:

The New Religion, or the Shakers

ORIGIN AND BELIEFS OF THE SHAKERS

In the early eighties the Indians of the Skokomish reservation began to lose faith in their old tamahnous as a religion and also as a method of curing the sick.[1] Protestants, Catholics, religious people, and people of no religion, rough loggers with whom they worked, and cultivated people, all united in one thing, and that was to call their tamahnous very foolish; and in progress of time it had its effect. The Indians began to lose faith in it. But the Indian is a religious being. He must have some religion. When he gives up one he must have another. When these gave up the tamahnous, a new religion appeared which has been called the Shakes, and its followers the Shakers, from the fact that during their services, their hands, arms, and even heads, often shake exceedingly fast. It is evidently an affection of the nerves, and based somewhat on the same principle in human nature as the jerks were, which occurred in the Southwestern states seventy-five years ago. It is also akin to the Messiah craze of the Dakota Indians of 1890, having a Messiah in it, but being much more civilized and with no thought of war.[2] It fairly began in 1882, but there were some preliminaries which finally connected themselves with it and which I will first mention, partly for this reason and partly because they show the workings of the Indian mind.

Revelations

Big Bill. A full account of this Indian is given in my "Ten Years at Skokomish," chapter 22, from which I take some of the following.

Big Bill was one of the better Indians of the Twanas. In the forties or fifties he had received some instruction from the Catholics, and been baptized by them, and although no vestige of Catholic ceremonies was seen among these Indians when I came here, yet they had not forgotten all their instruction. When in 1875 I went to their logging camps to hold prayer meetings, he seemed to be a leading one in favor of Christianity. When I offered to teach them how to pray, sentence by sentence, the other Indians selected him as the one most suitable to pray. I never knew anything objectionable in him, except that

427

he clung to his tamahnous, and at times he seemed to be trying to throw that off. When sick, often he would have nothing to do with an Indian doctor, although he was related to some of them; then again, he would call for their assistance.

In time consumption took hold of him, together with some other disease, something like a bloody flux, and he wasted away. He wanted to join the church and be baptized. We made some allowances for his superstitions and received him into the church. He came to church as long as he was able, although he lived two miles away, and always seemed glad to see me. But his sickness was long and wore on his mind. His nervous system became affected. Before he died he saw strange visions. They combined Protestant and Catholic teachings, and old native superstitions, and had reference largely to heaven. He told me considerable of them, and seemed hurt that I did not believe them to be as valid as the Bible. Among other things, he saw an old friend of his, named Sandyalla, who had died many years previous, and his friend taught him four songs. They were mainly about Heaven, and there was not much objection to them except that this species of spiritualism was mixed up in them. He taught them to his friends.

When he was no longer able to come to church, he instituted church services at his house, twice on each Sabbath and on Thursday evening, to correspond with ours. A Catholic Indian, Billy Clams, on the reservation often visited him, and some of his services were combined with those of Big Bill. When I visited him I was well received, singing and holding services in my way. Thus affairs became considerably mixed. He died in June 1881, and his relations went through with a long service which they had prepared of the combined Catholic services and those revealed to Big Bill, of songs, lighted candles, prayers, the sign of the cross, and various ceremonies.

He had two brothers, David and Joe Dan, and a brother-in-law, Dick Lewis, the latter being head chief, who had also received some Catholic instruction years before, and who professed to lean that way. Previous to the death of Big Bill, when I asked them to come to church, they excused themselves by saying that they attended church at his house. But after his death they continued these services, and when I asked them why they did so, they replied that their brother's last words were very precious to them, and they must get together and talk about what he had said, and sing his songs.

To prove that Big Bill's revelations came from heaven David told me that he prophesied, relating several things that he said afterwards came to pass. I had previously preached to them that prophecy was one proof that the Bible came from God, hence this was brought up as evidence of the divinity of these revelations. Big Bill, however, never told me of these prophecies, and David only told me of them after the events occurred, then saying that Big Bill had said they would thus occur.

The one good thing which resulted from these revelations was that Big Bill gave up his tamahnous or Indian doctors, and advised his relations to do the same, saying that in his visions he had learned that God did not like such things.

After the death of Big Bill, I had some talk with his brother David in regard to the matter, trying to learn why it was that his instructions seemed to have such a firm hold on them. In one of these talks he gave me the following account as a part only of these visions.

On one Sabbath evening Big Bill's stomach began to fill with blood. Dick Lewis and wife, Big Bill's wife, and David's wife were with him. David was absent at Lillewaup. Big Bill began taking out the blood, and as he did so he felt very badly, and told his wife she must stay in another room from the one in which he was. Then he stood up in his bed and took out the blood, and he also thought he had better die; that it was no use for him to live any more. He took a handkerchief and tied it to a post, and thought he had better hang himself. When he had done so and was about to hang himself, he heard some one speak, and turned and saw it was his grandfather. He turned and tried to see the person speaking, but could not do so. As he was looking toward the window, he saw a light coming up the road. Then he forgot his handkerchief, and about hanging himself. He turned back and some one stood by his side and said, "I am the one that called you. I am Sandyalla, your brother."

The light that Big Bill saw was the buttons on Sandyalla's coat, which appeared to him shining through the window. Then Sandyalla gave Big Bill a cup and said, "You must take this and drink it." But Big Bill did not look quick enough or take it fast enough, and Sandyalla said, "You have done wrong today and I am going to arrest you." So he took the cup which he had given to Big Bill, and fixed it in some way, and it became handcuffs. This was done because Big Bill had planned to hang himself, which is very wrong. He put the handcuffs on to Big Bill. The women before mentioned took the handkerchief, and fixed it some way on his wrists, so that they were all tied up. Big Bill said to the woman that he must take the kerchief, and tie it up above. His wife said, "We must take you to some other room with your feather bed." But he said, "You better not do it, as I am in trouble." Then he had a trunk for his pillow and a soap box under his back all night. Big Bill knew when they took out his breath, and put it on one side of him.

When Big Bill looked toward Sandyalla, he saw something like a string leading up to heaven. Sandyalla took the end of this string and put it into the end of Big Bill's mouth. Sandyalla also put his mouth to the end of the string, and talked towards God. Big Bill would also be talking, and he would understand him. Sandyalla put the cuffs on Big Bill's hands and said, "This hand is very bad, and I am going to put the handcuff on tight." He also put the other handcuff on the other hand, but loosely, as he said it was not so bad. Sandyalla then said to Big Bill, "I have been trying very hard to plead for you, so that you can enter Heaven. You have been sick five years now, and every year I have said to God, O let him live a little longer. Because you wanted to hang yourself is the reason I arrest you. Only six of us, your relations are in Heaven. The place is far off from this place. We six feel sad that all of you on earth do not turn to God. When daybreak comes I am going to fix you some way."

Then Big Bill, as if he were waking up, said to the women, "Are you going to leave me now? You must take hold of my right hand." Joe Dan, Dick Lewis, and the women then went and shook hands with Big Bill.

Again Sandyalla said to Big Bill, "Why do you want to stay and live in this wicked world? There is a happy land above. Everything is ready for you up there." Big Bill thought within himself though he said nothing, "One thing God does not like, that is for the tamahnous man to doctor me." Sandyalla said, "O that is nothing. God does not care.

When I was here on earth with you and God was just ready to take me up to Heaven, they used to doctor me. It is not because they want to kill you that they tamahnous over you, but they like you, and they want to cure you. One thing only God does not like. The tamahnous man goes to work, and says he is going to draw out the sickness. This he does not like. Where do you think you got this disease? In this world? No. God gave it to you, and no Indian doctor has a right to say he can cure you. If an Indian doctor goes to a sick man, the first thing he ought to do is to pray to God, and ask God's help in curing him. Do you suppose this is the first time I have come to you? For the last five years since you have been sick I have been with you every Sabbath. If God likes any person, man, woman, child, he gives them sickness for a good while, so that he thinks about God, sings and prays, and at last God takes him up to heaven. Jesus is about you, so is Satan and all his hosts, and Jesus is trying hard to get you to his home. Your grandfather wanted to come to see you, but could only come in the night. He was the person you saw talking to me at the window. He cannot come in the daytime. For this reason I leave you in the daytime. God's angels, and the devil's angels come together in this world, on God's Sabbath, only we do not see them. All that are good and go to heaven, are the same ones whom God sends down to this world, and all the bad comes from the bad world, so as to try to get the people.

"Every Sunday God sends his angels down and they write all that the good people do in their book. The devil does the same in regard to bad people. His angels write down all that the bad people do in their book. When people think about what is good the angels write it down. When people say naughty words, the devil's angels are around and write it down, with their names. If a man steals, no matter how small a thing, or drinks, the devil's angels write it down. When a person remembers God, his angels write it down. When a good person is about to die, God sends his angels, and the devil does the same and they all watch the sick person. God says to the devil, 'You just leave my people alone. See how many times he has done good to me.' When a bad man is about to die, the devil shows the book and says 'O God, you must leave this man to me. See how many times he has drunk, see how many times he has fought.'

"The richest men here, whites and Indians, do not think about God, but poor men think about him, and are counted his servants. Here in this wicked world, God sent all the Indians to be down under the whites. He made all nations like plants. But Adam and Eve missed one thing, so God made them poor. Do you suppose all the people made the children? No! God only loans them to you. When a babe comes to this world, God claims it, till the boy is big enough to know what is good and what is bad. Then God lets him go. When any one gets a child and takes his hand and slaps him, then God thinks, 'O those people do not take good care of the child.' So God takes it back and it dies. Now from this time, you must tell all the people they must not slap their children, but get a nice switch and pray God to make the child good, then switch the children, then when done take the switch up to the house. If you tell the people to pray before they switch the children, then hang it up, and if they do wrong again, pray and make them look at it. This will frighten them, they will cry, and feel that God has helped them."

As his brother was lying down, he heard something fall down, and he said it was the wickedness or sins of one of the Indians. Then Big Bill turned and saw that it was a ball, a foot through with sharp things around it. Sandyalla said, "That is just the way when people sin. That round ball is like the bad words the Indians say; little words as pins, and at last they quarrel. Now you see how that ball was, as when one person says bad words to another, like taking a pin from the ball, and throwing it at another. Hence, saying bad words is a very bad thing.

"Everybody that dies, having been shot or cut up with knives, God takes up above. When Jesus was here on the earth, the people speared him, and the blood flowed down, so when Jesus sees any one here cut or shot, he has pity on him, good or bad, and takes him to heaven."

Nearly midnight, Sunday night, Sandyalla had the handcuffs on Big Bill's hands, and his hand began to swell up and was black as polished stone. The other hand was all right, as it was loose, for Sandyalla said it was not as bad as the other. The women then said to Dick Lewis, "We must go and loosen the kerchief, that is the reason it is swelled up." Dick Lewis went and looked at it, but it was loose. Big Bill said, "Do you suppose the handkerchief is what my hand was fastened with. No it is the handcuff." About midnight Sandyalla said, "I'll loosen the handcuff." Then Big Bill said to the people, "Now loosen the kerchief." So they let it loose. After Sandyalla said he was going to loosen the hand-cuff, Big Bill spoke to the people about the kerchief.

Then David's wife saw smoke coming out of every joint of his fingers. It looked like bluing. This smoke was all the bad things that Big Bill used to do. They were now forgiven, and so the smoke came out from his hands. Then Sandyalla said to Big Bill, "It is nearly morning now. I am about to leave." David's and Big Bill's wives went out doors and saw that it was nearly morning but they said we will not tell him that morning has nearly come. Everything that Sandyalla said, Big Bill said.

Then Sandyalla said, "Do you suppose I do not know that morning is coming, and so you do not want to let us know." Then he said to Big Bill, "I am about to leave you now. Tomorrow, Monday, will be a bad day. If you Indians do not turn to God, perhaps he will turn the world upside down, and make you Indians into some other kinds of things, and make the birds to live. What do you think, when you hear the birds singing in the morning. They sing because another day has come, and they thank God for the day. All cedar trees are good in God's sight, for cedar is good for most everything. If you take cedar and sink it down in water, make it stay there for years, and then let it loose, it will come up, because it is good in God's sight. Now from this time when you take a cedar canoe to go on a journey, you must always pray to God not to tip over; for if you do not you will surely tip over, because cedar is good in God's sight. Another tree God likes is the pine. Now if I leave you, you must send some one to bring in some cedar and pine boughs to hang inside your house, and when you see them you will think about God and think good. Keep them there until the last day, when he will take you up home."

When Sandyalla was there, they brought in a coal oil lamp. He was afraid of it, as when they make a fire on the beach he is afraid of that. When Big Bill was kind of dizzy, he looked and saw the coal oil lamp, and it looked like a big fire, as when the wind is blowing it from one side to the other. Sandyalla said to him, "That coal oil is a very bad bad thing. It helps the devil to burn hotels and stores, so it is bad. Now if I leave you tomorrow morning you must get some candles and have them burning both sides of you, for sin is dark, and the candles are like light to God. From this time you must tell all the Indians when they get sick, they must not get coal oil, but candles to light them. Now I am going to leave you. During five weeks you will be doing good to your people, and when the five weeks end, God will draw you up to himself, on a Sabbath day. After you die, while you are lying, no bad man or woman will walk around you, because the angels will guard you."

When he was about to leave, Big Bill heard something like writing on a piece of paper. He said to Big Bill, "Now I have your name down in a book, and I am going up to Heaven, and your name will get up to Heaven, before your soul gets up there." After he had written Big Bill's name in the book, he said, "Now look here. When any man, woman, and child gets a name, they must keep it, and not change it, because if they are good God will write it in his book. So they must keep it till they die. Now I have your name written in the book, and it is going home to your heavenly father. After your soul gets up to Heaven, you will have everything you need up there. Here in this wicked world you have to work very hard to get a living, but up there you will not have to do anything, but will have all you want."

After Sandyalla had taken the name, he rubbed it in his hand, and Big Bill saw that it was made something like an egg. Then Sandyalla said, "Your name will reach Heaven before I get there." Big Bill saw him take the egg, and put it on the end of a string or wire like a telegraph, and send it up. At the same time he sang this song, and taught it to Big Bill.

> "I'm going home to Heaven to sign my name.
> "I'm going home to Heaven, where my name is written.
> "I'm going home," being repeated.

This is one of the songs that Big Bill left to his friends.

It being nearly morning Sandyalla said, "I am going home now," and he touched the handcuffs, and they dropped off as when you touch ice that is hanging down from the eaves of a house. As he left he gave him another song as follows:

> "By and by I will go to that happy land, by and by I will reach that happy land. Where my heavenly father dwells. Holy land is the name of that place where I shall soon go."

These lines repeat considerably.

Toward the latter part Big Bill was out of his head and dreamed, talking mostly in English. Then he made up some more songs.

"You are going to make a road for us,
   Up to the land above.
   You are going to the land, the good land,
   Where we will soon go."
"Ho land (holy land) Ho land,
   Go along and be the way."

After awhile he dreamed again, and the voice said, "Not very long now and I shall take your soul up above. Before you die, you must teach all these songs to your brothers and sisters, and when you are dead, they must sing them all when you are lying in your coffin."

Late in the afternoon he dreamed and saw some more visions. The last time he saw a vision he turned to see the person, but the voice said, "You must not turn this way. If you do your face will get all black." The last time Big Bill was dreaming he was talking in English all the time, and the voice said he must not close his eyes, for if he did, he would never see again.

Then Big Bill heard another person (at least there seemed to be two, but they would not allow him to look) who said, "Well Bill, how many souls have you taken." Bill did not answer, but the other person said, "Well, Bill has saved five souls."

When Big Bill waked up he said that his people must kneel down and pray for one hour and a half and angels came from heaven. When the hour and a half was passed, the angels left and Big Bill did not die then. The people did not know who these five persons were to whom Big Bill had been speaking. When they left they left these songs.

This was the statement as David gave it to me, though he said it was not all, as it was long. It had a strong effect on the people. It became plain to the Agent and myself that the Indians were losing faith in their tamahnous, and were about to jump somewhere into some other religion, where we could not tell. We tried to induce them to jump our way and I induced them to come to church, where they were allowed to sing their songs and speak, after I had spoken. But after a few weeks they became dissatisfied with it, and ceased to come and some of our people were nearly as much dissatisfied with their actions. It was hard to reconcile Congregationalism with Protestant–Catholic Spiritualism. So they held their services, but in a year or so it seemed to be waning in interest for lack of life.

John Slocum. He was an Indian who lived on the Skokomish reservation in 1874 when I first came here and for two or three years afterwards, but left for Squakson because he did not receive a patent to his land, and was afraid he would never get it. His original home was about the Squakson reservation, and he talked that language. In November 1882 he was carrying on a logging camp a few miles above that reservation and about fifteen from Skokomish, when he was taken sick. But the following from the *Tacoma Ledger* gives as full an account of the result as I have seen.

   John Slocum was an Indian of sporty proclivities. He had a powerful and consuming
   thirst for fire-water, which absorbed Jamaica ginger or pain-killer in lieu of whiskey or

alcohol straight. He also was the most confirmed gambler of his tribe, and there never was an Indian horse race in which he was not prominent. One October day he fell sick in his mind. He thought about his wicked ways and was sad. Then, at 4 o'clock one morning to all intents and purposes, he died. For six hours he remained in this lifeless condition. Then he sat up and proceeded to tell his people his experience. He had died, so he said, and his soul had parted from his body. As it arose from the lifeless clay it looked back and saw its former habitation as though it belonged to someone else. John then went on to say he went to heaven. There was a big fence around it, and he looked over. Inside were many of his friends who had crossed the gloomy river of death, but the majority were not there. John inferred they were in another place. An angel came out to meet him and said, "John, you've been a pretty bad Indian."

John said he thought so too.

"There are just two things you can do now, John," said the angel. "You can go down to hell or you can go back to earth and preach to your people."

John preferred the latter proposition, as the angel pictured in burning language a hell which even exceeded John Calvin's idea. Then the angel and the wandering Indian soul sat down outside the fence and the angel told John what he must tell his people. In the first place he must instruct them not to drink whiskey. That was foremost. Then a code of morals was laid down. Lying, gambling, cheating, and horse-racing; and licentiousness were among the vices prohibited. The code was a simple one and one which the Indian mind could comprehend.

After John had learned it all, he was put back into his body and immediately came to life, to the great wonder of his people. He straightway began to preach and within four weeks had a small church erected.

Many Indians were present when he was sick and apparently dead. They said that his neck was broken and that he remained dead for about six hours, when he returned to life, jumped up, ran off a short distance, and soon began to converse with the people. Whether it was a case of suspended animation or not is a question. A white man, a near neighbor of his, who saw him before his apparent death, while he thus lay, and after his resuscitation, said that he believed that the Indian was playing possum. But the Indians believed that he really died and rose again.

This created considerable talk and interest among the surrounding Indians, but still did not have any great effect until the next August.

After consultation with other Indians, especially on the Skokomish reservation, who favored him, it was decided to hold a big meeting. The Indians of the surrounding region were urged to go. They were told that they would be lost if they did not, that four women would be turned into angels, that persons would die and be raised to life again, and that other wonderful things would be done. (David, Dick Lewis, and the followers of Big Bill entered heartily into this meeting.)

Many went, about half those on the Skokomish reservation being among the number, and they did hold a big meeting. Women did go around trying to fly like angels, four persons were said to have died; and with the power which was said to have been given them from above, others were said to have brought them back to life again. This was a mixture of trying to perform miracles, as in Bible times, to prove the divinity of their religion, and some of the ceremonies of their old black tamahnous. This was a secret society of their savage days, in which they became very rigid, and out of which they came in the course of time.

The followers of this new religion dreamed dreams, saw visions, went through some disgusting ceremonies a la mode the black tamahnous, and were taken with a kind of shaking. With their arms at full length, their hands and fingers would shake so fast that a common person not under the excitement would hardly shake half as fast. Gazing into the heavens, their heads would also shake very fast, sometimes for a few minutes and sometimes for hours or half the night. They would also brush each other with their heads, as they said, to brush off their sins, for they said they were much worse than white people, the latter being bad only in their hearts, but the Indians being so bad that the badness came to the surface of their bodies and the ends of their fingernails, so that it could be picked off and brushed off. While thus brushing each other, sometimes they did it lightly and sometimes so roughly that the person brushed was made black for a week and sometimes sick. In connection with this they held church services, prayed to God, believed in Christ as a Savior, and said much about His death, and used the cross, their services being a combination of Protestant and Catholic services; but at first they almost totally rejected the Bible, for they said they had direct revelations from Christ, and were more fortunate than the whites, who had only an old antiquated book. After having kept up this meeting for about a week they disbanded and went to their homes, but did not stop their shaking or services. They sometimes held meetings from six o'clock in the evening until about midnight, lighting candles and putting them on their heads for a long time. They became very particular about making the sign of the cross many times a day, when they began to eat, as they asked a blessing, and when they finished their meal and returned thanks, when they shook hands with anyone, and they shook hands very often when they went to church and prayer meeting on Thursday evening, and at many other times, far more often than the Catholics do.

On the Skokomish reservation their indiscretions caused the death of a mother and her child and an additional loss of time and property to the amount of $600 or $800 in a few weeks. It also became a serious question if the constant shaking of their heads would not make some of them crazy, and from symptoms and indications it was the opinion of the agency physician, J. T. Martin, M.D., that it would do so. Accordingly, on the reservation the authority of the Indian agent was brought to bear, and to a great extent the shaking was stopped, though they were encouraged to keep on in the practice of some good habits which they had begun, of ceasing gambling, intemperance, their old incantations over the sick, and the like. Some at first said that they could not stop shaking, but that at their prayer meetings and church services on the Sabbath their hands and heads would continue to shake in spite of themselves, but after a short time, when the excitement had died away, they found that they could stop.

But about Skookum bay, Mud bay, and Squaxon, the shaking continued, and it spread to the Nisqually and Chehalis Indians. It seemed to be as catching, to use the expression of the Indians, as the measles. Many who ridiculed it at first, and fought against it, and invoked the aid of the agent to stop it, were drawn into it after a little and then they became its strong upholders. This was especially true of the medicine men or Indian doctors and those who had the strongest faith in them. The shakers declared that all the old Indian religion and especially the cure of the sick by the medicine men was from the devil, and they would have nothing to do with it. Those who at first originated and upheld it were among the more intelligent and progressive of the uneducated Indians. Very few of those who had learned to read and had been in Sabbath school for a considerable length of time were drawn into it. It was the class between the most educated and the superstitious who at first upheld it. They seemed to know too much to continue in the old style religious ceremonies, but not to know enough and too superstitious to fully believe the Bible. Consequently, at first the medicine men were bitterly opposed to it.

The order came, however, from the Indian department about this time to stop all medicine men from practicing their incantations over the sick, and when a respectable number of the Indians had declared against the old style of curing the sick, it seemed to be a good time to enforce this order of the department, as there was sufficient popular opinion in connection with the authority of the agent to enforce it. This was done. And the medicine men almost entirely joined the Shakers as their style was more nearly in accordance with the old style than the religion of the Bible.

As it spread, one Indian, Big John, went so far as to declare himself to be Christ, again come to earth, and he rode through the streets of Olympia with his hands outstretched, as Christ was when he was crucified, at the head of several score of his followers. But he was so ridiculed by some other Indians and whites for this, that he gave up the idea and simply declared himself to be a prophet who had received a revelation from heaven. At first his was a separate sect from that of John Slocum, but they afterwards combined.

When the order was enforced on the reservations stopping this shaking, a few broke it, Big John being among the number. He was a Twana Indian, but for many years has lived with his wife's people, among the Squaksons. He was accordingly put in jail. His followers believed that the Supreme Being would open the jail and let him out, but in this they were disappointed.

As an evidence of the truth of the religion, they uttered prophecies. The first was that a great tidal wave would come in the spring of 1884 and overwhelm all the region. Disappointed in this, they next prophesied that the world would come to an end July 4, 1884, and many were frightened, but hardly as many as were frightened by the prophecy of the tidal wave, because that prophecy had failed to come true. Many of the Shakers, however, gathered on the Fourth to see the end, but the world stood. They then said that they had made a mistake in the year, and that the event would occur July 4, 1885, but by the time that day arrived, the people generally had lost faith in their prophecies, and not much note was taken of the prediction, and since that time I have heard very little of prophecies.

Mowitch Man. As this religion spread, another Twana Indian, Mowitch Man, one of the very few who had two wives and had some influence, was roused to adopt some religion. It consisted partly in following that of John Slocum, but largely in his own dreams. For a short time he affiliated a little with the others, but he was rather too dreamy for them, and there came a complete separation. His church lived not much more, however, than a year, partly dying for want of real life and partly perhaps because he had two wives, for the other Indians did not believe such a one to be a fit leader in religion. He gave me the following, which had been revealed to him in his dreams. God said to him, "I think about the Indians, Mowitch Man, I shall go everywhere to teach the people soon, so you tell the people to have strong hearts and get ready for me." One of his prayers was as follows, he standing up and raising his right hand. "O God, our Father, I give thanks to you. Please have pity upon us. Please take us to Heaven, where we will never die." Another one was as follows: "O God, our Father, soon we will go to Heaven where we will always live, and never die. Only God is our father, take care of us. We will never die in heaven."

LATER HISTORY OF THE SECT

But to return to the Shakers [*Tacoma Ledger*]

For several years on the Skokomish reservation there was very little of the shaking or this mode of worship, except secretly when persons were sick. Still their intercourse with those off the reservation, who sometimes hold a special gathering and meetings when their followers grow cold and careless, and their native superstition kept the belief in it as a religious form in their hearts, so that lately, since they have become citizens, and hence are free from the authority of the agent, the practice of it has become more common, especially when persons are sick.

In fact while it is a religion for use at all times, yet it is practiced especially over the sick, and in this way it takes the place of the medicine men and their mode of curing the sick. At enmity with that it has no single performer, though it often has a leader who can pray the best, yet in his absence another can take the lead. But like that it has much noise. Especially do they use bells to ring, and these are rung over the person where the sickness is supposed to be. The rest who are present use their influence to help in curing the sick one, and so imitate the attendants of an Indian doctor; for they get down on the floor on their knees and hold up their hands, with a candle in each hand, sometimes for an hour. They believe that by so holding up their hands the man who is ringing the bell will get the sickness out much easier than he otherwise would. They use candles, both when they attempt to cure the sick, and also during their general services, for fear they may be easily tempted, as they believe coal oil lights to be satan's light.

In another point they also resemble their old religion; for a long time before a person is taken sick they foretell that the spirit of the person has gone to heaven. They also profess to be able to bring back the spirit of the person, and to restore it to him, so that he will not die as soon as he would have done had this not been done. Both of these things are what they professed to do by their old tamahnous or religion.

Still like Christians they believe in a Supreme Being, in prayer, the Sabbath, in heaven and hell, in man as a sinner and Christ as a Savior, and it leads its followers to stop drinking, gambling, betting, horse racing, the use of tobacco and the old style incantations over the sick. During these years, however, some of them have fallen from grace.

It has been a somewhat strange freak of human nature. A combination of morals and immorals, of Protestantism, Catholicism, and old Indian practices, of dreams and visions—of what the mind may do under certain circumstances, a study in mental philosophy.

Yet it is all easily accounted for. These Indians have mingled with whites for a long time, nearly ever since most of them were small. All classes of whites have made sport of their religion, the infidel, the profane man, the immoral one, the moral one, and the Christian. The Bible and God have been said to be against it. Consequently, they lost faith in it. But the Indian must have some religion. He cannot go without one. These are not ready to accept that of the Bible in all its purity. They wanted more excitement. They, like the Dakota Indians more recently, saw that Christ was the great center of the most powerful religion, of the most powerful, intelligent, successful, and wisest nations with whom they came in contact. Consequently, they originated one that would fill all these required conditions, and when a few leaders had originated it, a large share of the rest were ripe to accept it. But having had more Christian teaching than the wild Dakotas, it took a somewhat different form, with no thought of war, and with more of real Christianity.

After the Indians became citizens, the sect became much stronger. As Rev. M. G. Mann, the Presbyterian missionary, had labored at Mud Bay, Chehalis, Nisqually, and Puyallup for about fifteen years, some of the leaders applied to the Presbytery for licensure. The request was taken under consideration, but the way did not seem to be clear to grant it. Hence, they afterwards applied to the County Clerk or Auditor of Thurston County for the same, who granted it as far as civil authorities could and the Shaker church hence became a legal church. The following additional from the *Tacoma Ledger* gives considerable of their later history. The sect

owns church edifices at Mud Bay, Oyster Bay, Cowlitz, Chehalis and Puyallup. It has a dozen ministers.

On June 6th and 7th, 1892, Judge James Wickersham, who acts as attorney for the Indians, assisted them in forming a regular organization. This was done. Louis Yowaluck was elected head man and John Slocum, Louis Yowaluck, John Smith, James Walker, Charles Walker, Jack Simmons and Bill Jones were elected elders.

The religion is a combination of Roman Catholicism, Protestantism and "tomanamus" or Indian "medicine." A report was sent the government by Agent Eells on the subject, and one of the departments at Washington pronounced the scheme of religion similar in some respects to the messiah craze among the Sioux. The sect acknowledges God, and His Son Jesus Christ, as the Savior of the world, but does not accept the Bible, saying: "What do we need with that? Our John Slocum was in heaven just twelve years ago and he can tell us all about it."

They use the same argument with regard to morality. Certain it is that they are moral in character and sober, but they are evidently in a measure fanatics.

Their form of religion is a mixture. They have preaching and divine worship and chant hymns. They say grace before and after meals; cross themselves when shaking hands and when worshipping. They place candles about the dead and hang up Roman Catholic pictures of the saints in their dwellings. They believe in faith cure and Christian science to a certain extent, but still retain faith in the medicine rattle. When a person is sick they ring bells, pray and go through many performances of the old Indian "tomanamus," or medicine men.

Their form of baptism is unique. Instead of using water to wash away the sins of the penitent they rub him. If he is a particularly hard customer they rub so hard that they frequently rub the clothes off him.

The name Shaker was applied to them because at times in their worship, when they work themselves into a religious frenzy, they wag their heads in a peculiar manner, which often terminates in their being unable to stop. Then they go on shaking all over, their nerves being in a completely unstrung condition.

Inasmuch as the sect is orthodox in some respects it has been suggested that it affiliate with some church. The visit of the Indians to the meeting of the Presbytery was in line with that suggestion. No action was taken, however. The Indians who were here were Louis Yowaluck of Mud Bay, the head man; John Slocum of Oyster Bay, he who claimed to have the revelation; Lyell Wa-ha-wa of Cowlitz, Jack Simmons of Puyallup and James Walker of Chehalis.

One of the odd features of the religion is the manner in which John Slocum, the original leader of the sect, has yielded that position to Louis Yowaluck. The latter is by nature a leader and has gradually gone forward until he is recognized as the head of the church and is looked up to by the Indians as a sort of ruler. John Slocum, whose Indian name is Squi-sacht-un, acknowledges Yowaluck's authority and seems satisfied with the arrangement. He goes on preaching his simple doctrine of hellfire and damnation for sinners and a happy heaven for true believers, with as much vigor as when he first came back from his tour to the heavenly regions. He holds out his short moral code to the Indians, and calls on them to foresake their evil ways and come into the fold.

Since the citizenship of Indian property owners was declared the sect has been growing rapidly.

Indian Agent Eells, in talking about the sect to a *Ledger* reporter yesterday, says: "The Indians are very earnest in this religion of theirs and seem to take much pride in it. The doctrine appears to be a step towards Christianity from the old Tomanamus worship, but it is a short step. They have many commendable customs, but the Indian mind gets queer ideas and often gets carried away thereby. These people see visions now and then, and become possessed of various sorts of hallucinations. Several of them thought they were given divine power to fly, and accordingly jumped off high buildings and were quite seriously hurt. Their faith-cure doctrines they do not carry to great extremes. They retain some of the old Tomanamus customs, as shown by placing the patient on the ground, and howling and praying about him. The physician at the Cowlitz reservation says he thinks several children have been killed by that method of treatment.

"I had an Indian policeman known as Sandy, one time. He was a very good man, but he joined the sect and began to have hallucinations which unfitted him for work. I was obliged to call him in and relieve him of his authority. He took the matter good naturedly, as he was a very sensible Indian. When I was leaving I said to him: 'Sandy, why do you go off with those foolish notions? You get almost crazy over them.'

"He drew himself up and said: 'Crazy! Look at me. Do I look crazy? No. I'm not crazy, I'm better Indian. You know I'm better Indian. I don't drink whiskey, I don't swear, I don't do nothing bad no more. I'll tell you all about it. I went to these people's meetings to make fun. I used to stand around and laugh at them. Bimeby I got to feeling queer inside. I went off behind a stump and prayed, and I knew that I was going to be a good Indian. You say we are crazy because we rub people. One time I was down in Olympia; I saw a procession come down the street. There was a big long man in front. He was all dressed in white. He waded down into the bay and he took a woman with him and he ducked her down under the water. Then he took another and he ducked her. I didn't say nothing; I just whistled. Now you people wash your sins away with water and we rub them away, and yet you say we are crazy.'

"He had me there," laughed Mr. Eells in conclusion, "and I could say no more."

Sam Yowaluck is at the head of the faith-cure branch of the work, and claims to have performed some wonderful cures on both Indians and whites. He was converted by John Slocum, and says he was told in a vision that he could become a medicine man.

Judge Wickersham has been attorney for the sect for two years, and believes thoroughly in the Indians' honesty of purpose. "There can be no doubt in the world," said he, "that they have done great good. In all my experience with them I have known but one of the whole sect that touched whiskey. They do not drink, gamble or swear, and they are virtuous in all other respects. There is nothing unorthodox about their belief, except Slocum's visit to the heavenly regions."[3]

To the Indians the sect is known as the "Tschadam." By the whites it has been dubbed the Shaker religion, though its doctrine is not the same as that held by the Shakers of the eastern states.

It now numbers about 600 members, comprising Indians from all the tribes in western Washington, and is reaching out into the Yakima country.

A large amount of their work is curing the sick. Sometimes they cure and sometimes they do not. Some people, I believe, have died who would have lived had it not been for their methods. Yet every cure they effect makes them have a firmer faith in it. It is said that a Quinaielt boy visited the Chehalis reservation recently, where he was induced to accept it, and when he returned to Quinaielt he told his teachers, "I can now pray like thunder and lightning."

My opinion of its curative properties is largely the same as in regard to tamahnous. Some would recover any way, and some are helped because of the faith they have in it.

Of its future I think it will retain a hold of its followers, until the rank and file of them become a minority among the Indians. Very few of those who read and write on the Skokomish reservation and have been to church and Sabbath School accept it—only two. When these shall be a majority or perhaps even when in the minority, they shall have the influence of a majority and really rule, the Shaker religion will go much as the tamahnous went.[4]

The following is John Slocum's prayer. "Our God is in Heaven. If we die he will take our life to Heaven. Help us so that we shall not die. Wherever we are, help us not to die. Our Father who is there always have a good mind to us."

His song is as follows:

1 O Sha-ak Bad tca-tl
   O Sha-ak Bad tca-tl
2 Aas kwa a-hwa-to-mo-tle
   O Sha-ak-Bad tca-tl
3 Tu-hwal ti Sli-tca tli, etc. (Chorus)
4 Tu-hwal sa-u-ha-li-tca tle, etc.
5 Klo-hoi tca-tl ha li, etc.
6 Tu hwal Sha-ak- Bad tca-tle, etc.

Translation
1 O God, our Father above
2 Help us always
3 As long as life lasts
4 Until we have life hereafter
5 Through God our Father.

The leader starts the first line tolerably fast and alone, and the whole crowd sings the second line, very loud and holding to each word very long.[5]

Editor's Notes

VOLUME 1

Preface

1. The Preface and Chapter I are slightly modified as "The Indians of Puget Sound," in *American Antiquity*, v. 9, no. 1, January 1887. Another version is "The Indians of Puget Sound," *Pacific Magazine*, v. 3, no. 8, April 1891.

2. There are several standard ethnographies, which are listed here. These cover in many cases the same topics under the same titles as Eells does in this volume:

Edward S. Curtis, *The North American Indian*, v. 9 (Norwood, Mass., 1903). While he has specific chapters on the Twana and the Clallam, Curtis often speaks of the Northwest region in general.

William W. Elmendorf, *The Structure of Twana Culture*, Washington State University Research Studies, Monograph Supplement 2 (Pullman, 1960).

Erna Gunther, *Klallam Ethnography*, University of Washington Publications in Anthropology, v. 1, no. 5 (Seattle, 1927).

Hermann Haberlin and Erna Gunther, *The Indians of Puget Sound*, University of Washington Publications in Anthropology, v. 4, no. 1 (Seattle, 1930).

Marian W. Smith, *The Puyullap-Nisqually*, Columbia University Contributions in Anthropology, v. 32 (New York, 1940).

A body of literature has continued to develop concerning the principal groups discussed in this book. For the Twana in particular William W. Elmendorf's on-going work should be noted:

"Twana Kinship Terminology," *Southwestern Journal of Anthropology* 2 (1946): 420–32.

"The Cultural Setting of the Twana Secret Society," *American Anthropologist* 50(1948):625–33.

"Word Taboo and Lexical Change in Coast Salish," *International Journal of American Linguistics* 17(1951):205–8.

"An Almost Lost Culture," *Washington State Revue* 2(1958):2–6.

Skokomish and Other Coast Salish Tales (Parts I–III), Washington State University Research Studies 29(1961):1–37, 84–117, 119–50.

"Skokomish Sorcery, Ethics, and Society," in *Systems of North American Witchcraft and Sorcery*, ed. by Deward E. Walker, pp. 147–82 (Moscow, Id.: University of Idaho, 1970).

"Coast Salish Status Ranking and Intergroup Ties," *Southwestern Journal of Anthropology* 27(1971):353–80.

"Coast and Interior Salish Power Concepts: A Structural Comparison." *Arctic Anthropology* 14(1977):64–76.

"Coast Salish Concepts of Power: Verbal and Functional Categories." In *The Tsimshian and Their Neighbors of the North Pacific Coast*, ed. Jay Miller and Carol M. Eastman, pp. 281–91 (Seattle and London: University of Washington Press, 1984).

3. In keeping with the editorial requirements of his times Eells supplies only minimal bibliographic information when citing sources. Where possible I have provided the full source at first citation. In this case:

George Vancouver, *A Voyage of Discovery to the North Pacific Ocean and Round the World*. 3 vols. (London: J. Edwards, 1798).

4. Charles Wilkes, *Narrative of the United States Exploring Expedition, 1838–42*. 5 vols. and Atlas (Philadelphia: Lea and Blanchard, 1845).

5. George Gibbs, *Reports of Explorations and Surveys, to Ascertain the Most Practical and Economical Route for a Railroad from the Mississippi River to the Pacific Ocean*. Made under the direction of the Secretary of War in 1853–54, Executive Document no. 91, House of Representatives, 2nd Session of Congress, Washington, D.C., 1854; *Tribes of Western Washington and Northwestern Oregon*, Contributions to North American Ethnology, v. 1, Department of the Interior, Washington, D.C., 1877; and *Alphabetical Dictionary of the Chinook Language* (New York: Cramoisy Press, 1863).

6. W. Fraser Tolmie and George V. Dawson, *Comparative Vocabularies of the Indian Tribes of British Columbia*, with a map indicating distribution (Montreal: Dawson Bros., 1884).

7. Ross Cox, *Adventures on the Columbia River* (New York: J. and J. Harper, 1832).

Gabriel Franchere, *Franchere's Narrative of a Voyage to the Northwest Coast in the Years 1811–1814; or, The First American Settlement on the Pacific*, trans. and ed. by J. V. Huntington (New York: Redfield Co., 1854).

Alexander Ross, *Adventures of the First Settlers on the Oregon or Columbia River* (New York: Smith, Elder and Co., 1849).

James G. Swan, *The Northwest Coast; or, Three Years' Residence in Washington Territory* (New York: Harper and Row, 1857).

Chapter I

1. Eells' spelling has been made consistent in the text but it has not been modernized; materials previously published in article form have not had the spelling altered. (His original spelling of Clallam, for example, has been retained; whereas in published form it appears as Klallam.) Detailed treatment of Twana and Klallam names and spellings are to be found in Elmendorf 1960 and Gunther 1927. A more general survey of place and tribal names is provided by Leslie Spier, "Tribal Distribution in Washington," in *Coast Salish and Western Washington Indians*, IV, ed. by W. W. Elmendorf and June Collins (New York: Garland Publishing Co., 1974), prepared for the Indian Claims Commission.

Chapter II

1. Chapter II appears in slightly modified form as "Traditions and History of the Puget Sound Indians," *American Antiquity*, v. 9, no. 2, March 1887. Another version is "The Indians of Puget Sound," *Pacific Magazine*, v. 3, no. 9, May 1891.

2. A modern short summary of early visits giving several sources unavailable at Eells' time is Erna Gunther's *Indian Life of the Northwest Coast of North America As Seen by the Early Explorers and Fur Traders During the Last Decades of the Eighteenth Century* (Chicago: University of Chicago Press, 1972).

3. The "Stevens" treaties and the Indian wars Eells describes in this section are usefully illuminated by a recent biography of Stevens by Kent D. Richards, *Isaac I. Stevens: Young Man in a Hurry* (Provo, Utah: Brigham Young University, 1979). The classic history that would have been

available to Eells is Hubert Howe Bancroft, *History of Washington, Idaho and Montana* (San Francisco: The History Co., 1890).

4. The nature of Indian policy and administration for the reservations that Eells describes during his own lifetime is best seen in the unpublished memoirs of his brother, Edwin Eells, who was Indian agent from 1871 to 1894. These are in the Washington State Historical Society Library, Tacoma.

Chapter III

1. This chapter is slightly modified as "Decrease of Population Among the Indians of Puget Sound," *American Antiquity*, v. 9, no. 5, September 1887.

2. "The Decrease of the Indians," *American Antiquarian*, v. 25, no. 3, May/June 1893. In this later article of the same title Myron reports the population of the Twana to have declined still further, to 170. The tone of this article is one of defense against accusations that it is somehow the missionaries who have caused this decline.

Chapter IV

1. Chapter IV is slightly modified as "The Puget Sound Indians," *American Antiquity*, v. 9, no. 4, July 1887. This break in sequence of the presentation is presumably part of the basis of his dissatisfaction with S. D. Peet (see Preface).

2. Hubert Howe Bancroft, *The Works of Hubert Howe Bancroft*, vol. I: *The Native Races* (San Francisco: A. L. Bancroft and Co., 1883).

3. A discussion of this topic is found in Erna Gunther's *Ethnobotany of Western Washington: The Knowledge and Use of Indigenous Plants by Native Americans*. Revised Edition (Seattle and London: University of Washington Press, 1973).

4. An ecological analysis of more modern style is Wayne Suttles' "Variation in Habitat and Culture on the Northwest Coast," in *Man in Adaptation: The Cultural Present*, ed. Yehudi A. Cohen (Chicago: Aldine, 1968).

Chapter V

1. Chapter V has not been previously published separately except as excerpted in "The Twana, Chemakum and Klallam Indians of Washington Territory" (1887).

Chapter VI

1. Chapter VI has not been previously published separately except as excerpted in "The Twana, Chemakum and Klallam Indians of Washington Territory" (1887).

2. See also T. T. Waterman and Geraldine Coffin, *Native Houses of Western North America*, Indian Notes and Monographs, Museum of the American Indian, Heye Foundation, New York, 1921.

VOLUME 2

Chapter VII

1. This chapter has not been previously published separately except as excerpted in "The Twana, Chemakum and Klallam Indians of Washington Territory" (1887).

2. Photographs and commentary on matting, basketry, and other items of material culture are found in T. T. Waterman, *Notes on the Ethnology of the Indians of Puget Sound*, Indian Notes and Monographs, Museum of the American Indian, Heye Foundation, New York (completed in 1921 but not published until 1973). The previously cited standard ethnographic monographs: Curtis (1903), Gunther (1927), Elmendorf (1960), Haberlin and Gunther (1930), and Smith (1940), all have extensive discussion of material culture and should be compared to the following chapters.

Chapter VIII

1. Chapter VIII has not been previously published separately except as excerpted in "The Twana, Chemakum and Klallam Indians of Washington Territory" (1887).

Chapter IX

1. Chapter IX has not been previously published separately except as excerpted in "The Twana, Chemakum and Klallam Indians of Washington Territory" (1887).

Chapter X

1. Some of the material in this chapter is discussed in "The Stone Age of Oregon" (1889) and excerpts appear in "The Twana, Chemakum and Klallam Indians of Washington Territory" (1887).

2. Eells wrote "The Thunder Bird" (1882), but I think here he may oversimplify his identification of artistic symbolism. The Northwest Coast has a rich and complex set of such artistic conventions, which he may not always have comprehended.

3. Archaeological knowledge was rudimentary in Eells' time. For a readable general illustrated survey, see *Exploring Washington Archaeology*, by Ruth Kirk, with Richard Daugherty (Seattle and London: University of Washington Press, 1978).

4. W. J. Hoffman, "Poisoned Arrows," *American Anthropology* 4(1891):67–71.

5. See Wayne Suttles, "The Early Diffusion of the Potato Among the Coast Salish," *Southwestern Journal of Anthropology* 7(1951):272–288.

VOLUME 3

Chapter XI

1. Chapter XI is modified as "Puget Sound Indians, Fifth Paper," *American Antiquarian*, v. 10, no. 1, January 1888.

2. See T. T. Waterman and Geraldine Coffin, *Types of Canoes on Puget Sound*, Museum of the American Indian, Heye Foundation, Miscellaneous Series 11, 1921.

3. See Wayne Suttles, "The Persistence of Intervillage Ties Among the Coast Salish," *Ethnology* 2(1963):512–25.

Chapter XII

1. This chapter is modified as "Indians of Puget Sound, Sixth Paper," *American Antiquarian*, v. 10, no. 3, May 1888.

2. Here as elsewhere in his writings Eells seems largely unaware of the complex social networks and the structure of wealth accumulation (often borrowed from kinsmen) and redistribution. Elmendorf (1960 and 1971) gives some help with the Twana, and Gunther (1927) with the Klallam.

3. No date is provided for this clipping included in the notebook.

Chapter XIII

1. This chapter has not been previously published except as excerpted in "The Twana, Chemakum and Klallam Indians of Washington Territory" (1887). Small portions of the chapter appear to have been published in newspaper form but neither the paper nor the date is indicated.

Chapter XIV

1. Chapter XIV has not been previously published separately except as excerpted in "The Twana, Chemakum and Klallam Indians of Washington Territory" (1887).

Chapter XV

1. Chapter XV has not been previously published separately except as excerpted in "The Twana, Chemakum and Klallam Indians of Washington Territory" (1887).

2. Eells included some ten pages of colored outline maps of Europe and other schoolboy efforts, which I have omitted.

Chapter XVI

1. Chapter XVI has not been previously published separately except as excerpted in "The Twana, Chemakum and Klallam Indians of Washington Territory" (1887).

2. No paper or date is given for this clipping.

3. Eells included at this point a number of examples of printing done at the reservation in the form of meeting programs and the like. These have not been reproduced here. He also attached portions of bibliographies of the Chinook and Salishan languages and a few additional background references. While not reproduced in this volume, these references are:

James C. Pilling, *Bibliography of Salishan Languages*, Bureau of Ethnology, Smithsonian Institution, 1893; and *Bibliography of the Chinookan Languages*, Bureau of Ethnology, Smithsonian Institution, 1893.

Elwood Evans, *History of the Pacific Northwest, Oregon, and Washington*. 2 vols. (Portland: North Pacific History Co., 1889).

Caroline C. Leighton, *Life at Puget Sound* (Boston: Lee and Shephard, 1884).

Charles Nordhoff, *Northern California, Oregon, and Sandwich Islands* (New York: Harper and Bros., 1874).

VOLUME 4

Chapter XVII

1. Portions of this chapter were published as "The Thunder Bird," *American Anthropologist*, v. 2, no. 4, 1889; other parts in "Myths of the Puget Sound Indians," *American Antiquarian*, v. 12, no. 3, 1890; "Traditions of the Deluge Among the Tribes of the North West," *American Antiquarian*, v. 1, no. 2, 1878.

2. The additional references cited by Eells are:

Pierre Jean de Smet, *Oregon Missions and Travels over the Rocky Mountains in 1845–46* (New York: E. Dunigan, 1847).

S. D. Peet, *The Religious Beliefs and Traditions of the Aborigines of North America*, Transactions of the Victoria Institute, v. 21, London, 1888.

Garrick Mallery, *Pictographs of the North American Indians*, Fourth Annual Report, 1882–83, Bureau of Ethnology, Washington, D.C., 1886.

Erminnie A. Smith, *Myths of the Iroquois*, Second Annual Report, 1880–81, Bureau of Ethnology, Washington, D.C., 1883.

Franz Boas, "Notes on the Snanaimug," *American Anthropologist* 2(1889):321–28.

A. F. Chamberlain, "The Thunder Bird Among the Algonkins," *American Anthropologist* 3(1890):51–54.

Franklin Hamilton Cushing, "Primitive Copper Working: An Experimental Study," *American Anthropologist* 7(1894):93–117.

3. One cannot help but wonder, since he took the care to mark some of the proverbs "not true," whether he means to imply that the others *are* true.

Chapter XVIII

1. Chapter XVIII has appeared in modified form as "Aboriginal Place Names in the State of Washington," *American Anthropologist*, v. 5, no. 1, January 1892, and small portions in unidentified newspaper clips.

2. James Wickersham, *Is It "Mt. Tacoma" or "Rainier": What Do History and Traditions Say?* Tacoma Academy of Science, Puget Sound Printing Co., Tacoma, 1893.

Chapter XIX

1. Chapter XIX has not been previously published except for "Twins Among the Indians of Puget Sound," *Science*, v. 20, no. 504, September 1892, and portions of unidentified newspaper clips.

Chapter XX

1. Chapter XX has been previously published, modified as "The Potlatches of Puget Sound," *American Antiquarian*, v. 5, 1883, and in Eells, "Ten Years at Skokomish" (1886).
2. No date is given for either newspaper excerpt.

VOLUME 5

Chapter XXI

1. Chapter XXI has not been previously published except as excerpted in "The Twana, Chemakum and Klallam Indians of Washington Territory" (1887) and portions in "Ten Years at Skokomish" (1886).

Chapter XXII

1. Portions of this chapter appear in "Ten Years at Skokomish."
2. See again Elmendorf (1960) and Gunther (1927) for discussion of social organization. Neither Eells nor anyone else fully understood the complexities of the rank-oriented Northwest societies at this time.
3. Edwin Eells in his unpublished memoirs expresses considerable concern that citizenship and this loss of control would lead to debauchery.
4. Elwood Evans, *History of Pacific Northwest, Oregon and Washington* (Portland: North Pacific History Co., 1887).
5. I have omitted a very lengthy article, "Seattle," taken from the *Seattle Post-Intelligencer* of March 26, 1893, as being peripheral to the main text.
6. The source of this newspaper clip is unidentified.
7. Edwin Eells notes in his memoirs that Stanup on this second occasion was in opposition to Eells and had become a leader in attempts to sell Puyallup lands. Edwin Eells was in fact accused of murdering him!
8. Eells had inserted here a clipping undated and unidentified as to paper describing the death of Stanup and an undated clipping from the *Seattle Post-Intelligencer*, titled "Poor Old Angeline, Only Living Child of the Grat War Chief Seattle." Both are omitted.

Chapter XXIII

1. Portions of this chapter appeared as "The Religion of the Indians of Puget Sound" (1890).

2. Eells also published "Do-Ki-Batt, or: The God of the Puget Sound Indians" (1884).

3. Eells, in "The Worship and Traditions of the Aborigines of America" (1885), makes an attempt to demonstrate that the basic ideas of the Bible are universal either because they are "innate" or, more probably, because all men come from a single source—extreme diffusion.

4. L. H. Morgan, *Ancient Society* (New York: World Publishing, 1887). Morgan makes many comparisons similar to those cited by Eells in this work.

5. Eells also published "Idolatry Among the Indians of Puget Sound, Washington Territory" (1885).

Chapter XXIV

1. Portions of Chapter XXIV appeared in "The Religion of the Indians of Puget Sound" (1890).

Chapter XXV

1. Chapter XXV has not been previously published except as fragments cited in "The Twana, Chemakum and Klallam Indians of Washington Territory" (1887) and "Ten Years at Skokomish" (1886).

VOLUME 6

Chapter XXVI

1. This chapter was previously published only as fragments in "The Twana, Chemakum and Klallam Indians of Washington Territory" (1887) and in "Ten Years at Skokomish" (1886).

2. Edwin Eells narrates the same incident in his memoirs.

Chapter XXVII

1. Chapter XXVII was previously published in part in "Ten Years at Skokomish" (1886).

2. Eells was the principal source for the Shaker section of James Mooney's *The Ghost Dance Religion and the Sioux Outbreak of 1890*, Fourteenth Annual Report, 1892–93, Bureau of American Ethnology, Washington, D. C., 1896.

3. No date is given for the inserted clipping.

4. The church, of course, still exists on the Skokomish Reservation as well as elsewhere.

5. Eells included a final chapter on archaeology, which has not been reproduced here. The text is a repeat of his "The Stone Age of Oregon" (1889) and both text and drawings duplicate coverage elsewhere in the volume. Eells himself made a note questioning the desirability of its inclusion.

Myron Eells as Ethnographer:
An Appraisal

WILLIAM W. ELMENDORF

Professor Emeritus, University of Wisconsin-Madison

Research Associate, Anthropology, University of California, Davis

As HIS BIBLIOGRAPHY indicates, Myron Eells was a very prolific writer on ethnology and on the history of Pacific Northwest Indian missions. Among his ethnographic works "The Indians of Puget Sound" was regarded by its author as his magnum opus. The final version, completed in 1894 after several preliminary revisions, was deposited in the library of Whitman College, Washington, after the author's death in 1907.

This manuscript, as edited by George Castile, now appears in print nearly a century after its completion. It concentrates and organizes as a coherent whole most of the material in a series of earlier and often obscure publications that appeared during Eells' lifetime. As noted in the Editor's Preface, Eells expressed himself as never satisfied with the form in which these early versions appeared, and for years wished to see his ethnographic account of western Washington Indians published as a single detailed whole. In its present form this work offers perhaps more sheer data on various native peoples of the Puget Sound region, especially the Twana of Hood Canal, than does any other single source.

Appraising the quality, rather than the quantity, of Eells' data as ethnographic reportage turns out to be a more complex matter than appears at first sight. During the years in which I collected and wrote ethnographic data on the Twana Indians, from the late 1930s to the mid 1950s, I became well acquainted with most of Myron Eells' published writings, and although citing some of these as essential sources, particularly on the Twana (e.g., Elmendorf 1960:570), I tended to regard most of his work with a jaundiced eye, as the ethnocentrically biased productions of a missionary-reformer, whose facts might be of interest to a modern, positivist, objective anthropologist, but whose interpretations could largely be dismissed. I now look at that "scientific" cocksureness of my younger days as involving more naivety than science.

Like many other present-day ethnologists interested in the nature and interpretation of cultural reportage, I have come to realize that Eells as ethnographer was essentially part of his ethnography, and that furthermore this holds true of all descriptive analyses of "foreign" or "exotic" cultures, past or present. Eells was not trained as anthropologist or ethnographer. His education was that of a Christian missionary with a secondary interest in history, particularly the history of western American Indian missions. He came to ethnography, as did most other ethnographic writers of his period, as an amateur trained in other fields. Any estimate of what he did in describing the ways of the native American peoples among whom he found himself must take these background facts into account.

Just as we should appraise a biographical work partly in terms of the biographer, or a work of art in terms of the artist, so should we today in the 1980s look at an ethnographic work of a century ago with reference to the experiences, role, and motivations of the person who wrote it. It is easy, and proper, to criticize a work of this kind after decades of hindsight, and Dr. Castile, while appreciating Eells' contribution, has succinctly pointed out some weaknesses in his interpretations. In his Preface, Castile notes, for example, that "Eells was not always an accurate observer and very often he did not fully understand what he saw. . . . He did not, for example, seem to fully understand the ceremonial life of the people he lived among" (p. vii).

I agree with this, but feel that we must here distinguish observing from understanding. As an observer I would give Eells fairly high marks. He seems to strive for accuracy in reporting what he saw, and a great deal of what he saw could not be directly witnessed after the close of the nineteenth century. His work has therefore the value of at least an attempt at careful reporting of customs and conditions now vanished.

As for understanding ethnographic observation, this ideally entails a detailed knowledge of the culture being described, so far as possible from the viewpoint of participants in that culture—a knowledge not only of their observable behaviors, but of the rules, concepts, goals, and values motivating that behavior. It is here that Eells frequently falls short, in poor awareness of these cultural intangibles, and in often substituting for this essential knowledge of conceptual contexts stereotypic notions of his own and of the culture in which he grew up.

Examples of such stereotyping abound in Chapters XXIII–XXVII on religion, as in his discussion of "idols", and in Chapter XXI his remarks about an "evil spirit which killed the deceased." In view of the mutual aversion between the missionary and native shamans, and the resulting ignorance of the complex theories of Coast Salish shamanism on the missionary's part, such erroneous projections of stereotypes about primitives are not unexpected. These aspects of Eells' work could be summed up as interpretations sometimes shrewd and cogent, but perhaps more often biased by the outlook of a Christian missionary and cultural reformer, working in the last quarter of the nineteenth century.

In any appraisal of his ethnographic work we must see Eells against the background of his times. As Castile notes, Myron and his Indian Agent brother Edwin Eells mirrored the sentiments and motivations of their period toward native Americans. It was a time when U.S. governmental and religious authorities were determined to "civilize" the Indians under their control as rapidly and thoroughly as possible. These civilizing efforts were prevailingly combined with a mix of ignorance and misconceptions regarding the native cultures to be altered and replaced.

Among nineteenth-century agents of this attempt at cultural transformation Myron Eells was one of a limited number of exceptions to the prevalent employment of cultural blinders. His motives were certainly reform and religious conversion, but he did take a sympathetic enough interest in the ways of the southern Coast Salish peoples with whom he had direct contact to attempt a detailed description of both their then disappearing aboriginal customs and the rapidly changing conditions characterizing these Indian societies at the time of his missionary work. In fact, some of the most interesting and enduringly valuable portions of the present work are those depicting the changes in native cultures during the early reservation period, roughly 1870–1900. The transition styles described in some of these sections are of real value to any study of culture change and culture contact. A good example is Chapter VI, on housing.

Eells' own preface tells us that he "tried mainly to describe the Indians as they formerly were, with frequent allusions . . . to their present condition." This balancing of a somewhat indefinite but essentially mid-nineteenth-century ethnographic baseline with eyewitness accounts of rapid change during the last quarter of the century is one of the real values of his work. Eells was there, from 1874, and saw the changes at first hand. He was also close enough to an earlier pre-reservation generation to be able to report a good deal of valid data on earlier customs. However, it is here, in his treatment of "aboriginal" culture that a modern reader frequently finds Eells viewing his subjects and their modes of thinking and behaving through missionary-reformer spectacles.

So, if some of Eells' material seems not to accord with what twentieth-century anthropologists have come to regard as a respectable ethnographic standard, these shortcomings should be evaluated against not only the times in which this missionary-author worked, but also with regard to his own role as an observer and describer. That role was ostensibly devoted to conversion, to eradication of native beliefs and behaviors and their replacement by ways approaching norms of late nineteenth-century white American rural society.

The times in which Eells began his ethnographic studies, the 1870s and 1880s, afforded few ethnographic models, Boasian or Malinowskian, such as later generations were able to use. I do not know on whom, if anyone, he consciously modeled his descriptive accounts. There seems to have been a good deal of originality in his approach. He refers to earlier works of Vancouver, Wilkes, Gibbs, and others whose writings often concentrated on southern Northwest Coast peoples other than the subjects of his study. But none of these sources presents the kind of detailed data, derived from a quarter-century of intimate contact with his subjects, that Eells' does.

Like all ethnographers Eells was part of what he sought to describe, and, as we have seen, some of his description veers from the putatively objective standards of modern ethnography. Yet, measured against later and presumably more "scientific" work he does not fare too badly as a reporter of what he actually witnessed in western Washington Indian communities of the 1870s to 1890s.

His reportage was that of a particular person at a particular time, with particular reasons for his involvement with his southern Coast Salish peoples. Other descriptions by other observers might well have differed from that reportage, had there been any to furnish comparable ethnographic information during the same period and on the peoples involved, above all the Twana of Hood Canal.

We are accustomed today to instances of replicated ethnographic accounts not in good correspondence, when reported by different ethnographers. One thinks of the different Zuni of Ruth Benedict and of Li An-Che, or the Arapesh of Margaret Mead and Reo Fortune, or the recent much publicized confrontation of Derek Freeman's Samoa with that of Margaret Mead. Cases could be multiplied. All this is to say that like any observer of an "alien" culture, Eells reported his findings through a process of selection, omission, and emphasis colored by his own personal and cultural background and motivations. Some of those motivations, above all the drive for religious conversion, were not those of later ethnographers.

Probably the most immediate comparison here would be between Eells' account, devoted in large part to the Twana Indians, and my general ethnographic account of these same people (Elmendorf 1960). The former material dates from 1874 to 1894, mine from fieldwork at intervals between the mid-1930s and the mid-1950s, derived from a small number of elderly informants, one of whom was highly knowledgeable on matters having to do with pre-white religion and shamanism. I would rate my account as more tightly organized, more explicit about the general context of aboriginal culture, and more detailed and accurate in some topics, particularly those of religion and ritual.

In these latter subjects, as remarked above, Eells never really grasped the underlying ideas of native religion, and the mutual antipathy between him and native shamans precluded his deriving much reliable data from those sources. On the other hand, his prolonged firsthand contact with the people he described, at a time when knowledge of earlier culture was general among at least the adult Indian generation, gives his record special value apart from the distortions noted above and in the Editor's Preface.

One other comparative difference between Eells and the later Elmendorf account is worth mentioning. Because of anthropological and linguistic training I approached Twana culture in part through the native language, exploring linguistic forms so far as possible to define native meanings. Eells seems to have had no formal academic contact with the then embryonic subject of cultural anthropology, and he was, alas, no sort of linguist at all. He confessed himself, in other writings, unable to master any of the native languages of the peoples he worked with, and instead fell back on the meager resources of the regional pidgin, the so-called Chinook Jargon.

An example of the deficiencies of this kind of linguistic approach is his use, in discussing native supernaturalism, of the Jargon term *tamahnous*, which I heard as both *tamánawis* and *tamánamis*. This, like other terms in this pidgin, covers a very broad range of meanings: "anything supernatural," "supernatural power," "guardian spirit," "ritual concerned with spirit power," and the like—a whole complex of concepts which must be defined and distinguished in native terminology. Use of this Chinook Jargon term obviously contributes to the vagueness of Eells' interpretations of native religious beliefs and practices.

One other feature of the present work is worth noting. This is Eells' tendency at times to overgeneralize and to present data without sufficiently specifying their provenience.

That is, some portions refer to peoples and customs over the whole Hood Canal, Puget Sound, and Strait of Juan de Fuca region. While there were indeed some general features of native culture common to this entire area, it was nevertheless one in which much variation in native cultures existed. Eells was really aware of this, and perhaps more often refers specific details to Twana or Klallam or Squaxin, but some of his accounts are generalized for this ethnically diverse section of western Washington. I must add, however, that Eells did not overgeneralize to the frustrating extent of most of Edward Curtis' later work covering the Strait of Georgia and all of western Washington (*The American Indian*, vol. 9).

In what follows I note some specific points that particularly caught my attention.

The description of Twana canoes in Chapter XI seems curiously incomplete. In Chapter XV ("Art") the account of nineteenth-century carvings imported from the north, done by northern carvers, is very interesting as an illustration of diffusional processes perhaps stimulated by white contact with native peoples. Chapter XVI ("Writing and Books") has interesting documentation on acculturation through schooling in the late nineteenth century.

Chapter XVII ("Literature") on oral tradition and mythology gives mostly sketchy versions not as narrated by native sources. Chapters XIX ("Domestic Life") and XX ("Potlatches") contain valuable observations regarding tribal intermarriage and types of wealth-giving feasts. Eells' "small feasts" with distribution of presents are actually distinguished in Twana terminology as *syílaxab* from his "potlatch," which is *s'íwad.* There is a good deal of value here in the descriptive accounts.

The observations in Chapter XXI ("Funeral Customs") on variance, to some extent over time, are interesting and confirm my impression from informants of a good deal of change in burial customs during the nineteenth century (Elmendorf 1960:455). There are some details here which I did not hear about in my later Twana work. Chapter XXII ("Government and Political Economy") has some cogent and correct observations on how white Euro-American concepts were imposed on the very different systems of local Indian social and political organization.

But in Chapters XXIII–XXVII ("Religion") there are, as remarked earlier, numerous misleading "white" stereotypes in interpreting native belief systems, along with much significant information, the latter mainly from direct observation. The equating of the native world-changer, in Twana *dúkwibał*, with Jesus, which I heard again from informants in the 1930s, appears to have struck Eells as possible evidence of the appearance of the Christian Savior in this area. He is, however, somewhat noncommital in advancing this view. Throughout, partly because of his use of that vaguish and broad Chinook Jargon term and concept of "tamahnous", Eells tends to confuse shamanism with other systems for manipulating supernatural power. Worth noting in Chapter XXVI are the very interesting observations on Eells's belief in the psychological value of native curing treatments, coupled with his strong disapprobation of these same practices, expressed here and elsewhere.

The final chapter (XXVII, on the Shaker religion) presents first-rate historical source material for events leading up to and into the early development of the Indian Shaker

Church at Skokomish. In particular, the account of the Skokomish religious movement anticipating and preparing for the reception of the Shaker doctrines and practices—Big Bill's revelation and following—does not seem to have appeared in anything like this detail in later sources.

As a summary assessment I see the main anthropological value of Eells' work in his eyewitness reporting rather than in the descriptive ethnography, which is sometimes good and detailed but sometimes vague or overgeneralized. His interpretations of native customs are also at times naive and culture bound, particularly in his discussions of native world view, belief systems, and religious rituals. He did better in reporting the rapid and thorough cultural changes going on under his eyes during the last decades of the 1800s. Above all, Myron Eells was an assiduous and obviously highly motivated observer and recorder of the customs of the peoples whom he was attempting to convert to Congregational Christianity.

There is a certain amount of irony, as Castile notes, in the fact that Eells' years of missionary work did not finally result in any great success in obtaining converts for his church at Skokomish. In fact, during the next twenty years after its appearance on the Skokomish Reservation in the early 1880s the new Shaker religion seems to have flourished at the expense of Eells' congregation. Rather than his goal of converting the Skokomish Reservation community Eells seems in his missionary efforts to have played the role of preparing his Skokomish people for their rapid acceptance of, and adherence to the new Shaker creed. But we can be grateful for Myron Eells' outpouring of energy in his historical and ethnographic writings, and grant him a good rating for what he actually contributed to our understanding of local native American cultures during a time of rapid change.

Davis, California
June 1985

Bibliography

REFERENCES CITED

American Missionary Association
1895   "S'Kokomish Mission." *The American Missionary*, v. 49, no. 2, p. 38.
Amoss, Pamela
1978a   *Coast Salish Spirit Dancing: The Survival of an Ancestral Religion.* Seattle and London: University of Washington Press.
1978b   Review of Myron Eells and the Puget Sound Indians, *Pacific Northwest Quarterly*, v. 68, no. 4, pp. 188–89.
Barnett, H. G.
1957   *Indian Shakers: A Messianic Cult of the Pacific Northwest.* Carbondale: Southern Illinois University Press.
Castile, George P.
1981   "Edwin Eells, U.S. Indian Agent, 1871–1895." *Pacific Northwest Quarterly*, v. 73, no. 2, pp. 61–68.
1982   "The 'Half Catholic' Movement: Edwin and Myron Eells and the Rise of the Indian Shaker Religion." *Pacific Northwest Quarterly*, vol. 73, no. 4, pp. 165–74.
Codere, Helen
1950   *Fighting with Property: A Study of Kwakiutl Potlatching and Warfare, 1792–1930.* American Ethnological Society Monograph 18. Seattle: University of Washington Press.
Eells, Myron
1883   "Justice to the Indian." Paper read before the Congregational Association of Oregon and Washington. Portland: G. H. Himes.
1886   *Ten Years of Missionary Work among the Indians at Skokomish, Washington Territory, 1874–1884.* Boston: Congregational Sunday School and Publishing Society.
1893   "The Skokomish Indians." *The Home Missionary*, v. 65, no. 11, pp. 557–59.
1894a   *Father Eells.* Boston: Congregational Sunday School and Publishing Society.
1894b   "Report of S'Kokomish, Washington." *The American Missionary*, v. 48, no. 9, p. 333.
1894c   "Skokomish Agency, Washington." *The American Missionary*, v. 18, no. 4, pp. 166–167. (Misprinted and is v. 48).
1898   "Pacific Coast Religion." *Oregonian*, July 9, 1898. Portland, Ore.
1899   "Mission Work on the Skokomish Reservation." *The Indian's Friend*, v. 2, no. 6, pp. 8–9.
1903   "The Decrease of the Indians." *American Antiquarian*, v. 25, no. 3, pp. 145–49.
Eells, Edwin
1887   "Nisqually and Skokomish Agency, August 20, 1887." In the Annual Report of the Commission of Indian Affairs, 1887.
1888   "Puyallup Agency (Consolidated), August 22, 1888." In the Annual Report of the Commission of Indian Affairs, 1888.
1902   Letter to Myron Eells, April 20, 1902. Whitman College Archives.
1916   Untitled manuscript memoirs. Washington State Historical Society, Tacoma.

Eells, Ida

1947   *Mother Eells: A Story of the Life of Myra Fairbank Eells.* Mimeograph, Whitman College Library.

Elmendorf, William W.

1946   "Twana Kinship Terminology." *Southwestern Journal of Anthropology* 2:420–32.

1948   "The Cultural Setting of the Twana Secret Society." *American Anthropologist* 50:625–33.

1951   "Word Taboo and Lexical Change in Coast Salish." *International Journal of American Linguistics* 17:205–8.

1958   "An Almost Lost Culture." *Washington State Review* 2(2):2–6.

1960   *The Structure of Twana Culture.* Washington State University Research Studies, Monographic Supplement 2. Pullman, Wash.

1961   *Skokomish and Other Coast Salish Tales* (Part I–III). Washington State University Research Studies 29:1–37, 84–117, 119–50.

1970   "Skokomish Sorcery, Ethics, and Society." *Systems of North American Witchcraft and Sorcery,* ed. Deward E. Walker, pp. 147–82. Moscow, ID: University of Idaho.

1971   "Coast Salish Status Ranking and Intergroup Ties." *Southwestern Journal of Anthropology* 27:353–80.

1977   "Coast and Interior Salish Power Concepts: A Structural Comparison." *Arctic Anthropology* 14(1):64–76.

1984   "Coast Salish Concepts of Power: Verbal and Functional Categories." *The Tsimshian and Their Neighbors of the North Pacific Coast,* ed. Jay Miller and Carol M. Eastman, pp. 281–91. Seattle: University of Washington Press.

Gunther, Erna

1927   *Klallam Ethnography.* Seattle: University of Washington Press.

Prucha, Francis Paul, ed.

1973   *Americanizing the American Indians: Writings by the "Friends of the Indians," 1880–1900.* Cambridge: Harvard University Press.

Prucha, Francis Paul

1976   *American Indian Policy in Crisis: Christian Reformers and the Indians, 1865–1900.* Norman, Okla.: University of Oklahoma Press.

Richards, Kent P.

1979   *Isaac Stevens: Young Man in a Hurry.* Provo, Utah: Brigham Young University Press.

Ruby, Robert, and John A. Brown

1976   *Myron Eells and the Puget Sound Indians.* Seattle: Superior Publishing Company.

Taylor, Theodore W.

1971   *The States and Their Indian Citizens.* Washington, D.C.: Bureau of Indian Affairs.

Washburn, Wilcomb E.

1975   *The Assault on Indian Tribalism: The General Allotment Law (Dawes Act) of 1887.* Philadelphia: Lippincott.

White, Leslie

1963   *The Ethnography and Ethnology of Franz Boas.* Texas Memorial Museum, Bulletin 6. Austin: Texas Memorial Museum.

WORKS BY MYRON EELS

The following is a list of Myron Eells's principal works dealing with the Indians of Puget Sound, which, wholly or in part, contribute to this volume:

1877   "The Twana Indians of the Skokomish Reservation in Washington Territory." *U.S. Geological Survey Bulletin,* v. 3, no. 4, pp. 57–114.

1887 "The Indians of Puget Sound," first paper. *American Antiquarian and Oriental Journal*, v. 9, no. 4, January, pp. 1–9.

1887 "Traditions and History of the Puget Sound Indians." *American Antiquarian and Oriental Journal*, v. 9, no. 2, March, pp. 97–104.

1887 "The Puget Sound Indians," third paper. *American Antiquarian and Oriental Journal*, v. 9, no. 4, July, pp. 211–19.

1887 "Decrease of Population among the Indians of Puget Sound," fourth paper. *American Antiquarian and Oriental Journal*, v. 9, no. 5, September, pp. 271–76.

1888 "Puget Sound Indians," fifth paper. *American Antiquarian and Oriental Journal*, v. 10, no. 1, January, pp. 26–36.

1888 "Indians of Puget Sound," sixth paper. *American Antiquarian and Oriental Journal*, v. 10, no. 3, May, pp. 174–78.

1889 "The Twana, Chemakum and Klallam Indians of Washington Territory." Smithsonian Institution, Annual Report for 1887, pp. 605–81.

1890 "The Religion of the Indians of Puget Sound." *American Antiquarian and Oriental Journal*, v. 12, no. 2, March, pp. 69–84.

1890 "Myths of the Puget Sound Indians." *American Antiquarian and Oriental Journal*, v. 12, no. 3, May, pp. 160–65.

1891 "The Indians of Puget Sound." *The Pacific Magazine*, v. 3, no. 8, April, pp. 391–96; no. 9, May, pp. 450–55.

Other published works primarily concerned with Indian affairs:

1878 *Hymns in the Chinook Jargon Language.* Portland: George H. Himes.

1878 "Mounds in Washington Territory." *American Antiquarian and Oriental Journal*, v. 1, no. 1, April, p. 13.

1878 "Three Christian Boys and Their Letters." *The American Missionary*, v. 32, no. 4, April, p. 118.

1878 "Sunday School Progress—An Indian Festival—Temperance and Order." *The American Missionary*, v. 32, no. 5, May, pp. 148–49.

1878 "Traditions of the 'Deluge' among the Tribes of the North-West." *American Antiquarian and Oriental Journal*, v. 1, no. 2, July, pp. 70–72.

1879 "The Late Indian War and Christianity." *The American Missionary*, v. 33, no. 1, January, pp. 20–21.

1878 "Indian Music." *American Antiquarian and Oriental Journal*, v. 1, no. 4, April, pp. 249–53.

1879 "School and Church Work at Dunginess." *The American Missionary*, v. 33, no. 4, April, pp. 120–21.

1879 "The Spice of Missionary Life." *The American Missionary*, v. 33, no. 6, June, pp. 181–83.

1879 "The Religion of the Clallam and Twana Indians." *American Antiquarian and Oriental Journal*, v. 2, no. 1, July, pp. 8–14.

1879 "A Tour among the Clallam Indians." *The American Missionary*, v. 33, no. 11, November, pp. 342–44.

1880 "Indian Aid to the Whites in the Wars on the Northwest Coast." No. 1. "The Cayuse War." *The Council Fire*, v. 3, no. 5, May, p. 79.

1880 "The Yakima War." *The Council Fire*, v. 3, no. 6, June, p. 83. (Incorrectly attributed to Edwin Eells.)

1880 "The Chemakum Language." *American Antiquarian and Oriental Journal*, v. 2, no. 10, October.

1880   "S'kokomish, Washington Territory." *The American Missionary*, v. 34, no. 7, July, pp. 214–16.

1880   "Indian Aid to the Whites in the Wars on the Northwest Coast: The Nez Perces Mining Trouble." *The Council Fire*, v. 3, no. 9, September, pp. 141–42.

1880   "S'kokomish Agency: Field and Work." *The American Missionary*, v. 34, no. 10, October, pp. 308–9.

1881   "Indian Aid to the Whites on the Northwest Coast: The War with Joseph's Band of the Nez Perces." *The Council Fire*, v. 4, no. 6, June, p. 84.

1881   "The Twana Language of Washington Territory." *American Antiquarian and Oriental Journal*, v. 3, no. 4, July, pp. 296–303.

1881   "Work on a Short Tour." *The American Missionary*, v. 35, no. 10, October, pp. 308–10.

1881   "Indian Schools." *The Council Fire*, v. 4, no. 11, November, p. 171.

1882   *History of Indian Missions on the Pacific Coast: Oregon, Washington and Idaho.* Philadelphia: The American Sunday-School Union.

1882   "New Church at Dunginess." *The American Missionary*, v. 36, no. 7, July, p. 215.

1882 "Religious Interest at S'kokomish." *The American Missionary*, v. 36, no. 11, November, p. 341.

1883   "The Potlatches of Puget Sound." *American Antiquarian and Oriental Journal*, v. 5, January-October, pp. 135–47.

1883   "Church and Sabbath School Work at S'kokomish, W.T." *The American Missionary*, v. 37, no. 3, March, pp. 83–84.

1883   "Catholic Missions: Recent Changes." *The American Missionary*, v. 37, no. 7, July, pp. 211–12.

1883   "Justice to the Indian." Read Before the Congregational Association of Oregon and Washington, July 14, 1883. Portland: Geo. H. Holmes.

1884   "Census of the Clallam and Twana Indians of Washington Territory." *American Antiquarian and Oriental Journal*, v. 6, no. 1, January, pp. 35–38.

1884   "Another Criticism on Our Platform." *The Council Fire*, v. 7, no. 1, January, p. 13.

1884   "The Indian Problem." *The Council Fire*, v. 7, no. 4, April, pp. 60–61.

1884   "S'kokomish Agency, W.T." *The American Missionary*, v. 38, no. 5, May, pp. 152–54.

1884   "Do-Ki-Batt: or: The God of the Puget Sound Indians." *American Antiquarian and Oriental Journal*, v. 6, no. 6, November, pp, 389–93.

1885   "The Worship and Traditions of the Aborigines of America: or Their Testimony to the Religion of the Bible." *Journal of Transactions*, v. 19, pp. 3–41. London: Victoria Institute.

1885   "Idolatry among the Indians of Puget Sound, Washington Territory." *The Museum*, v. I, no. 1, (May-August), pp. 42–44.

1886   *Ten Years of Missionary Work among the Indians at Skokomish, Washington Territory, 1874–1884.* Boston: Congregational Sunday School and Publishing Society.

1886   "The Indians of Puget Sound, Utensils for Eating and Drinking." *American Antiquarian and Oriental Journal*, v. 8, no. 1, January, pp. 40–41.

1889   "The Stone Age of Oregon." Smithsonian Institution, Annual Report for 1886, pp. 283–95.

1889   *Hymns in the Chinook Jargon.* 2d edition, revised and enlarged. Portland: David Steel.

1889   "The Thunder Bird." *American Anthropologist* (o.s.), v. 2, no. 4, October, pp. 329–36.

1890   "Worship and Traditions of the Aborigines of America: The Beings of the Spirit World," pt. 1. *Washington Magazine*, v. 1, no. 5, January, pp. 164–70; pt. 2, v. 1, no. 6, February, pp. 216–20.

1890   "Worship and Traditions of the Aborigines of America: Man as a Religious Being." *Washington Magazine*, v. 2, no. 1, March, pp. 20–22.

1890   "Worship and Traditions of the Aborigines of America: The Sinful Soul." *Washington Magazine*, v. 2, no. 2, April, pp. 49–51.

1890 "Worship and Traditions of the Aborigines of America." *Washington Magazine*, v. 2, no. 3, May, pp. 88–90; v. 2, no. 4, June, pp. 115–17.

1890 "Worship and Traditions of the Aborigines of America: The Deluge." *Washington Magazine*, v. 2, no. 5, July, pp. 134–35.

1890 "Worship and Traditions of the Aborigines of America." Washington Magazine, v. 2, no. 6, August, pp. 169–73; v. 3, no. 1, September, pp. 196–99.

1890 "Jade in America." *American Antiquarian and Oriental Journal*, v. 12, no. 5, September, p. 289.

1890 "Worship and Traditions of the Aborigines of America." *Washington Magazine*, v. 3, no. 2, October, pp. 213–16; no. 3, November, pp. 239–43; no. 4.

1890 "Worship and Traditions of the Aborigines of America." *Pacific Magazine*, v. 3, no. 4, December, pp. 286–92.

1891 "S'kokomish Mission, Washington." *The American Missionary*, v. 45, no. 4, April, p. 132.

1891 "Indian Doctors of Puget Sound." *American Antiquarian and Oriental Journal*, v. 1, no. 2, August, pp. 11–13.

1892 "Aboriginal Geographic Place Names in the State of Washington." *American Anthropologist* (o.s.), v. 5, no. 1, January, pp. 27–34.

1892 "Shaking Religion." *The American Missionary*, v. 46, no. 5, May, pp. 157–58.

1892 "Twins among the Indians of Puget Sound." *Science*, v. 20, no. 504, September, pp. 192–93.

1892 "Indian Teachers Institute." *The Northwest Journal of Education*, v. 4, no. 1, September, p. 9.

1893 "Teachers Institute among the Indians." *The American Missionary*, v. 47, no. 1, January, p. 14.

1893 "One Soweth and Another Reapeth." *The American Missionary*, v. 47, no. 1, January, p. 13.

1893 "Superstitions among Christian Indians." *The American Missionary*, v. 47, no. 1, January, p. 14.

1893 "The Indian School Question." *The Northwest Journal of Education*, v. 4, no. 6, February, pp. 116–17.

1893 "The Skokomish Indians." *The Home Missionary*, v. 45, no. 11, March, pp. 557–59.

1894 *Father Eells, or the Results of Fifty-Five Years of Missionary Labors in Washington and Oregon: A Biography of Rev. Cushing Eells, D.D.* Boston: Congregational Sunday School and Publishing Society.

1894 "The Abolishment of Agencies." *The Indian Advocate*, v. 3, no. 11, February, p. 6.

1894 "S'kokomish Agency, Washington." *The American Missionary*, v. 48, no. 4, April, pp. 166–67 (misprinted v. 18).

1894 "The Chinook Jargon." *The American Anthropologist* (o.s.), v. 7, no. 3, July, pp. 300–312.

1894 "Report of S'kokomish, Washington." *The American Missionary*, v. 48, no. 9, p. 333.

1895 "Honorable Record for Indians." *The American Missionary*, v. 49, no. 2, February, pp. 38–39.

1896 "Busy Day of an Indian Missionary." *The American Missionary*, v. 50, no. 3, March, p. 96.

1898 "Religious Movements of Pacific Coast Indians." *Minutes of National Congregational Council, July 8, 1893.* Portland. Reprinted in *The Oregonian*, July 9, 1898, Portland.

1899 "Mission Work on the Skokomish Reservation." *The Indians' Friend*, v. 11, no. 6, February, pp. 8–9.

1900 "Fur Hunters and Missionaries." *Northwest School Journal*, v. 2, no. 8, April, pp. 4–12; no. 9, May, pp. 1–7.

1902 "A Busy Sabbath at an Indian Mission." *The American Missionary*, v. 56, no. 8, August, pp. 374–75.

1903 "The Decrease of the Indians." *American Antiquarian and Oriental Journal*, v. 25, no. 3, May/June, pp. 145–49.

1903 "Home Life of the Indians on Puget Sound." *The American Missionary*, v. 57, no. 6, June, pp. 167–71.

1909 *Marcus Whitman, Pathfinder and Patriot*. Seattle: The Alice Harriman Co.

Myron Eells wrote extensively on matters other than Indians and their missions, but these references are not given here. While the list above may not be exhaustive, it does indicate the bulk of his journal and book publications. Eells wrote for a number of religious newspapers, in particular *The Pacific* of San Francisco and *The Pacific Advance* of Seattle, and others such as *The Word Carrier*; many of these refer to Indian matters.

He was a prodigious newspaper correspondent writing regularly in his local *Union City Tribune* and *Mason County Journal*. He wrote frequently for papers such as *Port Townsend Argus*, *Oregonian* (Portland), *Seattle Post-Intelligencer*, *Tacoma Ledger*, *Tacoma Herald*, *Saturday Mail* (Seattle), and *Seattle Argus*. The total of his newspaper correspondence is difficult to assess. In 1902 when, as was his custom, he attempted to reckon up his accomplishments at the beginning of the year he estimated that he had written 1,250 newspaper articles, and he did slow down in the remaining four years of his life. The estimate is probably low. Certainly his own reckoning of his published articles in 1906 is incomplete and we may conclude he neglected the record of clippings even more.

INDEX

Italicized numbers refer to illustrations.